MOBILIZE!

MOBILIZE!

Why Canada Was
Unprepared for the
Second World War

LARRY D. ROSE

FOREWORD BY J.L. GRANATSTEIN

DUNDURN
TORONTO

Editor: Jennifer McKnight
Design: Jesse Hooper
Printer: Webcom

Library and Archives Canada Cataloguing in Publication

Rose, Larry D., author
    Mobilize! : why Canada was unprepared for the Second World War / Larry D. Rose ; foreword by J.L. Granatstein.

Includes bibliographical references and index.
Issued in print and electronic formats.
ISBN 978-1-4597-1064-1 (pbk.).-- ISBN 978-1-4597-1065-8 (pdf)--ISBN 978-1-4597-1066-5 (epub)

    1. Canada--Armed Forces--History--20th century. 2. Canada--Armed Forces--Mobilization--History--20th century. 3. Canada--Military policy--History--20th century. 4. Canada--History, Military--20th century. 5. World War, 1939-1945--Canada. I. Granatstein, J. L., 1939-, writer of added commentary II. Title.

D768.15.R65 2013   940.53'71   C2013-903921-X
                                             C2013-903922-8

1 2 3 4 5   17 16 15 14 13

We acknowledge the support of the **Canada Council for the Arts** and the **Ontario Arts Council** for our publishing program. We also acknowledge the financial support of the **Government of Canada** through the **Canada Book Fund** and **Livres Canada Books**, and the **Government of Ontario** through the **Ontario Book Publishing Tax Credit** and the **Ontario Media Development Corporation.**

Care has been taken to trace the ownership of copyright material used in this book. The author and the publisher welcome any information enabling them to rectify any references or credits in subsequent editions.

J. Kirk Howard, President

The publisher is not responsible for websites or their content unless they are owned by the publisher.

Printed and bound in Canada.

VISIT US AT
Dundurn.com | @dundurnpress | Facebook.com/dundurnpress | Pinterest.com/dundurnpress

Dundurn	Gazelle Book Services Limited	Dundurn
3 Church Street, Suite 500	White Cross Mills	2250 Military Road
Toronto, Ontario, Canada	High Town, Lancaster, England	Tonawanda, NY
M5E 1M2	LA1 4XS	U.S.A. 14150

This book is for
Michael Kevin Brennan, MD, FRCPC

"History with its flickering lamp stumbles along the trail of the past, trying to reconstruct its scenes, to revive its echoes, and kindle with pale gleams the passion of former days."

— WINSTON CHURCHILL, 1940

CONTENTS

FOREWORD

The Second World War was unquestionably the greatest national effort of the Canadian people. With a population of only 11 million, Canada put 1.1 million men and women in uniform, fielding the third largest air force and the fourth largest navy in the world, and a powerful overseas army of two corps with five divisions and two additional armoured brigades. The casualties were terrible, but significantly lower than in the Great War, and there was better care at every level than in the first conflict.

At the same time, Canadian industry produced the goods, churning out trucks and tanks, aircraft and ships, and armaments, shells, and bombs of every type. Farmers, miners, and forestry workers did their mighty bit too, and Canada supplied its own people with food — and much of the Allied world too. Moreover, the nation became so wealthy it could give away billions of dollars to its allies. The Gross Domestic Product doubled between 1939 and 1945, reaching some $11.5 billion, there was full employment, as much overtime work as everyone could handle, and families actually ate better than in the Thirties, despite food rationing. It was an exceptional period, the years when Canada altered almost completely.

No one could have predicted this turnaround in the 1930s. The Great Depression had sucked the life out of the nation. Unemployment in some years reached 25 percent, there was no state system of welfare, and men roamed the country, hitching rides on boxcars in search of work that could earn them enough for a meal. Provinces defaulted on their bonds, political parties peddled fanciful nostrums, and the nation's leaders had no real answers to offer to the crisis, most cutting government spending and hoping for an economic miracle that never seemed to arrive.

In such straitened circumstances, it was not surprising that Canada's military sank into utter irrelevance. The great host that had emerged from the Great War in 1919 was no more, though much of its equipment, now obsolete, still filled militia armouries. The regular army numbered only a few thousand, the navy and air force together adding another 5,000 to 6,000, and the reserve forces were completely untrained. There was literally no modern equipment — no tanks, no light machine guns or anti-aircraft weapons, and the Royal Canadian Air Force still flew biplanes. The Royal Canadian Navy did have a few modern destroyers, but "few" was the operative word.

None of this would have mattered if the world had been peaceful. But the 1930s was the heyday of dictatorships. In the Soviet Union, Josef Stalin ruthlessly killed his opponents, spread subversion around the globe, and built a huge army. In Italy, Il Duce, Benito Mussolini, attacked Ethiopia, and postured on the world stage. In Spain, the fascist leader General Francisco Franco crushed the legitimate government's forces and wreaked vengeance on trade unionists and democrats. In Japan, the army attacked China and made its plans to conquer Asia. And in Berlin, Adolf Hitler, the Fuhrer, was making Nazi Germany, allegedly disarmed after its defeat in the Great War, into the most formidable military power in world history.

Canada preferred not to look. The nation and its leaders, nominally independent of Britain since the Statute of Westminster in 1931, turned their eyes away from developments abroad and looked inward. There was no money to prepare for war, and even if there had been, Canadians were sadly divided. French-speaking Canadians still smarted from the wounds of conscription in 1917 and 1918, and the idea of going to war again had no support from the Church, business, the young, or the provincial government. Indeed, many young Quebecois looked to fascist Italy as a model worthy of emulation — in Rome, at least, there was order and support for traditional values. In English Canada, opinion also was divided. Conservative imperialists still looked to Britain for a lead, but London was more than slightly uncertain of its course. Farmers worried more about the persistent drought than overseas adventures, students preferred peace to war, and voted for this in university debates. Few in Canada studied international affairs, many in the churches were outright pacifists, and hope for the League of Nations as a panacea still existed, despite all the evidence to the contrary of its ineffectiveness.

Curiously, few scholars have looked deeply at opinion and attitudes in Canada in the Depression years. They have studied politics and parties, but not ventured into analyzing why there was so little public pressure on government to make an effort to prepare the Canadian forces for the conflict that many could see approaching. It is time to lift the veil.

Larry Rose is not a scholar, not a trained historian. He worked in television news for many years and, puzzled by the country's lassitude before 1939, he found himself drawn to Canada's interwar years. Why were we so unprepared? Why did no one realize that if we went to war, men would die unnecessarily because of the lack of numbers, training, and equipment? Why?

Rose set out to read the documents and memoirs, to interview the (few) survivors, and to put together his narrative account. As readers will discover, he brings a fresh eye to the story, always finding the apposite phrase and the right quotations to bring the past alive. But for all his skill, he cannot bring back the dead, those who fell at Hong Kong and Dieppe, those lost at sea, those shot down over Britain in the first years of the Second World War. The moral of Larry Rose's story is that unpreparedness exacts its price in blood, and that lesson regrettably is one that Canadians never seem to learn.

J.L. Granatstein

Dr. Granatstein is a distinguished research fellow of the Canadian Defence and Foreign Affairs Institute and author of many books, including *The Oxford Companion to Canadian Military History* and *Canada's Army: Waging War and Keeping the Peace*.

ACKNOWLEDGEMENTS

M any people and organizations have assisted in the preparation of this book. Thanks to Dr. Jack Granatstein who has responded to queries and offered encouragement and advice over several years, read the manuscript, and written the foreword. Thanks also to David Archer and the 48th Highlanders Regiment Museum in Toronto; Bruce Barbeau and the Royal Regiment of Canada Museum; Duncan Bell; Dan Bjarnason; John Boileau; Angus Brown; Michael Carr-Harris (son of W/C Brian Carr-Harris); Leah Cross of CTV Atlantic; Lieutenant Commander Bill Dziadyk; the University of Victoria Library and staff members John Frederick and Chris Petter; Dr. William Glover; Charles Groos; Dr. Stephen Harris of the Directorate of History and Heritage, who responded to queries and offered advice while the Directorate helpfully provided photos; Michael Hayes (son of Captain G.H. "Skinny" Hayes); Roland Klein; Elizabeth Klinck; Master Corporal Mark Kowalovski at the Royal Canadian Dragoons Photo Archive; Penny Lipman and the Royal Canadian Military Institute Library; Dr. Wilf Lund; Colonel Brian MacDonald; Jean Matheson and Library and Archives Canada; Dennis McIntosh for support, advice, and reading the manuscript; Jonathan MacInnis of CTV Atlantic; Fraser McKee for reading the manuscript; Ross McKenzie and the Royal Military College Museum; editor Jennifer McKnight and the Dundurn team; Eleisha McNeil; Colonel Allan Methven; Lieutenant Colonel Leo Morin; Earl Wotten and the Ontario Regiment Museum; Bruce O'Connor; Robin Rowland for encouragement and for assistance with files on Sutherland Brown; Peter Moon for reading the manuscript; John Packman; Fred and Stella Price; the Royal Canadian Air Force Memorial Museum at CFB Trenton; Justice Grant Radley-Walters; Alain Rivet, who read the manuscript; Lieutenant Colonel

Archie Steacy; Al and Grace Stapleton; Randy Smye; Ray Soucie of CNMT/ HMCS Sackville — Canada's Naval Memorial Trust; Brigadier General Garry Thomson; the excellent Toronto Reference Library and Toronto Public Library; Maxine Weber; the late Rear Admiral Robert Welland, who offered generous advice and assistance; and the late Peter Worthington (son of Major-General F.F. Worthington), who responded to numerous questions.

Finally, thanks go to my amazing partner, Michael. Any errors are mine.

CHAPTER ONE

WAR STATIONS

It was Friday evening at the start of the long Labour Day weekend. Even so the 48th Highlanders of Canada, part of Canada's reserve army, had soldiers on duty at the towered and turreted University Avenue Armoury in Toronto.[1] A good thing, too. The phone rang and Captain Eddie Ganong Jr., the orderly officer, reached for the receiver and heard an electrifying, once-in-a-lifetime message: "MOBILIZE!"

Ganong called the Highlanders' commanding officer, Lieutenant Colonel John Chipman, and the two began a telephone fan out, ordering key members of the regiment to report to the armoury first thing the next morning. Chipman and Ganong, quickly joined by several others, worked into the early morning hours to complete the job. To their enormous frustration, many people could not be reached because they had tried to squeeze in a weekend getaway and were out of town. One officer on the phone list had his plans thrown into turmoil. Trum Warren was going to be married in a few days and he was getting ready for his stag party. When Warren was phoned, his company commander ordered, "I want you down at the armouries at eight sharp tomorrow morning." Warren was there, among the first of thousands of young Canadians to find out that personal hopes and plans were in for a shake up.[2]

The 48th Highlanders mobilized on a history-making day: September 1, 1939. Early that morning the Luftwaffe had bombed the Polish town of Wielun, and minutes later the old German battleship *Schleswig-Holstein* opened fire on the city of Danzig on the Baltic. They were the opening shots of the Second World War. Eleven German tank divisions, forty infantry divisions, and one cavalry brigade — 1.8 million troops in all — swarmed across the Polish border. It was called Operation White, an attack from the north, west, and south. Blitzkrieg.

Only hours after the attack began the Canadian Press news agency in Ottawa telephoned Prime Minister William Lyon Mackenzie King's duty officer to report the news. It was the middle of the night Ottawa time so aides decided it was useless to wake the prime minister. There was nothing he could do. Oscar Skelton, under secretary of state for external affairs, called him sometime after six a.m. to pass on the latest information. It was received in silence.[3]

The cabinet met at nine that morning and quickly declared a state of "apprehended condition of war," giving the government powers to meet any emergency.[4] An order was sent out that provided blanket approval for steps that had already been taken by the armed forces, which included cancelling leaves for regular soldiers and authorizing the call up of reserves.[5] Parliament would be recalled.

While most things went smoothly, there was at least one big bureaucratic snarl. Reserve soldiers mobilized on September 1 were actually just on temporary duty. If they wanted to do wartime service, reserve and regular soldiers all had to re-enlist in a new army organization to be called the "Canadian Field Force." The whole idea was to avoid anyone being conscripted. However, at the last possible moment the cabinet changed the name to the "the Canadian Active Service Force" (CASF). Hundreds of pre-printed forms and templates with "Canadian Field Force" on them — $65,000 worth — had to be chucked out and new ones printed.[6]

Among the 300 infantry, artillery, signals, cavalry, engineer, and support formations mobilized that day was a reserve unit from the eastern shores of Lake Ontario, the Hastings and Prince Edward Regiment (the "Hasty Pees" for short). One member of the Hasty Pees was Howard Graham, a company commander and in civilian life a prominent lawyer. When he was phoned by the regiment's commander, Lieutenant Colonel Sherman Young, Graham hadn't heard the news from Poland. "Hello, Sherman, what's new?" Graham asked. "We are mobilized as of one minute past midnight tonight. Get into your uniform."[7] Celebrated writer Farley Mowat was at that time a pint-sized second lieutenant in the Hasty Pees. He said the regimental armoury had been "an empty and dusty vault," but the new message set off a detonation.

> In Marmora, Trenton, Madoc and a half dozen other towns, [men] ... threw down their shop aprons or stripped

off their mechanic's overalls and rushed to their local company armouries ... in pool rooms and beer parlours men were silent for one long instant, and then they crowded to the doors.[8]

In Listowel, in south-western Ontario, one man in the 100th Battery, an artillery reserve unit, was Gunner George MacDonell, who had joined the reserves about a year before.[9] He was phoned and went right to the armoury. Within days he had decided to join the Canadian Active Service Force. "Talk about an exciting time! No more high school for me — I was employed on more serious business." MacDonell had been living with his uncle and aunt after his parents' separation and then his mother's death. It was a difficult time for his relatives in the midst of a depression to cope with the addition of another family member. It would be the perfect time for MacDonell to get out on his own. But the young man's plans were derailed, at least temporarily. He may have been a strapping six feet but he was still only seventeen years and three weeks old and his uncle said he was too young to join the army as a full-time soldier. MacDonell then ran away from home to London, Ontario, lied about his age, and enlisted successfully in the Royal Canadian Army Service Corps, even though he did not know what the service corps did.

In the Permanent Force, with all leaves cancelled and training courses terminated, instructors and everyone else hurried back to their units. One regular, Donald Parrott, was due to leave the Princess Patricia's Canadian Light Infantry in a few days to return to civilian life at the Madsen Lake gold mines. When he heard of the attack on Poland he returned to the Fort Osborne barracks, put his uniform back on and applied to join the CASF.[10] Officer Cadet Ned Amy returned to the Royal Military College (RMC) in Kingston, Ontario, as soon as he heard what happened. Amy had finished up his first year of studies at the college the previous spring. "Everybody was gung-ho to get out of college and get into the army or the air force or the navy."[11] He was a long way from finishing his education at RMC, but before long cadets like him were given early commissions and he suddenly became Second Lieutenant Edward Alfred Charles Amy, posted to the Armoured Fighting Vehicle School at Camp Borden, Ontario. The young man from Newcastle, New Brunswick, who described himself as five-foot-two and three-quarters knew boom all about tanks, but he was about to learn.

EXTRA

If You Don't Get The Bulletin, You Don't Get All the News Nor the Pictures

Edmonton Bulletin
AN INDEPENDENT NEWSPAPER IN PUBLIC SERVICE

THE WEATHER

WHEAT CLOSE

EDMONTON, ALBERTA, FRIDAY, SEPTEMBER 1, 1939

WAR

POLAND IS INVADED BY NAZI ARMS

DANZIG IS IN HANDS OF HITLER

NAZI WARPLANES BOMB WARSAW

NO BOMBING OF CIVILIANS, PLEADS F.D.R.

Hitler Orders Battle

LONDON SAYS WILL FULFILL OBLIGATIONS

The army mobilization was part of an enormous and meticulously crafted plan called Defence Scheme No. 3 meant for just such an occasion. All details were put into a "War Book," which provided for mobilizing a force that combined units from both the tiny regular army and the much larger army reserve. Not all the reserve units would be mobilized, only the best ones. After that it was up to the government in Ottawa to give its approval, but the plan was for two entire divisions to be formed, each with about 16,000 members and, in addition, a Canadian Corps headquarters to command them.

The plan called for the only three regular infantry battalions in the army — the Royal Canadian Regiment (RCR), the Princess Patricia's Canadian Light Infantry (PPCLI), and the Royal 22e Regiment — to be distributed one to each brigade in the First Canadian Infantry Division. Reserve units filled out the remaining six infantry battalions. Among the reserve units selected were the 48th Highlanders and the Hastings and Prince Edward Regiment from Ontario, the Seaforth Highlanders from Vancouver, the Edmonton Regiment (later the Loyal Edmonton Regiment), the Carleton and York Regiment from New Brunswick, and the West Nova Scotia Regiment. The division included the First, Second, and Third Field Regiments and the Royal Canadian Horse Artillery (RCHA), along with medium and anti-tank artillery units. There were signals troops, three field companies of engineers, and service corps members. One group — No. 1 Provost Company in Ottawa — was made up entirely of RCMP volunteers. Though they were going to be part of the Canadian Active Service Force, all units would keep their names, badges, and traditions. That was in sharp contrast to the mobilization during the First World War in which each unit was set up from scratch — a plan that turned into a colossal mess.

The First Division reservists included some outstanding individuals, among them Bert Hoffmeister and Cec Merritt of the Seaforths, and Graham of the Hasty Pees. In 1939 Hoffmeister was a major and in civilian life a lumber company sales manager. Eventually he became a major general and commander of the Fifth Canadian Armoured Division. Merritt, a six footer who appeared to have been assembled from concrete blocks, was an RMC graduate and lawyer.[12] He would win the Victoria Cross at Dieppe. Major Graham after the war became a lieutenant general and chief of the general staff (CGS). However, the vast majority of volunteers were simply ordinary Canadians. George MacDonell was a high-school student, Graham Chatterley of Toronto owned a barbershop, while another volunteer, Hugh Caldwell of the Seaforths, was a milkman.

Conspicuously absent from the mobilization and from the First Division were the Royal Canadian Dragoons and the Lord Strathcona's Horse, the two regular army cavalry regiments. An earlier version of Defence Scheme No. 3 had called for an entire cavalry division to be mobilized, but a few months before the war the reality had finally sunk in that the cavalry would have no place on the battlefield. If anyone had hoped for tanks in place of the cavalry, they would have been disappointed. In the Canadian army in 1939 there were tank regiments, but none of them had any tanks. Two tanks had arrived in Canada in 1938 and by late summer 1939 there were fourteen in all but they were only for training.[13] As for radio sets there were only a few and they were mostly obsolete. The tanks mostly used signal flags.

The mobilization order sent out to Captain Ganong and all the others may have been a shock, but it was not really a surprise because the Polish crisis had been building for months. There was, however, one completely unexpected turn of events on August 23, when German Fuhrer Adolf Hitler signed the Molotov-Ribbentrop Non-Aggression Treaty with the Soviet Union. The very idea was mind boggling. Hitler had been a vituperative enemy of communism while anti-fascist propaganda gushed out of Moscow. The treaty said that if war came the Germans and the Soviets would not attack each other and the two would carve up Poland. It meant there would not be a two-front war for Hitler.

While thousands of soldiers were sent scrambling into operation on September 1, they were not actually the first troops to be called out. Earlier in August the government had issued General Order 124, the "Precautionary State of the Defence Scheme," which summoned detachments of soldiers to protect vital installations. The *Vancouver Sun* noted on August 26 that west coast units had been activated. "LOCAL MILITIA VOLUNTEERS GO INTO UNIFORM," it reported. Members of the reserves included two artillery units, the 15th (Vancouver) Coast Brigade and the 1st Anti-Aircraft Regiment. Suddenly Vancouver residents passing along Burrard Street near the downtown saw guards posted around the Seaforth Armoury.

Coast artillery batteries were also manned and ready for action at Esquimalt outside Victoria.[14] They were meant to protect against the unlikely prospect of a "bolt from the blue" attack by a German cruiser. On August 26 the small Royal Canadian Navy minesweeper *Comox* made its way to the north end of Vancouver Island to protect the northern entrance of the Inside Passage. The prospect of a 470-ton minesweeper facing a 10,000-ton German cruiser must have been sobering for the crew of *Comox*.

Those called out to duty on August 26 numbered about 10,000 in all, stationed outside armouries, power plants, and airports across the country. It seems hard to imagine Nazi saboteurs wreaking havoc on Regina, but the Regina Rifles had a guard of four officers and forty-four other ranks at the city's airport, just in case.[15]

In reality, the vision of saboteurs stalking the Canadian heartland at night was not completely ridiculous. In the last week of August a group of 700 German-Canadians rallied in Maple, Ontario, to support the German cause, waving swastikas and singing the Horst Wessel Song, the anthem of the Nazi Party.[16] One day later a brawl broke out at a Toronto industrial plant, leaving a German-Canadian employee injured. Shop workers threatened to quit en masse if five Germans working there were not fired. A scene at the Canadian National Exhibition in Toronto revealed the anger of many ordinary Canadians.

> Germany's pavilion… was quietly taken down on September first as a crowd of onlookers watched. Posters proclaiming Germany's virtues and statues symbolizing its growing power were consigned to the trash bin. No one in the strangely quiet crowd of over a thousand citizens moved to stop the workers. Inside the International Building, however, citizens were more boisterous, cheering a CNE employee who had climbed a ladder to pull down the letters spelling out Germany.[17]

By September 3 sweeping provisions of the government's Defence of Canada Regulations were put into effect. They included waiving the right to trial, bans on some political and religious groups, and some publications, all aimed at rounding up fascists, communists, and potential subversives. Many men were picked up by local police in the next eighteen months, including more than 1,300 arrested by the RCMP.[18] They included 586 Italians (105 released) and 763 German immigrants (127 released), along with known Communists

(87 released) and members of other ethnic groups, including Ukrainians and Poles.[19] The most famous person arrested later on was Montreal mayor Camilien Houde, who spent most of the war in detention in Petawawa, Ontario.[20] The Communist party was banned in 1941 but the ban was lifted a year after Hitler's attack on the Soviet Union.[21]

The Royal Canadian Navy and the Royal Canadian Air Force had also been part of the emergency plan, but the two services were covered by different legislation than the army. The Naval Service Act required Parliament to meet within fifteen days of the reserves being called out.[22] Both services took urgent steps toward war readiness without the legislation being enacted immediately. Leaves for regular force members were cancelled. The air force dispatched a senior officer on an urgent mission to Washington to buy aircraft from the United States. Also, a licensing deal was signed to have what became an iconic training plane, the Harvard, built by Noorduyn Aircraft in Montreal.[23]

For the navy, Halifax was an urgent priority because of the possibility of German cruisers or submarines appearing on the east coast. Several German warships, including two "pocket battleships," were already lurking somewhere in the Atlantic. The obsolescent coast artillery guns protecting Halifax could fire only about 10,000 yards to seaward. Newer and better guns had been ordered from Britain but there were interminable delays and they had not been delivered.[24]

The Halifax Rifles, a regiment in the Non-Permanent Active Militia (the formal title of the army reserve), organized guards at eight separate locations including the airport, the Joint Services Magazine, the Halifax shipyard, the Imperial Oil Refinery, and the water supply reservoir.[25] The regiment had been creative in using telephones, messengers, the local radio station, and even alerts flashed on theatre screens to call members for duty.

In New Brunswick, brothers Fred and Harold Price and their father, Irvine, were among those called out on August 26. The members of the New Brunswick Rangers were sent to the waterfront in Saint John to patrol the boundaries of the largest floating dry dock in the British Empire and one of the few existing in Canada.[26] Along with the military, civilian agencies responded to the crisis. Within a few days and without instructions from anyone, municipal officials in Saint John started a voluntary partial blackout at night, directed by local police and 100 special air raid wardens appointed by the mayor.[27] In Halifax, Eaton's store began advertising special green blackout curtains.

The RCN had some coastal minesweepers on the east coast, but just one major warship was available — the 1,300 ton destroyer HMCS *Skeena*. The only other destroyer in the Atlantic, HMCS *Saguenay*, was undergoing a refit that included installing new anti-submarine gear. Reinforcements were needed so two ships were summoned urgently from the west coast. The ships got the message while they and two other destroyers were visiting the Pacific National Exhibition in Vancouver. Suddenly there were whispered conversations and guests were ushered ashore. The ships had been on short notice to leave, but it didn't take more than a few minutes to get going. Aboard HMCS *Fraser* and HMCS *St. Laurent* smoke immediately poured from the funnels, awnings were furled, boats hoisted, and booms and gangways secured.[28] Family, clothing, and unpaid bills were left behind. *St. Laurent* and *Fraser* were soon cracking along at twenty-five knots toward the Panama Canal en route to Halifax.[29]

Fred and Stella Price

The picture of Fred Price looks as if it was taken in 1918, but it is actually from September 1939. Little had changed in the army in uniforms and equipment in the interwar years. Three members of the Price family, all in the New Brunswick Rangers, were mobilized in 1939.

Terry Higgins, Copyright 2013

Supermarine Stranraer. The coastal patrol aircraft was described by pilots as a "Gentleman's aircraft." It did what you wanted, but in its own good time.

As part of its east coast defenses the Royal Canadian Air Force had No. 5 Squadron, a regular force unit based at Dartmouth, Nova Scotia. No. 5 Squadron's crest was emblazoned with the motto "Volando vincimus" (By Flying We Conquer), but conquering with the aircraft it used, the Stranraer flying boat, was going to be a tall order. The biplane presented little threat to any maritime intruder, its short range limiting it to scouting the approaches to Halifax harbour. Like the RCN, the air force started moving in reinforcements, such as they were. A squadron of near-useless Northrop Deltas was moved from Ottawa to Sydney, Nova Scotia.

On September 1 the Naval Service Headquarters (NSHQ) in Ottawa finally dispatched a warning signal to RCN destroyers and coastal commanders: "Ship warheads and be in all respects ready for action. Do not start an engagement until ordered from NSHQ but be prepared to defend yourselves in case of attack."[30]

On Saturday, September 2, people in Ottawa opened the newspaper to read "BRITAIN AND FRANCE MOBILIZE, POLAND SEEKS AID AGAINST FULL GERMAN ATTACK." The whole front page and many inside pages were plastered with stories.[31] On an inside page of the *Citizen*, Ontario Conservative leader George Drew said Canadians are "offered a choice between barbarism and civilization." Another headline read: "BRITAIN SENDS WARNING — HITLER MUST WITHDRAW OR FRANCE AND ENGLAND ARE AT WAR." One story said, "The Canadian government ... rushed with all possible speed its preparations for war." It added, "The Dominion of Canada will march with Great Britain." Despite that the prime minister had said emphatically and repeatedly that only Parliament would decide whether Canada would go to war or not. Canada was not at war, at least not yet. On an inside page was the news that Parliament would not meet until September 7.

In Toronto on September 2, a rain-soaked and humid day, the 48th Highlanders held their first parade since mobilization. The priority was to get all members who wanted to be in the Canadian Active Service Force signed up and given a medical exam. The medical officer was among those who had been out of town on Friday night but still by the next day, September 3, a temporary medical board was set up at Grace Hospital in downtown Toronto. The first thirty-eight volunteers were examined, including Captain Ganong, a long-time Highlander, a lawyer, and, if the name sounds familiar, a member of the famous chocolate-making Ganong family.* The signing up routine was repeated at dozens of armouries across the country.

On Sunday, September 3, Britain and France declared war. The news was telegraphed to Canada early that morning when most people were still in their beds. In several cities, including Toronto, newspapers printed special editions.

> The streets were only just beginning to come to life when British Prime Minister Neville Chamberlain's words were cabled to newspaper offices … Many people learned of the declaration [of war] as they passed by newspaper offices where extras were displayed. Street car drivers stopped their buses to allow travelers to read the latest bulletins.[32]

That afternoon thousands of Canadians across the country heard a message from King George VI on the radio.

> In this grave hour, perhaps the most fateful in our history, I send to every household of my peoples, both at home and

---

* A second member of the extended Ganong family was Lieutenant Colonel Hardy N. Ganong, commanding officer of the Carleton and York Regiment and later a major general.

overseas, this message, spoken as if I were able to cross your threshold and speak to you myself. For the second time in the lives of most of us, we are at war … I ask you to stand calm, firm and united in this time of trial. There may be dark days ahead … but we can only do the right as we see the right and … with God's help we shall prevail.

Among those listening to the message were young Jim Edwards, his brother, two sisters, and their parents in Battleford, Saskatchewan. For weeks Jim had been following the crisis in Europe and, that day, Britain's war declaration. He immediately wanted to join the air force and become a pilot, but he hadn't finished high school. His pals thought he would be a good fighter pilot. For one thing, there was a kind of joke, a trick of Jim's. He would stand on a rise outside Battleford and look at the post office tower with its large clock face a mile away and read the time on it. Jim was a crack shot, too.[33]

On that same day the government in Ottawa declared a state of emergency, back dated to August 25. It already had extensive powers but now new regulations were put in place for the control of exports, shipping and prices, postal censorship, and calling out of naval and air force units. The minister of national defence approved a new warning to the navy and air force and army coastal units. It said, "You can fire on any blinking German who came within range of our guns," but he added, "we are not at war."[34]

Only hours after German forces began their attack on Poland, off the northwest coast of Ireland, the German submarine *U-30* sighted a ship zigzagging in an area off the normal transatlantic shipping route. The boat commander, Oberleutnant Fritz-Julius Lemp, had been informed by radio about midday that Germany was at war so his patrol immediately took on a new urgency. Lemp attacked, scoring a direct hit amidships with at least one torpedo. *U-30* dived for safety, but later in the fading light Lemp decided to try to identify the vessel, finding that it was the 13,000-ton British passenger ship, *Athenia*. Commanded by the historically named Captain James Cook, *Athenia* was en route from Britain to Canada and the attack was a tragic mistake. Lemp had been under strict orders not to attack civilian ships because at that point Hitler was still hoping for a deal with Britain and France to bring a quick

Just a few months before the war, the entire regular army had consisted of 4,169 officers and men. You could have put them all in Toronto's hockey mecca, Maple Leaf Gardens, two and a half times over. The reserve army was nominally much better off with 51,000 members, but that number was a complete fiction. Thousands were just names on a list and the reserve army was likely as much as 50 percent under strength.[42] When the 48th Highlanders held their parade on September 2 there were thirty officers and 251 other ranks on the drill square. Even accounting for those who did not show up, the Highlanders were far below their authorized strength of about 800.

The reservists were mostly untrained. On the outbreak of war one officer had described them as basically a mob, "an organized mob, in uniform." They could march on a parade square but couldn't defend it.[43] Much later, Ned Amy commented on the lack of training, saying, "It would have been tragic if we had been shunted off into battle in 1939. Absolutely tragic."[44] The main role of the regular army was not to form an operational force, but to train the part-time reservists. In the years before the Second World War, the regular army had only trained together once in 1938 and that was a shambles. Like the reserve regiments, the regular battalions were vastly under strength. The Royal 22e Regiment had an establishment of 773 members, but in 1939 actually had only 184 all-ranks.[45]

The government had started a modest rearmament program in 1936, but the army was emphatically last on the priority list. Apart from the moth-eaten uniforms for the Regina Rifles and everyone else, there were few trucks and medical supplies. When the war broke out the Edmonton Regiment could outfit less than half its members with boots while the Carleton and York Regiment had only sixty-six pairs.[46]

As far back as March 1938, the *Financial Post* newspaper had published a scathing article entitled "Canada's Defence Farce."[47] It said Canada had a "bow and arrow" army, but even worse, it was running out of arrows. It pointed out a startling array of shortages of ammunition and equipment. It said the army reserve "is armed with rifles, machine guns and other equipment used during the Great War. Without exception they are all obsolete." The article concluded, "No nation of our population and wealth in the whole world today is so badly equipped as we are.…"

The standard infantry weapon, the .303 Short Magazine Lee-Enfield (SMLE) bolt-action, magazine-fed rifle was still serviceable but little changed from the First World War. If extra weapons were needed, the army would have to rely on thousands of the dreaded Ross rifles in storage and untouched since 1918. They were great on a target range but hopeless in the field. There was also a scattering of Lewis machine guns of Great War vintage, and in addition five mortars, eighty-two Vickers machine guns, twenty-nine new Bren guns, and twenty-three useless anti-tank rifles.[48] These shortages could have been avoided if Parliament had been willing to spend far more on rearmament than it had.[49]

There were 100 batteries of field artillery and seventeen batteries of medium artillery, along with coast batteries and an anti-aircraft regiment.[50] All told there were about 800 men in the regular artillery. There were 14,000 gunners listed in reserve units, which meant there were probably about 7,000 actually in the flesh. New artillery designs had been a feature of weapons development in the interwar period — notably in Germany. However, the Canadian artillery would be far outranged by the new guns, as it still trained on First World War weapons — eighteen pounders and 4.5 inch howitzers for the field batteries.[51]

One of the artillery reinforcements rushed to Halifax as the war began was the 4th Anti-Aircraft Battery, a Permanent Force unit from Kingston, Ontario. It was equipped with the only eight serviceable anti-aircraft guns in the entire country.[52] They had been converted to anti-aircraft as a "temporary" adaption in 1918. Modern height-finders or predictors were non-existent, leaving one officer to describe the relics as "useless for war and of little value for training."[53]

The Royal Canadian Navy had just 1,500 regular officers and sailors, or, if you added in all the reserves, 3,500. Its six destroyers were fairly new and capable ships while the officers and sailors in them were well trained. But if you took the destroyers and the four minesweepers and spread them over two long coasts, they hardly constituted a naval threat. Add in two more small vessels and a sailboat used for training (a sister ship to the *Bluenose*) and the whole lot was sometimes referred to as the "baker's dozen fleet." Two of the ships from the Pacific coast had been moved to the Atlantic, but that still meant only four destroyers based at Halifax.[54]

Neither of the two operational bases, Esquimalt on the west coast, or Halifax in the east, had much changed since 1910. In terms of barracks and training schools the navy was unable to support operations much larger than those that existed when the war broke out. One writer commented that "the RCN lacked the essential base for a self-sufficient navy" while "experienced staff, specialist and technical expertise, scientific liaison, training facilities and organization, shipbuilding and repair capacity, dockyard facilities and logistic support--scarcely existed."[55]

True, there had been a great deal of work before the war to organize a worldwide convoy system. The Royal Navy orchestrated most of it, but the Royal Canadian Navy had spent a lot of time and effort in setting up its part of a convoy system for merchant ships. That at least was well in hand.

The scale of everything in the Royal Canadian Navy in 1939 could be judged from its head office. Naval Service Headquarters in Ottawa took up a single floor in the six-storey Robinson Building at 72 Queen Street. As if meant to confuse any passing German spy, there was a deli on the main floor, a Department of Agriculture office specializing in swine on the second and third floor, while the government's radio licensing branch was on the fifth. On the navy's floor, only the chief of naval staff, Rear Admiral Percy Nelles, had his own office and beside him a ponderous safe used to keep both secret documents and the admiral's tea caddy.[56] Everyone else sat elbow to elbow in a common room.

The reality also was that the Royal Canadian Navy was simply a branch plant of the Royal Navy. It was also the most "British" of the three services. As historian Joseph Schull noted:

> Its ships were British; it wore RN pattern uniforms; personnel training above new entry training was conducted in Britain by RN instructors; its doctrine and tactics came from RN manuals and were refined in exercises with British fleet units; it followed RN customs; and, with no real fighting tradition of its own, the RCN proudly embraced those of the RN, with occasions like Trafalgar Day marked by enthusiastic celebrations in the ships and shore establishments of the Canadian navy.[57]

The British couldn't be blamed for Canada's dependence. Through the 1930s the RN had offered assistance in a thousand different ways. It supplied Canada with good destroyers at knock-down prices and it provided officers — including Robert Welland aboard HMS *Fame* — with training they could never have had in Canada. Apart from the size of its fleet, the Royal Navy had enormous experience, leadership, and a worldwide planning and intelligence network. The Royal Canadian Navy reaped huge benefits.

But at a price. Who could be surprised that since the RN did all the heavy lifting it wanted to call the shots. Later in the war, if it came to deciding whether a Canadian or a British commander would take charge of a joint operation, most often the British wangled it so that one of their own would run "the show."[58] Although four senior RCN officers had attended the Imperial Defence College during the interwar years the instruction they received reflected British attitudes toward centralized imperial defence. That may have been strategically sound for the empire but not necessarily for Canada. The RCN was stuck with a lot of other Royal Navy policies, priorities, and perceptions. One was that in the Royal Navy gunnery officers ruled while anti-submarine specialists were headed for career suicide. Anti-submarine warfare was a side show.

MILESTONES

JANUARY 28, 1939 — Former Prime Minister R.B. Bennett sailed for Britain after surrendering his seat in the Commons and retiring to private life in England. He was later named Viscount Bennett.

APRIL 30, 1939 — Television in the United States made its formal debut at the World's Fair in New York City with a presidential address by Franklin D. Roosevelt.

AUGUST 20, 1939 — Armoured forces under the command of Soviet General Georgi Zhukov decisively defeat the Imperial Japanese Army forces in the Japanese-Soviet border war in Inner Mongolia.

The Royal Canadian Air Force suffered from the same basic problems as the other two services, even though it had been the government's first priority in rearmament. It had only 4,100 officers and men, including reserves, 275 aircraft, and twenty-three different types of planes.[59] Supposedly there were twenty-three squadrons, but almost none fully trained or ready to go.[60] However, it is another number that is most telling: the air force started the war with only 235 pilots.[61] That was a legacy of cutbacks in the midst of the Depression.

The prime minister was horrified to find that on the outbreak of war the RCAF was unable to send a single squadron to Europe and, in the event, the first squadron was only sent in January 1940. Another of the great handicaps was that the RCAF had only been a military service since 1935, while before that it was mainly the government's flying service concentrating on fighting forest fires and mapping.

The saddest episode in the entire mobilization was the attempt to rush No. 3 Squadron to war stations in Halifax. It looked like a pie-in-the-face comedy.[62] On August 26 the squadron was ordered to take its seven Wapiti light bombers from its home base in Calgary to Halifax. The Wapiti was a hand-me-down from the Royal Air Force, a single engine, open cockpit biplane that would not have been out of place in the skies over France in 1918. The Wapiti ("What-a-pity" to the crews) chugged along at about 210 kilometers per hour. With the receipt of the warning order on August 26, the squadron left Calgary, but there were never-ending mechanical problems. By the time they got further east, two aircraft came down with engine trouble at Millinocket, Maine, and, when the weather closed in, nearly found themselves interned in the United States.[63] In all it took eleven days for all the planes to arrive in Halifax.

Although nearly all the twelve air force reserve squadrons went on full-time duty on September 3, they did so with extremely limited equipment.[64] No. 110 (Bomber) Squadron in Hamilton, Ontario, had four tiny DH-82A Moth training planes and seven qualified pilots.[65] One regular squadron flew the Armstrong Whitworth Atlas, an army co-operation biplane that first flew in 1925. The Northrop Delta, referred to earlier as being sent to the east coast, was originally a racy civilian aircraft, but by this time was converted to operate on floats and carry — in a pinch — one machine gun. Its fuselage had an alarming habit of cracking in a hard landing. The best planes the air force had were twenty Hawker Hurricanes. They were too short ranged for operational use in Canada but with them the RCAF could do modern pilot training, plus they were a morale booster.

It wasn't long before there was some pay off for that RCAF shopping mission to the U.S. In what became a famous episode, some aircraft found their way to Canada despite the American neutrality laws. The RCAF bought several Douglas Digby twin engine bombers and American pilots flew the first two of them to a field in Sweet Grass, Montana. One of the RCAF officers present was Claire Annis, a later air marshal.

They landed over the brow of a hill where we were waiting and then taxied up to a barbed wire fence separating a Canadian field at Coutts, Alberta from the adjacent American field. The Americans got out and shook hands with [Squadron Leader R.C.] Gordon; everyone was in civilian clothes. The wire was then cut, a rope thrown across the border to be tied on the aircraft, as a team of horses dragged them over the line. The ground sloped towards our side and the first *Digby* began to roll quite rapidly causing considerable tension among the bystanders. Fortunately someone managed to get onto the step of the aircraft and after quite a struggle succeeded in putting on the brake.[66]

Additional Digbys, Lockheed Hudsons, North American Harvards, and other aircraft were towed across the border at Emerson, Manitoba.

While the army, navy, and air force scrambled to their war stations in August and early September 1939, a political drama was being played out behind the scenes in Ottawa. There was a dangerous divide that Prime Minister King had been grappling with ever since he returned to office in 1935. What would happen if English Canada demanded that Canada declare war, but French Canada, fearing conscription, refused? King relied heavily on Quebec support, so on this question could the government split in two and collapse? The situation had the real potential of triggering a breakup of the country. The English-French split had already had a dramatic effect on rearmament. Increases in defence spending were enormously unpopular in Quebec. Defence spending, Quebeckers argued, was evidence that Canada to going to join Britain in a European war which, in turn, would mean conscription. Among the questions French Canadians asked was about Canada's geography. Was it located in Europe?

Since 1935 Prime Minister King had hoped that war in Europe could be avoided, endorsing appeasement as a solution. He had shunned proposals for United Empire defence and joint British-Canadian arms purchases because of the French-English divisions. At the same time he faced a second dilemma, because until the beginning of 1939, English opinion was much against a

European war as well. His stock answer about whether Canada would go to war was "Parliament will decide." That was bafflegab because he was the one running Parliament, but it kept his options open.

By the beginning of 1939, with war appearing increasingly likely, King had realized his stalling could not continue. He had been working to achieve a consensus — Canada would join Britain if war was declared, but most importantly there would be no conscription. There had been speeches in Parliament and meetings among ministers to find an accommodation.

There had been a series of meetings dating back to the beginning of 1939, but one vital session was on August 24 as the ministers decided what the cabinet would "recommend" to Parliament about declaring war. No one around the table said Canada should stay out of war if it came, but there were still reservations about exactly what Canada should do. Joseph Michaud, a French-speaking New Brunswicker, said declaring war was one thing but there should be no military activity outside Canada. English Canadian cabinet members were not going to have that. The influential Norman Rogers, labour minister and MP for Kingston, said immediate action was essential. If Britain went to war, Canada must declare war too and Canada should say so publically. National Revenue Minister James Ilsley was even more emphatic, saying Canada should make its plans known immediately, a view shared by Defence Minister Ian Mackenzie.[67] Then came the crucial moment. Ernest Lapointe, the minister of justice and the most powerful and respected Quebecker in King's government, supported declaring war, *so long as there was no conscription.* The prime minister was "immensely relieved."[68] Not everyone was in entire accord — differences remained — but there were no threats to resign. King concluded, "we were of one mind and united" on how to proceed. Parliament would be recalled.

The premature newspaper headline of September 2 that assumed Canada was at war may have confused some people, but it wasn't only Canadians who were unsure. On September 5, U.S. President Franklin Roosevelt personally phoned the man he called "Mackenzie" to get the real story. (King was "Rex" to his friends, but somehow Roosevelt had fastened onto "Mackenzie."[69]) "We are having a discussion here," he told King, "is Canada at war?" King replied that only Parliament could decide that and it had not met yet. Roosevelt was nervous about whether the U.S. could send military supplies to Canada because of the Neutrality Act, which outlawed supplying arms to combatants. Roosevelt was relieved to hear the news from King first hand. Sales could continue, at least for the time being.[70]

For years public opinion in the United States had overwhelmingly favoured staying out of any European war. A measure of American feeling came in October when aviation hero Charles A. Lindbergh delivered a radio address arguing that Canada was endangering the United States by entering the European war. The *New Yorker* magazine mocked the isolationists in a September issue, writing, "Our people dislike Hitler and they want him soundly beaten by a couple of other fellows."[71]

Parliament met in an emergency session on September 7. Governor General Lord Tweedsmuir read the Speech from the Throne that urged a quick decision to declare war.[72] The fact that Parliament would decide the question at all was the result of a fundamental change in Canada's constitutional standing eight years earlier. The Statute of Westminster of 1931 had given Canada broad new powers, including those over foreign policy.

Since the cabinet was united and the Liberals had a majority, the outcome of the motion to declare war was a foregone conclusion. Still, there was tension. Senator Arthur Meighen, a former Conservative prime minister, said in the upper chamber that when Britain was at war Canada was at war and no independent declaration was needed. "Either we are part of the British Empire or we are not," he said. Co-operative Commonwealth Federation leader, J.S. Woodsworth, a lifelong pacifist, was resolutely against it. Two Quebec Liberals broke with their leader, accusing King of slavishly following the British. The two dissenters called for a formal vote, but their call was drowned out by a chorus of "nays." Parliament had decided without a recorded vote — it would be war.

The government cabled the text of the war declaration to King George for his signature. At Buckingham palace there was fussing over exact wording. A little-known diplomat and sports fanatic, Lester B. Pearson, was trying to sort out the problem with the monarch's secretary while the king himself popped in and out of the room offering suggestions. Finally, he signed. The Royal Proclamation declared that a state of war with the German Reich existed in Canada. An extra edition of the *Canada Gazette* published at 12:40 eastern time on September 10 carried the official word. For the second time in twenty-one years Canada was at war against Germany but it was the first time the country had made that declaration of war in its own right, and just one week after Britain's declaration.

Across the country there was little flag waving and few outbursts of emotion. The decision was observed with ambivalence by many immigrant communities and grudgingly in Quebec, but it was roundly supported by the vast majority of Canadians. The *Globe and Mail* headlined, "DOMINION COMMITTED TO STAND WITH BRITAIN IN FIGHT AGAINST HITLER." Armed forces chiefs notified all major units of the declaration. The telegram from Naval Service headquarters used a pre-set code word for its message: "GRAPNEL GERMANY REPETITION GRAPNEL GERMANY."[73] Meanwhile, the RCAF's first wartime mission was flown along the east coast that very day.

Ahead lay stupendous challenges. For all three services the lack of equipment, training, and leadership would hobble the fight against Germany for months to come, even years. How had that happened? Was this what Canadians wanted? It had been a grim battle for all three services simply to survive, a battle that went right back to the end of the First World War.

CHAPTER TWO

CLOSE TO THE VANISHING POINT

In 1919 after the First World War, Britain had hundreds of military aircraft scattered around all over France and Britain. Many were new or almost new, but what to do with them all? The British decided to give many of them away in what came to be called the "Imperial Gift."[1] Canada got more than 100 planes — trainers, fighters, and flying boats. The Canadian army got a post-war bonanza as well, with tons and tons of rifles, artillery, and ammunition it had in stock in Europe shipped home. But how much of this stuff would Canada need in a world in which the prospect of any future war seemed non-existent?

Air Force Workhorse. The Avro 504 was the basic air force trainer in Canada after the First World War and performed many other duties as well. Its top speed was eighty-five miles per hour.

The answer was fairly straightforward for the new planes. They could be used for mapping and forest fire patrols, opening up the north and mining exploration. There could be a small Canadian air force too. The aircraft that started arriving in 1919 included eight British Felixstowe flying boats from 1917 and two Curtis H16 flying boats. The H16 was the first in a family of long-range seaplanes that would later begin international air travel. The Gift also included a sampling of fighter planes, among them a new Sopwith Snipe, while a few German planes were thrown in as trophies. Perhaps most important of all were sixty-two Avro 504 trainers, which became a workhorse throughout the 1920s.[2]

The new air force would build on wartime experience. Almost all Canadian flyers served with British forces. There had been moves to set up separate Canadian formations, including two RAF squadrons, but by that time the war was almost over. In September 1918 the Royal Canadian Navy had formed its own — the Royal Canadian Naval Air Service — but it never saw action.

The new air force could also cash in on the reputation of Canadian pilots who had astounded the world between 1914 and 1918. There were three Victoria Cross winners: Billy Bishop, William Barker, and Alan McLeod. All three survived the fighting, but McLeod, who had won the Victoria Cross while still a teenager, died of the Spanish flu after the war. To administer both civil aviation and the military air force, the government set up a civilian air board, which held its first meeting in June 1919.[3] The Canadian Air Force was approved in February 1920. It was not until 1935 that the air force started switching over from mostly civilian duties to being a military service. It then faced a near impossible battle to prepare for any future war, setting up a military administrative structure, getting new equipment, and gaining experience in military flying.

It has been said that the steps to nationhood are measured in short shuffles and long bounds.[4] The First World War, and especially with such victories as Vimy Ridge, made for very long bounds for Canada. The nation had been transformed during the war years, but the price had been ghastly. Sixty-five thousand Canadians and Newfoundlanders had died while the wounded numbered 138,000. British dead were 723,000, French 1.4 million, and Germans 2.1 million. By one count an average of almost 900 Frenchmen and 1,300 Germans were killed every single day of the war.[5] But even then, those numbers did not portray the real picture.

Thousands were blinded or maimed for life, while uncounted others faced what is called today "post-traumatic stress disorder." There was also political damage to the country. There was a calamitous conscription battle, which included rioting in Quebec City in March 1918 that left dozens injured and five dead. Meanwhile, after the war nearly a quarter of the veterans were left unemployed. Added to that, the Winnipeg General Strike of 1919 was shattering. The Spanish flu killed as many as 22 million people worldwide. The first symptoms showed up in Canada in September 1918 and within a month cities like Brantford, Ontario, reported 2,500 cases. With the devastation of the war and all the problems after it, Canada was a troubled post-war nation. Above all there was a powerful collective memory among Canadians that the country had to stay out of any future European conflict.

MILESTONES

JANUARY 2, 1924 — The Canadian Red Ensign becomes the official flag to fly over Canadian government buildings.

JULY 1, 1927 — Prime Minister William Lyon Mackenzie King delivers Canada's first network radio broadcast, addressing the nation from Parliament Hill as part of Canada's Diamond Jubilee celebrations.

SEPTEMBER 7, 1929 — The Schneider Trophy race was won by Britain with a Supermarine plane powered by a 1,900 horse power Rolls-Royce engine. It was an ancestor of the renowned Spitfire.

MAY 17, 1929 — The first Canadian to save his life by parachute was Canadian Vickers test pilot Jack Caldwell, who parachuted from a spinning Vedette flying boat.

Given the anti-war climate of 1919 and with no prospect of war even faintly on the horizon, it was a daunting task to muster any support for the Canadian army. The job of designing a new post-war army was given to General Sir William Otter, the first Canadian-born chief of the general staff. Some veterans suggested there should be a regular army of 30,000, but there was not a drop of political support.[6] After examining the options, Otter's commission settled for a mostly part-time army that would have basic training, inadequate equipment, and few, if any, modern arms. Mechanization and the likelihood that any future war would mean a highly mobile battlefield were simply ignored. On paper, at least, there would be eleven infantry and four cavalry divisions. Otter also tried to settle conflict over whether post-war units would keep the First World War unit names or return to the familiar pre-war units. In the end there was an awkward compromise with many of the pre-war unit names remaining. Exceptions included the 22nd Battalion of the First World War which later became the Royal 22e Regiment.

Along with the reserve army, there would be a small Permanent Force (PF) of full-time soldiers, including two cavalry regiments, the Royal Canadian Dragoons and Lord Strathcona's Horse. In the infantry were the Royal Canadian Regiment, Princess Patricia's Canadian Light Infantry, and 22e Regiment (later the Royal 22e Regiment, the famous "Vandoos"). The same three units would be mobilized in September 1939 as part of the First Canadian Infantry Division. There was a knock-down drag-out battle over the Royal 22e Regiment, the one and only French speaking PF unit. The military wanted the Vandoos but prevailed only after the cabinet turned down the army recommendation five times.[7]

After a brief flurry of enlistments in the reserve in 1919 and 1920 interest fell off dramatically. There were supposed to be 150,000 officers and men enlisted, but, in a reality that continued throughout the entire period, many units existed only on paper, while most could hardly make up a couple of companies. In 1924 the Regina Rifles had sixty all-ranks.[8] In the PF most units were also far below authorized strength. The RCR in 1921 had thirty-six officers and 458 men, and the PPCLI twenty-five officers and 269 men. In June 1931, the actual strength of the Permanent Force was 3,688 against the authorized establishment of 6,900.

The gear brought back from Europe was enough to equip five divisions, so the equipment situation initially was very good. There were 142 field guns, along with 500 rounds of ammunition for each one.[9] There were 106,000 Lee-Enfield rifles. It was too expensive to bring back everything, so thousands of horses the army had used were sold to the Belgian government for next to nothing, while 1,250 swords, 5,000 revolvers, and almost 1,300 bicycles were sold at auction. In another decision with a long shadow, two battalions of tanks in Canadian service were returned to the British.

It's a bit of an exaggeration, but not much, to say that the weapons and equipment the army had in 1939 were about what the army had in 1920, except that moths had devoured hundreds of the uniforms, a good number of the Enfield rifles had just worn out, and the artillery rounds had all been fired.

* * *

The Royal Canadian Navy had been established in 1910 and equipped with two aged cruisers, HMCS *Niobe* and HMCS *Rainbow*.[10] During the early part of the First World War a naval force of six vessels was bolstered by a regatta-like fleet of yachts, trawlers, drifters, or whatever else came to hand. Another ship, HMCS *Shearwater*, joined the RCN in 1915. The small size of the Canadian navy meant that it could do little against the German threat, particularly in 1917–18, when U-boat activity targeted Canadian fishing vessels and coastal freighters off Newfoundland and Nova Scotia. About 9,500 Canadians and Newfoundlanders eventually served in the RCN in the First War, with the service commanded by Sir Charles Kingsmill. He was born in Guelph, Ontario, but had served for many years in the Royal Navy. HMCS *Niobe* was damaged in the Halifax explosion in 1917 and was retired in 1920.

After the war the RCN lived on the knife edge of extinction. The navy's budget in the early 1920s was cut to $1.5 million — barely enough to keep the destroyers *Patrician* and *Patriot* in commission along with four trawlers. In 1922 there were only fifty Canadians in the navy along with 450 sailors borrowed from the Royal Navy in Britain. The crews of *Patriot* and *Patrician* were entirely British.

In 1923 both the Royal Canadian Naval Reserve (RCNR) and the Royal Canadian Navy Volunteer Reserve (RCNVR) were established.[11] The RCNR was small, made up mostly of civilian officers and sailors working on merchant ships. The RCNVR was larger and turned out to be an inspiration, the brainchild of Commodore Walter Hose, who succeeded Kingsmill after the war. Hose knew that with the pitiable amount of money available the navy couldn't operate a serious fleet or even a serious squadron but the key, he felt, was to keep the navy alive in local communities. So the RCNVR with its amateur sailors, boating enthusiasts, and landlubbers was set up in every major Canadian city. To begin, the authorized strength was 1,000 all-ranks. Toronto, Montreal, and Winnipeg had 100 all-ranks, while fifteen cities, including Calgary, Charlottetown, Edmonton, Halifax, Ottawa, and Vancouver, had a "half company" of fifty members. They had no buildings of their own and met mostly in garages or empty offices. Starting the half company in Vancouver was delayed when it was discovered that the nautical experience of the proposed commander, Lieutenant J.W. Hobbs, included rum running.[12]

Despite its budget limitations, most summers' reserve sailors would take part in training cruises. Some of them were very young, including Seaman Cadet Alex Jardine, who was fourteen when he joined.[13] Arthur Hewitt and William Mansfield, boy seamen, recalled the navy in the 1920s.

> We lived in *Naden* [the shore base at Esquimalt, on the west coast] in great barren barrack-rooms and the Officer of the Watch came around with the Petty Officer of the Watch, and the usual routine. The PO of the Watch always carried a lantern, leading the parade and they had to open all the bloody windows in the place. It was cold as charity in October or whatever, and so as soon as they'd gone, of course, you'd close all the windows. But there was no heat in there anyway. It really was a very uncomfortable business. We sit back and laugh about it now, but in those days we thought it was really pretty doggone grim.[14]

In Ottawa, the wartime Unionist government continued in office after 1918, but the election of December 1921 brought a Liberal government to power under Prime Minister King. Earlier, as Opposition Leader he had vehemently opposed most defence spending. He asked, "Where does the Minister expect invasion from? ... defence against whom?"[15] In 1922 Chubby Power, a First World War veteran and Quebec Liberal, called for a cut of $300,000 in original army training estimates.[16] The Liberal caucus went further demanding an additional $100,000 in training cuts and $300,000 in other reductions. In addition, the new government cut the estimates for the new Air Board by 43 percent. The next year at a disarmament conference in Washington the Liberals announced a sudden 40 percent cut in Canada's naval budget.

The Liberal government did make one significant change in 1922, passing a new National Defence Act. One minister would be responsible for all three armed forces. However, defence spending continued to decline until in the fiscal year 1924–25 when it was less than $13.5 million. Even at that the budget drew sharp criticism from many quarters including opposition MP Agnes Macphail, who was particularly outraged at the tiny budget for army cadets. That, she said, "creates a bombastic military spirit of toy soldierism."[17]

By the mid-1920s the regular army and the reserves had been relegated to the nation's peripheral vision, so much so that in 1924 the government considered turning all drill halls over to the public for community use. Many Canadians had a low opinion of the military. Calgary citizens in the 1920s thought Lord Strathcona's Horse members were "the scum of the earth."[18] Promotion was so slow that one officer who joined the Toronto Scottish in 1929 calculated that, given peacetime conditions, he would rise to command the regiment in 2032.[19] Pay for private soldiers was $1.70 a day in 1923 but that was reduced to $1.20 the next year.[20]

There was no money for the badly needed new armouries. In Regina, several militia units led by the Regina Rifles had to raise their own funds for a new building, which finally opened in 1929.[21] With minuscule budgets and little public support, the army reserve slipped to a point in the late 1920s that one regimental history described it as being "close to the vanishing point."[22]

While most of the flying heroes who returned to Canada after the war did not remain in the Canadian Air Force (CAF), William Barker, VC, was one who did, at least initially. He was an enormously popular commanding officer at the main air force base at Camp Borden between 1922 and 1924 and lobbied hard to make the CAF a fighting air force.[23] Uniquely, Barker had won twelve gallantry awards, including the Victoria Cross, Distinguished Service Order and bar, the Military Cross and two bars, the French Croix-de-Guerre, two Italian Silver Medals of Military Valor, and three mentioned-in-dispatches. Eventually, seeing there was so little government support, Barker resigned, later dying in a civilian air crash in 1930.

On April 1, 1924, the Canadian Air Force became the Royal Canadian Air Force. Until then the CAF had worn its own dark blue uniforms and its own badges, but everything was replaced with British Royal Air Force pattern including the RAF motto "Per Ardua Ad Astra" (Through Adversity to the Stars). Ironically, everything that was uniquely Canadian was thrown out while British customs and training were back. The RCAF began with sixty-two officers and 262 men, about half of them stationed at Borden. Seaplane bases included Dartmouth, Nova Scotia (a former U.S. Navy station), Lac St.-Jean, Quebec, and Jericho Beach, now a part of Vancouver. The Royal Canadian Air Force continued its focus on aerial photo surveys and forestry patrols, along with some northern exploration. A future chief of the air staff, Roy Slemon, recalled, "I never saw a weapon or fired a machine gun."[24]

There was still a romance and mystique about flying in the 1920s. There had been so many record breaking "firsts" that captured the imagination of people in Europe and North America. Among the most famous was the first non-stop transatlantic flight by John Alcock and Arthur Brown in June 1919. Their twin-engine Vickers Vimy bomber set out from Lester's Field in St. John's, Newfoundland, encountering one heart-stopping danger after another — ice, snow, and fog. At one point Brown climbed out on the wing to knock ice off one engine. The pair was unhurt in a crash landing in Clifden, County Galway in Ireland. They were lionized as heroes, winning more than £11,000 in prize money and being knighted by King George V.

The first trans-Canada flight was in 1920. Several aircraft and crews were used in relays, with the operation starting in Halifax and ending in Vancouver ten days later.

The achievement delighted Canadians and focused intense interest in aviation. In 1927 Fowler Gobeil, later a Second World War Hurricane pilot and wing commander, was in awe of flying when he started his career. Gobeil was an RMC graduate originally from Ottawa. When he arrived at Camp Borden, even the sight of the instructors was thrilling. "When I first saw one of these gods, dressed to kill in long boots, whipcord riding breeches, a beautiful 'maternity jacket,' complete with medal ribbons — well, I just damned near keeled over in a dead faint. THAT was really living."[25]

The RCAF was involved in operations in the high Arctic that were extraordinary for their time. In 1927 and 1928 a long series of flights over several months reached the south shore of the Hudson Strait. Considering the open air cockpits, the unreliable aircraft, and the rudimentary instruments, not to mention the lack of aerial maps, these were singular achievements. The flights were not without mishap. In January 1928, Squadron Leader T.A. Lawrence set out from Wakeham Bay en route to Nottingham Island, but a heavy snowstorm forced him to land in a small inlet near Deception Bay. For nine days storms battered the area while Lawrence and his crew lived off survival rations. In what sounds like a needle in a haystack scenario, Flying Officer Brian Carr-Harris located the missing Fokker aircraft on January 16, landed, and helped make it airworthy. Everyone returned to safety.[26] Carr-Harris was one of a daring and resourceful group of pilots in the 1920s and 1930s and, at the same time, an example of how often the Canadian military tradition runs in families. The Carr-Harris clan had an extraordinary association not just with the forces but with the Royal Military College. Brian's father was Robert Carr-Harris, a professor of civil engineering and architecture at the RMC from 1879 to 1897. Robert had eight children from two marriages and additionally had two nephews, nearly all of whom attended the RMC.[27]

The King government was determined to use the country's Atlantic and Pacific "moats" to shut Canada off from trouble. The League of Nations was supposed to deal with international disputes but King was wary of it in case it might drag Canada into some international maelstrom. This policy gave vent to one of the most widely quoted and dubious statements of the interwar period. At a League of Nations meeting in Geneva, the Canadian Government Leader in the Senate, Raoul Dandurand, said Canada did not have to worry about the international situation. "We live in a fire-proof house, far from inflammable materials. A vast ocean separates us from Europe."[28] King also worried that if the League didn't manage to drag Canada into another European war, British Empire leaders in London would. Some empire leaders promoted a combined empire defence policy with a united empire military command in London. King would have none of it. He said the primary responsibility of the dominions was to protect their own ports and coastlines.[29]

Some hoped that military cutbacks in many countries and spending limits on the German armed forces augured well for peace. The Treaty of Versailles after the First World War limited the German navy to 16,000 officers and men, twelve cruisers, and twenty-four destroyers. Meantime, the Americans put on a big push to cut naval forces among Pacific and Asian powers. With the signing of the Washington Treaty of 1922 the U.S. scrapped seventeen battleships and stopped construction on others, there were limits on the tonnage of new ships, and Britain scrapped 657 ships, including twenty-six battleships and battle cruisers. The British cuts were significant because they meant that Britain could no longer put a big squadron in the Pacific. The decision, not incidentally, had a part in the Canadian disaster at Hong Kong in 1941.

There was something of a tidal change in the late 1920s for the Canadian forces, but it did not last long. By 1929 the budget had climbed back to $21 million. At this point the navy faced a desperate situation because *Patrician*

Maritime Command Museum

HMCS Saguenay on July 31, 1931. It was one of the two warships built in Britain expressly for the RCN.

and *Patriot* had become all but unseaworthy. However, the chief of naval staff, Walter Hose, and Defence Minister J. Layton Ralston, a former commanding officer of the Nova Scotia Highlanders, pulled off a coup. The two persuaded the government not only to replace the ships but to do so with two state-of-the-art destroyers.[30] The original plan was to have them built in Canada, but the cost would have been 60 percent higher than in Britain so they were built in the UK. The new ships, which became HMCS *Saguenay* and *Skeena*, were ordered in 1929 and built to Canadian specifications. The ships had reinforced hulls for operations in ice, improved heating for cold weather, and better ventilation for hot weather. *Saguenay* and *Skeena* arrived in Canada in the summer of 1931.

As the 1920s wore on, the glue-and-fabric planes of the Imperial Gift wore out. Their light construction and Canadian winters helped reduce most to scrap by 1929. There was only enough money for three new types. The air force was able to buy the Vickers Vedette, a wooden flying boat that looked like a large canoe with wings. It was the first plane designed and built in Canada, with sixty of them completed starting in 1926.[31] In time the Vedette compiled a proud record because most topographical maps in use today are based on photos taken from it. Another new aircraft was the Atlas army co-operation plane. Its range was so limited that even a flight between Ottawa and Camp Borden required a refueling stop. The Armstrong Whitworth Siskin fighter was flashier, but the RCAF could only afford twelve of them. The biplane Siskin had been introduced in the Royal Air Force in 1924 as the first aircraft with an all metal frame. It had a top speed of only 156 miles an hour, not much better than First World War fighters, but according to Fowler Gobeil flying it was a vivid experience. "[It] had a fourteen-cylinder radial engine of some 300 HP ... Everything was right out where the pilot could see it working — push rods pumping up and down, rocker arms pivoting in plain sight, oil blowing back over the windscreen ... A real threshing machine of a motor."[32]

The plane became famous in Canada because of the Siskin Flight aerobatic team. The three planes performed more than 100 demonstrations across Canada and in the U.S. starting in 1927. At the Canadian National Exhibition air show in 1929, the top guns of the RCAF wanted to put on a performance to remember, but the result verged on the suicidal.

Dave Harding, an RAF exchange officer in charge of the flight, decided that the team would add razzle dazzle by having the planes spin in formation. Ernie McNab, later the first RCAF pilot to win the Distinguished Flying Cross during the Second World War, said, "We had one practice at Camp Borden consisting of No. 1 and 2 wing men moving out two spans from the leader picking a point on the horizon, putting the aircraft in a right hand spin coming out on the picked point on the third turn." McNab said he never heard of anyone in the United States or Britain who even dreamed of anything quite so mad. "But," he said, "they didn't have a Dave Harding and two dumb wingmen."[33] Despite the risk, all survived. The Siskin was scrapped by the RAF in 1932 but it was a measure of the hard times that the aircraft remained in front line service in the RCAF until 1938.

One episode in the 1920s, little known at the time, exploded into news headlines decades later. At its centre was a mind-boggling prospect: war between Canada and the United States. Today it seems mad, but there really was a Canadian plan, called Defence Scheme No. 1, to invade the United States. It was mainly the work of one man, Buster Brown, more formally Brigadier James Sutherland

Brown, the director of military operations and intelligence from 1920 to 1927. Brown's military career began in 1895 when he joined an Ontario reserve regiment as a fourteen-year-old boy bugler.[34] He attended Royal Military College and became an outstanding staff officer in the First World War. He remained in the army as a lieutenant colonel after 1918, leading to his appointment in 1920 as director of military operations. It was then and remains today the job of the military to prepare for all kinds of contingencies, most of which never happen. Brown was ordered to prepare a series of contingency war plans, including the possibility of war between the United States and the British Empire.[35]

While such a war seems to be wildly improbable today it was, indeed, credible because of the American fear of a war in the Pacific. The Americans worried that while they had been allies of the British in the First World War, so too were the Japanese and that in the event of a Pacific war, Britain might remain neutral or perhaps even hostile. Ernest King (later the commander of the U.S. Navy and a five star admiral) said in 1933 that Great Britain had historically suppressed maritime competition. King, a notorious Anglophobe anyway, called Britain a potential enemy of the U.S. and predicted, "the questions of trade, of shipping, and of naval strength may lead to war."[36] A key point for Canada was that the Americans were not going to allow the Japanese to use remote parts of the British Columbia coast to stage an attack on U.S. territory. The Americans might stampede across the Canadian border to stop it.

This was the backdrop to Buster Brown's plan. He wrote 200 pages of analysis emphasizing that if it came to war, virtually the only chance Canada had would be to conduct a pre-emptive strike. That would allow Britain weeks or months to send reinforcements from India or Britain. According to Defence Scheme No. 1, Canada's Pacific Command was to occupy Spokane and Seattle in Washington state and Portland, Oregon, while the Prairie Command would take Fargo, North Dakota, and then Minneapolis. The seizure of Albany and the Adirondacks was delegated to the Quebec Command, while the maritime unit was charged with taking Maine. Brown was not a man of half measures. He and several subordinates, wearing civilian clothes, risked a diplomatic incident to carry out reconnaissance trips across the border into New York state and Vermont.

While the whole idea of a Canadian invasion may seem beyond belief, the Americans, astonishingly, were planning the very same thing in reverse.[37] Their plan was called "War Plan Red" and it had the approval of the Secretary of War. The countries involved were given colours as code words with Canada designated as "Crimson." Crimson would be the ideal target for a U.S. invasion, the plan said, as a way of indirectly attacking the British. The plan listed roads that could be used in British Columbia including Highway 99, "the best practicable route to Vancouver." (The Canadians planned to use the same road going the opposite direction.) One part of the American plan was actually put into operation. Congress gave the U.S. military $357 million to build airfields near the Canadian border and disguise them as civilian airports. The airports were built. To the Americans' horror the plan was inadvertently published by the Government Printing Office in 1935 and ended up on the front page of the *New York Times*.

As for the Canadian plan, its Achilles heel was that it required fifteen divisions, well over 200,000 troops. Once district commanders and high level staff officers saw that, the whole thing collapsed. It was financially impossible.[38] By the 1930s it was revoked and most records of it were destroyed. That might have been the end of it but its existence was disclosed publicly in the early 1960s, exposing its author to widespread ridicule in the news media.[39]

The defence scheme did have one other point of interest as part of a brief debate about what kind of army Canada should have.[40] If implemented, Buster Brown's plan would have meant that the army would have operated in Canada's vast expanses and would have had to operate during Canadian winters. That would have required a much different army than, for example, an expeditionary force in Europe. It would be a "national" army as opposed to a branch of the Imperial Army. Since 1919 the army had been searching for a viable role Buster Brown's solution was looked at but not seriously and not for long. Instead the army (though not the government) began to focus more and more on the worsening situation in Europe.

The end of the 1920s marked the emergence of the man universally regarded as the most outstanding Canadian military figure of the era, Andrew George Latta McNaughton. James Eayrs said "McNaughton dominated his colleagues in the military establishment as a great oak dominates a scrub forest."[41] McNaughton was brilliant and had charisma to burn. He was perhaps the most intellectually gifted officer ever to wear a Canadian uniform.[42] McNaughton was born in Moosomin, east of Regina, in 1887. In 1900 he went to Bishop's College in Lennoxville, Quebec. He joined a cadet corps that was resplendent in uniforms topped with slouch hats and armed with ancient Martini-Henry rifles. Many other military officers had gone to Royal Military College but, unusually, McNaughton attended McGill University. He studied electrical engineering, taking a master's degree and then joined the university faculty. In 1909 he also joined the militia and on the outbreak of war was a major in the 3rd Battery, Canadian Field Artillery. McNaughton saw front-line combat and was wounded at Ypres and Soissons, but by 1916 he was back near the front lines as a lieutenant colonel.

In 1917 he became Counter-Battery Staff Officer of the Canadian Corps — an extremely high-profile job — and was in charge of locating and neutralizing enemy guns. His later glittering reputation was based on a number of artillery operations, including an astounding feat in August 1917.[43] McNaughton had gone up in a barrage balloon to see the terrain behind German lines only to be in the line of fire of one piece of extremely long-range heavy artillery. The gun was causing havoc all along the Canadian lines. After a hair-raising time getting to the ground, McNaughton resolved to take it out.

The weapon was a stupendous railway-mounted thirty-eight centimeter gun, which might have belonged on a battleship. It would be enormously difficult to hit because when the Germans fired it, they used the smoke and the flash of other smaller guns fired at the same time to hide it. When not being used, it was hidden in a tunnel. McNaughton's plan involved using hundreds of men, laying special roads and platforms and bringing new twelve-inch howitzers right up to the front lines, the only way they could get within range. He then used a novelty — three widely spaced teams of men with sound ranging microphones to locate the gun. The next time it fired those teams were able to get a good fix and the Canadian guns responded, as McNaughton related later.

> They knew they had a good location. Ten or fifteen yards, that's near enough for a two-thousand-pound shell, quite near enough. In due course they got another check and called for fire. I think they [the Canadian artillery] fired four or five rounds altogether and they reported a direct hit. Nobody believed it.[44]

Aerial photographs the next day confirmed the strike and the railway gun would fire no more.

McNaughton went on to repeat that kind of spectacular work, most famously at Vimy Ridge. His counter-battery fire there was said to have eliminated 83 percent of the enemy guns before the Canadian troops left their trenches.[45] A senior British general, Sir Frederick Pile, said McNaughton was probably the best gunner in the world: "his ideas were colossal."[46] After the war Sir Arthur Currie led a successful campaign to keep McNaughton in the army. Post-war, McNaughton attended Staff College at Camberley in England in 1921. A string of subsequent appointments all ended with outstanding assessments ("doing splendid work"), indicating that McNaughton was not only on the fast train to the top, but on the express.

By 1923 he was deputy chief of the general staff. If there were difficulties they may have been that he missed the opportunity to command large formations in the field.[47] Despite his military achievements, some said McNaughton remained not a soldier, but rather a scientist at heart. Even while rocketing through the senior ranks of the military, he continued his scientific work and was credited with inventing the cathode-ray direction finder in 1926.[48] In January 1929, Andy McNaughton, the man from Moosomin and McGill, the dazzling ballistician with the blue-steel mind, became the new chief of the general staff. He was forty-two years old.

CHAPTER THREE

The Dazzling Ballistician and the Unspectacular Sailor

Until the autumn of 1929, business had been booming in Canada, but the Wall Street crash on October 24, 1929, touched off a decade-long catastrophe. Not many had seen it coming. Edward Beatty, president of the Canadian Pacific Railway, said earlier in the year he'd never seen the country looking better while Alberta Premier John Brownlee said, "at no time since the formation of the province have conditions, both in Alberta and Canada, been more auspicious."[1] One prominent American economist had said only a short time before that "stock prices have reached what looks like a permanently high plateau."[2] The crash destroyed the life savings of thousands, collapsed businesses, and drove some municipalities to bankruptcy. The total provincial income in Saskatchewan dropped 90 percent in two years while in Newfoundland a British-appointed commission ran the government. There was strange weather across the country, including years of prairie drought, while in 1932 the winter was so cold that Niagara Falls froze completely solid.

By the summer of 1932 one-fifth of all Canadians were on relief. Canadian governments poured a billion dollars into aid, but it seemed pitifully meagre to recipients. Fear of political unrest grew. In 1933 one communist-led labour protest in Stratford, Ontario, ended with the Royal Canadian Regiment being sent in. When the regiment arrived with a number of small Carden-Loyd machine gun carriers, it caused a sensation. One newspaper described them as "baby armoured military tanks."[3] In 1934 alone there were forty-three protests and demonstrations in Toronto serious enough to be reported in the Toronto papers.[4]

Amid this disaster the luckiest man in the country may have been William Lyon Mackenzie King. He and his government were defeated in an election in July 1930, and, while it must have been a devastating blow at the time, he was out of office for the worst of the Depression. Conservative leader Richard Bedford Bennett became prime minister. Bennett had pledged during the campaign that if elected he would beat the Depression or "perish in the attempt." Bennett was unmarried but an admirer of women and a man who, while shunning liquor, consumed chocolates by the pound.[5] He was from New Brunswick but made his name after joining Senator James Lougheed's law firm in Alberta in 1897. Historian Charles Stacey says that in these dismal times, it didn't help that the new prime minister was rich or that he looked like a cartoonist's version of a tycoon, while in Pierre Berton's view, Bennett "not only looked like a bloated capitalist, he was a bloated capitalist."[6]

The Depression not only led to the defeat of the King government, it transformed the political landscape in Canada. The Communist Party gained new members and new visibility while socialist, labour, and co-operative groups banded together to found the Co-operative Commonwealth Federation (CCF) in 1932. Its "Regina Manifesto" was aimed at overcoming the Depression by building a socialist economy to replace the capitalist order. The CCF contested its first election in 1935, electing seven MPs.

The Depression had profound effects in Europe. After the First World War, Germany had suffered greatly in the Treaty of Versailles. The German government and the post-war republic were shaky but for several years a solid political middle gave at least a modicum of stability. That political centre was wiped out by the ghastly inflation of the 1920s and just in case anyone had been spared, again by the Depression. Adolf Hitler was sworn in as Chancellor of Germany on January 30, 1933. Few expected much from him but his brilliance as a political operator didn't exclude using street thugs to kill or frighten opponents. Soon Hitler repudiated sections of the Versailles Treaty, which left the French horrified but unwilling to do anything to stop him. Similarly the British sat on their hands while the Americans locked themselves up in Fortress America.

In the wisdom of the time, the only way out of the economic mess for the government was to cut back on every conceivable expense, and Prime Minister Bennett did just that. In June 1931, he made $2 million in spending cuts. Just before the crash the new chief of the general staff, General McNaughton, had managed to put through an army vote of more than $11 million, the highest figure in the 1920s. It was roundly criticized by both J.S. Woodsworth and Agnes Macphail, who wanted to abolish the Department of National Defence altogether.[7] After the crash, even the smallest military spending decisions reached absurd levels. A proposal to buy some new kitchen equipment at Camp Borden was kicked all the way up to McNaughton. In a memo dated March 23, 1931, he decided, "I think that the O.C. [Officer Commanding] has made a case for the dishwashing machine, the mixing machine, and the toaster in addition to the bread slicer." Those items were approved but others on the same list were rejected.[8]

There were army cutbacks, but the government feared cutting too deeply because of possible unrest, similar to the explosive situation in Stratford, Ontario.[9] It was different for the RCAF and so came the "Big Cut." That was the name used for the decision to chop seventy-eight officers, 100 airmen and 110 civilians from the air force — about one-fifth its entire strength. The Siskin Flight, with its breathtaking aerobatics, was disbanded. Spending for military and civil aviation was sliced from $5.2 million to $1.7 million, crippling the RCAF for years to come.[10] One of those who lost his job was Kamloops, British Columbia, native Frank Miller, who had only pinned on his pilot's wings a few months before.[11] Miller was a civil engineering graduate from the University of Alberta, exactly the kind of young officer the air force wanted, but that wasn't enough to save him. "The earth fell in," Miller said. "I was kicked out."[12]

There was no warning about the cuts, nor was the chief of the general staff even consulted. The air force was ordered to stop flying for other government departments unless they paid. There would be no more new aircraft or engines, no more construction work at the Trenton, Ontario, air base, and no more air mail contracts. At the country's most important air base, Camp Borden, flying came to a near standstill while refresher courses for civilians were wound up. Those who did survive the cut considered themselves lucky. Brian Carr-Harris, the pilot of Arctic rescue fame, was just glad to have a job, even though he was supporting his wife and children and two adult relatives on his skimpy air force pay.[13] The RCAF might have hoped that was the end of it but the whole process began all over again for the 1933–34 budget year. The government demanded a further cut of $1 million.[14] In the end the government voted $1.4 million for civil and military operations, lower than the year before and the lowest figure since the early 1920s.[15]

Amid the wreckage there was one consolation. Chopping its civilian roles moved the RCAF a step closer to being a strictly military force although it would still be 1935 before a full transformation took place. At the same time the air force knew that there were revolutionary developments in aviation which would also change its role dramatically. With the advances in aircraft carriers, there was now the possibility of planes appearing off Canada's coast without warning. That meant that the air force had to have permanent, rather than reserve, squadrons for coast defence. It would take just too long to mobilize a reserve squadron in an emergency. A vivid demonstration of the new power of aviation came in 1930, although it was in the form of an airship rather than an airplane. More than a million people came out to stare at the breathtaking British dirigible *R-100*, which flew from Cardington, England, to Montreal in seventy-nine hours. It carried fifty-five people.[16]

Even with no new money the air force reorganized what it had into seven regular force squadrons. Each coast would have one squadron of flying boats and one bomber squadron. There would be a fighter squadron in Montreal to reinforce the east coast and a unit in Winnipeg to boost the west coast. An army co-operation squadron would be based in Ottawa.[17] Coast defence was beginning to take on new importance.

In reality not much could be done right away because of the decrepit fleet of planes on strength. The Siskin, Wapiti, and Atlas were antiques while other aircraft could carry little or no armament and were limited to observation or training. No. 4 (Flying Boat) Squadron in Vancouver used Vickers Vedette and Vancouver* aircraft but mostly for anti-smuggling patrols and aerial photography.[18] The RCAF also estimated that between 1930 and 1935 it would have to write off 143 aircraft because of crashes or because they were just worn out. However, there would only be money for eighty-two replacements. At that rate the air force was flying toward extinction.

Despite having no money to do it with, the RCAF set up an air force reserve in 1932. The Non-Permanent Active Air Force established squadrons in Toronto and later Vancouver and Winnipeg. It was a shoe-string operation. There were, for example, no planes until 1934. At that point five small de Havilland Moth basic trainers were assigned to each squadron.[19] The reserves

---

* The Canadian Vickers Vancouver of 1929 was a twin-engine flying boat, originally designed for forest fire patrol. The biplane had a metal hull manufactured from a new Alclad material: sheets of corrosion-resistant aluminum bonded to a metal alloy. Other aircraft of the period were made of wood and fabric.

were fortunate to have some experienced people to call on including men such as Wilfred Curtis, whose career may be unique in Canadian military history.

Curtis served in all three armed services and after the Second World War rose to become an air marshal and the RCAF's chief of the air staff. Born in Havelock, east of Peterborough, Ontario, in 1893, he had worked for the Royal Bank of Canada.[20] In 1914 he tried to join the Royal Naval Air Service (RNAS), but wasn't immediately accepted and joined the army reserve in Ontario in the meantime. Finally, he was accepted, trained, and began front line flying with the RNAS. So by the end of the war he had served both in the army reserve and in the Royal Navy where as a pilot he was credited with thirteen victories and awarded the Distinguished Service Cross and Bar. Curtis returned to Canada and set up an extremely successful insurance brokerage company in Toronto. He re-joined the Toronto Scottish Regiment as a captain because at the time there was no air force reserve. He had kept up his pilot's qualification so when No. 10 Squadron was set up in Toronto he joined it. He switched to full-time RCAF service in 1939.

Canadian War Museum

A unique career. Wilfred Curtis (left) had naval, army, and air force service. After the Second World War he was chief of the air staff, RCAF.

61

MOBILIZE!

* * *

With unemployment reaching disastrous proportions, the Bennett government began casting about for ideas about how to cope. General McNaughton suggested the regular army open work camps for unemployed men. Bennett approved and so began perhaps the most controversial government initiative of the Depression: the Unemployment Relief program. With army officers and NCOs running the show, new air strips were built out of the bush, new armouries built in some cities, and new RCAF buildings constructed in Trenton.

The relief camps eventually housed 170,000 unemployed. Single, homeless men were given shelter, food, and clothing and were paid twenty cents a day. The program was initially accepted, but before long that all changed. The low pay and the semi-military character of the operation were soon sneered at, the men referring to themselves the "Royal Twenty Centers." If the aim was to curb radical politics, it failed, and eventually the whole thing became hugely unpopular. The "On-to-Ottawa Trek" of 1935 hoped to take the desperate situation of the unemployed to the halls of Parliament. As many as 1,000 men set off from Vancouver and, jumping aboard freight trains, reached Regina. There, on orders from Ottawa, they were stopped by police, but when officers tried to arrest a number of speakers at a protest meeting it touched off a riot. One policeman was killed, forty protesters and five citizens were wounded, and 130 men were arrested.

The relief program undoubtedly had some positive effects for the military. It was the Depression-era equivalent of infrastructure spending. Some, including First World War Victoria Cross winner George Pearkes, thought that without it the army might have faded out of existence altogether.[21] However, one of the great criticisms of the McNaughton years was that the unemployment program completely diverted the army from serious military training.

By the early 1930s most of the army equipment from 1918 was in desperate need of replacement.[22] McNaughton told the defence minister that neither the regular nor reserve forces were capable of defending Canadian shores any longer, McNaughton estimating that, for one thing, it would cost about $6 million just to bring ammunition stocks up to what they had been in 1920. Despite the appeals, the government expenditures were reduced in 1931 while in 1932–33 spending was cut to its lowest level since 1913.

Almost the only new purchase was the Carden-Loyd machine gun carrier, the vehicle that made its startling appearance in Stratford, Ontario.[23] The army had been so worried that its arrival would be seen as aimed at quelling riots (actually, there for just that purpose) that it ordered a clamp down on publicity. In July 1931, National Defence Headquarters advised one military district to keep the existence and movement of the Carden-Loyds out of the press.[24] They were to be referred to as "carriers" and not tanks. Emphasis was to be placed on their role as transport vehicles for machine guns and their crews, replacing horse-drawn wagons.

Most armoured vehicles of the time were small, but still the Carden-Loyd looked more like a toy than anything else. It was only eight feet long and four feet high, smaller than a compact car. Despite the admonitions of defence headquarters, it was generally known by the dainty name "tankette." If it looked like a do-it-yourself project, it was. An early version was assembled by the British military engineer Major Giffard LeQuesne Martel in his garage using spare parts. The tracked Carden-Loyd carried a crew of two and was armed with a .303 Vickers machine gun. The armour was thin and there

Department of National Defence, Directorate of History and Heritage

Missed opportunity. Ford and Chevrolet each offered similar armoured vehicles to the Canadian army in 1934. Both, including the Chevrolet, shown here, had a crew of four, carried a Vickers machine gun, and had a top speed of more than thirty miles per hour. Only prototypes were produced.

was no overhead protection. With only twelve of them ordered, it was hardly enough to equip even a single squadron and, in the event, they were divided up among the regular infantry regiments. The prospect of forming a miniature armoured force or a mechanized infantry company evaporated.

The purchase of the Carden-Loyds was one of only three faint attempts to acquire armoured or mechanized vehicles before 1938. One glimpse of new equipment came in 1934 when the cavalry tried out two new armoured cars. They were formidable vehicles capable of fifty kilometers per hour. Ford and Chevrolet built one each at their own expense, hoping for orders, but none came. In addition to those two, in the spring of 1935 the General Supply Company of Canada wrote to NDHQ offering to produce the Disston Tractor Tank — a Caterpillar diesel tractor with an armoured tank body built around it. It had a fully-rotating turret mounting a short .37-mm cannon and a machine gun. Top speed was 6.5 miles per hour. If not needed as tanks they could be converted back to tractors. At a price of $21,000 each, they were half the cost of a British light tank but the army said they were too slow and they were left as just another might-have-been.[25] As Desmond Morton put it, "Canada's soldiers could see tanks, anti-tank guns, armoured cars and machine gun carriers — but only in the newsreels."[26]

As far back as 1921, General McNaughton had emphasized the role mechanization would play in a future war, saying battle would be "faster-moving, harder-hitting and with a very long range of action."[27] He was an advocate of mobile warfare and motorized equipment, however — crucially — that advocacy took second place to his views about "the scientific soldier."

> I believe that when the time comes for us to mechanize, we will find that we have great natural advantages to our credit; as a nation our young men are well educated; they are used to handling machinery of all kinds; they do not lack initiative; and, after our experience in the Canadian Corps, I do not think we need to defer to any one in our ability to organize and work together.[28]

This was a significant issue. McNaughton's approach sounded good but what he was really saying was equipment wasn't that important because in an emergency there would be equipment. The "scientific soldier" would be able to figure it out then. What he really did was simply kick the can down the road. Budgets and the Depression were crippling problems, but McNaughton's inability to come up with better leadership and alternative training left enormous gaps in the army's training before September 1939.[29] The time for an army to train for battle isn't when a war begins, but long before that. While the German army at that point had little armour or mechanization, that did not stop it from conducting extensive training on how armoured strike forces should be employed.[30] There was widespread use of mock tanks and armoured vehicles.

While posted to England, a number of Canadian officers saw British tanks, and as time went on there was vigorous debate among some officers in Canada on armoured and mechanized warfare.[31] As we will see in chapter six, there were exercises in 1936 that attempted this kind of training, but mostly it was done by individual commanders rather than by doctrine laid out or mandated by the top brass or the result of an overall plan of action. In these years the army did not have a practiced understanding of what the war of 1939 might look like.

The problems were not simply with armour or mechanization. It was difficult for the artillery, for instance, to do anything but basic training. In some years there was no summer training camp, but, even if there was, gunners were often limited to firing only five rounds for each gun in their two weeks in the field. Artillery shells, as Jack Granatstein has commented, were just too valuable to actually fire.[32] While the 3rd Medium Battery, Royal Canadian Artillery, and two RCHA batteries were equipped with some trucks in 1929 and 1930, there were no funds to buy any modern anti-aircraft equipment. A speaker at the annual meeting of the Canadian Artillery Association in 1933 reported, "Unfortunately the latest anti-aircraft equipment is foreign to most of us. It differs from what we hold at present almost as much as the smooth bore cannon of the Middle Ages."[33]

Other branches had similar problems. In 1931 the Regina Rifles regiment was one of several units that did not hold a summer camp. Meantime, one reserve officer in another unit said:

> We had a Mechanical Transport unit … [that] had no equipment whatsoever — absolutely none. From 1926 until the outbreak of war we never had one item of mechanical

transport issued to us. Not a motorcycle, not a van, not a truck. ... Training was possible only by using our own imagination and ingenuity.[34]

In January 1931, Armand Smith became the commanding officer of the Wentworth Regiment in Hamilton, Ontario, and kept the regiment going after that almost singlehandedly.[35] Smith was a member of the E.D. Smith jam family and C company was established at the company's plant; the rifle range was in the canning plant basement and the parade square was in the shipping yard. E.D. Smith trucks carried the soldiers to Niagara-on-the-Lake for summer camp. Many members of the regiment, including Fred Woodcock, who would go overseas once the war began, were E.D. Smith employees. In the town of Winona, the regiment was a cornerstone of the community.[36]

In Vancouver, the British Columbia Regiment in April 1934 had 126 all-ranks, down almost forty from the year before.[37] It was typical of many regiments. As of June 1931, the number of men in the reserve army was nominally 51,200, compared with an establishment of 134,800. The Permanent Force was supposed to be nearly 7,000 all-ranks, but its actual strength in March 1931 was only 3,688.[38]

In light of negative public attitudes, little equipment, and almost no money for training, it was a wonder that any of the armed forces members even bothered. "I don't know why we did it," said one reservist. "It became our hobby. ... Those who kept the unit together did so at great personal cost in time and money, and ... in the face of much public jeering at 'Saturday Soldiering.'"[39]

Canada's army, air force, and naval forces have been involved in battles of all kinds all over the world but maybe the most bizarre in our entire history came in 1933 when the army tried to wipe out the Royal Canadian Navy. There were no bullets, no attacks at dawn, but it was a hammer-and-tongs battle all the same.

It had been brewing for years, starting back in 1923 with a turf war when the three separate military departments were combined into a single Department of National Defence. With the amalgamation, the army's Major General James MacBrien tried to make himself departmental chief of staff with final authority over all three services.[40] That was challenged by Commodore Walter Hose, the director of naval services, who refused to acknowledge MacBrien as his boss.[41] Crucially, Hose was supported by a deputy minister, who simply ignored MacBrien's power grab. The clash became so bitter that MacBrien resigned in 1927. Hose stayed on and his title was later changed to chief of the naval staff, indicating that he was an equal to the new army commander.

Round two began when McNaughton took over as chief of the general staff in 1929. McNaughton did not feel himself confined to the mere realm of land battles, instead lobbing opinions on, and trying to exercise authority in, air and navy strategy too. McNaughton pushed for army control because it was the largest of the armed forces and the only one with a developed staff and nationwide command system.[42] McNaughton was also extremely well plugged in politically, having — rather quietly — written some speeches for Prime Minister Bennett.[43]

In 1930 McNaughton had persuaded Bennett that at an upcoming Imperial Conference, he alone should speak for all three services. McNaughton then tried to lever that into a deal to have the army and air force get the lion's share of the new budget in preference to the navy. That performance was repeated in 1932 when McNaughton convinced the government that Canada could

Library and Archives Canada

Battle for survival: Walter Hose (left) struggled to keep the Royal Canadian Navy afloat. Chief of the General Staff Andy McNaughton (right) attempted to wipe the RCN out, favouring the air force for coastal defence.

best meet its obligations at the Geneva disarmament conference by making massive cuts in the naval estimates and only token reductions in the army and air force budgets.[44]

By 1932 the navy had only its two new destroyers and two others that were at the end of the operational life, so the next budget would make or break it. In May 1933, the Bennett government wanted another $3.6 million cut from the armed forces, but it had not decided where the chops would be made. McNaughton, again acting as a super chief of staff, said that cutting each service equally would leave all three crippled.

McNaughton was a champion of air power. He was among those who were inspired by the idea that it would render the traditional role of sea power obsolete.[45] The navy's coastal patrols could be better done by aircraft. At the same time the air force would not have to be large and expensive since civilian pilots could be quickly trained as military pilots. And finally, he felt that in a crunch the Royal Navy would move in and assume control of Canadian coastal defence anyway, so why bother with a tin pot Canadian navy?[46] The McNaughton solution therefore, was to save the army and the air force, but, if necessary, wipe out the navy. As he put it, "the Canadian Navy as presently constituted is not an answer to any problem of Canadian defence."[47]

On June 1, 1933, McNaughton laid out his views to the prime minister and listed where the proposed budget cuts should come. When the meeting ended it appeared the decision was made and that McNaughton had won. The cabinet decided that $3.7 million would be cut from the three services as demanded and that the navy's share would be $2 million. Earlier the navy's budget had been tentatively set at only $2.4 million. However, by the time the review began the budget year was already underway and some of the money had already been spent, so that a $2 million cut in the midst of a budget year meant, effectively, the navy budget would be zero. McNaughton was most of the way to sinking the navy.

McNaughton's adversary in all this was the quiet and reserved Commodore Walter Hose, who is not much remembered today but should be. In 1933 he saved the navy.[48] If someone wanted to invent a fictional naval hero they might start with the early years of Walter Hose. He was born at sea in 1875. His father was the Anglican Bishop of Singapore and his parents were on board a Pacific & Orient ship on their way to India at the time he was born. In 1890 Walter Hose joined the Royal Navy at age fourteen and was sent to HMS *Britannia*.

Hose and other youngsters went off by themselves and, after learning the basics, boarded a warship to travel to the remotest corners of the earth. They were picked on mercilessly as they went, but, if they survived that, they learned how to become the best fighting sailors in the world.

Hose spent most of the next twenty-one years at sea. He was a capable officer and while his assessments were positive, they were not enough for him to reach flag rank. Compared with the gold braided rulers of the king's navy, his career was unspectacular. So, in 1909, seeking new challenges, Hose contacted the head of the Canadian Naval Service. He was offered command of the elderly cruiser HMCS *Rainbow* and transferred to the RCN in 1912.

When the First World War began Hose managed to get *Rainbow* operational despite the lack of a trained crew. The vessel became the first RCN ship ever to go to sea at wartime. Later, he seized some German merchant ships as prizes. In 1920 Captain Hose was summoned to Ottawa as acting director of the Naval Service and appointed director in 1922. In the next years he demonstrated an abundance of political acumen, talent, and ambition. Hose had two great achievements before 1933. The first has already been mentioned — the establishment of the RCNVR. The other success was in convincing the government to buy HMCS *Skeena* and *Saguenay* in 1929. Two good ships do not a navy make, but it is difficult to imagine what the RCN would have looked like without them.

Now the stage was set for the showdown with McNaughton. In 1933 Hose sent a number of memoranda to the government arguing against the proposed budget cuts.[49] Hose said that the air force was not, as McNaughton claimed, able to perform coastal patrols as well as the navy. Planes could not operate in poor weather, could not board or seize a vessel at sea, and had a much more limited range than a ship. If convoys were needed, air patrols would not be as effective and were impossible at night.

On June 23, 1933, Hose was summoned to appear before the treasury board. The commodore put his job on the line, making it clear that if the navy suffered further substantial cuts he could not continue. Could he not "lay up the ships for a bit?" He argued that the loss of trained sailors and officers combined with tying up ships at a dock for years would be the end of the service anyway. This was the moment of decision — either choice would have enormous long-term consequences. The board backed down. One member said, "I'm convinced. You've made your case clear to me."[50]

That should have ended the battle, but, like a suspense novel, there was one final twist on the last page. Even after everything, the government again wavered. At that point fate intervened in the form of a senior British admiral, whose name sounds right out of Gilbert and Sullivan. Admiral Sir Reginald Aylmer Ranfurly Plunkett-Ernle-Erle-Drax, RN, the commander-in-chief of the America and West Indies station, happened to arrive in Ottawa.[51] Questioned about the government's plans to cut budgets, Admiral Drax underlined the importance of sea power and the absurdity of having a navy with no ships. That was that. In the end the naval budget for 1933–34 was cut by $200,000, not the $2 million proposed by McNaughton. Hose's forceful personality and political touch saved the RCN. The unspectacular sailor had defeated the dazzling ballistician.

One last note. Despite their official and long-standing animosity, it is remarkable that McNaughton and Hose were friends off duty. "We fought all day and fished all night," said McNaughton.[52] Hose was promoted to rear admiral and retired in June 1934. The budget battle was his final victory.

After the First World War there had been hope that international disputes would be resolved by the League of Nations, but it turned out to be a complete failure. In 1931 the Japanese army began to occupy the Chinese province of Manchuria, which the League didn't stop. When Italy's Benito Mussolini invaded and annexed Ethiopia, the League looked even weaker. Canada didn't help by disavowing oil sanctions proposed against Italy. New disarmament talks in Geneva in May 1934 broke up when Hitler withdrew Germany from the conference.

The weakness of the League and the developments in several world capitals led Britain to make a significant decision in 1932. It abandoned the "Ten Year Rule," an official opinion recorded each year that no major war would be expected in the following ten years. The rule had been a catch-all excuse for all kinds of defence cuts. The decision to drop it marked the first step toward British rearmament. In July 1934, Parliament approved expanding the Royal Air Force, increasing the number of home defence squadrons from fifty-two to seventy-five, and aiming for a total of 128 fighter squadrons within five years. This was the period that marked the birth of the Spitfire and Hurricane.

The rebuilding of the Royal Air Force had a dramatic effect on some Canadians. The Big Cut had decimated the RCAF, so dozens of aspiring

Canadian pilots made their way to Britain instead. Some went on to out-standing careers in the RAF, including Wing Commander Johnny Kent who joined in 1935. Kent, from Winnipeg, got his flying license in 1931 at age nineteen and his commercial license two years later. His RAF flying before the war included the near suicidal job of making more than 300 deliberate airborne collisions with various experimental barrage balloons. He became one of the legendary Battle of Britain pilots while flying with No. 303 (Polish) Squadron.

Britain's biggest problem was that it had never recovered financially from the wreckage of the First World War and yet its costly colonial and empire responsibilities remained. One admiral called Britain, "a gouty giant."[53] At this time the defence of the empire was still the top priority. While RAF and Royal Navy rearmament gathered speed, it was not until 1938 that the British army switched its priorities from fighting brush fire wars in the far corners of the empire, to a possible battle in France or Belgium.

The British frequently pouted that the dominions were not help at all in defence. Mostly the British paid little attention to Canada, but there were two questions that did matter. First, if Britain were dragged into a European war, would Canada help or not? And second, why didn't Canadians at least look after their own back yard? That last was nothing new. As far back as 1862, during debate on a Militia Bill, the *Times* of London had said, "If Canada will not fight to protect its independence, neither will England.... If they are to be defended at all, they must make up their minds to bear the greater part of the burden of their own defence."[54] Maurice Pope, later a lieutenant general, commented that when he attended Imperial Defence College in 1936, one of the candidates said that Canada's contribution to imperial defence should be five cruisers and twenty-five air squadrons.[55]

A brutally frank view of Canada as seen through British eyes came from Sir Maurice Hankey, a civil service mandarin who visited Canada as part of a tour of several empire countries in 1934.[56] While noting "fervid Imperialism" in Australia and New Zealand, Hankey was struck by "a calculating aloofness" of Canada. It seemed to him "extremely dubious" whether Canada would ever support Britain in a new European war. Everywhere there were highly vocal isolationists and "disloyalists." With an election coming up in 1935, the politicians seemed cautious, timid, and helpless while French Canadians were bitterly hostile to Imperial defence. He went on, "in the prairies there are great blocks of unabsorbed aliens (Ukrainians, Russians, Poles, etc.) who have absolutely no sense of loyalty to the empire." As for English Canadians, many had "fallen on hard times and are in a bitter, resentful frame of mind." At the Canadian Institute of International Affairs, where left wing thought was prominent, people would talk "a lot of dreadful slop."

Hankey's comments show that while the political situation in Europe was far from clear in 1934, the top minds of the British government were already looking at the possibility of war. Preparing for it would take years of planning and preparation. The British were not merely musing about what to do, they were taking action on rearmament. Some of their actions preceded those in Canada by three years. It raises the question of how it was possible that the Canadian government could only begin rearmament in 1937 when all it had to do was watch what was happening in London in 1934. Canada's progress on rearmament could not have given the British much to cheer about. Having twenty-five air force squadrons for empire defence or for anything else was beyond the most ardent dream of the RCAF in 1934 while there were not going to be five cruisers, nor, indeed, any cruisers in the Royal Canadian Navy before the war.

Nevertheless, the Royal Canadian Navy was clearly committed to empire defence. There was no NATO in the 1930s, so the only collective strategy Canada had was to be part of British Empire defence. That was fine with Commodore Percy Nelles. With Hose's retirement, Nelles, an ardent, unrepentant Anglophile, was appointed the new chief of naval staff. The bantamweight Nelles did not have a hard time getting the job; he was the only one qualified.[57] He was a competent and experienced, if uninspiring, leader, but the fact that there was no one else was a measure of the lack of depth in the navy's leadership.

Nelles was born in Brantford, Ontario, in 1892 and was among the first group of Canadian naval cadets in 1908. He made his name as second-in-command of the British cruiser HMS *Dragon* during a South American tour in 1930. Part way through the voyage the captain dropped dead, so Nelles became acting captain and finished the cruise. He came home to take command of HMCS *Saguenay* on its commissioning in 1931. He was sent to the Imperial Defence College in 1933 and was then appointed assistant chief of the naval staff at the end of that year. Nelles was determined to continue his predecessor's unwavering campaign to re-equip the RCN with a fleet of modern destroyers.[58] His conviction was that cruisers were simply too large and too expensive for the RCN, but the destroyer was at least a blue-water fighting ship that had enormous versatility.

Each year the Canadian destroyers demonstrated what they could do when they joined Royal Navy exercises in the Caribbean. One year the Canadian ships were part of the attacking force on an enemy fleet made up of the battleships *Nelson*, *Rodney*, and *Malaya*, along with the aircraft carrier *Furious*. But no matter the enemy force, each exercise followed the same pattern. The RCN trained neither as a sovereignty patrol force, nor against submarines or aircraft; instead, it operated as part of the RN in the clash of two armadas — big fleet operations. As Commander Kenneth Hansen has argued, the clear result was that "the selection of destroyers as the basis of Canada's interwar fleet had the effect of keeping the RCN relevant to the needs of the RN battle fleet."[59]

The iron determination of Nelles and others, combined with the training in the Caribbean, were designed to forestall any attempt to reshape the navy into a navalised version of the Fisheries Protection Service. Smaller (and cheaper) ships such as sloops or cutters could have done the job of sovereignty protection with perhaps one bigger cruiser for protection against surface raiders. In fact, that was exactly the recommendation of Britain's first sea lord later on.[60] Having destroyers and using them in big fleet training, to the exclusion of all else, was a double edged sword, however. It showed that Canada was part of the British Empire's collective security blanket which — true enough — Canada needed. Not incidentally, it fit perfectly with the "more British than the British" sensibilities of Percy Nelles and guaranteed that the RCN was going to be a branch plant. In the meantime, Nelles joined virtually the entire array of gold braid in the Royal Navy in thinking that the submarine threat had mostly been taken care of.[61]

MILESTONES

DECEMBER 11, 1931 — The British Parliament passes the Statute of Westminster, giving Canada greater independence, including control of foreign policy.

FEBRUARY 9, 1933 — The Oxford Union Debating Society passes a resolution: "That this House will under no circumstances fight for its King and country." The vote is 275 to 153.

NOVEMBER 30, 1933 — General Sir Arthur Currie, the commander of the Canadian Corps in the First World War, dies.

SEPTEMBER 26, 1934 — The 82,000-ton liner *Queen Mary* is launched in Britain. It becomes a troop ship during the Second World War.

* * *

Prime Minister Bennett had said in 1930 that he would conquer the Depression or perish in the attempt and after five years it was clear he was perishing. As Maurice Hankey had noted, a federal election was coming up. The Depression had reached its nadir in 1933 and the economy was beginning to show faint signs of life. Still, the relief camps — the opposition called them slave camps — had become a national symbol of Bennett's failures. The "Bennett Buggy," a car with the engine taken out and pulled by a horse, was a common sight on the prairies. For decades the cry of the prairie farmer, whatever plague or misfortune he suffered, was "God damn the C.P.R.," but by 1935 the prime minister had replaced the evil railway as the target of the farmers' scorn. It didn't help that the Conservatives suffered from internal divisions as cabinet minister H.H. Stevens left to form the Reconstruction Party while some other Tories switched to support the Liberals. Bennett did what he could to clear the deck. He ejected McNaughton from the top army job because the work camps had made him a political liability. He was shuffled off to be the head of the National Research Council.

The end of McNaughton's term of office as chief of the general staff in 1934 brought with it disappointment. In the beginning there had been the hope that revolutionary ideas were at hand. Few senior officers had been so highly regarded; he was just the man to re-invigorate the army. The Depression had undoubtedly dashed many plans. However, there was more to it than that, including the ugly confrontations over the relief camps and then the tangle with the navy. After five years the evidence was that McNaughton's ideas were strictly conventional. This had been the time to professionalize officer training, side-track the deadwood, and make sure that armoured warfare and the use of aircraft were an integral part of training. Little of that happened; it was a missed opportunity of far reaching proportions.[62] Also important to the future battlefield was that McNaughton pushed the infantry and the cavalry (or future armour) to the background in favour of the artillery. Of the seventy-five Canadian officers who were awarded PSC (Passed Staff College) as graduates of Camberley or Quetta Staff College, only seven came from the cavalry. Even though the infantry was far larger, the artillery and infantry were each awarded twenty-one vacancies.[63] The result was that apart from the artillery, combat arms were unready for senior command in 1939.

Because of the Depression, McNaughton had concluded that Canada had to have a military organization that would not disrupt the economic life of the country.

> We need no large standing army nor any large force for very quick mobilization. We need rather to be able to assure the possibility of creating large forces, sea, land, and air, on reasonable notice. It follows that a citizen Militia with a small Permanent Force for instructional duties, and possibly ... an effective coast defence organization, is what is required in the way of land forces and if this is so, no radical change in our present system is necessary.[64]

Not having any standing army meant that there was no quick reaction force for an emergency. It was quite clear that the government would have never have authorized spending for any such force. Still, if McNaughton imagined that a small, highly trained, permanent-force nucleus would do the job, the answer was it was only ever "small" and never highly trained at least in modern warfare.

There was another failure too but in this case McNaughton's worthy efforts were defeated by the politicians. As early as 1929, McNaughton had tried to promote building an arsenal in Quebec. There was a small arsenal that made small arms ammunition and limited quantities of field artillery shells, but McNaughton championed a much larger operation that would also manufacture guns and carriages up to four-inch calibre. His view was "I regard it as in the highest degree important."[65]

Despite McNaughton's push, in early 1930 the Liberals refused to authorize any new arsenal, despite it being a basic requirement in any emergency. Apart from the cost, the idea of the government being in the arms business was seen as too ugly. "Canadians, under a Liberal government, would not become Merchants of Death," said Desmond Morton, "even in their own interests."[66] Later some work was done as an unemployment relief project but weapons production was delayed repeatedly.

The issue resurfaced again in 1937 when then chief of the general staff, Major General Ernest Ashton, reviewed the whole matter for the defence minister. Ashton pointed out the difficulty the army had because of the small size of Canadian production and long delays in getting equipment and ammunition from Britain. He concluded that, in the light of the desperate international situation, it was out of the question simply to wait until Britain could meet Canada's needs. At the same time he said existing neutrality legislation in the United States made that country a doubtful proposition. The only effective course of action, he suggested, was "the setting up in this country of an armament industry designed to diminish our dependence on external sources of supply."[67] However, there was little progress.

If McNaughton's full plan had been carried out earlier, one estimate is that the cost of the arsenal would have been between $30 million and $35 million. By 1944 the government had spent $130 million in constructing plants for the production of ammunition, bombs, and mines, while another $130 million had been invested by the Crown in the gun and small arms industry.[68]

Despite the disappointment of the McNaughton years, there was one great achievement, although it was not finished by the time he left his post as CGS. It was a top-to-bottom, no-holds-barred shake up of the structure of the reserves and the Permanent Force. It was impossible to maintain fifteen divisions, which, in any event, existed only on paper. It was far better to reduce the establishment to seven divisions — six infantry and one cavalry. McNaughton would have settled for a nucleus of two divisions equipped as a core force to be expanded on mobilization, but even that was hardly possible.[69] McNaughton wanted to cut back the number of cavalry regiments to make the whole army a more balanced force. Consideration had to be given to coastal threats, but, more importantly, the army had to focus on a possible war in Europe. Despite his best efforts, his attempts ran into a nightmare of special interests and bureaucratic delays and was not finished by 1935.

The army and air force were in worse condition at the end of 1934 than when McNaughton had been appointed CGS. As a valedictory message, McNaughton had prepared a synopsis of the situation as he saw it. It was scathing. His memo to the government became one of the most vivid descriptions of the military at the time and one of the most quoted. The memo was titled "The Defence of Canada," and in it McNaughton reviewed the existing dangers the country faced and the manpower and equipment available. Once it had been read, no government could ever say it had not been warned or that it didn't know what the real situation was.

As for the air force:

> There are only 25 aircraft of service type in Canada, all of which are obsolescent except for training purposes; of these, 15 were purchased before 1931 and are practically worn out. The remaining 10 were procured in 1934 from the Air Ministry at nominal valuation; they are old army co-operation machines.... Not a single machine is of a type fit to employ in active operations. Not one service air bomb is held in Canada.[70]

However, his principal message was his overview of the army:

> As regards reserves of equipment and ammunition, the matter is shortly disposed of. Except as regard rifles and rifle ammunition, partial stocks of which were inherited from the Great War — there are none.
>
> As regards equipment, the situation is almost equally serious, and to exemplify it I select a few items from the long lists of deficiencies on file at National Defence headquarters.
>
> There is not a single modern anti-aircraft gun of any sort in Canada... The stocks of field gun ammunition on hand represent 9-minutes' fire at normal rates for the field guns inherited from the Great War and which are now obsolescent.... The coast defence armament is obsolescent and, in some cases defective in that a number of the major guns are not expected to be able to fire more than a dozen or so rounds. To keep some defence value in these guns, which are situated on the Pacific Coast we have not dared for some years to indulge in any practice firing.... About the only article of which stocks are held is harness, and this is practically useless.

CHAPTER FOUR

THE FAT LITTLE CONJUROR

In the general election of October 14, 1935, William Lyon Mackenzie King's campaign slogan was "King or Chaos." It was a reference to the economic misery of the Depression and to the R.B. Bennett Conservatives, but the "chaos" might just as well have referred to the voting itself. It was an election in which 894 candidates were running. There were the familiar party names, the Liberals and Conservatives, but there was also the new Co-operative Commonwealth Federation. The ballots also listed candidates from Social Credit, the Reconstructionists (a breakaway Conservative party), Liberal-Labour, Labour, Liberal-Progressives, United Farmers of Ontario-Labour, Socialists, and Communists. It was a wild free for all.

King, of course, was on pins and needles about the outcome. The night before the vote he and his friend, Joan Patteson, sat down for a séance. The two conjured up the ghosts of King's grandfather, William Lyon Mackenzie, and his grandmother, Isabel Mackenzie.

> No presence could be more real than those who spoke with us tonight. It all ended as I would wish with grandfather and grandmother Mackenzie in at the close. I went to bed shortly after midnight confident of victory tomorrow, with a majority of from 45 to 60.... [1]

In some elections the spirit world did no better than bad pollsters in predicting King's future, but this time the "Other Side Polling Company" was mostly right. When the votes were counted King's program of modest economic change and a vote split among Conservatives handed the Liberal party a thumping victory — 171 seats to the Conservatives' thirty-nine. The win marked only the second time in Canadian history that a defeated prime minister had returned to office.[2] Significantly, King won fifty-nine seats in Quebec, meaning the Quebec caucus made up a significant voting bloc in the Liberal Party and in Parliament. King won fifty-six seats in Ontario.

William Lyon Mackenzie King, a brilliant political leader but also Canada's strangest prime minister. He was the central figure in the struggle for rearmament from 1935 to the outbreak of war in 1939.

Library and Archives Canada

The victory marked the beginning of thirteen continuous years in office for King. From 1935 onward the country began to recover its economic strength, only to be shaken and then transformed by war and after that transformed again by a post-war social revolution that included government services like the Baby Bonus.

While King was enormously respected and Canadians voted for him again and again, and while his achievements in the following years in office may have been monumental, the truth is mostly what people talk about today — if they talk about him at all — is that he was so weird. His character and habits have invited vitriolic pot shots to this day. Perhaps the bitchiest and most acidic description of King was that of diplomat Charles Ritchie who pictured him as "a fat little conjuror ... with flickering, shifty eyes and an appliqué smile."[3] He has also been called "one of the dullest dogs in Canadian history (at least until his diary was uncovered)"[4] and a man who combined "unswerving self centredness with terminal halitosis."[5] Left-wing poet F.R. Scott — admittedly no friend — described King's method of operation as a "cult of mediocrity" that operated on the notion, "Do nothing by halves / Which can be done by quarters."[6]

In 1935 King was a dumpy sixty-year-old with thinning grey hair. He was devious, nitpicking, and obsessed with hidden messages in the hands of clocks. He was not much loved in the way, say, Laurier was loved. He suffered from chronic insecurity. He even found it painful to watch himself in news-reels. "I do not like my appearance anywhere," he wrote in his diary. "A little fat round man."[7] He was alarmed about the Group of Seven painters and new-fangled women's bathing suits, and under his pudgy face lurked a shameless tightwad. He was "unmilitary," never quite getting military ranks right nor having much understanding of the military.[8] But even with all that and much more piled on, King was always something of an enigma. There was something about him you couldn't quite put your finger on. His longtime friend Violet Markham wrote, "those who knew him best will be the first to admit that in some respects his character was baffling."[9]

King's most unusual legacy was his diary, unique in Canadian history. While it was withheld in the early years after his death, by 1980 the entire opus had become public. It is staggering in length — 30,000 pages with King scribbling away until just three days before he died.

As Charles Stacey said, King inhabited two worlds, a public world of pol-itics and at the same time, a strange, private world populated by his family, his innumerable women friends, and the spirits of political titans of yore. He worshiped his mother, kept a shrine to her in his private library, and his greatest burden was meeting her expectations. Certainly no other woman, especially potential wives, could live up to her, which is likely why he remained unmarried. As Jack Granatstein says, "She drove him. She made him what he was; a narrow, frustrated, sexually inadequate, power-mad man."[10]

Starting in 1933 King spent hours and hours in the world of séances, seated beside "the little table" at his Ottawa home, Laurier House.[11] On his sixtieth birthday, December 17, 1934, King received good wishes from a galaxy of dead Canadian leaders while among "visiting" British politicians was the former Prime Minister William Gladstone. Of course, many in England and in Canada were addicted to table rapping, séances, clairvoyance, palmistry, and crystal gazing. Many prominent figures in Britain such as Sir Arthur Conan Doyle, the creator of Sherlock Holmes, were ardent advocates. But King almost never let the séances intrude into his decision making. The entire ritual was more to confirm what he already believed and calm his insecurities than to give new direction.[12]

Among his greatest obsessions was with a series of dogs, all named Pat. His diary entry for July 14, 1941, tells that the prime minister was upset. King was at his country estate Kingsmere and his Irish terrier, "the truest friend [he] ever had," was dying. King cancelled a cabinet meeting to sing "Safe in the Arms of Jesus" to his dying dog. Abnormal? Says Granatstein, "Abnormal in the sense only that there isn't a wife to talk to every day, so he talked to the wretched dog."[13]

King was a famously wooden speaker, but journalist Bruce Hutchison, who knew him well, said his spontaneous speeches, though rare, were much better. His prepared addresses "maintained his own antique style of classic rotundity, convoluted sentences, occasional florid passages, grand and wooden gestures."[14] Leonard Brockington, the ablest Canadian speaker of his time, was hired to add "even a faint wash of colour" to King's speeches, but when the prime minister got his hands on them the "brilliant hues of that superb orator were systematically dulled into a steady gray [sic]." For reasons no one knew, any speech draft presented to him could not include the words "challenge," "sober," or "decent." King was not a memorable phrase maker in the mold of Churchill, but his comments included the successful "King or chaos" election slogan and his all-purpose response in the 1930s to questions about war: "Parliament will decide." In the conscription controversy during the war he commented, "not necessarily conscription but conscription if necessary," but even that was cribbed from a Toronto newspaper.

But to leave a picture of him simply as King the Strange or King of the Occult would be totally misleading, because in politics King was the titan of his era.[15] He was extraordinarily shrewd, a man who could and did dominate such alpha males as C.D. Howe. He was a political operator of the first rank and when it came to running things on Parliament Hill, a wily manipulator of his caucus, his cabinet, and his government.[16] According to Harry Ferns, who worked in the prime minister's office a bit later, King had a "preternatural sense of what was up in the House of Commons and could anticipate a question before the opposition had even thought of it."[17] As Bruce Hutchison said, he was "seismographic in registering every tremor of public opinion." He could be as ruthless as a mafia don. Normally he was an inveterate procrastinator and delayer of difficult decisions, but by one description he could be a "reckless plunger" if the occasion required.[18] He gave no quarter to the opposition and smashed the career of Arthur Meighen. He rode his secretaries to nervous breakdowns, but was oblivious about it because he was a workaholic himself. When he landed in political trouble, newspaper writers may have howled, political opponents may have wagged fingers, Royal Commissions may have delivered denunciations, but he survived them all and kept on surviving for the next thirteen years. He was he was far and away the most crucial decision maker of all in the coming struggle over Canada's rearmament.

It sometimes looks as if his last name was "Mackenzie King," a double-barreled name without a hyphen, but his family name was just King. His famous grandfather was William Lyon Mackenzie, the radical newspaper man, first mayor of Toronto, and old rebel leader in the Upper Canada Rebellion of 1837. King cherished his grandfather's memory his whole life long.

Willie King was born in what was then Berlin, Ontario — now Kitchener — on December 17, 1874. Busy Berlin, the locals called it, was crowded with German language newspapers, German church services, German choirs and clubs, and, as of 1897, a stone bust of Kaiser Wilhelm on display in a central park.[19] King spoke almost no French and knew little about francophone Quebec, but in his early political career he delivered a speech in fluent and well-accented German.[20] All that German influence may account for King's later belief that the

German and British empires could live peacefully together. The Germans and British did in his hometown.

King attended the University of Toronto, the University of Chicago, and Harvard and finished with five degrees including one in law and a doctorate in political economy. When he was twenty-six years old and attending Harvard he was given time and money to visit Europe. He stopped at numerous German cities, including the capital that in his German-language speech he had called "the old, beloved city of Berlin." His claim to fame was becoming, still in his twenties, Canada's first federal deputy minister of labour, and he was considered a young sensation in Ottawa. He got the job in 1900 as the result of his university work and articles he had written on sweatshop labour conditions. He remained deputy minister for eight years mainly conciliating industrial disputes.

In the general election of 1908 King ran in his hometown as a Liberal and was elected. He joined the Laurier cabinet in 1909, only to be defeated in a new election in 1911. From 1914 to 1919 he was a troubleshooter in industrial disputes in the U.S. and an advisor to J.D. Rockefeller Jr.[21] King then resumed politics, and although he lost in 1917, he was elected Liberal party leader after Laurier retired. King first became prime minister in December 1921. He was prime minister through most of the 1920s until 1930 and then opposition leader until his 1935 political rebirth.

In late 1935 he and his government took office with King needing every bit of such interest as he had in military affairs. Canada's situation was plain enough. As General McNaughton had said, the country was basically defenseless, or as James Eayrs put it, King had inherited "armed forces without arms."[22]

The new prime minister appointed Ian Mackenzie, a British Columbian who operated at the shallow end of the political pool, as his defence minister. Mackenzie was energetic in parliamentary debate, but one polite summary says his papers don't appear to show that he was "closely and constantly concerned" with what went on.[23] Mackenzie was a First World War veteran, and, while the prime minister liked him, he also knew that Mackenzie was a bad boozer. Mackenzie also had an almost impossible challenge — to put defence on the agenda at a time when few others in the country showed an iota of interest.

The new chief of the general staff, Major General E.C. Ashton, ensconced in the Woods Building just steps from Parliament Hill, aimed a barrage of memoranda at Mackenzie to make sure the minister knew about the situation in the army and air force.[24] Shortly after the election McNaughton himself phoned one of William Lyon Mackenzie King's advisors as a reminder about the CGS's final memo. Mackenzie was alarmed. The resulting memo he sent to the prime minister described the army and the air force as being in a "most astonishing and atrocious condition."[25]

A later report to Parliament included what McNaughton had said but also added equally grim news about the navy. In an apparent reference to the situation in the Pacific, Mackenzie noted that Canada did not possess adequate forces to guarantee its neutrality in a shooting war.[26] Assuming that a danger existed on just one coast, the minimum force required for effective naval patrol, the navy believed, would be six destroyers, four minesweepers, and twelve auxiliary vessels. In October 1935, Canada possessed two effective destroyers, two due for the scrap heap, and one minesweeper. As a result, Mackenzie said Canada was incapable of defending its coastal cities, or shipping in the area, against a determined attack by even a single raiding cruiser. Equipment for such defence, whether by land, sea, or air, "simply did not exist." He added, "The organization and armament of the Canadian forces had little relation to the recent development of the art of war." In summarizing the basic problem the King government faced, Charles Stacey said, "At no time since 1919 had the Dominion had a genuinely realistic defence policy; the variations as between successive ministries had been simply varying degrees of neglect," while the public had simply been indifferent to it all. A long and expensive rebuilding process lay ahead.

Despite the Mackenzie memo and Ashton's work, nothing much changed for months after King took office. What is more, King did not actually see the McNaughton memo for nearly a year. This seems unaccountable, except that King had only a tiny staff at a time long before hundreds of civil servants toiled in the prime minister's office or the Privy Council office. So the first opportunity to seize the issue of the desperate shortcomings of the military simply slipped by.

What the military had to work with was the previous Estimates of the department, those for 1935–36. They had amounted to about $30 million, but nearly $12 million of that was for unemployment relief programs. Spending for the army was $10 million, an increase of about $1.3 million from the year before. The navy would receive $2.4 million and the air force, including civil aviation, would increase by about $1 million to $3.7 million.[27] For the first time in many years the budget tide was changing, but the new money was barely enough to begin making up the enormous shortcomings of each of the forces.

It didn't help that before the new government had barely taken office the international situation blew up. Italy invaded Ethiopia. The issue was taken to the League of Nations, but it was not clear what the international body might do. It could call for military action to either punish Italy or kick the Italians out of Ethiopia, and if either of those things happened that could trigger a new European war. Would there be a French-British military campaign to stop Italy? If so, would Canada be dragged into it?[28]

The prime minister saw at once that military intervention by the League could mean calls for a new Canadian army force sent overseas, similar to the Canadian Expeditionary Force of the First World War which, in turn, could mean a reprise of the conscription crisis of 1917–18. Quebec cabinet ministers, including King's Quebec lieutenant, Ernest Lapointe, hoped that the League of Nations could settle the issue, but in any event wanted no military solution that involved Canada. Meantime, Nova Scotian James Ilsley was among King ministers who took the opposite view. This was the time to stop the dictators in their tracks. It came down to either Canada supporting military sanctions, in which case Lapointe would resign, or it would not support military sanctions, in which case Ilsley and possibly others would resign. So here was the dilemma that was to torment the government for the next four years. Many in French Canada were completely against any new military adventure against Italy or later Germany. If you don't want to be part of a new European war, why do you need to rearm?

King's response to the Ethiopian invasion was precisely the same one he would follow in the years to come. He hoped that the League would only call for economic but not military sanctions. "My own feeling is that, if Canada carries out her part with respect to the economic sanctions, we should not be expected to go further. … Our own domestic situation must be considered first, and what will serve to keep Canada united."[29] In other words, a key element of King's strategy was simple avoidance. He would delay and avoid doing anything until it was *absolutely* necessary. In this case it worked, because the question of sanctions was never actually put to a vote. The outcome was that nearly every nation in the League condemned Italy's action, but none of them, including Canada, lifted a finger to do anything about it.[30] The Ethiopian crisis had left in its wake two key points. First, it became clear that Europe was increasingly divided between fascist states and the Western democracies, and second, it showed that when the chips were down, Western democracies preferred to look the other way.

The crisis also gave King a convenient excuse for putting off action on rearmament at home. In a later review of events, the prime minister said that since this country had called on Italy to withdraw and on other nations to implement greater disarmament it would be hypocritical for Canada to begin a major rearmament campaign. Rearmament might be misinterpreted both at home and abroad. King told Parliament:

> as a Government we felt it unwise to arouse discussion in this House on matters of defence, especially when there was the possibility that our actions would have been entirely misunderstood by other countries as well as our own. We urged the Minister of National Defence not to press for moneys to make good the depletions and deficiencies in defence to the extent he deemed necessary until the ... European situation ... had somewhat cleared.[31]

More positively, King also had decided to conduct a thorough review of both defence policy and estimates and have a cabinet committee look into the matter. Appointing a committee hardly counts as decisive action, except that in this case the committee was made up of the prime minister himself, the justice minister, finance minister, and defence minister — clearly, a heavyweight crew. The decision signalled that defence questions were being regarded with "new seriousness" in Ottawa.[32] In the months ahead the committee met with top military officials with the result that there was a modest budget increase, but, crucially, not for another year. The issue of rebuilding the military was on the table, but even so there were not going to be any quick fixes. In his view, this was not an emergency that required immediate attention.

The estimates for 1936–37, that is, the first estimates put together by the new King government itself, were presented before the cabinet review was finished. The figures were almost the same as the previous year, at just under $30 million.

However, they did include a special supplementary estimate of $5.2 million allotting more money to the navy and more than $1 million in additional funding to the air force. Earlier in 1935, the RCAF had been able to order a few new aircraft — six Westland Wapiti and four Shark torpedo bombers. In addition, Boeing Aircraft, which at that time had an operation in Vancouver, was contracted to build enough additional Sharks to equip two squadrons.[33] As well, in 1936 the first of the Supermarine Stranraers* were ordered. While the Stranraer was new, the other two planes were old hat. According to pilot Larry Dunlap, the Wapiti — the same aircraft that made its hapless way to Halifax on mobilization — "glided like a brick." He called it the "worst apology for an aircraft that it has ever been my misfortune to fly."[34] Unfortunately, Dunlap aired that opinion in front of Wing Commander Lloyd Breadner, the man who ordered the planes. Breadner's reaction was incandescent. However, the RCAF picked the planes because the air force didn't have any money for anything better.

The open cockpit Wapiti had a two-man crew, two machine guns, and could carry 600 pounds of bombs, and was meant for sleepy outposts of the empire. Its origins were unlikely. At the end of the First World War, Britain had dozens of biplane wing sets left over from DH9A aircraft, so Westland designed a new fuselage and the two parts were simply slammed together. The second aircraft, the Blackburn Shark, was a torpedo bomber whose Armstrong Siddeley Tiger engine was hopeless. A second batch of planes used better Bristol Pegasus engines.[35] The Shark was being used on floats, where its limitations were amply revealed. In one test two 100-pound bombs were put under the wings so it could be used as a regular bomber, but no matter how long the take off run, the Shark was able to climb to only about 100 feet. The bombs were put aside. The limited number of new planes meant the RCAF had to continue operations with both the Siskin fighter and Atlas ground co-operation aircraft.

The air force was still operating with a skeleton staff. As of March 1935, it had 794 all-ranks in the regular force and 308 in the reserves.[36] The regular ranks included Aircraftsman Gerry Bell, very likely the first black member of the RCAF. He joined in 1931 and in 1935 was posted to No. 19 Squadron in Hamilton.[37] As with the army, money was so tight that air force reservists received only token pay. The reserve squadron in Toronto (later 440 Squadron) estimated that pay was only available for fifty-four hours per person in 1935,

---

* The Stranraer had many nicknames. On the west coast it was sometimes called "the flying centre section of the Lion's Gate Bridge."

and thirty-six hours in 1936. All money except what was earned at summer training camp was turned over to the squadron.

As for the navy, its two relics — HMCS *Vancouver* and HMCS *Champlain* — were finally going to be retired, but the possibility of replacements remained vague. The new budget did not include any money for improving naval shore installations despite the fact that the naval magazine at Esquimalt had been declared a menace to the surrounding community as long ago as 1905. Despite the lack of money and everything else, somehow a loyal core of officers and men remained in the services. Among the promising young officers from these years was Harry George DeWolf. In July 1935 he was appointed assistant director of intelligence and plans and was promoted lieutenant commander.[38] He had enlisted in the navy at fourteen, and while he spent years at sea, he never really overcame seasickness. By the time of his promotion DeWolf had just turned thirty-two years old.

One of the pervasive problems for the RCN during the Second World War was that most officers hated paper pushing jobs and avoided them at all cost. That meant a service-wide weakness in administration, especially when the navy had to expand quickly. However, DeWolf was getting the opportunity to learn skills that would be essential for a career at the top. A second promising officer was Leonard Murray. Between 1922 and 1939 he spent a third of his time on attachment to the Royal Navy so that he could be given more challenging leadership positions.[39] Starting in 1934 Murray was assigned to be a senior officer in Halifax where he ran, among other courses, summer training for the reserves.

MILESTONES

FEBRUARY 12, 1935 — A historic document entitled "Direction and Location of Aircraft by Radio Methods," is submitted to the British Air Ministry by Radio Research Station staff member A.F. Wilkins and Robert Watson-Watt. It was an important step in the development of radar.

SEPTEMBER 1935 — In Germany, an ME 109 took to the air. Because of delays in the Jumo engine, it was powered by a British Rolls-Royce Kestrel engine. Features included automatic wing-slots, a small, light airframe, and enclosed cockpit.

MOBILIZE!

* * *

In July 1935, *Maclean's* magazine ran an article called "The Germany I Saw" by businessman B.W. Keightley.[40] "Everyone seems to be busy in Germany," Keightley enthused after a visit to Leipzig and Berlin. He added that if new elections were held in Germany Hitler would undoubtedly win, hands down. Keightley said, "So far as the great majority of average German citizens are concerned, the present Nazi regime is what they wanted and voted for; and now that they have it, they are entirely satisfied with it." Keightley didn't mention that opposition to Hitler was being ruthlessly stamped out. The article was naïve in the extreme, but his comments probably represented what many ordinary Canadians and Europeans believed about Germany in 1935. The country had been a basket case, but Hitler's tough love was turning it around.

By the time Keightley's article was published, Hitler had already repudiated the restrictions on German rearmament in the Treaty of Versailles. Germany was producing 265 planes a month, and by the end of 1935 it had produced almost 2,000 combat aircraft. The German government also began compulsory military service to build up its army to thirty-six divisions. In the navy, Commodore Donitz was appointed commander of U-boats while Germany began a U-boat building campaign. The original plan was to build 268 boats by 1939, but, fortunately for Canada, Britain, and the Allies, the actual number constructed was fifty-eight.

In the summer of 1936, U.S. President Roosevelt made a formal state visit to Canada that included talks with Prime Minister King. For some time Roosevelt had been developing a "good neighbor" policy. Before the visit he had commented, "Our closest neighbors are good neighbors. If there are remoter nations that wish us not good but ill, they know that we are strong; they know that we can and will defend ourselves and defend our neighborhood."[41] Speaking at the Citadel in Quebec City, Roosevelt said he could hardly think of Canadians or Americans calling each other "foreigners." It helped form a new idea that in future the two countries might find themselves co-operating against a menace from abroad.

While Roosevelt sent an important message about bringing the two countries together, a second message carried a more pointed message: "War

Plan Red" had not been forgotten entirely. The continuing Japanese expansion in the Far East was still causing the Americans deep concern. Roosevelt told Prime Minister King privately that if Canada were unable to secure the west coast, American forces might have to do so.[42] He asked King for a highway across Canadian soil so that American forces could move quickly to Alaska in a crisis. The prospect that the United States could be attacked from Canadian territory had also been raised the year before during Congressional hearings in Washington.[43] Even if Canada remained neutral that could cause problems. "Neutrality involves responsibilities as well as rights," one officer said. "If [Canadians] did not take steps to carry out the laws of neutrality we would have to do so, I imagine."

A year later top American commanders visited Alaska and British Columbia and were dismayed by the poor state of Canadian defenses. A Canadian memo in 1936 said "As Canada is, for practical purposes, incapable of resisting such a United States invasion there would be no course open except the humiliating one of accepting the violation of its sovereign rights."[44]

Even at the time of "War Plan Red" the problem was not new. As early as 1921 Canadian army officer and journalist C.F. Hamilton had contended that American might become "an uncommonly ugly neighbor" if Canada could not safeguard its neutrality against Japan.[45] In the same period, the Ottawa *Evening Citizen* also editorialized that the United States had to look to its own interests. If Canada was not doing its share, it was because the government had "virtually disbanded" the Royal Canadian Air Force. Canada could afford to ignore its responsibilities no longer "unless the pretense of nationhood is to be completely abandoned."[46]

On November 26, 1936, the British cabinet decided to speed the Royal Air Force expansion program, aiming to complete it in two years instead of four. That came after the British received the news that the German air force would be as large as the RAF within one year. There was also a move to re-equip — although not expand — the British army. In another decision the government created "shadow factories" built by public money and managed by industrial companies. They were meant to duplicate what any factory could do so that if it were destroyed in an attack, the production could continue. Earlier in 1936 the cabinet had approved expanding the Royal Navy.

Preliminary work was started on a new class of battleship, which became the King George V class. However, it was 1937 before the keel was actually laid, and as an indication of the lead time required to build capital ships, the King George V was not finished by the time the war broke out in 1939. As might have been obvious to any defence planner in Ottawa, it was already too late to begin some rearmament programs.

Even with these moves in Britain, in the Commons in November 1936, renegade Conservative Winston Churchill attacked the government's rearmament program as inadequate. He said the government was "decided only to be undecided, resolved to be irresolute, adamant for drift, solid for fluidity, all-powerful to be impotent." The Labour Party held just the opposite view. In March 1934, Labour leader Clement Attlee said, "We on our side are out for total disarmament." In July of the same year Labour tried to censure the government over its planned RAF expansion. On May 22, the day after Hitler claimed that German rearmament offered no threat to peace, Attlee asserted that the German leader's speech gave "a chance to call a halt in the armaments race."

On March 7, 1936, German troops reoccupied the Rhineland, which had been a demilitarized zone. Germany had political control of this area, but it was not allowed to put any troops into it. Commanding the leading company of SS-Leibstandarte was Captain Kurt Meyer, who would become infamous in 1944 as the commander of an SS regiment that murdered unarmed Canadian prisoners. The reoccupation of the Rhineland was a huge gamble for Hitler. However, as it turned out, France was going through yet another political crisis at the time and did nothing. Most people in Britain were blasé, saying the territory was essentially Germany's anyway. The event is a watershed in European history. It has often been said that the reoccupation was the last moment when Hitler might have been stopped in his quest for expansion. Heinz Guderian, the German tank expert, said after the Second World War that if the French had intervened in the Rhineland in 1936, "we should have been sunk and Hitler would have fallen." Hitler himself later called the forty-eight hours after the march into the Rhineland, "the most nerve-wracking" of his life.

In Ottawa the prime minister found out the ominous news about the Rhineland when he got a call from an Ottawa newspaper. King relayed the news to other ministers at a cabinet meeting. "There was complete silence on the part of all," he wrote afterward. "No one had anything to say."[47] Former Prime Minister

R.B. Bennett, at this time opposition leader, agreed with King that a debate in Parliament would not be helpful and it didn't happen. However, commenting on the events in Europe, Canadian officer Maurice Pope said, "on this date a Second World War became inevitable."[48]

CHAPTER FIVE

CANADA IN A MAD WORLD

On August 26, 1936, the power players of the William Lyon Mackenzie King cabinet and the military top brass gathered around a table in Ottawa.[1] Scattered around the room were Prime Minister King; Charles Dunning, a former Saskatchewan premier and at this point the federal finance minister; Ian Mackenzie, the defence minister; and Ernest Lapointe, the formidable justice minister. They met with the chief of the general staff, Major General Ernest Ashton, Commodore Percy Nelles of the navy, and Air Commodore George Croil, the air force commander. Croil was an unusual character. His previous jobs included running a tea plantation in Ceylon and, during the First World War, being a pilot for T.E. Lawrence — Lawrence of Arabia.

The politicians were likely in a grumpy mood since in sitting down they had to put aside the day's distasteful news headlines. Maurice Duplessis and his Union Nationale government were being sworn into office in Quebec that very day. After thirty-nine years in government, the Liberals had suffered a landslide defeat in a provincial election. On the military situation King had finally seen the McNaughton memo. He wrote, "the impression left on my mind was a complete lack of any real defence. I felt we must get aircraft and equipment & look after our coasts — defend our neutrality, & be prepared to mobilize industry."[2] King recorded what happened next.

> General Ashton gave a review of the existing situation, which was splendidly presented. I formed a quite different conception of his abilities — a very clear mind. Commodore Nelles read his report of conditions re naval defence. It was well prepared.... [Air] Commodore Croil of the air force

impressed me very favourably ... the impression left on my mind was one of the complete inadequacy of everything in the way of defence — the need in view of changed methods of warfare, of having some coast armament against raiders, chance attacks by sea and air. [But] It is going to be extremely difficult to do anything effective without a cost which this country cannot bear.[3]

Both King and Lapointe knew that any spending on national defence would be a tough sell in any part of Canada, but especially in Quebec. Lapointe was especially emphatic that no money be spent for Canadian forces to be sent abroad. Finance Minister Dunning wanted to know where the money would come from. The prime minister may have already made up his mind about what he wanted anyway, but the cabinet committee finally gave its support for the outline of a new defence program. With everything on defence stuck in a Sargasso Sea for months, events suddenly jolted ahead at neck-snapping speed. The prime minister took the proposal to the full cabinet that same afternoon. He said despite the finance minister's protest the cabinet, "generally accepted the view that we must take action at once, & next step to get a practical scheme for consideration."[4]

That next step would be what, in today's parlance, would be called an "action plan." It was duly prepared and the result, according to James Eayrs, is "one of the key documents of Canadian history."[5] Accompanied by a windy title, "An Appreciation of the Defence Problems Confronting Canada with Recommendations for the Development of the Armed Forces," the plan was delivered on September 5. It included a striking conclusion: "the possibility of a major war is becoming more apparent. Indeed, the realization is growing in many minds that the cessation of hostilities in 1918 was but an armistice."[6]

All services contributed to the report, but it was largely written by Colonel Harry Crerar, the director of military operations and intelligence, the same man who became commander of the First Canadian Army in the middle of the Second World War. In 1936 Crerar was on the way up. He was forty-eight years old, a contemporary of Bernard Montgomery and Andy McNaughton, trim, with thinning hair and a moustache that was just so. He was bright and, thanks to a bequest on his mother's death in 1919, comfortably well off.[7] Crerar has been described as "an emotional man," but if so he rarely showed it. Like King, there was an aura of dull grey about him.

Library and Archives Canada

Hamilton, Ontario, native Harry Crerar was able but ruthlessly ambitious. He made key decisions in the Hong Kong and Dieppe disasters but survived to become commander of the First Canadian Army.

Crerar was from Hamilton, Ontario, and had worked for the Ontario Hydro-Electric Power Commission before the First World War. He was a graduate of the Royal Military College and served in the First World War, ending up as a lieutenant colonel. Like McNaughton he stayed in the army after 1918. He was able, but was also fiercely, ruthlessly ambitious, and it didn't hurt that he was in the artillery rather than the cavalry. Not long after the First World War he was sent off to Camberley Staff College in England, where he excelled. As a mark of the dreary pace of promotion, even a man with his abilities was still stuck as a lieutenant colonel for fifteen years.

Even today the report that Crerar and the others wrote is gripping. It repudiated isolationism outright. It said the developing crises in the Far East and in Europe should worry Canada "no matter how reluctant that concern may be." It noted that in the Pacific the Americans had decided on a crash naval rebuilding program. It acknowledged the view expressed by President Roosevelt that if Canada could not protect itself the Americans might arrive uninvited to do the job. As for Europe, the report said if it came to war, both Canada and the U.S. would likely be a part of it.

> In spite of a sincere desire to hold herself aloof from partici-
> pation in the war of 1914-1918, the United States was inev-
> itably dragged in. It is suggested that in the event of another
> world war the same force would again bear the same com-
> pelling influence, possible with even great intensity. It seems
> unlikely, therefore, that in such circumstances Canada can
> hope to remain at peace. It follows that the dispatch overseas
> of Canadian Forces may again be necessary.[8]

For the armed forces the report prescribed an urgent five-year rebuilding program. The navy should go from two to six modern destroyers plus four minesweepers and get the increase in manpower to provide crews. The report proposed a twenty-three-squadron air force and raising air force personnel numbers from 1,100 to 3,700. For the army, the outline called for two infantry divisions that could be quickly mobilized and sent to either the Pacific or Atlantic for coast defence if needed. Unstated was that if the army's mobile force could be moved to the coast or from one coast to the other, there was no reason it couldn't also be sent overseas. For the army that was a crucial bit of camouflage. The army's view was, "the most serious or important military issue for which we, in this country, require to be organized ... concerns itself with the mobilization and dispatch of a Canadian Expeditionary Force to take part in an empire war of the first magnitude."[9]

The price tag would be about $65 million in the first year and about $200 million over five years.[10] By standards of later budgets and the size of the developing threat, that's the kind of money it would take to make up for years of chronic supply shortages and lack of new equipment. However, in terms of previous budgets, the costs were simply staggering. The figure for the first year alone was three times the defence estimates for 1936–37.[11] The prime minister was horrified, saying $50 million might be the most that could be delivered in the first year.[12] All this revealed an underlying problem that dated back to 1919. The "floor" set earlier was so low that even a large spending increase would, in reality, not be enough to make a significant difference.

The cabinet met again on September 10 — by coincidence three years to the day that Canada would declare war on Germany. King wrote later that he, himself, was the one pushing hardest to get higher spending approved. All the French-speaking members except Lapointe wanted to leave things as they were.

The military may have had high expectations, but when the time came, its hopes crashed to the ground. The 1937–38 defence budget was ultimately not $65 million as Crerar had proposed, and not $50 million as the prime minister had suggested *might* be possible, but rather $36 million. It was "rearmament lite." Even then, getting $36 million took prime ministerial prestidigitation to "shape" how the increase would be presented to the public. As King said:

> Excepting Mackenzie, I myself presented, I think the strongest case for immediate coast defence, taking the ground that as a Canadian citizen, I thought we owed it to our country to protect it in a mad world ... both on sea and in the air, alike on the Atlantic and Pacific Coasts. I stated it was humiliating to accept protection from Britain without sharing on the costs, or to rely on the United States without being willing to at least protect our neutrality. That we had no enemies, but owed it to ourselves and subsequent generations to lay foundations on which they would have to build. I told Mackenzie he might have to extend his five year program to ten years.[13]

In the end, the key element of the program was to stress that the money was strictly for home defence. It was the only politically acceptable solution. King thought protecting the country "in a mad world" was important, but his colleague, Chubby Power, at first thought it might cost the Liberals the entire province of Quebec in any new election.

The home defence posture was accompanied by a second policy of King's in an attempt to limit political criticism. If anything about sending forces overseas popped up, King had a ready response saying he had made "no commitments" and would make none. In a speech in Geneva King said the British Commonwealth was held together by ties of friendship, similar political institutions, and a common attachment to our democratic ideas but in terms of military commitments, "the Canadian parliament reserves to itself the right to declare, in the light of circumstances existing at the time, to what extent, if at all, Canada will participate in conflicts in which other members of the Commonwealth may be engaged."[14] For the next three years King would oppose any deal that even remotely suggested that Canada was going to send troops overseas. It was just too divisive.

MILESTONES

MAY 28, 1936 — British scientist Alan Turing submits "On Computable Numbers" for publication. He later becomes one of the key figures in decrypting the Enigma machine.

JULY 14, 1936 — RAF Bomber Command formed.

AUGUST 1, 1936 — Adolf Hitler opens the Olympic Games in Berlin.

In early 1937 the government introduced the new defence estimates in the House of Commons. On February 19, the prime minister delivered his first major statement on defence policy since the election. King said he regretted that the estimates had revealed the extent of unpreparedness, however, if the real situation had not been stated, Parliament and the public would continue to believe that the country was safe. But, in fact, it was not safe.

King said the spending would involve buying two (not four) destroyers for the navy, and as for air defence: "the entire air force appropriation may be considered as replacement." In other words, the air force was in such a state of calamity, the rebuilding would have to start from scratch. One provision in the estimates was a real shocker. The government moved the air force to the top of its spending priority list. As for the army, while the money would buy some more guns and ammunition to protect Canadian coasts, there was no question of equipping an expeditionary force for overseas service.

Ian Mackenzie's comments underlined those of the prime minister. "There is no idea whatever of sending a single Canadian soldier overseas in any expeditionary force," he said, deftly ignoring the capability of the "mobile force" being able to move to Europe if needed. He added "there is not a single cent providing for that in the estimates … [there is] provision only for the defence of Canada."[15] He called the defence spending proposals "a Canadian defence policy for the direct defence of our Canadian shores and our Canadian homes."[16]

There was a whiff of genius in terms of public opinion in the way King set up the defence policy and the budget. Certainly, home defence was an essential requirement, but saying there would be no commitments to Britain or to any European war would obviously appeal to isolationists, pacifists, and neutralists. The isolationists, in King's view, were growing in numbers in French Canada.[17] "No commitments" might appeal to them all because they fervently wanted Canada to stay out of any war. But mostly, like a gleaming new car, King's policy had curb appeal for the majority of English Canada because it did not rule out participation in a war in some circumstances. It didn't say Canada would not commit itself to supporting the empire in the right situation.

The policy was by no means heroic. Likely many English Canadians were exasperated by a prime minister to whom clouds of obfuscation were second nature. Of course the policy of no commitments was also simply a device for putting off decisions that might divide the country. The slogans "no commitments" and "Parliament will decide" only meant that the government would decide when it was good and ready. It had a majority in Parliament and it could decide any time it wanted. But it sounded good.

After King's speech in Parliament he received plaudits from many quarters, including from Vincent Massey, a former Liberal bagman and King's appointee as Canadian High Commissioner to London. King replied, "I hope members of the British Government will realize that in taking the step we did, our Government ran the risk of splitting the Party in half…. I had finally to settle differences between members of the Administration which seemed irreconcilable."[18] His message to Massey was undoubtedly to score political points in London, and, of course to trumpet his own role, but it also showed the importance of national unity as a factor that was severely crimping rearmament.[19]

King's plan put the official opposition Conservatives in a quandary. They thought Canada was foot dragging on empire defence and wanted more spent on the military. Leading Conservative George Drew said: "There has been no attempt whatever to face the situation in terms of reality either in regard to the Naval Service or the Air Force."[20] However, such was the disorganization and lack of unity in the party that in the end the Conservatives chose to remain silent in the Commons. It was a different matter for Grant MacNeil of the Co-operative Commonwealth Federation, a First World War veteran and now a pacifist. "The real danger is that we may assist in setting the stage; in erecting, as it were, a scenario of fireworks which may be set off at any moment by a madman or a fool." MacNeil quoted General Sir Maurice Wilson: "when we prepare for war we get war."[21]

Even so, there was other opposition as well. An ardent skeptic of rearmament was Dr. Oscar Skelton, King's rabidly anti-Imperialist foreign affairs advisor. Canadian opinion, Skelton thought, was still under the control of "an older, jingoistic, British-oriented minority which had the power, public position, and wealth to carry the dominion into a British war whatever the sentiments of the majority."[22] One anti-military voice was the left-leaning magazine *Canadian Forum*, which, although it had only a tiny circulation, had many influential contributors including Dr. Norman Bethune. *Forum* lashed out time and again against defence expenditures, its February 1937 issue saying: "In a rapidly re-arming world we have, we are told, to protect our own shores. This is humbug." The article said isolation from Europe is "a policy not of cowardice but of common sense."[23] When it came for Parliament to decide, as many as sixteen Quebec Liberals voiced opposition to the defence increases, but in the end a CCF amendment opposing them was defeated 191 to seventeen.

The new role for the Royal Canadian Air Force had far reaching consequences. The RCAF would get more money, but, more crucially, the government was determined to make it Canada's first line of defence. The decision followed the British government, which in 1933 made the RAF its number one rearmament priority. In Canada the army had long been the dominant force in Canada, the largest of the armed forces in size and budget, but from this point on the air force would have first crack at new equipment and expansion. In the 1936–37 budget the RCAF got about $4.1 million, $1 million more than in 1935–36. Although army spending was higher — totalling $11 million — its increase was small.[24] In time the RCAF would overtake the army in total spending.

Even if it was not the complete answer that General McNaughton had trumpeted earlier, the air force did provide clear advantages in coast defence. Aircraft could be moved quickly to either coast if a threat developed. It was also easier to expand the air force than, say, the navy because of the long lead time needed to build new ships. For King, pushing the air force was a "modern" approach.[25] He was very likely influenced in his thinking by British Prime Minister Baldwin whom King met in October 1936.[26] The British prime minister said training air crews and having plenty of aircraft was "the essential of modern warfare."

The armed forces then set about implementing the home defence policy, looking first at coast defence. The air force would provide reconnaissance and bomber aircraft, the army coast artillery and the navy, its destroyers. Building up coast defenses was an enormous undertaking. The army had coastal fortifications at Halifax on the Atlantic and Esquimalt on the West Coast but with the money available it could only upgrade the West Coast. Because of the threat of a U.S.-Japanese war, it was given priority.

The RCAF had two coastal seaplane bases, one at Jericho Beach in Vancouver and the other at Dartmouth, Nova Scotia. At the beginning the cheapest solution was to expand existing seaplane bases so the Vancouver base was updated beginning in 1936–37. The only land plane base in B.C. was at Patricia Bay, today the site of the Victoria International Airport. However, starting on March 1, 1936, Sea Island Airport — today's Vancouver International Airport — became a new base and the headquarters of the newly established Western Air Command. Officers there would take charge of West Coast air defenses.

The result of all the focus on B.C. was that the Atlantic coast was largely a British protectorate. By the time the war started almost nothing had been done in the Atlantic region. At the same time the requirement for coast defence trumped any other army equipment purchases. It was able to make only limited progress on mechanizing tanks or on increasing the strength of the regular army.[27] Boosting the small size of the regular army — which totalled 3,509 men in 1935 — was not a top priority. Plans to buy new uniforms and a new light machine gun were postponed. In a supreme irony, as a result of both the lack of a domestic armament industry and of Britain's inability to deliver new equipment because of its own demands, as much as $3.7 million of the new appropriations remained unspent at the end of the fiscal year.[28]

While the RCAF was on the road to modest rearmament it still had only twenty-three military aircraft in the entire air force and had still not really recovered from the Big Cut.[29] There were two early acquisitions. Never mind getting hot new fighters or bombers, a top priority was simply to get a new basic trainer. The air force had been using the de Havilland 60 Moth but in May 1936, Phillip Garratt, a First World War pilot, became general manager of de Havilland Canada and designed a Canadian version of the newer Tiger Moth. It incorporated changes requested by the RCAF, including an enclosed cockpit for winter flying, a padded instrument panel, and other refinements. About eight months later de Havilland won a long sought order for twenty-six Tiger Moths to be built at Downsview, on the edge of Toronto.* Twenty Northrop Delta planes built by Canadian Vickers were also bought. (When the war began they were dispatched to the east coast.) The Delta was a high performance photographic aircraft built from an American civilian design. It looked racy but it proved to be near useless in 1939.

Terry Higgins, Copyright 2013

The Northrop Delta was a racy design, but turned out to be too lightly built and was near useless once war began. It was soon discarded.

---

* Eventually more than 1,600 Canadian Tiger Moths were built by de Havilland, equipping more than twenty flying schools during the Second World War.

The navy made important progress thanks not so much to the new government money as the generosity of the British. The Admiralty in London agreed to replace the two decrepit Canadian destroyers with two C-class destroyers, similar to the existing *Saguenay* and *Skeena*. The used but usable ships — which became HMCS *Fraser* and HMCS *St. Laurent* — were capable vessels built in 1931 and 1932.[30] They were immediately available at knocked down prices, $978,500 each.

Author Farley Mowat once referred to the RCN's situation as "a pitiful handful of little ships — a navy that the Swiss could very nearly have outmatched."[31] The new ships were a boost for the RCN, but that still meant there would be only two destroyers on each coast. Since ships had to be tied up for replenishment, repairs, or crew training, many times there would only be one destroyer patrolling, or often none at all. Except for small minesweepers, there were no reserve ships or reinforcements, except what the Royal Navy could supply.

An example of how desperate the navy reserve was for equipment was described by one sailor in the reserves in 1936. "The only training aid we had was a model of the foc'sle and cable arrangements of HMS *Hood*, which wasn't particularly helpful for those of us who were destined to go to small ships. There was a rifle range in the basement and the only permanent staff was one retired RN chief petty officer."[32] There was some sea training for the fortunate few. For men like Fred Sherwood, who joined the naval reserve in Ottawa in 1932, summer training at sea could last up to four months. By 1936 he was able to get a watchkeeping certificate, which qualified him to be in command on the bridge of a ship.[33]

Being kicked to the bottom of the government's priority list was not the only shock for the army reserve in 1936. In that same year some historic and colourful regiments were wiped off the order of battle. Work on the massive reorganization had begun under McNaughton but it took a lot of finesse to overcome bitter resistance. Finally, in May 1936 it went ahead.[34] The new plan reduced the number of divisions from fifteen to seven — six infantry and one cavalry plus additional support groups. It killed off dozens of units, but most of them existed only on paper anyway. It also rebalanced the army, which until this time had far too many cavalry regiments, not enough artillery, and no tank units.

The seven divisions would meet the heaviest probable commitment for home defence, including allowance for a mobilized "field force."[35] The 123 infantry battalions were cut in half, but new machine gun battalions doubled their number to twenty-six. Artillery field batteries rose from sixty-nine to 110, medium batteries increased from twenty-five to thirty-one, and anti-aircraft batteries from one to six.[36] There was an increase in the number of Royal Canadian Engineer units as well as Royal Canadian Corps of Signals.

Every effort was made to preserve battle honours, traditions, and unit names, but it was a messy affair. The Border Horse, which came from communities on both sides of the Saskatchewan-Manitoba border, including Brandon, lost its identity when it was amalgamated with the 12th Manitoba Dragoons. Les Chausseurs Canadiens, based in the Quebec City region, were also gone. The Kootenay Regiment, from the southern interior of British Columbia, including the smelter city of Trail, was erased as an infantry battalion. However, it magically re-emerged as the 24th (Kootenay) Field Brigade, Royal Canadian Artillery.[37]

The Wentworth Regiment, which had been so loyally supported by the Smith jam family, was split. One company became a field artillery battery while the rest was combined with the Royal Hamilton Light Infantry. The Royal Grenadiers and the Toronto Regiment combined into what became in time the Royal Regiment of Canada, later one of the Dieppe regiments.

Although the cavalry was cut back, for the first time the new reserve roster included four armoured car and six tank regiments. Four existing infantry battalions — the Argyll Light Infantry in Belleville, Ontario, the Ontario Regiment in Oshawa, the Three Rivers Regiment, and the Calgary Regiment — became tank formations. A fifth unit, the New Brunswick Regiment (Tank), was formed from remnants of the 7th Machine Gun Battalion in Moncton. The Essex Tank Regiment was created from scratch.

Of course, there were no tanks or armoured cars to equip any of them, nor would there be until 1940. However, the creation of new regiments at least recognized the tank as a weapon of the future. New members could only drool at the establishment that called for sixty-six tanks, eleven wheeled cars, nine trucks, and twelve motorcycles for each regiment.[38] The army sensibly chose to develop closer links with Canada's auto industry by selecting Windsor (home of Ford and Chrysler) and Oshawa (General Motors) for the location of two of the new formations. For the first time members in some tank units began wearing what became their signature headdress, the black beret. The Essex Regiment, not having any traditional headdress, wore them at the regiment's inaugural parade on August 20, 1937, in Windsor.[39]

Since they had no equipment, the units had to improvise. All the 2nd Armoured Car Regiment in Winnipeg had was a vehicle mock-up built by the Dominion Bridge Company. It had no engine so the soldiers pushed it onto the floor of the Minto Armoury to practice mounting and dismounting drills.[40] The 8th New Brunswick Hussars had been cavalry, but that summer was an armoured car regiment, trained without horses for the first time in its history. Their new mounts were thirty-one privately owned vehicles. Regimental members were ordered, perhaps in jest, not to wear spurs when cars were being used.[41] As for other training, Corporal George Lawrence of the 8th Hussars found that one of the usual instructions he received was to "go down to the Q.M. Stores and draw a truck load of imagination."[42]

The regular Royal Canadian Dragoons ran exercises in 1936 that explored the possibilities of mechanized warfare. In August and September at St. Jean, Quebec, the Dragoons combined training of horses, an armoured car, machine guns, and motorized reconnaissance. The motorized reconnaissance force was made up of at least ten private cars owned by the officers.[43] These were useful but the cars were restricted to roads and none of the vehicles had radios. More importantly, there was no doctrine to teach from. The Dragoons history notes that most RCD members were not much impressed by what they saw. One member said, "It never entered my mind that sooner or later we would all be mechanized," while another thought what happened was "more of a curiosity than anything else."[44] In the meantime many in the army continued to have their minds locked in the past. In the mid-1930s, Howard Graham of the Hasty Pees still had to pass a horse riding requirement to qualify as an infantry major. Graham passed but was told not to show his marks to the horse.[45] Not long before the war, Royal Military College Cadet Robert Bennett was told there were three things an officer had to do: first, look after his horse, then look after his men, and if there was time, look after himself.[46]

The Canadian Tank School, which like the armoured regiments had no tanks, was created in November 1936 and was initially located in London, Ontario. Major General Ashton, a tank advocate, picked Major F.F. Worthington of the PPCLI — known to all as "Worthy" — as commanding officer. During 1937 and 1938, Worthington attended a year-long course at the Royal Tank Corps School in Bovington, England.

The artillery tried to use its obsolete anti-aircraft guns for training. As outlined in the McNaughton report, the guns were thirteen-pounder Mark I pieces, "temporarily adapted" during the First World War. There were no modern height-finders or predictors.[47] One west coast officer recalled that the RCAF refused to tow drogues for the anti-aircraft gunners to shoot at in training because without fire-control equipment it was just too risky.[48] One blunt spoken regular officer was Chris Vokes who was posted to do army cooperation work with the RCAF at Camp Borden and Trenton in 1936. In one joint exercise, he said the anti-aircraft guns were pieces of pipe nailed onto scraps of wood.[49] Vokes said the RCAF knew little and cared less about ground force cooperation. Still, here and there were tiny glimpses of the future. Howard Graham got his first ever flight in an airplane on one exercise. He was among fifteen people taken up in a Ford Tri-motor airplane to look for identification strips on the ground. They were used to indicate where troops were located. "We could tell … that aircraft and ground movement in a big way was going to be part of any new war."[50] For the Royal Canadian Army Service Corps, the last Horse Transport parade was held in 1936 as the corps slowly began mechanization.

However, for most part-time soldiers the reserve army was as much a social organization as anything. The pomp, uniforms, and parades of military life were all great for boosting morale. The 15th Alberta Light Horse, according to Fred Scott, concentrated more on fielding a good polo team than any training for war.[51]

It was something of a marvel that Robert Welland was able to join the Royal Canadian Navy in 1936.[52] A bit like winning the lottery, except that enormous skill was involved. Welland, you'll recall, was the young Canadian officer aboard HMS *Fame* when the liner *Athenia* was torpedoed in 1939. At that time he had been in the navy for three years. But back in 1936 Welland was a high-school student, one of hundreds of young Canadians who wrote gruelling civil service exams hoping to become officer candidates in the RCN. For many in the midst of the Depression, passing those exams was virtually the only hope for a paying job. Welland studied German, did exceptionally well in high school, and had served a stint in the Manitoba Horse reserve regiment. Of the hundreds across the country who applied, only eight young men were accepted in the RCN that year. He was one of them. The next year the number was lowered to six.

Earlier on, when he was fourteen, Welland had written on a piece of paper that he intended to become the captain of a warship and an admiral. Seventy years later, living in retirement in Surrey, British Columbia, he still had the paper. He had achieved both his dreams.[53] Wanting to join the navy might have been a considerable leap for a boy from Oxbow, Saskatchewan. He had never even seen the ocean. However, his father had been with the British Pacific & Orient shipping line before moving to Canada, and his tales of the sea helped kindle his son's imagination.

The 1936 cadets were an extraordinary group. Among them was Ralph Hennessy, whose father and other family members had been in the army.[54] The Hennessys were Catholics, but when a navy career beckoned young Ralph was hurried over to the Anglican Church because a lot of senior navy officers were Anglicans. There was also William Landymore who, at twenty, was two years older than the others and had already spent two years at Royal Military College. In addition to Welland, both Hennessy and Landymore also went on to become admirals after the war.[55]

Courtesy Robert Welland

Robert Welland, one of the best-trained young RCN officers on the outbreak of war. In a nationwide competition in 1936, he was one of eight officer candidates selected to join the RCN. In the 1960s he became a rear admiral.

The Royal Canadian Navy had no means of training any of the eight young men of 1936, or any other year, for that matter, and instead they were all sent to the Royal Navy. They started as cadets, below the status of an able seaman. By Welland's own description, in the next three years he slept in a hammock and pushed a wire brush up ten foot-long boiler tubes, learned about anchors and cables and how to handle them on a stormy night, read Morse code at thirty words a minute, was part of the crew of a six-inch gun that hurled shells twelve miles, sailed a twenty-seven-foot whaler around Tobago, navigated a 10,000-ton cruiser from Aden to Singapore using his own sextant, learned the rules about how to duck hurricanes, and, perhaps once or twice, danced with the taxi girls in Penang.[56] Welland later added to this account, saying that while it was true he and other crew members had fired the six-inch gun, it was a rare event. His ship, HMS *Emerald*, was on a mission to show the flag and had to look immaculate for the various sheiks and potentates. Firing the gun cracked the paint.[57]

While officers and men who joined the navy before the war provided a critical mass of experience in 1939, and an even more critical mass when it expanded after that, not all naval careers started with the Royal Canadian Navy or the regular Royal Navy. In 1936 a young man from Winnipeg had his heart set on a career in the British merchant navy. Has father had died and his family lived in modest circumstances, but thanks to money from an aunt, Godfrey Harry Hayes set out from his home town for London to join HMS *Conway*.[58] Dating back to 1829, Conway was the home for Britain's merchant navy cadets at a time when its merchant navy was huge, with as many as 3,000 ocean going ships and another 1,000 coasters. Growing up Hayes had been called "Skinny," which he hated, but didn't much care for "Godfrey" either (what do you call a person named Godfrey for short?). He hoped to call himself "Harry," but someone recognized him as soon as he arrived in Britain, called him "Skinny," and it stuck.

A speech by Viscount Elibank, a member of the British House of Lords and a hard liner on empire defence, triggered a furor in Canada in the summer of 1936. He accused Canada of being an imperial freeloader. In a speech in Calgary, Elibank said, "We have got to make up our minds whether we are going to stay in the Empire or out of it."[59] The speech touched off huffy rebukes and expressions of dismay by the Canadian government and editorialists. A British cabinet committee in 1936 recommended that the self-governing parts of the empire should be immediately requested to help reduce the load of imperial defence.

The government in London decided to put its case directly to two members of the Canadian cabinet, Finance Minister Charles Dunning and Defence Minister Ian Mackenzie, when they were in the U.K. discussing defence contracts. The two met with the chiefs of staff and British minister, Sir Thomas Inskip. The British outlined their grocery list: Canada should buy (and not expect the loan of) two more destroyers, modernize coast defenses and anti-aircraft defenses, spend more to equip and train the army reserve, and develop mobile land forces so that, acting with the RCAF, they would be able to repel coastal attacks. The British also hoped that if war broke out Canada would contribute a supply of pilots and military specialists, including telegraphers and medical staff. The two Canadians were sympathetic, but Dunning said that above all there would be no Canadian commitment at this stage to any European war that might break out. Dunning said there was a strong feeling among Canadians that "they must have the right to decide for themselves."

Neither was there any progress on a British proposal to set up an early and small version of the British Commonwealth Air Training plan. It didn't help that the program was essentially an RAF-run scheme to recruit Canadians for British service.[60] To King, signing it would be a "commitment" — a red flag to pacifists and neutralists in Parliament. It would imply that Canada was doing back room deals to ensure that if war came to Britain, Canada would be already committed because of agreements already signed. Popular British writer Len Deighton has commented:

> It would not be true to say that the Battle of Britain was decided by flying training. And yet it would not be very far from the truth. Just as the all-metal monoplane had to be created from scratch, so was the new sort of fighter pilot like no other aviator.
>
> One of the worst set-backs suffered by the pre-war RAF was the repeated refusal of Mackenzie King, the Canadian Prime Minister — from 1935 onwards — to discuss the Empire Air Training Scheme.[61]

The British government also wanted to set up a shadow armaments industry in Canada (that is, duplicates of those in Britain) with active Canadian government assistance as soon as possible. The British feared that if war broke out air attacks would cripple their own industry, and they knew that the American neutrality laws might prevent getting supplies from the U.S. King was agreeable to the British government placing its own orders for munitions and war equipment, including aircraft plants. Even this approval, however, included a caveat that any plant was subject to Canadian nationalization if needed and prohibition of exports if the Canadian government felt it was necessary. Neither would the Canadian government act as a broker in deals between the British government and individual Canadian manufacturers. King later told the British privately that it would be unthinkable for Canada not to take part in a war if Britain were attacked, but public deals — commitments — were another matter.

Yet, the reality was that the military ties between Canada and Britain were so strong, and at so many levels that they represented a powerful institutional commitment to Canada joining Britain's side in any new European War. Oscar Skelton, the under-secretary of state for external affairs, wondered "How many hypotheses make a commitment"?[62] Canada's armed forces were, except for basic instruction, almost entirely trained by the British, as shown by Robert Welland's training. Canada followed British practice on virtually everything — organization, training, equipment, and communications. One air force officer, George Howsam, said the extensive British training that Canadian officers received in the interwar years was "a godsend." He said, "Without it, we'd have been absolute neophytes."

There were strong links in the post of director of naval intelligence and plans in Ottawa, a job filled by a Royal Navy officer. It was a crucial appointment that amounted to the incumbent being in some respects the second-in-command of the Royal Canadian Navy. The director's job was to provide a link to the Admiralty in London reporting about North America for Britain's worldwide intelligence network. From 1929 onward there were regular conversations between Canadian Naval Service headquarters and the Royal Navy's nearest operational admiral, the commander-in-chief of the America and West Indies station.

There was a wide range of information and intelligence the British provided to keep Canadian forces "in the loop" with latest developments. There were also specific agreements at the political level about Canadian action to support British forces, should war involving both countries break out. As early as 1929 the Canadian government stated privately that the British would be able to base the commander-in-chief of the America and West Indies squadron at either Esquimalt or Halifax to direct Imperial Naval Forces he commanded. Further, two decades before, the Canadian government had agreed to give British vessels full use of the dry docks at Halifax and Esquimalt in peace or war. That was still in effect in 1939.

Another deal to which both the Bennett and King governments agreed was that on the outbreak of war several Canadian-flagged passenger ships would be converted to being British armed merchant cruisers. The Canadian government would look after peacetime storage and upkeep of the equipment and weapons needed to make these vessels operational. As Norman Hillmer notes, the entire setup involving all three forces in myriad ways "constituted a formidable limitation on Canada's freedom of action should Great Britain become involved in a major war."

The perception that Canada was not only an ally of the British but a branch plant was not helped by occasional evidence of patronizing attitudes on the part of British officers. A letter in 1937 from the chief of the Imperial general staff to his Canadian counterpart was addressed to the "Chief of the Canadian Section, Imperial General Staff, Ottawa, Canada."[63]

The British, to their credit, spent a good deal of time and treasure helping out Canada and its beleaguered armed forces, but in return, it hoped for military, naval, and air forces to be there when the time came, but, of course, strictly under British command and control. Who could blame them? RCN sailors joked that they were members of the "Royal Colonial Navy" and it was largely true, and it was the same for the Royal Colonial Air Force and the Colonial army too.

While the King government and the armed forces struggled to deal with the threats of war that might be coming in Europe or the Far East, even in 1936 it was hard to escape the shadow of the past. On July 26, 1936, came another painful reminder of the ghosts of 1914–18. Thousands of Canadians in France, at a place with heroic but painful memories. Vimy. On that day the majestic Vimy Memorial, eleven years in the making, was dedicated by King Edward VIII. At the ceremonies the young King Edward was joined by 3,000 or more

Canadian veterans; a sea of spectators. Among them was Mrs. Charlotte Wood of Winnipeg.[64]

That sun-filled July day, Mrs. Wood was wearing a beret and the medals won by five of her sons who died in the Great War. Two others were wounded but survived. In all she had eleven sons serve in the British or Canadian forces, while the family also had one daughter. Charlotte Wood was British by birth and married Frederick Louis Wood, a widower with six small boys. Later the couple had six other children. Some of the eldest remained in Britain but the parents and the younger children moved to Gunn, a town northwest of Edmonton in 1905. After the death of her husband she moved to Winnipeg.

Among those attending the dedication of the Vimy Memorial in 1936 was Mrs. Charlotte Wood. Eleven of her sons served in the First World War and five of them died.

Just before the formal ceremony at Vimy Mrs. Wood met the king who commented, "Please God, Mrs. Wood, it shall never happen again." The dedication of the memorial, and the presence of so many families demonstrated that in 1936 memories of the First World War were still fresh, still filled with pain.

CHAPTER SIX

EXPANDING TORRENTS, HUFF DUFF,
AND THE FIRST LETTER OF OBSCENE WORDS

In 1936 a science-fiction movie called *Things to Come* scared the pants off people in Europe and North America. Based on a novel by British author H.G. Wells, it was all about a singularly frightening future war. The film, which incidentally starred Toronto-born actor Raymond Massey, portrayed a bombing attack on one city that touched off a global war. The fighting went on for decades and civilization entered a new Dark Age. The story included the use of poison gas and foreshadowed submarine-launched ballistic missiles. In Wells's book, the flashpoint was a violent clash between the Germans and Poles at Danzig. The movie provided just one glimpse of a number of controversies in the 1930s about war. It is often thought that nothing much happened in military development in the decade, but that is most definitely not the case.

The film reflected widespread fears at the time because it was released not long after Britain's "Air Panic of 1935."[1] The "panic" was based on alarmist stories in the British press about Germany's new Luftwaffe. Britain, the newspapers declared, was vulnerable. British air planners thought that, if war came the Luftwaffe might launch a preemptive attack to wipe out London. A later estimate included a bit of math. It said that the Luftwaffe could possibly deliver 3,500 tons of bombs on London in the first twenty-four hours of a war; each ton would cause at least fifty casualties. Indeed, a few years later when the war actually did break out, the expectation even then was that as many as a quarter of a million casualties could be expected in the first twenty-four hours.[2]

The single most memorable line about the future of air power was "the bomber will always get through."[3] It was widely quoted and almost everyone on both sides of the Atlantic believed it. The phrase, used by British politician Stanley Baldwin in a speech in 1932, was based on a simple idea. At the time, twin-engine bombers were faster than single-engine fighters, and so bombers could arrive over a target at high altitude, deliver an attack, and escape before any defending fighters could be sent to attack them. The bombers would almost be back home before the fighter could climb from the ground to the bomber's altitude. Even if a fighter did intercept, the argument went, the bomber's heavy defensive weapons would shoot it down. Baldwin said that in the first five minutes of a future war, any town within reach of an airfield could be obliterated.

There were many air power advocates at the time, including Billy Mitchell in the U.S. and Major General Sir Frederick Sykes in Britain. At one point Sykes described a scene similar to that in *Things to Come*. "Huge day and night bombers will assemble at the declaration of war to penetrate into the enemy's country" with the result that "an enemy's industries will be destroyed, his nerve centres shattered, his food supply disorganized, and the will power of the nation as a whole shaken."[4] Perhaps the most influential writer of them all was Italian General Giulio Douhet, whose book *The Command of the Air* was published in 1921.[5] Douhet was among the earliest writers to portray the true potential of air power, stressing the ability of aircraft to fly over ground troops and attack the enemy heartland. Similar to Sykes's view, the resulting terror and panic would cause resistance in the enemy population to collapse. Douhet's conclusion was that air power could win a war all by itself.[6] The idea gripped air force leaders and politicians alike (and continued to do so right through the Second World War).

Douhet and the others were enormously influential in Germany, while the architect of the Royal Air Force between the wars, Air Chief Marshal "Boom" Trenchard, was also a Douhet advocate.[7] One writer thought, "It may be said, without straining verity, that bombing was what the RAF was all about…. It is chiefly for that reason … that cooperating with the army and navy went right out of fashion between the wars."[8]

In Canada, the air power debate was followed closely. As early as 1924 Wing Commander J. L. Gordon, a bilingual officer from Montreal, attended RAF Staff College and later Imperial Defence College.[9] Gordon wrote a report that echoed the view of the Royal Air Force, stressing the importance of bombing attacks even at the expense of army or navy co-operation. Andy McNaughton was well aware of new developments as shown by his argument that the navy was redundant in coast defence. One Canadian officer, Flight Lieutenant G.R. Howsam, pointed out that aircraft carriers could sail to within a few miles of the Canadian coast then send off attacking forces to bomb major cities.[10] Newspapers and magazines began carrying stories claiming that Canada's Pacific coast cities were vulnerable. Toronto MP Tommy Church told Parliament that enemy aircraft "could be upon us before you could say 'O Canada.'"[11] A Canadian defence policy statement in 1938 noted:

> We are by no means immune to air attack today. Very definitely, at the moment, attack by airships from an overseas base, or by aeropanes [sic] launched from ships, is a probability. Direct attack by aeroplanes from an overseas base is also possible, and it will only be a short time before such will become probable.... Even if peace continues, records of today will be normal performance five or six years hence.[12]

If there had been any doubt about air power's impact on Canada, a reminder came in 1934 with the flight of ten American B-10 aircraft commanded by Colonel Hap Arnold. The flight was clearly a trial run in the event of a U.S.-Japanese war. The aircraft went from Washington, D.C., to Alaska, with stops in Regina, Edmonton, Prince George, and Whitehorse. It was amicable enough, but the flight was a reminder, if anyone in Ottawa needed it, of American military power. What would Canada do the next time the request was made for such a flight, and the next after that? A further demonstration of American air power came in 1935 when Boeing unveiled its four-engine XB-17 which later developed into the legendary B-17. The U.S. Army Air Corps tested the plane in a spectacular flight from Seattle to Dayton, Ohio, a distance of 2,100 miles, at a record-breaking 232 miles per hour.

Although many of the dozens of other aviation breakthroughs did not have a direct effect on Canadian rearmament, a few of them might be mentioned as a measure of the revolutionary change of the period. Among the greatest achievements was radar, which became such a vital part of the Battle of Britain. From the first non-military experiments in Britain, the detection and location of aircraft by radio beams made such rapid progress that by 1940 an operational chain of coastal radar stations covered the east and south of Britain. At 10,000 feet, intruders could be detected at ranges of between fifty and 120 miles. It was effective because it was part of a sophisticated command and control network that received the raw radar plots and rapidly applied them to direct fighter aircraft to their targets. Timing in introducing the system was everything. The developments had just begun working before the Battle of Britain, so Germany had little opportunity to develop countermeasures.

Another vital element in time for the Battle of Britain was the all-metal, high-performance monoplane fighter. For years public interest in aviation had been focused on record-breaking flights and prestige air races, which had led to phenomenal progress in aircraft performance. Speed was important because it meant that with fast fighters the bomber might not always get through. That new fighters arrived at all in Britain is surprising. Fighters, in Boom Trenchard's view, should be kept to the lowest possible numbers, and then only as a concession to weak-kneed civilians. In terms of aircraft, the Spitfire, Hurricane, and their German equivalent, the Bf 109 were all in advanced design stages by 1933. The RAF issued specification F5 34 for a new fighter plane built around the fast-firing American Browning machine gun. It was to have an enclosed cockpit, eight Brownings with 300 rounds per gun giving a total firing time of about fifteen seconds, and as well retractable undercarriage and oxygen for the pilot. The Spitfire's elliptical wing and the famous Rolls-Royce Merlin engine combined to allow a top speed of 360 miles per hour, faster than several contemporary fighters. Over the interwar years, engine power increased from about 225 horse power in 1918, to 500 horse power in the early 1930s, and finally to more than 1,000 horse power for the Hurricane and Spitfire. Meanwhile, the British had something the Germans didn't — higher octane fuel.

Aviation was not the only world that was being transformed.[13] Canadian soldiers may have still been armed with their First World War Lee-Enfield rifles and dressed in the same tunics worn on the Western Front, but dazzling new ideas about land warfare were being presented that were aimed at overcoming static trench warfare. Among the most visionary ideas were the "expanding torrent" and the "indirect approach," concepts outlined by Captain Basil Henry Liddell Hart, the British military historian.[14] Liddell Hart served in the infantry in the First World War, but left the army in 1927. For many years he was a writer with the *Daily Telegraph* and the *Times* newspapers in London, and his output of books and articles and letters was an expanding torrent of its own.

The indirect approach held that direct attacks against an enemy firmly in position almost never worked and should never be attempted. To defeat an enemy you must first upset his equilibrium then launch the main attack. The indirect approach favoured the use of surprise and flanking manoeuvres to overrun command and control centres of the enemy, rendering their fighting forces ineffective and demoralized. The expanding torrent involved concentrating forces at a single point of attack and then pouring a torrent of them past a breakthrough point in a rapid and deep strategic penetration. Really, he was talking about the German blitzkrieg of 1939, and famously, the Germans were among his avid readers.

Liddell Hart was also a proponent of tanks, and in 1925 he wrote that they should be concentrated and used in a single mass. This idea is also often linked to a second advocate of armour, Major General J.F.C. Fuller. Of course, tanks had been used in the First World War and their potential was notably shown at Cambrai in 1917, but their future role on the battlefield was debated.

Another revolutionary notion was mechanization. For the first time, it was proposed to put troops on trucks to conduct operations faster and over longer distances than had ever been possible before. In 1927, combining tanks and mechanized infantry, the British put into the field the Experimental Mechanized Force, the first armoured formation in history designed for independent operation. However, afterward their commitment to tanks and a mechanized army faded. In Canada, armour vanished into a void after the war when tanks being used by Canadians were not brought back to Canada. Except for the Carden-Loyds and a few trucks, the army had no money for mechanized equipment. It is especially unfortunate that the army was not able to adopt at least trucks on a larger scale. Once war broke out, Canada produced 710,000 trucks for the Canadian and British armies, but there were relatively few in the Canadian army before the war. Still, many officers, including Dan Spry, a young lieutenant, were at least aware of what was being discussed. "We studied General J.F.C. Fuller's writings in detail.... We were thinking and training in terms of mobile warfare even if we didn't have the equipment with which to do it."[15] Nevertheless, with the exception of one summer exercise in 1938, there were no large-scale mobile exercises to try out new ideas. As well, most officers studied ideas on their own without the help of any Canadian army doctrine.

While there was no Canadian army college for senior officers, there was an attempt to take part in the cut and thrust of new ideas. Major Ken Stuart, later a lieutenant general, became the editor of *Canadian Defence Quarterly* (*CDQ*) in 1929, a journal meant to stimulate thinking in both the regular and reserve armies. Stuart encouraged officers to write and had books reviewed. The journal included a remarkable exchange by two young officers, Captain Guy Simonds and Lieutenant Colonel E.L.M. Burns. The two debated about the organization and tactics of armoured formations, posing questions that would be raised in precisely the same terms by General Bernard Montgomery following the desert campaign of 1942. Neither was afraid to criticize or offer alternatives to current British doctrine.[16]

Burns, one of the rare intellectuals in the Canadian army, was also a writer whose work, often under the pseudonym A.B. Conway, appeared in such magazines as *American Mercury*. In the *CDQ* he called for soldiers to have more practical uniforms and he was outspoken in calling the cavalry useless. Burns attended the British Army Staff College in Quetta, returning to Canada in 1930.

Simonds had dreamed of attending Royal Military College since childhood. At RMC he was a "star" from the beginning, dubbed "the Count" by his peers because of his aloof behavior. He graduated with the college's Sword of Honour in 1925. Simonds was among officers who benefited from training in Britain being posted to Camberley in England in 1936 and 1937 after earlier passing Staff College examinations.[17] Simonds had the opportunity, as he could not in Canada, to see large troop formations and modern weapons on exercises. He had also spent a summer attached to the British 2nd Division, commanded by Major General Archibald Wavell, a future field marshal. He was marked for future promotion when he returned to Canada in 1938 to join the instructional staff at RMC. Jack Granatstein commented "that two such men could be found in the tiny, stunted Permanent Force was incredible. Unfortunately, they and their few peers were vastly outnumbered by drones, the over-aged, the under-qualified, and the unhealthy."[18]

Radios were among the most notable shortages in the Canadian army in the 1930s. Like air power and armoured weapons, radio communication was about to revolutionize ground warfare. There had been some experiments with wireless military radios during the First World War. In one incident, a member of the Canadian 50th Battalion used an intricate wireless set called the Tyrell

H.W. No. 1, which had a range of more than seventy-five miles. The operator on the front lines was able to communicate with another station as far away as the Eiffel Tower in Paris.[19] In armoured exercises in Britain in the late 1920s tank commanders had used signal flags to communicate, but soon radio began to change the way commanders could move and control their forces.

Radio equipment may have been in short supply in the Canadian army, but at least the Royal Canadian Corps of Signals was established in 1921. Some reservists had civilian jobs with telephone or communications companies as operators, linemen, or wireless mechanics, which paid dividends for the army.[20] Meanwhile, the forces built up a small but critical pool of experts. Ottawa's Bill Megill enlisted in the Signals Corps as a recruit at the age of sixteen in 1923, but then left the army to study electrical engineering at Queens. However, in 1930 he returned, was commissioned, and used his engineering knowledge in the regular army Signals Corps through the 1930s.[21] Radios were temperamental and cumbersome, but there were a few small trials and novel training experiments. The Signals Corps history notes that in one exercise eight Austin roadster cars were fitted with No.1 Wireless Sets on the vehicle's instrument panel while batteries and other equipment were put in the rear.[22] One Ontario signals unit put radio sets on horseback in an attempt to provide the cavalry with mobile communication.

Just before the Second World War the Signals Corps had a few No.1 Wireless Sets that had been developed in 1933 and had a range of up to five miles. It was a forerunner of the No. 11 Set developed in 1938 — the first army radio manufactured in Canada. Northern Electric Company built 100 of them for the army. But when mobilization came in 1939 many of the signals units had still never been able to hold exercises in their assigned roles.

The war at sea was being transformed by the aircraft carrier. The sea battle that had been conducted at a maximum range of sixteen miles — the farthest a shell could be fired — expanded to 200 miles or more, the range of carrier aircraft. There had been attempts to launch planes from ships even before the First World War with HMS *Ark Royal*, the first warship to be built as an aircraft carrier in 1914. In the U.S. two huge carriers, *Yorktown* and *Enterprise*, were ordered in 1934 and the U.S. Navy had five carriers in 1939. Britain had seven carriers in operation in 1939 and five under construction. Germany ordered the 23,000 ton aircraft carrier *Graf Zeppelin* in 1935 and another after that but neither was completed. Of course as it became painfully obvious on December 7, 1941, the Japanese had spent tremendous effort developing both aircraft carriers and superb planes to put on board.

But for the Royal Canadian Navy the most important new developments were in anti-submarine warfare. As with the tank and airplane, the submarine had shown its worth in the First World War, so much so that by the end of 1916 U-boats had sunk 1,360 ships. Only the introduction of convoys overcame the submarine threat. The first step toward a new German U-boat fleet came in 1933 when a Finnish submarine, *Vesikko*, was built to German order. While so many other weapons and theories were changing in the interwar years, the U-boat was not changed much. New boats had stronger hulls and the boats could dive deeper but they were still essentially meant to fight and operate on the surface. Many could barely make five knots underwater.

One might have expected that with modest change in technology, the submarine would not have been much of a threat when the Second World War began, but there were several reasons why things turned out differently. Certainly, the fall of France in 1940 put German submarine pens much closer to the mid-Atlantic than they had been before so they could be much more effective and, as well, the German use of "wolf packs" — submarines fighting in groups — was revolutionary. But the most crucial reason was that the Royal Navy and the Royal Canadian Navy simply did not take the submarine threat seriously.[23] In Royal Navy fleet exercises, submarines were often ordered to withdraw after dark. The RN regarded the submarine service as a career dead-end, while Canada lacked trained officers and a submarine to conduct anti-submarine training. The Royal Navy felt that aircraft, convoys, and anti-submarine devices would be decisive. As then-Commodore Nelles put it, "If international law is complied with, submarine attack should not prove serious. If unrestricted warfare is again resorted to, the means of combating submarines are considered so advanced that by employing a system of convoy and utilizing Air Forces, losses of submarines would be very heavy and might compel the enemy to give up this form of attack."[24]

While there was not much change in the U-boat there was a world of change in anti-submarine technology, although it took years before some of it became effective and before it was deployed on RCN ships. The challenge for Allied navies was trying to find U-boats in the vast reaches of the Atlantic and, once they were located, to close in and attack them. The solution was provided by three different types of equipment: High Frequency Direction Finding (HF/DF or, more commonly "Huff Duff"), radar, and asdic/sonar.[25] Huff Duff was a series of shore stations that could intercept messages from vessels at sea. It was an absolute requirement for German submarines to keep in regular radio communication with the service's headquarters. So the Royal Navy's "Y" Service, its radio intelligence organization, set up listening stations in the British Isles, Iceland, Gibraltar, Newfoundland, and Bermuda to establish bearings for their transmissions. When a message was tracked at two different locations, a cross reference could be obtained. That information was sent to the Operational Intelligence Centre at the Admiralty that calculated the location of the U-boats. This was not a complete solution because the locations were often too far from Allied warships or aircraft to be of tactical use. The answer was to put Huff Duff equipment on warships, but their huge size prevented that until 1941.

Radar was used at sea to locate U-boats at closer range. As mentioned earlier in its use for aircraft location, it was invented in 1936. It was eventually used by allied navies for surface searching, fire control, and ranging, as well as navigation. Small ship-borne sets became possible when two British scientists invented the cavity magnetron in November 1939. When war broke out there was considerable research and production going on in Britain, but there was no radar industry in Canada. The National Research Council in Ottawa started developing a Canadian radar set in 1941, which became the SW1C (Surface Warning 1st Canadian) radar. However, it was almost a complete failure.

The third development was initially known as asdic, but later became better known by its American name, sonar. It was a sound transmitter mounted in a dome attached to a warship's hull. It sent out a high-frequency sound impulse — a "ping" — through the water and when the ping sound was returned to the source, a trained operator could locate a submarine and its bearing. Depth charges could then be used. Some original research on it was done by University of Alberta scientist R.W. Boyle in 1918.[26] There were many problems with sonar, however, including the fact that it wasn't on board all anti-submarine ships. While HMCS *Fraser* and HMCS *St. Laurent* had been equipped with asdic in 1937, the equipment was only just being installed on a third East Coast destroyer when the war began.

Perhaps the greatest problem with asdic/sonar was the Royal Navy's near total belief in it and its blindness to its shortcomings. "The Admiralty believed that asdic was 80 percent effective at locating submarines and naval officers interested in ASW — and there were not many in the late 1930s — regarded it as almost infallible."[27] Robert Welland, one of the few who was a qualified antisubmarine specialist early in the war recalled:

> Only a few officers knew all about asdic and even after I qualified in 1940, petty officers and sailors were not told all about it, and weren't allowed access to the books [as a security measure]. Only specialist anti-submarine officers knew all about the machine. Consequently, captains of ships didn't understand what the instrument was capable of doing and didn't know how to use the damned thing. So a lot of gung-ho guys in destroyers felt the world revolved around guns and torpedoes, when actually the most important instrument on board was the asdic. None of them had ever been trained on it — none.[28]

There were many other developments in the war at sea. The German navy produced the quintessential commerce raider, the pocket battleship. The British built many new ships, including the Tribal class destroyer, whose design was finalized in 1935. It was much bigger than earlier British destroyers and very fast at thirty-six knots. Although the Royal Canadian Navy had an obsession about the Tribals, they couldn't be built in Canada in the early part of the war. At the same time, the British needed every one they could build. In a telling comment about the RCN, historian Marc Milner notes, "Not being able to pull a fleet from a hat when you needed it" was clearly one of the perils Canada faced in 1939.[29] It was not until March 1940 that Britain allowed Canada to contract for two Tribals in British yards, with two more to follow in 1941. Canadian shipyards did later attempt to build Tribals, but the progress was so slow that the ships were not finished by the time the war ended.

Military and naval intelligence turned out to be one of the crucial fields in the Second World War. One of the most disquieting situations the Canadian military faced in the interwar years was that it was without any meaningful and independent intelligence service. Canada relied almost totally on the British.

There was the director of military operations and intelligence, but he had few independent resources.

> As 1939 dawned the Canadian government had no formally established method of gathering or producing foreign or military intelligence. Its knowledge of world affairs came largely through the good offices of the British Secretary of State for Dominions. The Foreign Office, the War Office and the Admiralty also provided diplomatic and military intelligence of some value, but eight years after the 1931 signing of the Statute of Westminster, Canada still gathered no intelligence of its own.[30]

There were attempts to combine the small intelligence assets of all three Canadian services into one unit. The most notable attempt came in March 1938, when Colonel Crerar, then the head of Military Operations and Intelligence, suggested a Joint Service Intelligence section be formed as a sub-committee of the joint staff.[31] However, neither the air force nor the navy liked the idea, seeing it as an army power grab.[32] The navy only appointed retired RNR officer Jean Maurice de Marbois as head of its intelligence section in August 1939. Following the declaration of war, an army service was further organized, but the Canadian Intelligence Corps as such was not created until 1942.

Code breaking became the focus of fierce attention on all sides. The United States was able to break some Japanese diplomatic codes before war in the Pacific broke out, but it was not enough to prevent the Pearl Harbor disaster. However, later the Americans had an enormous success with the Japanese military code JN-25. Using mathematical analysis, IBM punch-card tabulating machines, and a cipher machine, the U.S. was able to crack most of the code in time to make a crucial difference at the Battle of Midway in 1942.

Both sides in the war in Europe had successes and failures in code breaking. The German navy's cryptanalytic service, called Beobachtungs Dienst, or "B-Dienst" for short, was based in Berlin. In the first two years of the war the German navy gained more advantage from B-Dienst than did the Royal Navy from its work. B-Dienst had been listening to British fleet signals long before the war began and it also broke the British and Allied Merchant Ship Code used for convoys.

The greatest intelligence asset for the Royal Navy and the Royal Canadian Navy in the Battle of the Atlantic was the now famous ULTRA intelligence. However, it is important to note that for the most part the RCN was not given top access to ULTRA, with convoys rerouted on information from the RN.

The Enigma Cipher Machine. It was widely used in Germany and Italy, even by postal services. Breaking it turned out to be the result of brilliant mathematical work and espionage, but also the carelessness of German operators.

A German engineer as early as 1918 had developed a commercial cipher machine called Enigma.[33] From that point on to the end of the Second World War as many as 100,000 Enigma machines were made. The navy was the first branch of the German armed services to adopt it in 1926, while by 1928 the German army started using its own version. It was even used by the German railways and the Italian Navy.

British, French, and American cryptanalysts had no success in cracking Enigma but Polish Cipher Bureau did. In December 1932 the bureau received from French Military Intelligence two German documents and two pages of Enigma keys which were changed daily. A twenty-seven-year-old mathematics graduate, Marian Rejewski, made one of the most important breakthroughs in cryptologic history by using new methods to decipher the Enigma messages. After that, the Poles were able to decrypt a substantial portion of Enigma traffic. The Polish work was handed over to the French when Poland was overrun and then in 1940 given to the British. As a result Polish scientists deserve credit as among the victors of the Battle of the Atlantic.

British mathematical genius Alan Turing was able to improve on the Polish work. Also analysts were able to take advantage of the fact that some secret messages were sent both by Enigma and other methods, since small ships did not have Enigma. The information provided by the Bletchley Park cryptanalysts had an enormous impact on the Battle of the Atlantic. It has been estimated that evasive routing provided by ULTRA in 1941, following the capture of material from U-110, saved the Allies about 300 ships.[34]

Enigma was broken using a variety of methods, including grabbing the machines and codes when ships and submarines were captured. Apart from that Enigma should have been unbreakable, had its operating procedures been better and its operators more disciplined. But the British were able to take advantage of mistakes German users made. Despite their instructions, operators' message settings continued to be far from random as they picked letters close together on the keyboard, or picked girlfriend's names or the first letter of obscene words.

While the new ideas, new weapons, and new technology seemed to be everywhere in the interwar years, it is important to note that when the time came not all new ideas were believed and not all new technology adopted. A new war would be completely different than anything that had been seen before, but not everyone believed it and, crucially, those in key positions were among the most hidebound. The Japanese and Americans understood the power of the aircraft carrier, for example, more than the British. Meantime, in 1937 the Canadian Cavalry Association, a military lobby group which included retired senior officers, passed a series of resolutions which included calling on the Defence Department to supply all cavalry units, both horsed and motorized, with radio sets. But there were also resolutions for more horse shelters and swords for all mounted units.[35]

CHAPTER SEVEN

RIGHT UP THERE WITH JOAN OF ARC

London, in the summer of 1937, was the backdrop for one of the great pageants of the era — the coronation of George VI. The abdication crisis was over and now Britain and the empire could turn their loyalty to the new king. Leaders from around the world were invited to the coronation, while empire leaders were invited to both the coronation and an Imperial Conference afterward.

The Canadian delegation to both events included Prime Minister William Lyon Mackenzie King, Ernest Lapointe, and Ian Mackenzie, while among the Department of External Affairs officials was Lester B. Pearson, the same man who would scurry in and out of the king's office finalizing the Declaration of War in 1939. The coronation on May 12 was historic and memorable. It was also notable because of the number of "lasts," including that King George would be the last emperor of India and the last king of Ireland. The new king, the centre of apprehensive attention because of his insecurities and shyness, looked suitably regal during the ceremony. The coronation was seen for the first time by millions around the world in newsreels and was judged a great success.[1]

Prime Minister King arrived in London completely burned out from work. He was "fatigued" and the thought of having to make speeches in London "hung over my mind and spirit like a pall. Its effect had been paralyzing."[2] That might have been alarming, except that the word "fatigued" appears no less than 326 times in King's diary over a five year period.[3] Despite the fatigue and a cold, he took part in the coronation service decked out in his elaborate Windsor uniform as prescribed for Privy Councillors in the 1937 edition of *Dress Worn at Court*. The uniform consisted of a dark blue jacket covered in a riot of gold oak leaf embroidery and, as dictated in the instruction book, exactly nine buttons. White knee breeches, white silk hose, a black beaver cocked hat, and ceremonial sword completed the outfit. King was in his element.

The prime minister was among 10,089 Canadians who later received a coronation medal honouring the event. The recipients included everyone in the official Canadian delegation, surviving Victoria Cross winners, senior military commanders, the Governor General's staff, members of cabinet and their spouses, members of both houses of Parliament, mayors of larger towns and cities, judges, and provincial legislature representatives. Additional members of the military were also honoured, among them Captain Eddie Ganong, who a year before had been appointed adjutant of the 48th Highlanders in Toronto.[4]

With the elaborate services over there was serious work to be done at the Imperial Conference in light of the increasingly tense state of affairs both in Europe and the Far East. No matter how it was presented, the main question for debate by empire leaders boiled down to the same one that King had been dodging for years — calls for a united empire defence strategy.[5] Many at the conference might have agreed with Viscount Elibank the year before: when it comes to the empire, you're in or you're out.

When the conference began, the main case for Imperial defence was put forward by British cabinet minister Sir Thomas Inskip. He said the government had no reason to conceal the gravity of the international scene, nor how much it was counting on the dominions for help.[6] He then unveiled his "to do" list. Turning to Canada he said the British government needed help with munitions. American neutrality legislation meant the British could not obtain necessary supplies from the United States so Canada, with its industrial capacity and isolation from any theatre of war, could become the prime alternative supplier. Inskip went down his list, which also included foodstuffs.

In reply, Ian Mackenzie laid out the Canadian determination that there would be no commitments. Canadian public opinion supported the present government's policy of coastal defence and the money being spent on national defence was the maximum that the country would accept. He argued,

> The most important contribution they [Canadians] could render at this time, when dark shadows seem to be hovering over the world, was, as far as possible, to preserve *unity*

in their councils; to avoid any possibility of dissension, and to respect the heartfelt opinions and profound convictions of those who might differ from the policies which might, to others, be necessary.[7]

The arguments about coast defence and maximum acceptable spending may have been old hat but Mackenzie's comments underlined the principal argument that was becoming the King government's all-purpose trump card in such situations: national unity. It was, in essence, a threat. You want us to do more for defence? Fine, but it will break up the country. It was an argument that seemed impossible to refute and one that King would go on to use again and again.

Australia and New Zealand were in a different strategic situation altogether because both countries were in real danger if Japan decided to strike south. Both desperately needed the protection of the British fleet based in Singapore and British assurances that in a crunch the Royal Navy would not pull out. It was in their interest to have a common strategy with the British. The Australians called for a united policy in naval, air, military, munitions, financial, and supply fields as a deterrent to agression.[8]

In becoming the "Dr. No" of the conference, Prime Minister King insisted on refraining from making any commitments and went to astonishing lengths to enforce his position, ordering the Canadian military to restrict its contacts with its British counterparts. Members of Canada's joint staff committee and their secretary, Harry Crerar, had come to London, but they were given strict instructions to avoid any discussions with British officers that might lead to a possible Canadian commitment. King insisted there be no discussion of what measures British authorities might be considering for the defence of Newfoundland, at that time still a British colony. That was despite the painfully obvious fact that the island had great importance to Canada's own security.[9]

King was absolutely unmoved by any British, Australian, or New Zealander arguments. He was determined that Canada was not going to make public commitments to Britain, the empire, or the League of Nations that would limit its actions in any way. When the conference ended it was clear there would be no deal on united empire defence. That was that.

There remained only the problem of the final communiqué. In a word by word parsing of the statement the British had proposed, King ruthlessly eliminated any whiff of Imperial control over Canadian policy. Everything was watered down to such an extent that one writer described the eventual result as filled with the kind of meaningless platitudes that might be heard at "a dinner of the Royal Antediluvian Order of Buffalos."[10] C.P. Stacey notes, however, that as obstinate as King could be, his stand might have sounded familiar to an earlier prime minister. "There is a striking parallel with the evidence of Sir John A. Macdonald ... in 1880: do not ask Canada for military contributions when there is no enemy in the field."[11]

The Imperial gathering was notable as well for a significant leadership change in the middle of it. British Prime Minister Stanley Baldwin retired and in his place came a new prime minister and conference chairman — Neville Chamberlain. Baldwin, as chairman, had never had much to say except when it came to motions to adjourn for dinner, but Chamberlain was a different type altogether. He was a commanding presence, described as both "masterful" and "confident."[12]

Chamberlain had been in cabinet as far back as 1923 and most recently had been Chancellor of the Exchequer. Chiefly as a result of the new leader's performance at the meetings, King became a great admirer, even a devotee. With Chamberlain as prime minister, King could feel "greatly reassured about the future."[13] King also told a British friend about Chamberlain, "I marvel at the splendid manner in which he measures up to the exceptional obligations of his high office."[14] Speaking to Chamberlain privately, King delivered a *sotto voce* message. He said that if Britain were to become involved in a continental war, then Chamberlain could not expect Canadian support, but if Britain were directly attacked, Canada *would* go to war.[15] King now became an ardent supporter of the policy now most closely associated with the new British leader — appeasement.

After the coronation and the Imperial Conference came perhaps the most unlikely event of William Lyon Mackenzie King's long career. He went to Berlin to meet Adolf Hitler.[16] The idea took shape in discussions with then Prime Minister Baldwin before the coronation. King had suggested that the British leader visit Hitler to build up good will, but Baldwin demurred. Then the British Foreign Secretary, Anthony Eden suggested King should go and King decided he would. His decision may be explained by his long held view that the best way to defuse international conflict was by personal diplomacy, an idea which had led King to meet with Mussolini in 1928.[17] Before visiting Hitler King wrote to the Governor General advising, "I am not without hope that in however slight a way, Canada may be helpful."

The Berlin meeting was set up by the German ambassador, Joachim von Ribbentrop, one of the Nazi new guard. There was a surprising Canadian connection with Ribbentrop. He had lived in Montreal, Ottawa, and Vancouver from 1910 to 1914 and at one point had opened a wine importing business. While in Ottawa he was a frequent visitor to Government House and a member of the "Minto Six," a famous figure skating team of the time.[18]

In going to Germany, King apparently wanted to steer well clear of British "guidance." He, therefore, decided not to stay at the British embassy, lodging instead at the swanky Adlon Hotel on the doorstep of the Brandenburg Gate. Once in Berlin, King dutifully spent two days touring youth camps, work camps, and the 1936 Olympic stadium, while on June 29 he met Luftwaffe chief, Hermann Goering. The conversation was amicable but the subject at one point turned to Canadian independence from Britain. King assured the German leader that Canadian association with Britain was purely voluntary.

King in crowd. King was given VIP treatment in Berlin in 1937. King said the world would come to see Hitler as "a very great man." He was not the first nor the last world leader to completely misjudge Hitler.

The Luftwaffe chief then posed a sticky question: If the peoples of Germany and Austria should wish to unite and Britain tried to prevent it, would Canada feel bound to support Britain? King was at his obfuscatory best, saying Canada's attitude would be the same as for all other questions that might arise. Canadians would want to examine all the circumstances and make a decision on the facts as they were at the time.

Then on to the main event. Just after noon the same day, King was whisked to the old Presidential Palace to be greeted by a guard of honour. German attendants, resplendent in court dress, first showed him into what had been President von Hindenburg's office, complete with the late president's death mask on a desk. Then Hitler welcomed King in an upstairs room, the Fuhrer coming forward to shake hands. Those at the meeting included a covey of Hitler's military aides and assistants in the background and two men with King. So what might have been an intimate talk began with thirteen people in the room.

King started by describing his hometown of Berlin, Ontario, presumably dancing lightly over the fact that after anti-German riots during the First World War, it had been renamed Kitchener. He showed Hitler an album that included pictures of Kitchener. It is hard to imagine what Adolf Hitler, one of the world's most powerful leaders, his mind bursting with megalomaniacal plans to rip apart the map of Europe, must have thought about spending an afternoon leafing through King's picture book. The meeting then switched to substantive issues with the session lasting nearly two hours, long past the scheduled time. The two parted with King receiving an elegant case containing a picture of the German leader on which Hitler inscribed, "To his Excellency the Canadian Prime Minister Dr. W. L. Mackenzie King in friendly memory of his visit 29 June 1937."

Among the letters King wrote were ones to Neville Chamberlain and Anthony Eden.[19] These indicate that King outlined his views on military expenditures to Hitler with the prime minister saying they "could only do harm in the end." He told the Fuhrer:

> that I was a man who hated expenditures for military pur-
> poses; that the Liberal Government in Canada all shared
> my views in that particular.... I had found it necessary,
> however, in order to keep my party united, and to meet the

sentiment of the country to bring in increased estimates for expenditure on army, navy, and air services at the last Session of Parliament.[20]

King did deliver one vital message. On the question of Canada's status as a dominion, he said that in the event of war Canada would be free to go to war or not as Parliament might decide, but he made it plain that if Britain were attacked by a foreign power, Parliament would decide to fight at its side.[21] This was essentially the same message that King had given to Chamberlain. It was an important message for Hitler but it also showed King's reading of what the Canadian public would demand if pushed to the wall. King was looking two years down the road.

All that is straightforward enough, but other comments King confided to his diary are cringe-inducing. Quite simply he allowed himself to be hypnotized by Hitler.[22] King wrote, "I confess that the impression gained by this interview was a very favourable one." The German leader was a man of "deep sincerity" and "one who truly loves his fellow-men, and his country, and would make any sacrifice for their good." He forecast that "the world will yet come to see a very great man — mystic in Hitler." The Fuhrer was described later by King as basically a "peasant" but one who will "rank some day with Joan of Arc among the deliverers of his people."

King wrote a number of letters, including ones to Neville Chamberlain and Anthony Eden. Both British leaders acknowledged the importance of delivering the message about what Canada would do if Britain was attacked.[23] The correspondence was also seen by senior officials in the British Foreign Office where the reaction of at least one of them was scathing. "It is curious how easily impressed & reassured Hitler's visitors are when Hitler tells them that Germany needs to expand at somebody else's expense but of course does not want war."[24] King also wrote to the Governor General, Lord Tweedsmuir, about the prospect of war saying, "I am perfectly certain ... that the Germans are not contemplating the possibility of war, either with France or with Britain."[25]

Author Bruce Hutchison says the visit to Berlin was significant because it shaped King's subsequent views and actions. "The impression which King formed of the Fuhrer was one not only absurd but calamitous. It distorted all King's thinking."[26] Like others who subscribed to appeasement, King's views remained fixed, believing that the European problem would be solved by negotiations, by patience, by understanding. One could delay things such as rearmament because it would all work out in the end.

In sharp contrast, it is worth adding that Colonel Harry Crerar travelled to Berlin shortly before King did. Crerar's visit was unrelated to King's and Crerar travelled as a private citizen at his own expense. His judgment was that it would be one or two years before the German military would be ready for a major European war. "The over-riding impression which I took away … was that of a highly dynamic nation, determined before long to break its present bounds, and, consequently, increasingly dangerous to European and, indeed to world peace."[27]

MILESTONES

JANUARY 19, 1937 — Howard Hughes establishes a record flight from Los Angeles to New York City in 7 hours, 28 minutes, and 25 seconds.

APRIL 26, 1937 — Guernica is bombed in the Spanish Civil War.

SEPTEMBER 1937 — British Field Marshal Sir Cyril Deverell, chief of the Imperial general staff, visits German army manoeuvres, which include an attack by 800 tanks and 400 aircraft.

The government unveiled a new budget in 1937, and again it gave more clout to the RCAF. It was an extraordinary change for a service that had been flying its planes with only fumes in the gas tank two years before. It swamped an administrative system just too small to handle it all. There were only 1,107 full-time officers and airmen (an increase of only about 300 from 1935) along with about 500 reservists. Because there was not enough staff to move the avalanche of paperwork required, orders for new aircraft and equipment were delayed for months. Before new recruits could be signed up, trainers had to be trained. As Air Commodore Croil pointed out, "it is not possible to take full advantage of a sudden and relatively large increase in appropriations."[28]

The air force had already started with the basics by ordering a new elementary trainer. Then it turned to deal with an enormous backlog of equipment and supplies needed to simply keep existing operations going. They included spare parts, rations, clothing, motor transport, gasoline and oil, machine tools, new work shops, electrical equipment, parachutes, armament, bombs and ammunition, wireless equipment, overhaul equipment, and many others. The RCAF might have wished for immediate and dramatic changes, but instead its rebuilding included buying nuts, bolts, and fuel. If things looked bad for the short term, they were not going to improve much for quite a while. Croil thought that, even if funding remained the same for the next few years, the air force would still be able to equip and man only five Permanent Force squadrons by the end of 1941 with another five partly equipped. Additional squadrons would be added when manpower and equipment permitted.[29]

The paperwork jam up, the inability to expand quickly and all the rest had widespread repercussions. There were a limited number of new officers to bolster the air force. Among them was Leonard Birchall, who would become famous in 1942 as the "Savior of Ceylon."[30] Birchall had actually graduated from RMC in 1933 (College # 2364) but served for a time in the Signals Corps before transferring to the RCAF in 1937. But even with the additions, the air force would be desperately short of trained pilots, especially fighter pilots, by 1939. If war broke out then or before, the RCAF would be very restricted in what it could do.

In the next couple of years the RCAF intake was so small that Canadians continued to stream toward Britain to join the RAF, among them Ian Arthur, later a wing commander. The Winnipeg native was one of thirteen Canadians who were given short service RAF commissions after boarding a ship for England in August 1937. When war broke out in 1939 Arthur was already a pilot officer.[31] Only a month later he was posted to No. 141 Squadron in Scotland where there were no less than seven Canadian pilots, all from the western provinces.[32]

After dealing with the enormous supply shortages, the RCAF then turned its attention to buying additional new aircraft. That presented a tangle of challenges. Because of Britain's own rearmament program, many U.K. companies already had bulging order books so Canadians would just have to wait in line. The result was that proven types would be obsolescent by the time they were available. Choosing new and untested planes could be risky because many turned out to be duds. The Americans were developing some excellent new aircraft, but all the existing RCAF equipment, tools, and weapons were built to British standards while at the same time, as Sir Thomas Inskip had noted at the Imperial Conference, U.S. neutrality laws might be used to cut off supplies in the event of war. Ultimately, the RCAF stayed with mainly British planes, although they were mostly a sorry lot. Meanwhile, the Wapitis that had been ordered in 1935 were delivered and put into service as bomber trainers. No. 3 Squadron completed its initial air firing and bombing practice with them in the summer of 1937.[33]

The long term solution was that Canada had to develop its own aircraft industry. As it was there were only a few Canadian aircraft companies and they produced a mere handful of planes. Work on the Tiger Moth was underway and the Supermarine Stranraer flying boat had already been ordered at home. However, it would not go into service until 1938. But placing Canadian orders by itself was not going to result in a flood of new planes any time soon. If a plane was ordered in Canada, it meant an extra year had to be added to the delivery time because plants had to be set up or expanded, workers trained, and parts ordered before production really got underway.

Despite the maddening delays and setbacks, there was a milestone on September 21, 1937, when at last the air force was able to field an operational fighter unit. No. 1 Squadron at Trenton would begin focusing on training fighter pilots and developing tactics.[34] The new commander was Flight Lieutenant Brian Carr-Harris, the officer who had pulled off the dramatic high Arctic rescue in 1928. The squadron would require about two years to become operationally effective.[35] It was still stuck with the Armstrong Whitworth Siskin but it was all the RCAF had.[36]

For coast defence the RCAF had already undertaken a series of squadron moves dating back to 1933. Two coastal squadrons were operational. No. 4 (Flying Boat) Squadron had been established by combining several west coast detachments all equipped with Vickers Vancouver aircraft (top speed ninety-four miles per hour) while No. 5 (Reconnaissance) Squadron was in Halifax flying Fairchild 71s. The latter were near useless.

As for the reserve, new squadrons were formed in 1937 in Calgary and Quebec City.[37] They were the seventh and eight reserve squadrons in the country. In May 1937, No. 19 reserve squadron in Hamilton, finally got its first aircraft, a DH 60 Moth light trainer which allowed the squadron's handful of pilots to begin training. It was a start but No. 19 was supposed to be a bomber squadron and with a Moth there could be very little realistic bombing done. In May and June 1937 eight officers and sixty-three airmen from the squadron attended their first summer training camp at Borden. Members travelled by private cars rather than rail to save the Defence Department about fifty-five dollars.[38] No. 19 Squadron soon became No. 119 Squadron as, starting in November 1937, all reserve squadrons were renumbered in the 100 series.

For the Royal Canadian Navy February 17, 1937, was a day to savour. A crowd gathered on a dock in Chatham, England, for the commissioning of its newest ships, HMCS *Fraser* and *St. Laurent*. Those on hand could see the destroyers packed a lot of punch, including four 4.7 inch guns and eight torpedoes along with a twelve-pounder anti-aircraft gun. Before the RCN took them over both were equipped with new asdic gear, the first for the Canadian Navy. *Fraser* cast off for its new home with Captain Victor Brodeur in command, one of the very few senior French Canadian officers in the entire service in the interwar years. Brodeur's ship would head to Halifax initially and in 1938 move to the Pacific. *St. Laurent*, commanded by Lieutenant Commander R.E. Bidwell — later a rear admiral — also would make the west coast its home.

Maritime Command Museum

HMCS Fraser *was originally HMS* Crescent*, launched in 1932. It was another of the "used but usable" British destroyers taken up by the RCN and at bargain basement prices.*

While adding two ships to its fleet was significant progress for the RCN a brief comparison shows the real limitations of the service and how enormously the RN overshadowed the RCN. The British had introduced a comprehensive rearmament program in 1936 and Royal Navy estimates for that year provided for building two new battleships, one aircraft carrier, five cruisers, nine destroyers, four submarines, and six escort vessels. This is despite the fact that the RN had second priority for rearmament to the Royal Air Force.[39] In 1937 the RN added orders for three more battleships, two more fleet carriers, seven cruisers, sixteen destroyers, seven submarines, and three escort vessels.

In the summer of 1937 the Japanese launched a full scale invasion of China. By November China's most important port, Shanghai, fell to Japanese troops while Nanking, Chiang Kai-shek's capital, was taken in December. The Rape of Nanking has gone into history as one of the most shocking horrors of modern times. By the time the Japanese army was finished ransacking the city, the death toll may have reached a quarter million, while the number of women raped was estimated at 80,000. By the end of 1937 all major Chinese cities were captured by the Japanese, with Chinese casualties estimated at 4 million.

For those watching in Ottawa, Vancouver, or Washington, D.C., it appeared that sooner or later there would be a mighty collision between Japanese ambition and American interests. In March of 1937, before the Japanese invasion, King had travelled to Washington to hear U.S. President Roosevelt again promote building an Alaska highway saying the route would be "of a great military advantage" in the event of a clash with Japan.[40] The talks got nowhere but it was clear that building up troops, equipment, naval, and air forces on the west coast of Canada was becoming an urgent matter.

Roosevelt was not about to give up on the highway. Having planned a trip to Alaska, he decided to make a brief side trip to Victoria to talk about the issue. The president arrived on September 30, met by enthusiastic crowds and welcomed by a keen advocate of the highway, Premier Duff Pattullo. Roosevelt later described the Victoria stopover as "a great success" while adding that besides the highway, he wanted to coordinate U.S. and Canadian military plans for the defence of British Columbia and its coastline.[41] Roosevelt was not mollified by reports that Canada had increased defence spending, the president describing British Columbia's fortifications as "not only entire inadequate, but almost nonexistent."[42]

In the midst of this came an ominous development. On December 13, 1937, waves of Japanese warplanes attacked and sank the USS *Panay* near Nanking. It was an armed riverboat that had businessmen, diplomats, and their families on board. Several sailors were killed. The ship was marked with U.S. flags and the U.S. assumed the attack was deliberate. There was an explosion of anger in Washington, with Secretary of the Navy, Claude Swanson, telling the cabinet he wanted war and wanted it "right away." Subsequently, American tempers cooled and Japan offered compensation, but it triggered a series of U.S. actions, including a new invitation to King to go to Washington. It appeared likely he would be pummeled again about feeble west coast defences and the Alaska highway.

King, not for the first time, delayed, but several Canadian newspapers, possibly tipped by U.S. diplomats in Ottawa, ran stories on January 6, 1938, about the weak state of Pacific defences.[43] Other newspaper reports hinted America might build fortifications along its border. While King did not go to the U.S., a delegation of top Canadian military officials did go to meet secretly with their American counterparts. At one point U.S. Army Chief of Staff Malin Craig stunned the Canadians by suggesting that the U.S. might want air bases in British Columbia and that Canada's west coast should be incorporated into the American military command system. The United States offered to supply mobile artillery and aircraft. In the end there were no definite decisions made, nor did the Americans get any access to Canadian territory.[44]

Professor Galen Perras has speculated that Roosevelt's intent was no less than to bring Canada under the American defence umbrella.[45] For one thing, Roosevelt could certainly see that the British were much weakened in the Pacific. While the whole idea may have been a ploy to keep Britain from offering commercial or military help to Japan, Perras says British officials were convinced that Roosevelt was pursuing a long-standing American goal to detach Canada from Britain.

The entire episode had disquieting implications for Canada's national sovereignty. If push came to shove in the Pacific, there was the prospect that the U.S. would make demands that could not be resisted. Meanwhile, while military leaders in Ottawa saw the threat of a European war as an urgent priority, both they and the government felt compelled to continue work on Pacific coast defences. Canada's "rearmament lite" program left the army especially short of money, and whatever it did have had to be focused on the west coast. Even as late as the summer of 1939 a Pacific war still looked like a possibility.

Construction of artillery batteries in Stanley Park near downtown Vancouver and on Point Grey near the entrance to Vancouver Harbour continued. First-year spending was put at $895,000.[46] The coast artillery, meanwhile, faced long waiting lists at British factories.[47] Canada had relied totally on Britain and now, when it was most needed, the British couldn't deliver. For coast artillery, the best that could be done was relining three worn 9.2 inch barrels, a job that was finished in October 1938. As an interim measure several reserve guns held by the navy were handed over to the army. The army had hoped that as time went along it would have money for the west coast and coast artillery upgrades on the east coast as well. However, even that wasn't entirely possible. Prior to the war some B.C. coastal defences could be only improved by cannibalizing existing facilities elsewhere.

As vexing as the situation on the west coast was, and with the drum beat of President Roosevelt's demands continuing, still the greater danger appeared to be in Europe. As the decade progressed the prospect of war there went from being a dim possibility, to a probability, to a near certainty. However, since 1935 there had been a fiction about army mobilization plans. The government in Ottawa pretended that it had no plans to send two divisions to Europe and the army pretended that the two divisions it thought would be needed in Europe were for home defence. Finally, in 1937, there was a breakthrough on this disconnect. One writer called it the army's "masterstroke."[48] The Canadian army's plan for mobilizing two divisions was part of a document called Defence Scheme No. 3, by far the most significant of the army's pre-war plans. It was not new in 1937 by any means, Defence Scheme No. 3 dating back originally to the 1920s. The army reorganization of 1936 had been meant to reflect the defence scheme.

Of course, earlier there had been Buster Brown's Defence Scheme No. 1 and its hypothesis of war with the U.S. while Defence Scheme No. 2 had considered Canada being neutral in a war involving Japan. However, while Canada was rebuilding west coast defences, neutrality did not seem like the most likely scenario.[49] Defence Scheme No. 3 was significantly more important than either earlier plan. It outlined possible attacks the country might face and laid down detailed steps to be taken in an emergency. While most of the potential threats were obvious enough, the scheme also included among the possible threats, an attack by an airship. The scheme included the army's detailed plans for mobilizing two divisions of about 18,000 men each, getting them basic equipment and training, and sending them to the danger point in a reasonably short period of time. Although the plan included a cavalry division as well, as was seen earlier, that was dropped in the spring of 1939. The mobilized forces were to be called an "expeditionary force." Mobilizing two divisions, especially when they would be made up of mostly reservists, was a monumental undertaking. The mobilization plans included the Permanent Force units, but also identified the most efficient militia units for inclusion, and even noted individual commanders to be kept or replaced.[50] Those lists were revised each year. The plan also included what had to be done by other government departments and the RCMP.

The ultimate result of this work was a "War Book," completed in provisional form in May 1939. With that, nothing was required to launch the mobilization except sending telegraph or phone messages.[51] In the event, the mobilization of 1939 had its share of confusion and error, but still, without the scheme the mobilization could not have been possible. In any event, it was light years ahead of the 1914 mobilization.

Prime Minister King's statements in February, that everything in the new defence budget was for home defence, brought the disconnect between the government and the military to a head. The defence scheme was reworked yet again, with the expeditionary force submerged even further, apparently because it sounded too much like something that was meant to go to Europe. Its name changed to the "mobile force," which sounded the same but was evidently less politically objectionable. Nevertheless, any reading of the newly revised Scheme would show as plain as day that it opened the prospect of a European expeditionary force. Despite that the plan was duly dispatched to Defence Minister Mackenzie. After examining it, he carefully noted that the "dominant motif" of the plan was the defence of Canada but — in a crucial further comment — he said he realized, however, that the staff had to prepare for every possible contingency. He brushed over the mobile force and in March 1937, approved the plan both in principle and in detail.[52] This was a significant contribution to war preparedness. It should also be added that the army's own institutional goals were also represented in Defence Plan No. 3. In this case the army feared and tried to prevent a 1914 scenario in which Sam Hughes had completely displaced the existing army with an entirely new overseas army. The new plan would make that scenario unnecessary if war broke out. The army was convinced that while Japan and the Pacific represented real threats, the most urgent necessity — even if the government wouldn't say so publically — was a European war.

The "master stroke" was that the army now had a plan that it could implement in the event of all-out war in Europe. There would be a mobile force, however disguised. Whether the mobile force went to the B.C. coast or to Europe could be decided later. The military could continue planning for the possibility of an overseas war with at least ministerial approval.[53]

There still remained the awkward problem of the government's public position. Indeed, then Lieutenant Colonel Pope said, many of the requests for new equipment and supplies the army made at the time "strain[ed] the capacity of an archangel to make a convincing case" that they were just for home defence.[54] Still, one writer has noted that if this military policy had originated in the prime minister's office rather than in Mackenzie's, the scheme probably would not have been approved because it too obviously ran counter to the government's defence priorities.[55]

Finally, as an aside, it should be noted that the name "mobile force" remained one of the great misnomers of the time. Part-time troops could be "mobilized," but that did not make them "mobile" or a part of any "mobile force." It is ironic that the forces and the government continued to refer to a mobile force but that force had no transport to speak of, no tanks, and few motorized artillery units. In reality the mobile force was only mobile if you put everyone on a train. Otherwise it was only mobile up to a speed of three miles an hour, the speed a person can walk.

On a blistering summer day in 1937 the Calgary Highlanders marched out of its armoury and onto the road, on its way to its summer training at Camp Sarcee four miles away. The officers and men sang such First World War favourites such as "Tipperary." At least that's what they sang as long as there were any civilians around, but once they got out into the country, they could get away with rowdier fare.[56] The Highlanders had no summer uniforms but trudged along in heavy khaki doublets and kilts, plus their Lee-Enfield rifles and full web gear. Among the soldiers was Jeffery Williams, not yet eighteen. Williams was impressed with Camp Sarcee when it came into view but there was nothing much to suggest anything up to date. "It could have been 1914 or the Boer War or even Crimea," said Williams. "Long lines of white bell tents were interspersed with rows of large marquees. A horse-drawn battery raised clouds of grey dust from the main gravelled road."

The regiment was supposed to be 800 strong and there was a good turn out this summer but most winter nights parades the Highlanders were down to about 125, including twenty in the band. Everything they carried, wore, or used dated from the First World War. There was no transport of any kind. Williams had signed up a couple months before, saying there were plenty of signs that a war might come.[57] Joining was simple.

> An officer explained that there was no money to run the battalion, hence every officer and man made over his pay to [the regiment].... We would be paid only for going to camp.... First I filled in personal details on an attestation form, had a brief medical examination to ensure that I could walk, see, hear and cough, then swore allegiance to the King in front of the colonel.[58]

Williams was given a uniform including kilt, slacks, and a Glengarry bonnet, but he had to buy his own black boots. Not many new members knew much about a Highland regiment or for that matter much about the army either. On the first parade one recruit wore his kilt backwards. Fortunately, by the time summer camp came there was plenty of rifle and machine gun ammunition. There was some map reading work and other basic courses but Williams, echoing U.S. General Pershing, thought that the training basically boiled down to learning to "shoot and salute." Williams thought the most important thing was the experience of living in a military camp. At least while the camp lasted they were real soldiers.

The story of the Highlanders was much the same as most regiments at that time. One snap shot of the state of the army reserve's equipment in 1937 comes from the *Vancouver Sun*.[59] Referring to local regiments including the British Columbia Regiment, the Irish Fusiliers and the Seaforth Highlanders, writer Alan Morley commented,

> Bombs, rifle grenades and smoke grenades, major items in the army of the modern infantryman, are legendary objects

to Vancouver's militia. Tactical exercises are carried out on maps of England, as no one has ever seen a military map of Vancouver. Anti-tank-rifles (one to each platoon) and antitank guns (one to each company) are also things of mystery. No one knows what they look like. But that is all right, because the "mechanized" regiments have never seen a tank, either.

But in one way the Highanders and the Vancouver regiments were better off than the Permanent Force. There was no camp for collective training for the Permanent Force in the summer of 1937 because of a lack of money.[60] During that time, the three Permanent Force regiments remained at about two-thirds below authorized strength, each averaging about 250 and 350 officers and men.[61]

CHAPTER EIGHT

BREN GUN MISFIRE

In 1938 Adolf Hitler wiped Austria off the map. Hitler, Austrian-born himself, had always believed that it should be a part of Greater Germany. The Nazis had been carrying out a campaign of intimidation against Austria for months but the final crisis came in February when Hitler gave the Austrian chancellor, Kurt Schuschnigg, a list of ten demands. The chancellor's response was to order a plebiscite on whether or not Austrians wanted a separate country, a vote Schuschnigg believed would show strong support for independence. Hitler pre-empted that with a *coup d'etat*, ordering German troops to invade Austria on March 12. There was no military opposition, no bullets or shells, just kisses and flowers. The German soldiers called the operation, "Blumenkriege" — flower wars. The annexation of Austria was formalized the same day. When Hitler arrived in Vienna on April second, it looked like a Roman Triumph with several hundred thousand people crowded into the city to hear his speech. Britain and France protested about it all but, as Hitler predicted, they did nothing.

Meanwhile, German rearmament continued. There were elaborate training exercises for all services. Among the most notable was one in 1938 run by Admiral Karl Donitz. Groups of submarines practiced "wolf pack" attacks against convoys. The exercise was not much of a secret since Donitz wrote about it publicly in the magazine *Nauticus* in 1939. In May the leading German tank expert, Heinz Guderian, was appointed commander of mobile troops, a new position that included direct access to Hitler. Still, even by the time the Second World War began, and contrary to the general impression, only six out of 106 active and reserve German divisions were armoured, four were motorized infantry, and four were light. That is barely 13 percent of the army motorized and less than 6 percent armoured.[1] The top ranks of the German general staff approached mechanization and the creation of armoured forces with caution. Generals Werner von Fritsch and Ludwig Beck knew that Germany did not have enough fuel reserves for more than a few armoured divisions. Steel was in very short supply while some senior commanders, including Erwin Rommel, were opposed to armour anyway.[2]

In Canada there was anxiety about the Austrian invasion, but Prime Minister William Lyon Mackenzie King accepted the outcome without outrage or protest. He wrote, "I felt all along that sooner or later the annexation of Austria was inevitable."[3] Harry Crerar also thought the move was entirely expected, saying that his visit to Germany had left him with the view that Austria was "an imminent target of Nazi aggression."[4] Crerar thought at least there was one small consolation in Canada. "John Q. Public is at last getting behind the move for reasonable and efficient means of defence."[5]

Out in the Pacific, near Singapore, Robert Welland and other midshipmen continued their training aboard HMS *Emerald*. That included, on occasion, a visit to Captain Augustus Agar's quarters for a discussion of world events and defence problems. Agar, a Victoria Cross winner in the First World War, was much admired, even if he didn't like to fire the main guns because it cracked the paint. He was one among many officers who predicted that Britain would be at war with both Germany and Japan within five years. Agar decried the Royal Navy's building new battleships instead of aircraft carriers, saying the only consolation was that the Germans were "pissing away resources like us."[6]

About the same time, Skinny Hayes of Winnipeg was winding up his course at HMS *Conway* in Britain. In late August 1938 he joined his first ship, the small freighter *Silverfir*, part of the Silver Line. At his graduation he was offered and accepted a commission in the Royal Navy Reserve. The Royal Navy and the Royal Canadian Navy would soon be much in need of young officers who could navigate the oceans, even if they didn't know how to fight a ship — yet.[7]

While many eyes were on the ominous situation in Europe, Canadians were diverted for months by a headline-grabbing spectacle that became known as the "Bren Gun Scandal."[8] Except for sexual escapades, the affair featured a complete check list of political scandal. There were back room deals, a mysterious and murky company, documents handed over in plain envelopes, the scent of political corruption, a would-be arms merchant, and a former Olympic hockey star. It all wound up with the big finish — a royal commission.

The problem most certainly was not the Bren gun itself, which became an iconic weapon used right through the war and for decades afterward. The Bren gun mess can be traced back to 1935 when the British started looking for a new light machine gun. They tried out several designs and finally selected the Bren. Its name was made up of the first two letters of Brno, the Czechoslovak city where it was designed, and the first two letters of Enfield, the town where it was to be made in Britain. The Bren was reworked to fire the same .303 ammunition as the standard Lee-Enfield rifle — a big plus — and had an effective range of about 600 yards. It could theoretically fire up to 540 rounds per minute, although at that rate the barrel wouldn't last very long.

While the Bren came to be admired by soldiers, early on it was considered almost too accurate. The cone of fire was extremely concentrated, resulting in multiple hits on one or two targets but leaving anything around them untouched. Some soldiers preferred worn out barrels to spread the fire across a larger area.

The Bren gun. The light machine gun proved to be one of the iconic weapons of the Second World War but in 1938 it was also at the centre of the "Bren Gun Scandal."

Library and Archives Canada

The later Bren featured a distinctive curved box magazine, conical flash eliminator and quick change barrel. The Bren magazine required more frequent reloading than belt-fed machine guns such as the larger Vickers machine gun but the Bren was several pounds lighter and could be fired while standing and on the move. The Bren was also used on many vehicles including the Universal Carrier which became better known as the Bren Gun Carrier. The Bren gun went into service in Britain in 1937.

Since the Canadian army used almost entirely British equipment, the British informed Canadian officials about their plans for the Bren. The Canadian army acquired two prototypes in 1936 and Ottawa was impressed. The defence department wanted to buy it, estimating the army would need 7,000 guns, and thought it should be made in Canada to expand the country's industry. Funding for the Bren was put into the preliminary defence budget in 1936, but its final approval was delayed until 1938.[9] Two crucial years elapsed. For their part the British were happy to have Canada buy the Bren and have it made in Canada. It would be another "shadow factory" arrangement that the British were trying to organize. One big problem for the Canadian army was that ordering 7,000 guns would make each one too expensive, but if there was a British order as well, the unit cost would be much lower.

The possibility of making Bren guns in Canada for both Canada and Britain had been discussed at the Imperial Conference in 1937, but for Prime Minister King it was the same old problem. It would break the policy of no commitments.[10] The result was, as King's assistant Oscar Skelton commented, "for fear of leaving the impression of Anglo-Canadian collusion in defence production, King prohibited any public connection with the British on this matter."[11] It didn't help either that the prime minister was hounded by business leaders in pursuit of fat military contracts.[12]

Skelton also opposed the purchase with the peculiar reason that making weapons for the British might constitute a threat to Canadian autonomy. Once a Canadian munitions industry got started, he argued, control of it would be largely out of Canadian hands.[13] Skelton was also worried that it would enhance the authority of the military, saying that in view of the army's history in 1914, "this seems scarcely a reassuring reflection."[14]

While both the British and the Canadian army were both interested in the deal, it appeared to be going nowhere because of the prime minister's opposition and bureaucratic inertia. However, just offstage one man was working furiously to get the Bren gun made in Canada. James Hahn, the president of the John Inglis Company, wanted to manufacture Bren guns at his plant. Hahn was at this time in his mid-forties, square jawed with dark hair, and one of those inverted "v" moustaches that turned up regularly on Hollywood leading men of the time.

Hahn had an outstanding and even dashing army record in the First World War, wounded three times, winning the DSO and the Military Cross and Bar. He spent time in military intelligence, even going to Germany undercover.[15] He finished the war as a major and then went to Osgoode Hall Law School. His real interest, though, was not the law, but business — more particularly, the radio business.

In the 1920s commercial radio was becoming a fixture in Canadian homes. About 100,000 Canadians owned a radio in 1925, while only five years later that number had jumped to half a million. Canadians were intoxicated with such programs as *The Happiness Boys*, while as early as 1923 Foster Hewitt, a cub reporter with the Toronto *Star*, had started making "he shoots, he scores," part of the Canadian lexicon. Among the plethora of new companies that sprang up making radios was Hahn's DeForest Crosley Company. In a self-promoting newspaper article in the Ottawa *Citizen* in 1929, Hahn described himself as "one of the pioneers of the radio industry."[16] De Forest Crosley actually made a number of products including "electrical washing machines" and clocks, but its main business was radios. It offered such ritzy models as the Lancaster, more than four feet high and made with exotic Oriental laurel wood cabinetry.

Alas, the Depression pulled the plug on DeForest Crosley and the company was sold to Rogers Radio. Hahn then turned to a new business venture in 1936 when he and other investors bought the John Inglis Company of Toronto, which had been making precision tools and boilers, but it too had gone bankrupt. The Inglis plant was empty and Hahn thought it would be an ideal place to make Bren guns. He launched into the project full blast. He held discussions with military officials, including the deputy minister of defence, L.R. LaFleche, who was all in favour of a Bren gun deal. LaFleche was no anonymous bureaucrat, rather one of the few influential French Canadian military figures of the time.[17] Off went Hahn to England with a letter of introduction in his pocket from Defence Minister Ian Mackenzie. The British were interested, but as noted earlier, it was clear the Canadian government was foot dragging. The prime minister was not on board. Another roadblock was the truly mind-boggling civil service mindset.

As late as January 1938, that was on show at a meeting of the Interdepartmental Committee on the Control of Profits on Government Armament Contracts, which was then considering a possible Bren contract.

> It was suggested by one of the members that he thought Canada was in no immediate danger of being destroyed through, say, six months' delay. The only country that might now attack us would be Japan, and she is pretty busy at present, so that the sense of immediate danger is not real. The same member asked if the speed element was so vital that we cannot consider contracts in the course of the next few months, and contended that he would not be uncomfortable in this matter for a year.[18]

In 1938 Hahn returned to Britain to finalize a contract with the British and at least get that much done. Then, with LaFleche behind it, somehow the reservations that had been stalling the plan to supply Brens for Canada were finally pushed aside. There was a deal. On March 21, 1938, the minister of national defence put the details in front of his cabinet colleagues and an Order-in-Council was passed that day authorizing the contract.

What had actually happened only gradually emerged but one change may have made the difference between a deal and no deal. In the plan that was approved, both Canada and the British would sign separate contracts with Hahn. It required both countries to buy the Bren, but, strictly speaking, there were two separate deals.[19] Twelve thousand Bren guns would be made, 5,000 for Great Britain and 7,000 for Canada, at a price based on the cost of production plus 10 percent. That limit would solve the problem of profiteering. The government would supply the Inglis factory with left-over machinery that had been used to make the Ross rifle twenty years earlier. The agreement would seem to have been a watershed — providing significant progress on rearmament. There would be new jobs as a result and certainly Hahn must have been pleased. Perhaps he had a few moments to catch his breath and even celebrate, but if so, the celebration didn't last long.

The contract had not been tendered. Since no one else had been allowed to bid, there was an immediate buzz in Ottawa about political strings and political connections. That soon reached the ears of William Arthur Irwin, the tough-minded associate editor of *Maclean's* magazine. No one in Canadian journalism sniffed scandal like Irwin. A plain brown envelope arrived at *Maclean's* with all the details of the contract inside. Irwin saw clear discrepancies between what was in the contract and what the government said was in the contract.

Irwin unearthed a lot of new information, which made it obvious that Hahn had political help from a backbench Liberal MP, Hugh Plaxton. Just a few years before, Plaxton had been an Olympic hockey star and then a player with the Montreal Maroons, but after retiring he went into politics. He was elected a Liberal MP in 1935. It was Plaxton who had smoothed the way for Hahn to meet the deputy defence minister while Plaxton and his brother had gone to Britain with Hahn. The law firm handling Hahn's business was Plaxton and Company, where the MP had previously been a member of the firm and where he still maintained an office.

Then there was a mysterious company called Investment Reserves Limited. The role of Investment Reserves was not clear but it had bought shares in Inglis just before the Bren deal closed and presumably those shares would be worth a lot more once the deal was signed. One account summed it up by saying, "There seemed to be too many connections between Hugh Plaxton, MP, his previous law firm and its share of Investment Reserves."[20]

Maclean's wanted a "name" writer to put together a story, and it chose well-known figure George Drew. He was a hero from the First World War, serving as an artillery officer and being wounded to the point that he had only limited movement in his arms. Drew was a lawyer and an authority on national defence, having written the earlier article that had referred to Canada's "bow and arrow army." Drew sniffed a "stock profiteering boondoggle."[21] But there was a big problem with Drew because he was a prominent Tory and, as of 1938, the leader of the Ontario Conservative party (later an Ontario premier). So, much of what followed had the whiff of a Tory axe job.

A tradition still honoured by the Ottawa media today is that any big investigative news story is preceded by a campaign of leaks, rumours, and hype. It is how a big story becomes even bigger. Sure enough, in August there were leaks that *Maclean's* was about to drop a bombshell about the Bren contract. Finally, on August 25 the article, headlined "Canada's Armament Mystery" came out and the Bren Gun Scandal erupted into public view.[22] The article mainly targeted Defence Minister Ian Mackenzie, noting that while Mackenzie had said profits on the deal would be limited to 10 percent, Hahn had also claimed thousands of dollars in earlier expenses, including his trips to Britain. As for the deal itself, "the least that can be said is that the contract is extremely favorable to Major Hahn and his company."[23] Drew asked why Hahn was chosen when his industrial experience was confined to making radios. Men with years of experience in manufacturing rifles, he said, were available.

Drew implied that the contract was the result of Liberal party patronage. He also felt that arms manufacturing shouldn't be left to private companies because it was too obviously an opportunity for greed. Drew had lots of innuendo, but, apart from the contract not being tendered, there was not really a smoking gun. There was no proof, for example, that money had changed hands. Plaxton, the MP, might have been working simply to get jobs in his riding, which included the Inglis plant. Drew would have a more effective case for governmental procrastination. It had been known for almost two years that the army needed Bren guns and that the British government was interested in a joint contract with a Canadian manufacturer, but the decision had been postponed again and again because of King's determined opposition.

The horror of "Canada's Armament Mystery" gripped William Lyon Mackenzie King. Earlier he had danced with infamy in the Beauharnois kickback scandal of 1930. It had caused embarrassment for King and the Liberals and the prime minister was not about to let it happen again. Within a week King had a Conservative appointee on the Supreme Court named to head a Royal Commission. Mr. Justice H.H. Davis must be given all relevant documents, ordered the prime minister. Unlike today's Royal Commissions, with their lugubrious pace and bespoke-suited lawyers billing by the hour, the Davis Commission moved quickly. It began hearings on September 19, with the principal players parading to the witness stand at a brisk pace.

Drew did not do himself any favours as a witness, losing his temper and saying the Bren gun contract was "cloaked in fraud." MP Plaxton had trouble remembering much about key meetings. Hahn, testifying on October 27, pointed out that his bringing the British into the deal saved the Canadian taxpayer an enormous sum of money. Hahn was goaded in cross examination by *Maclean's* lawyers for his "good luck" in managing to get the bankrupt Inglis plant for a song. Other evidence showed that Hahn and Hugh Plaxton were "by coincidence" ushered into LaFleche's office at the precise moment the deputy minister was admiring a sample of the Bren gun.[24] The most extraordinary appearance was by Defence Minister Mackenzie who displayed a breathtaking ignorance of the entire deal.[25] Mackenzie signed the contract but hadn't really read it. He didn't know whether Hahn actually owned a plant, didn't know who Hahn's business partners were, and didn't know whether Hahn had had any previous relevant business.

After the last witness was heard, Justice Davis was speedy in reaching his conclusions, with his report released in January 1939. By great good fortune, and rather unaccountably, the government avoided the worst outcome. Davis's most serious criticism was that the contract had not been tendered. Evidence had shown that at least five other companies might have been in a better position to make the Bren gun. Davis's main recommendation was that a defence purchasing board be set up to eliminate any suspicion of profiteering in future. King promptly set up such a board only a few months later.

But, Davis said, there was no actual evidence of corruption or misconduct by either politicians or civil servants. The prime minister must have thought his most fervent prayers been answered. He and his ministers had avoided being named as crooks.[26] The exception was the deputy minister, Leo LaFleche, who was criticized for going far beyond his mandate in promoting the deal with Hahn. That criticism was hardly a surprise to the army. Although he had attempted to promote the Bren gun, LaFleche was considered an unguided missile. King, a past master at this kind of situation, knew the best strategy was to declare victory, commenting "there is no evidence ... that the Deputy Minister ... was guilty of any act of corruption or anything in the nature of corruption." This was charitable since it was clear that LaFleche had acted improperly. King's statement, if nothing else, showed that political spin doctoring has been part of the Ottawa scene for a long time.

For Ian Mackenzie, far worse than Davis's verdict was the court of public opinion. He was fatally damaged. His dreadful performance was out in public for all to see. King already knew that Mackenzie was drinking heavily, which, combined with his testimony, left Mackenzie a marked man. In his diary, King wrote,

> I feel extremely sorry for him but if he is undone, it has been his own undoing from the kind of habits that have been contracted through associations that are not too good. There was a time when I really believed that he might succeed to the leadership of the Party but that time has disappeared.[27]

King, in the time-honoured manner of political de-hiring, would wait until the whole thing blew over and ditch Mackenzie at a more convenient moment.

Other figures were not exactly covered in rose petals either. Drew's sensational allegations just looked like party bickering to the newspapers. The far away *Milwaukee Journal* had covered the scandal, but even it described commission evidence as "a spectacular demonstration of mudslinging."[28] MP Plaxton, meanwhile, lost the Liberal nomination in his riding before the 1940 general election.

However, in the end it wasn't just that Hahn, LaFleche, Plaxton, and Drew had been bruised or their reputations tarnished. And it wasn't that Ian Mackenzie's career as defence minister was wrecked. The greatest casualty of all was rearmament itself. Acquiring the Bren gun was the "largest and most significant single step toward the rearmament of the Canadian land forces taken before the outbreak of war. The only important progress made toward the goal of acquiring the armament of two divisions."[29] The contract went ahead, but many others were tainted. Every new proposal to buy equipment was sniffed at by King with deepest suspicion. The main result was that remarkably few items of equipment were produced in Canada for the Canadian forces before the war.[30]

Among the companies that tried to get new business from the British government was Ford of Canada. Ford was informed by the British that owing to the attitude of the Canadian government, the Air Ministry could not entertain its proposal to manufacture twenty-five or fifty aircraft engines for the RAF.[31] That is significant because while it was only a small test order, it might have opened the door to have aircraft engines made in Canada. Aircraft engines never were made in this country through the entire length of the war. Meanwhile, it was only in the last months before the war that the Canadian government took action to counter the British view that Canada was not interested in defence business. A delegation from the Canadian Manufacturers Association, helped by Ottawa and led by Andy McNaughton, was sent to the U.K. in the summer of 1939.

The first Bren guns were delivered by Inglis on March 23, 1940. By the end of the war Inglis had manufactured 186,000 of them.[32] The company was credited with doing an outstanding job.

MILESTONES

FEBRUARY 4, 1936 — Adolf Hitler abolishes the War Ministry and creates the High Command of the Armed Forces, giving him direct control of the German military.

OCTOBER 5, 1937 — In comments aimed at Japan, U.S. President Roosevelt calls for peaceful countries to "quarantine aggressive nations."

OCTOBER 25, 1936 — Rome-Berlin axis is formed. Italian dictator Benito Mussolini uses the term "axis" in signing a friendship treaty with Germany.

In 1937 Squadron Leader Frank Sampson of the RCAF was working at an unlikely job, flying anti-submarine patrols off Spain during the Spanish Civil War. The flights were meant to protect neutral shipping while Sampson himself was an exchange officer attached to No. 209 Squadron of the Royal Air Force and based in Malta. He was getting incredibly valuable operational experience with better and newer equipment than could ever be found in Canada. Later, he was able to pilot Sunderland flying boats, which became one of the workhorses of the Battle of the Atlantic.

Like the other Canadian forces, the RCAF provided only limited opportunity for operational training. Fortunately, however, Canadian airmen working with the British could get attachments to RAF squadrons. Senior officers could be sent on RAF training programs.[33] Apart from Sampson, Flight Lieutenant A.A. Lewis went to Britain in 1935 where some of his training included flying Whitley bombers on day and night cross-country missions, as well as doing bombing practices. Flight Lieutenant Ernie McNab — the young pilot in the Siskin air shows — was posted in 1937 to a fighter outfit and trained on Gloster Gauntlets. He learned about fighter interception using radio ground control and was pleased to find his training included live firing, because, in his entire RCAF career, he had never fired a gun before.

The policy of making the RAF the government's top priority began to show results. By 1938 the new fighters, including the Hurricane and the revolutionary Spitfire, were in operational service or close to it.[34]

This was all good news for RCAF officers on attachments, but as W.A.B. Douglas has noted, the re-equipment program did create some problems. Flight

Lieutenant McNab's unit continued training with its Gauntlets, but there was no point in his reporting further on this training because the new Hurricane's speed and armament so radically changed procedures that anything he reported to the RCAF would have soon been obsolete.[35] Still, Roy Slemon, much later an RCAF air marshal, said that because of the British training, by the time the war broke out "we had a fairly good idea of what was required, even if we didn't have the equipment to carry it out."[36] Officers were able to assume new key roles in the RCAF when they came home. Flight Lieutenant Lewis, on his return to Canada, was given command of No. 3 Bomber Squadron, while Squadron Leader Sampson later commanded No. 5 Squadron in Dartmouth, Nova Scotia.

The RAF experience was one thing, but equipment, training, and manpower at home were different matters entirely. Late in 1938 the regular air force still only had 249 officers and about 1,800 airmen, not even half its authorized strength.[37] The RCAF was plagued with aircraft and equipment shortages that limited training. The number of flying training hours increased more than fourfold between 1931 and 1938, but most of it was basic training. In 1938 only 1,700 hours were spent on combined operations training, compared to 22,500 hours on such activities as test, transportation, liaison, and the like.[38]

In 1938, squadrons, including No. 7 Squadron, a unit based at Rockcliffe outside Ottawa, had only three of its eleven officers, while thirteen airmen positions remained vacant.[39] The commander noted the squadron described as a "general purpose" unit lacked a clearly defined role if it came to a shooting war, and had not been told whether it would operate on land, water, or both. No. 8 Squadron was employed entirely on non-military duties. No. 3 Bomber Squadron moved from Ottawa to Calgary in October and began training initially with four Wapiti aircraft, and later with four more. The planes were armed, but only four had radios. No. 2 (Army Co-operation) Squadron was the busiest unit, working with militia units at Shilo, Petawawa, and St. Catharines, among other places, even though it was stuck with seven clapped out Atlas aircraft throughout most of 1938. In August the squadron joined No. 3 (Bomber) Squadron at Camp Borden to provide air support for the militia concentration. Still, during that training two of the Atlases crashed and one was a write off, and No. 1 Squadron was reduced to only three Siskins remaining in flying condition. No. 1 Squadron trained ineffectually with its Siskins until the following summer when they were finally sent into storage. For any significant improvement the squadron would have to wait for the arrival of the Hurricane fighter in 1939.

There was an upbeat note for some reserve squadrons. No. 111 Squadron in Vancouver had only six aircraft altogether, but it reported after summer camp that in 1938 the squadron "really started to shape up as a potentially operational unit."[40] Its planes were kept busy with camera gun practice, pinpointing, oblique and vertical photography, and "puff target" shoots. The last were bags of smoke chemical that were exploded electrically on the ground so that crews would have practice correcting artillery shooting.

The RCAF was not alone in dispatching officers to Britain. In April 1938, Frederic Franklin Worthington wound up a year at the Royal Tank Corps School in Bovington, and on his return was posted to take command of the Armoured School at Camp Borden.[41] Worthington was the army's leading expert on armoured warfare. His rank was a bit of complexity. He was Captain, Brevet Major, Acting Lieutenant Colonel F.F. Worthington. He was actually a captain, but a brevet major, which meant that his seniority in the rank was recognized but there was no pay, and as "acting lieutenant colonel" he could wear the rank insignia.[42] When he arrived at Camp Borden, Worthington had a training staff of about twenty-five all-ranks.

The fact that the school was at Borden marked a significant change. The armoured school had opened in 1936 in London, Ontario, but in 1938 it was moved to Camp Borden where there was much more room for field training. With that move there was a new name: the Canadian Armoured Fighting Vehicles School. There were no tanks, of course, and otherwise its equipment was comical. It had a single truck named "Old Faithful" made from junk, including an ancient Buick engine and a collection of bits and pieces.[43] Otherwise, there was a discarded artillery gun tractor called a Dragon and a mock up of a tank turret that could roll, yaw, pitch, and alter course, and from those names was called a "Rypa." That was it.

Even without tanks, work had begun on training the six new tank regiments. For a six-week period members of the Essex Regiment were lectured three nights a week on tank tactics and machine guns. During the summer the school organized more elaborate training with three regiments using thirty-one privately owned vehicles along with their horses for exercises. It was true that the battle between cavalry diehards — the British called them "the cavaliers" — and the tank advocates — "the garage hands" — was far from over.[44]

Still, with the cavaliers remaining unconvinced, the garage hands were about to get a boost.

In late summer, two British Mark VI light tanks arrived, the first in the Canadian army since 1918. In the 1936–37 defence preliminary budget, the army asked for 312 tanks. By 1937 it had enough money to buy nine and was begging the government for more, but it was only in 1938 that the first two appeared.[45] The Vickers Mark VIs were bigger than the Carden-Loyd

Nothing much escaped the attention of F.F. Worthington, shown here after the start of the Second World War. In 1939 he was likely the only tank expert in the Canadian army.

Library and Archives Canada

machine gun carriers, but were still only six tons with a crew of three impossibly wedged inside. Ned Amy called them "tiny little things."[46] While the tanks were armed only with two machine guns, at least the vehicles had arrived and now there could be the beginning of realistic training.

One of the first to see the new tanks was none other than the prime minister, who happened to be nearby at the time they arrived. On August 19, in the mid-summer heat, he was shown around Camp Borden and witnessed both cavalry and tanks in the field. He noted, "Life itself, I should think, would be hardly endurable in the tanks. Men must have some great ideal of service or heroism in their breasts to engage in the work."[47] If he had any illusions about how tough things were in the army, on that day he got a firsthand glimpse.

> I confess the effect of the visit was on the whole depressing.
> To begin with, such buildings as there are, are very dilapidated and out of date; firetraps, primitive kind of sanitary arrangements. The ground is overgrown with poison ivy; except a muddy stream, there is no water for bathing ...

In 1939 the Canadian army had fourteen light tanks similar to this Vickers Mark VI. Even after the war began some senior officers questioned how useful tanks would be.

While there was a new home for the armoured school and there were two tanks for training, by far the biggest asset for armoured warfare in Canada was the bulldog who ran the school, Captain, Brevet Major, Acting Lieutenant Colonel Worthington, who was among a mere handful of military leaders in Canada who could be called charismatic. He had his identity card made up with a picture of a monkey on it instead of his photo and raised hell when gate guards passed him without checking.[48] He could and would intimidate anyone, and even his son said, "Quite, sincerely, his eyes could blaze and I can't imagine anyone relishing his anger."

Worthy's early years were so calamitous, exotic, and seemingly impossible they sound like an Indiana Jones movie. He was born in 1890 in Scotland but his family later moved to California.[49] His father had been a surgeon but by grim misfortune both parents soon died, leaving Worthington an orphan at age eleven. The nearest relative was a half-brother working at a gold mine in Nacozaro, Mexico. Worthington travelled all the way to Mexico only to have tragedy strike again as the mine was raided by Pancho Villa's soldiers and his brother was killed. From this point Worthy was on his own, surviving by savvy street smarts, a string of unlikely but helpful strangers, and bountiful good luck.[50]

In the next years he was a sailor aboard a series of sailing vessels in the southern Pacific. By 1906 he was in San Francisco in time to survive the Big Quake, and afterward signed onto a steamer bound for China. He was a mercenary in wars in Guatemala and Nicaragua, and in 1913 was wounded in the Mexican Civil War. When the First World War broke out he made his way to Montreal and joined the Canadian army by mistake. On a Montreal street he saw members of the Black Watch in uniform and joined up, not realizing they were members of the Black Watch of Canada, not the Scottish Black Watch.

On the Western Front he saw tanks in battle on September 15, 1916, and became an armoured warfare convert. He won a Military Cross and Bar and Military Medal and Bar, a rare combination. Worthy returned to Canada — a country he barely knew — and decided to make his future in the post-war Canadian army as a Permanent Force officer. By 1927 he had married, and when a son arrived, Worthy even included the name "Vickers" — from the Vickers machine gun — in the boy's name. His soldiers had suggested it. So the child was Peter John Vickers Worthington, possibly the first boy ever named after a machine gun.*

Finally, in April 1938, F. F. Worthington returned to Canada and Camp Borden. He was determined that Canada, as far behind as it was in armoured warfare training, would be hell bent on catching up.[51] Considering he had about "a hundred new ideas a minute," he wasn't about to waste time.[52]

The excitement of new tanks and a visit by the prime minister were not the only remarkable events at Borden in the summer of 1938. There were also extraordinary exercises for Permanent Force members. For the first time in the interwar years, a skeleton Permanent Force infantry brigade was assembled in one place for a month. The units included the Royal Canadian Regiment and the Royal 22e Regiment, the Royal Canadian Dragoons, two standard artillery batteries of the RCHA, plus a medium artillery battery, signals units, and an improvised brigade headquarters. Although none of the regiments would have made up a full-sized battalion, almost no officers or enlisted men in the army had ever seen such a force before. Young officers like Dan Spry, originally from Winnipeg, welcomed the training as a chance to see first-hand the kind of mobile warfare described by General Fuller and others.[53]

Much of the equipment was in short supply, obsolete, or non-existent, but that was nothing new for most soldiers. One junior officer, Desmond B. Smith, said he spent most exercises in the 1930s holding a yellow flag to represent a machine gun.[54] Despite the tremendous advances made in wireless communication infantry, signallers still practiced with flags and mirrors or 1918 model field telephones.[55] Nevertheless, the Dragoons came with their one and only armoured car, two green painted civilian vehicles, and, of course, their horses.[56] Even something as mundane as water was a problem once the mock battles began. Field kitchen and water supply transport could only travel at a top speed of eight miles an hour and couldn't keep up with the combat formations if they moved.[57]

The exercises were a mess, a cavalcade of confusion and failure. W.A.B. Anderson, a Permanent Force artillery lieutenant, remembered what happened as "very unprofessional, play soldiering, full of old officers." The forces were "sloppily handled."[58] There were glaring deficiencies in even the most elementary tactics. The RCD reported:

> As a learning exercise, these manoeuvres were a great success, exposing a vast array of blunders and weaknesses by

---

[*] Peter Worthington served at the end of the Second World War, in the Korean War, and later became a prominent journalist in Toronto. Peter liked the name "Vickers" and passed it on to his own son.

the infantry as well as the cavalry, and in command and control of the force. Advances were unnecessarily slow, cooperation was lax, and combined tactics poorly applied by all of the arms.... Many of the same weaknesses that were to plague Canadians in action five years later were prominently displayed.[59]

None of this should have been a surprise. As Jack Granatstein noted, "Nothing more could have been expected from an army that, collectively, had spent most of the last two decades training the Militia and grooming horses."[60]

In the fall of 1938 several people in Victoria began to organize a new group that wanted to make a contribution to Canada's military. The members wanted to serve, but until this point they had been utterly ignored. The group was made up of women trying to establish themselves as an auxiliary military service. They met just a few weeks after Britain had decided to allow women in one branch of the British Territorial Army. One organizer in Victoria recalled that her group was organized without any government encouragement or support.

> There was much enthusiastic marching about and drill in the big armouries.... It was obvious to all of us that there was going to be a war and we jolly well better start preparing for it — women as well as men!...We formed almost at once into four divisions — Motor Transport, Commissariat (supplies), Red Cross First Aid, and Clerical. We also decided on a uniform for ourselves; a white shirtwaist, blue skirt, blue sweater and a beret with a blue badge and letters WVS (Women's Volunteer Service) in gold.[61]

For the most part, women had not been part of Canadian military service. However, there had been women nurses in war service as early as 1885, and they had made a notable contribution in the First World War. During that time there had been 3,141 nursing sisters serving in both Canada and overseas as members of the Canadian Medical Corps. Fifty-three nursing sisters died in service, including fourteen who drowned when a U-boat sank a Canadian hospital ship.

There were also women volunteers in the Canadian Red Cross, the YWCA, St. John Ambulance, and the Imperial Order Daughters of the Empire.

Women were active in a number of cities, determined to have their own branch in the army, one that would allow them to take roles other than nursing. The Second World War would be underway for close to two years before that happened.[62]

In August 1938 there was another high-profile visit to Canada by American President Franklin Roosevelt. In 1936 he had gone to Quebec City, but this time he was at Kingston, Ontario, to deliver one of the most important addresses ever by an American president on Canadian soil. In what became a famous declaration, Roosevelt pledged that "the people of the United States will not stand idly by" if Canada were threatened by another country. Clearly, as he had shown earlier, Roosevelt was still worried about Canada's lack of defences. Shortly after the visit ended, King promised that Canada would not allow the United States to be attacked via Canadian territory although he had no real way of backing that up.

CHAPTER NINE

A Total and Unmitigated Defeat

In the fall of 1938, the Munich crisis brought Europe to within a hair's breadth of war. People lived in acute anxiety for months hoping for peace one moment, despairing the next. As early as May 28, Adolf Hitler had sent a directive to his military chief of staff, General Keitel, stating the "unalterable intention to smash Czechoslovakia by military action." The deadline was October 1. Hitler had won by bluff and bullying in Austria, so he thought Czechoslovakia would be the same. By late July the British were aware that German pilots had been recalled from Spain. Something big was up.

Ostensibly, the main issue was the Czechoslovak Sudetenland, the border area that was home to 3 million ethnic Germans, but Hitler's real aim was to take over all of Czechoslovakia. There would be enormous benefits if that happened, including a weapons bonanza. It was the home of the renowned Skoda works, which turned out some of the best tanks, aircraft engines, and guns produced anywhere. Strategically, taking over Czechoslovakia would also change the whole military balance in the region because it would free up German divisions that otherwise would have to protect against the very considerable Czechoslovak army.

In late summer the Nazis provoked street demonstrations and protests. The Prague government was prepared to grant autonomy to the Sudeten Germans but to Hitler that was meaningless. At the same time Czechoslovakia had military alliances with France and the Soviet Union so there was a real prospect that an attack might escalate into another European war. In Canada Prime Minister William Lyon Mackenzie King wrote to the Governor General to say that war was an immediate possibility, but King felt "it will be found in the end that Hitler is for peace, unless unduly provoked."[1] On August 31,

King held a meeting with one of the Quebec ministers in cabinet, Chubby Power, and Ian Mackenzie to discuss events in Europe. King wrote that if war came to Britain, undoubtedly Canada would be drawn in. "I made it clear to both Mackenzie and Power that I would stand for Canada doing all she possibly could to destroy those Powers which are basing their actions on might and not right, and that I would not consider being neutral in this situation for a moment."[2]

When Power said that might mean Quebec members leaving the Liberal Party, King responded with a dire warning. He said the Quebec MPs should be the ones leading the province in its obligation to participate in any forthcoming war and that if Quebeckers refused, "that would be the end of Quebec."[3] In a later diary comment King was just as firm, saying, "our real self-interest lies in the strength of the British Empire as a whole, not in our geographical position and resources.... I am clear in my own mind that co-operation between all parts of the Empire and the democracies is in Canada's interest in the long run and in her own immediate self respect. The only possible attitude to be assumed."[4]

The British and French policy in dealing with Hitler was appeasement since the alternative was war. Appeasement enjoyed enormous support both in Britain and Canada. While King felt that Canada would have to join a European war if Britain were attacked, that was always a last resort. Until that moment came, King was among the most ardent appeasement supporters. Until late in 1938 the policy had a different connotation, one of "reconciliation." Many in Europe recalled the nightmare of the last war only too clearly while appeasement supporters strongly believed every attempt had to be made to avoid a new war. France had never really recovered from the First World War and the French armed forces were poorly led, split by factions and disorganization. In Paris one story making the rounds was that mountains of secret documents were hidden in a wind tunnel, but, unaware of their presence, someone started the fans. Thousands of pages scattered themselves all over a Paris suburb at a speed of 200 miles an hour. The quip was that it was "the first breath of fresh air that ever blew through the French Air Ministry."[5] Meanwhile, a British policy of "no commitments" to the continent would have sounded familiar to many Canadians. All Britain's army planning was not for Europe's defence but for the empire's protection.

As King had tried to do earlier, Neville Chamberlain believed the crisis could be defused by face-to-face negotiations with Hitler. At a cabinet meeting on September 17, the British leader described Hitler as an excitable but rational man with strictly limited aims. The British chiefs of staff, in a crucial assessment of the military situation, pointed out that Britain was not ready for war. It did not have military parity with Germany, let alone superiority.

Chamberlain's resolve to travel to Germany prompted King to send a message applauding the British leader's "striking and noble action." Chamberlain, taking his first ever long distance airplane flight, made his way to Germany on September 15 and again on September 22. He proposed to sacrifice part of Czechoslovakia for the greater good of peace in Europe. The Czechoslovak people, of course, had little to say about it. The French were eager to get off the hook from their treaty commitments. Nothing was resolved on the first visit to Berlin and Chamberlain, to his dismay, found on the second trip that Hitler only increased his demands. The Fuhrer threatened to march into Czechoslovakia within a week and Chamberlain returned to London without an agreement.

In Ottawa on September 23, Prime Minister King held a cabinet meeting to sound out ministers. He was surprised to find general agreement that if Neville Chamberlain failed, Canada should declare itself on the side of Britain.[6] However, Ernest Lapointe in Geneva cabled back that there should be no definite commitments made, and that if war came Parliament should be recalled.

The imminent prospect of war left the Canadian forces in enormous embarrassment — the Atlantic coast defences were simply not ready.[7] For one thing, the air force's projected east coast artillery co-operation squadron, designed to be spotters for the big guns, had not even been formed. The RCAF had to slam together an emergency plan. No. 2 Squadron had to shepherd its archaic Atlas light bombers from Ottawa to Halifax to fill the gap. To go with them the RCAF scraped together whatever odds and ends it could find, a total of thirty-nine planes in all. The only remotely modern aircraft were the six Shark torpedo bombers. The redeployment entirely cleaned out the rest of the country, leaving only primary trainers in central Canada and five obsolete aircraft on the Pacific coast. An air force memo later described the response as "pitiably inadequate."[8] It said what happened "drove home the almost hopeless position with which the country was confronted at the time."

The RCN also had severe problems but at least one bit of good timing. Some months earlier the cabinet had agreed to buy two more destroyers for the navy, bringing the total to six. There was no money in the budget, but instead funds were simply taken from the army budget and transferred to the navy's. King wrote in his diary, "I found that members of the Cabinet generally were wholly favourable to the purchase of the new destroyers.... [Government Leader in the Senate, Raoul] Dandurand was quite emphatic that the coast defences could be defended but not an increase in army estimates which might look to expedition overseas. I think that is now wholly out of the question."[9]

So in addition to *Skeena* and *Saguenay*, which had arrived in 1931, and the modern *Fraser* and *St. Laurent*, which had arrived in 1937, *Ottawa* and *Restigouche* were transferred from the RN the summer of 1938. The two arrived from Britain just as the Munich crisis was breaking.[10] As for anything else, the navy's cupboard was bare. The only other ships it had were two newly commissioned minesweepers and fewer than a dozen government craft that could be used as armed auxiliaries. Because of budget limits the navy lacked more than $2 million worth of basic equipment to outfit the destroyers and auxiliary vessels and install even the most rudimentary anti-submarine port defences. Admiral Nelles described what he saw as "near tragic."[11]

Called by most sailors "Rustyguts," HMCS Restigouche was built as HMS Comet in 1932.

In mid-September panicked calls were made to the United States about buying American military aircraft. On September 28, Air Vice-Marshal Croil dispatched a team to Washington on an air force version of that much loved Canadian tradition, a U.S. shopping spree. The team's orders were to buy as many military planes as they could get their hands on for $5 million. Air Commodore Ernest Stedman led the group — all in civilian dress — to Washington, telling the Americans the RCAF only wanted aircraft that could be delivered in three months. That was a tall order. The only planes that would fit that description were U.S. Army Air Corps aircraft just coming off the assembly lines. With enormous generosity the Americans allowed the RCAF to go ahead and take what it needed, excepting only a few experimental aircraft. The Canadian priorities were fifteen reconnaissance aircraft, eighteen long-range Douglas 18A bombers, and fifteen Seversky (later Republic) P-35 fighters. The P-35 was already obsolete in 1938, but it was the first single-seat American fighter to feature all metal construction, retractable landing gear, and an enclosed cockpit.

Meanwhile, back in Ottawa, King issued a public statement about the Czechoslovak crisis on September 26.

> The Canadian Government is continuing to keep in the closest touch with the grave developments in the European situation. The government is making preparations for any contingency and for the immediate summoning of Parliament if the efforts which are still being made to preserve the peace of Europe should fail. For our country to keep united is all-important.[12]

War hysteria gripped Britain.[13] On September 27, trenches were dug in London parks and gas masks were distributed. One of the leading hawks in the British foreign office, Sir Robert Vansittart, burned his private papers and stocked up on suicide pills. Prime Minister Chamberlain addressed the British on radio, making one of the most astonishing statements of his time. "How horrible, fantastic, incredible it is that we should be digging trenches and trying on gas-masks here because of a quarrel in a far-away country between people of whom we know nothing."

On September 28, the British fleet was mobilized. That evening Chamberlain was speaking to the House of Commons about the likely prospect of war. He had proposed going to Germany one last time for a four-power summit and, dramatically, at that exact moment word arrived that Hitler had agreed to a meeting. The house erupted in wild, prolonged acclaim, one MP describing the scene as "one of the most dramatic moments which I have ever witnessed."[14]

Chamberlain made his third flight to Germany on September 29. On arrival in Munich, the British delegation was taken directly to the Fuhrer's office for the meeting with the three other leaders: Hitler, French Prime Minister Edouard Daladier, and Italy's Mussolini.[15] In the early hours of September 30, the four reached an agreement allowing Germany to occupy the Sudeten areas. There would be peace but at a fearful price — Czechoslovakia would be dismembered.

With the deal reached, Chamberlain left for London. Importantly, in his view, he flourished a paper signed by Hitler saying that it was the wish of the British and German peoples that the two countries would "never go to war with one another again." Hitler declared he had made his last territorial demand. What Chamberlain wanted, and what he thought he had, was a framework so that diplomacy would replace brinkmanship as a way of settling European disputes.

Thousands of people were gathered at Heston Airport near London when Chamberlain returned. As the plane's door swung open, the crowd surged forward, erupting into pandemonium. Chamberlain waved his hat at the cheering throng. "I've got it," he shouted, referring to the agreement signed by Hitler. The nine-mile drive to London took an hour and a half and, as Chamberlain later recalled, the roads "were lined from one end to the other with people of every class, shouting themselves hoarse."[16] He declared it was "peace for our time" while later Chamberlain and his wife appeared on the Buckingham Palace balcony with the king and queen.[17] He received thousands of gifts, including dozens of his trademark umbrella.

The events in Europe were anxiously followed in Canada. Charles Stacey, later a distinguished military historian, was in Toronto. "Walking down Bay Street one actually sensed the fear of war in the air; certainly it was on the set faces of the passers-by. I have never had such another experience, before or since. And when the crisis was resolved — even though it was by the sacrifice of a weak and helpless democratic state — the sense of relief, and of momentary gratitude to the peacemaker Chamberlain, was equally overwhelming."[18]

The news came to Prime Minister King "like a reprieve to a condemned man."[19] He sent off a message to Chamberlain saying, "The heart of Canada is rejoicing tonight at the success which has crowned your unremitting efforts for peace. May I convey to you the warm congratulations of the Canadian people."[20] At this moment in Ottawa, someone suddenly remembered the team sent to Washington to buy aircraft. Stedman's blanket authority was temporarily stopped and then cancelled altogether, so he returned home with neither aircraft nor contracts.

The Munich crisis has been described by historian A.J.P. Taylor as the high water mark of Britain's appeasement policy.[21] In Chamberlain's eyes the agreement was a resounding success because there was an accommodation that changed the frontiers set in 1919 without a war. While immediate newspaper reaction and public comment in Britain and Canada was overwhelmingly in favour of the deal, there was an undercurrent of doubt. Had anything really been solved? Some were convinced that more demands from Hitler were coming. General Edmond Ironside, a senior British commander, resented cabinet ministers in London "trying to explain away our humiliation."[22] In British Parliament a number of speakers lashed out at both appeasement and Munich. Among them was a person King called "one of the most dangerous men I have ever known,"[23] the Conservative Party has-been, Winston Churchill, who commented:

> We have suffered a total and unmitigated defeat ... you will find that in a period of time which may be measured by years, but may be measured by months, Czechoslovakia will be engulfed in the Nazi regime. We are in the presence of a disaster of the first magnitude ... we have sustained a defeat without a war ... the terrible words have for the time being been pronounced against the Western democracies: "Thou art weighed in the balance and found wanting."

In Canada there was still support for Chamberlain, but Bruce Hutchison, for one, called it "peace by surrender."[24] Lieutenant Colonel Worthington was among many who said from then on most people knew the democracies were living on borrowed time.[25] Another critic was John Wesley Dafoe, the most influential journalist of the era. A staunch Liberal and editor of the influential *Free Press* in Winnipeg, Dafoe urged the government to prepare for war, which he predicted would begin in 1939. One scathing article he wrote was titled,

"What's the Cheering For?" He said the doctrine that Germany can intervene for the "protection" of Germans in any country, regardless of guarantees it had given, had "not only been asserted but made good." He said, "it has been approved, sanctioned, certified and validated by the governments of Great Britain and France, who had undertaken in this respect to speak for the democracies of the world."[26]

King at first rejoiced at the Munich agreement. For three years he had tried to convince himself that somehow he would be saved from the fateful decision of having to go to war, but Munich was a turning point — his appeasement policy began to suffer a slow but steady attrition.[27] From December 1938 his goal was no longer avoidance but rather finding a political formula so that if Canadians had to go to war they would do so as a united country.[28] However, in terms of rearmament, a lot could still be done in a "crash" campaign to rearm, but instead King and the Liberal government seemed to reflect a business as usual mindset.

At this point, public opinion in Canada was divided into several camps. Canadian Imperialists said if Britain went to war, then Canada would be at war. Many Conservatives, including George Drew, were ardent supporters of this view, demanding at the same time a vigorous rearmament program.[29] A second group was made up of many, or possibly most, English Canadians. Opinion differed but generally they that felt that if Britain were attacked Canada should join the battle. However, they said that a British declaration of war did not mean Canada was *automatically* at war. They did not want to be forced into going to war or be taken for granted.

A third group was made up of pacifists who wanted to avoid war under any circumstances, essentially turning aside the suppression of liberty in Germany. Pacifists included many in the CCF and Protestant church groups. In 1932 the United Church declared that "armed warfare between nations was contrary to the spirit and teachings of Christ."[30] Also expressing anti-war sentiments were some university students such as Hammy Gray of Nelson, British Columbia. He was a supporter of the Student Peace Movement at the University of British Columbia and did not believe Canada was threatened.[31]

Finally, the isolationists felt that Canada should avoid another European entanglement. Many of the 3 million French Canadians were in this group, saying that war would inevitably bring conscription. Some thought it was acceptable if English Canadians wanted to get themselves killed, but leave the French out of it. Francois-Albert Angers, a Quebec nationalist, wrote: "Deep in every English Canadian, if indeed he is a Canadian, slumbers an imperialist."[32] King's advisor, Oscar Skelton, also was an outspoken advocate of staying out of European conflicts. "It is incredible that we would tamely accept the role cast for us by some overseas directors, namely, that every twenty years Canada should take part in a Central European war, sacrificing the lives of tens of thousands of her young men, bringing herself to the verge of bankruptcy, risking internal splits and disturbances."[33]

King knew that because the country was so divided any declaration of war would be a dangerous business. However, as he had told Chamberlain earlier, if fighting did break out he was prepared to recall Parliament within two weeks and propose that Canada join the war.[34] King knew that in the final analysis he could not turn aside the English Canadian ties to Britain but in any event he was a strong believer that empire security was Canada's only option.[35] Or in the words of Charles Stacey, "These were the people whose opinions were decisive in 1939; and, incidentally Mackenzie King was one of them."[36]

In a new budget in November 1938, the RCAF got, for the first time, more money than the army. In a move that again showed King's determination to avoid overseas expeditions, the army came last in terms of budget increase. The prime minister described cabinet members as being united "in favour of keeping militia estimates to narrowest bound, increases to go to naval services and mostly to air."[37]

The final budget total was $64 million — the largest defence spending ever proposed in Canada in peacetime and almost double the outlay of the year before.[38] The air force got just less than $30 million, twice what it had the year before. The army got only $21.4 million. The navy received $8.8 million. The air force increase was dramatic, but even if it had got everything it asked for, it would still be more than 100 aircraft short of its plans to equip eleven permanent and twelve reserve squadrons.

The new money in 1937 and1938 did allow the RCAF to buy a considerable number of new planes from both British and Canadian companies. And finally, at the end of 1938, it was able to introduce the first of its Stranraer long-range flying boats into service. It was assigned to No. 5 Bomber Reconnaissance Squadron on the east coast.[39] It was the same aircraft that began patrols off the east coast at the start of the war. There was agonizing wait for other aircraft, as Canadian companies seemed to take forever to make deliveries while British firms were still backed up with British orders.

Among the new aircraft ordered in 1938 was the Westland Lysander army co-operation aircraft meant to replace the Atlas. The Lysander would be built in a new plant at Malton, on the edge of Toronto, managed by National Steel Car Ltd. Seventy-five were ordered, with the first one delivered in September 1939. The RCAF also contracted Fairchild Aircraft of Longueuil, Quebec, to build the twin-engine Bolingbroke to provide a much more modern coastal patrol plane than the Stranraer. Additionally, the RCAF had ordered twenty Hurricane fighters from Britain and they began to arrive at the start of 1939. There were also two orders from Britain that would provide a boost for Canadian aircraft production. The British ordered forty Hurricanes to be built at Canadian Car and Foundry in Fort William (now Thunder Bay), Ontario, and there would be larger orders later on.[40] There was a further contract for assembling eighty Hampden bombers for the RAF, while tentative plans were made for building 100 more.

The British orders were prompted by the formation of Canadian Associated Aircraft, which included six small aircraft makers: Canadian Car and Foundry, Fairchild, National Steel Car, Canadian Vickers, Fleet Aircraft, and Ottawa Car and Aircraft.[41] Many of the new factories would not be able to produce aircraft for months, as plants had to be expanded and new workers trained.

The new budget money and new aircraft ordered were not the only signs of the growing importance of the RCAF. One early result of the Munich crisis was the RCAF's becoming an independent service.[42] Air Vice-Marshal Croil's title had been senior air officer, which implied subordination to the army's chief of the general staff, but from this point on his title was changed to chief of the air staff. Since its inception the air force had been entirely dependent on the army for administration, pay, transport, medical services, and rations.[43] Now there would be a national command structure with Eastern, Western, and Air Training Commands set up.[44] In the meantime, three more reserve squadrons — the last ones before the war — were established in Halifax, London, Ontario, and St. John, New Brunswick. Each had five Moth aircraft along with two permanent officers and five airmen attached.[45]

MILESTONES

1937 — In Germany, Luftwaffe Chief Hermann Goering orders a halt to all work on the four engine JU-89 and DO-19 bombers. The decision ended German efforts to build a strategic bomber that might have been used in the Battle of Britain or later as the so-called "Ural Bomber."

FEBRUARY 4, 1938 — Hitler seizes personal control of the German army and puts Nazis in key posts.

OCTOBER 1938 — The British Air Ministry rejects Ronald Bishop's idea for a fast bomber built of wood. Mr. Bishop and de Havilland built it anyway and the Mosquito went on to become one of the most versatile military planes ever built.

While the money for the navy, including the poaching on the army budget, allowed the RCN to add new ships, the next step was uncertain. The cabinet examined the prospect of building major warships in Canada, but interest quickly evaporated when it got the cost estimates. By the end of the year the last of the four small minesweepers had been built and commissioned. The government approved the purchase of one more British destroyer, which, as before, was available at bargain basement prices thanks to the Royal Navy.[46] But Admiral Nelles said that was likely the last vessel the RCN could get on those terms because it was now becoming apparent that the British themselves were extremely short of destroyers. Still, achieving a fleet of six relatively modern destroyers with one more to come was a major accomplishment for the navy.

The army faced a most difficult situation, with James Eayrs describing its budget as "ruthless, arbitrary and inadequate."[47] The new money was not enough to cover payments for existing equipment orders.[48] Major General T.V. Anderson, the new chief of the general staff, had warned earlier that the slow progress the army was making was "little related to the grave situation which we now face."[49] Finally, Parliament did vote additional funds for improving Atlantic coast defences at Halifax, Saint John, and Sydney.

The budget included the news that that new uniforms to be called "battle dress" would be ordered. With additional funds, there would be more reservists by far taking part in two weeks of summer training in 1939 than in earlier years. However, there had not been money to buy new anti-aircraft guns or field artillery, meaning artillery regiments would still be equipped with First World War eighteen-pounders, but at least by this time many reserve artillery regiments had replaced horses with trucks.[50] New artillery recruits, including seventeen-year-old George MacDonell, the teenager who was too young to join the Canadian Active Service Force in 1939, would learn the basics, but still on the First World War hardware.[51]

At the same time, there were more examples of the incredible dedication of some army members. In Calgary, Donald MacLauchlan had wanted to be a soldier from the age of sixteen and had finally been able to join the Calgary Highlanders. But in 1938 he lost his job at the *Albertan* newspaper for taking off too much time to attend militia courses.[52] Many companies in the 1930s had little patience with employees who were missing work for any reason. Some outstanding regular officers, including Lieutenant Colonel E.L.M. Burns, were instructing in the new Advanced Militia Staff Course. It was meant for majors who were preparing for promotion to colonel and higher. Among the students was Lieutenant Colonel A.E. Walford, a Montreal reservist who commanded the 2nd Medium Artillery Brigade until the outbreak of war. He later became a major general and one of the most senior planners in the Canadian army in Europe.[53]

Any attempt to build up a Canadian munitions industry was sidetracked by other priorities. Only one arsenal in Quebec continued to turn out limited quantities of small-arms ammunition. Work was finally started on a new arsenal at Valcartier in 1934 as an unemployment relief project. In 1937 a new tool-and-gauge plant was opened at Quebec, and in 1938 a tracer-bullet plant was put into operation at the same place, but bigger projects were too far down on the priority list to be funded.

By 1938 Quebecker Jean Victor Allard was an old hand in the army reserve.[54] In 1929 he had wrangled his way into his hometown unit, the Three Rivers Regiment, at the age of sixteen. He quickly excelled and two years later he was asked to take the reserve officer training course. Two evenings a week for more than half a year Allard and a small group of other reserve stalwarts took military law, administration, tactics, and other subjects. He was commissioned as a second lieutenant on April 23, 1933.

Allard was orphaned when he was only seven years old, so he and his six sisters did not have an easy time. However, Allard had one priceless advantage that set him apart from many French Canadians at that time — he lived for a year or so in King's hometown, Kitchener, Ontario, and learned English. A bonus was that his courses at St. Jerome's College included physics and algebra, which were not studied much in high school in his home province.

After that Allard returned to Quebec, but had to scratch around for jobs because of the Depression. Still, he was able to pursue two completely different pastimes. He loved classical singing, had a fine voice, and performed at private and public events, but he also took advantage of every chance to pursue his training in the militia. There were obstacles including that in 1936 the Three Rivers Regiment became another of those tank regiments without tanks. However, between 1933 and the start of the Second World War, Allard spent what added up to two entire years on army training courses or exercises. That included the Militia Staff Course in Kingston while on his own he studied works by Clausewitz and Liddell Hart. By 1938 he was a well-trained captain.

Allard was not the only French Canadian in the military. Seventeen-year-old Gilles Turcot joined Les Voltigeurs de Quebec in 1935 and was expelled from the Seminaire de Quebec for doing so without permission.[55] Paul Triquet was turned down when he tried to join the regular army when he was seventeen, but a year later in 1927, he joined the Vandoos.[56] Dollard Menard graduated from Royal Military College in 1936 (Cadet # 2290).[57] He was six feet two inches, a broad-shouldered giant who later became famous at Les Fusiliers Mont-Royal as a fitness maniac. Another outstanding Quebecker was the gregarious and outgoing Julien Bibeau, a sales manager for the Maple Leaf Milling Company who became a member of the Maisonneuves. Fluent in English, a natural leader, and instinctive soldier, Bibeau became one of the outstanding battalion commanders in the Canadian army.[58]

These young French-Canadian officers, however, were the vast exceptions, not the rule, in the interwar years. They made up a tiny minority in the army. The unsurprising reality was that Quebeckers simply did not feel welcome in the unilingual world of the Canadian forces. Before the Second World War there were fourteen French-speaking units in the reserves, all of them infantry. English, however, was the principal language of command and administration. All foot drill was in English and so were all training manuals. Jean Victor Allard's officer training course was in English with translation provided by a senior NCO. French was used in the battalions only for instruction and social activities.[59]

In 1935 there were forty-five French-speaking officers in the regular army (only two were colonels or higher), compared to 375 English speakers.[60] In the Permanent Force the only French-speaking unit was the Royal 22e Regiment, and it was well under strength, making up just 4.4 percent of the regular force.[61] Such was the shortage of well trained French-speaking officers that even as late as 1941 the army was unable to find a single qualified French Canadian to command one of the brigades in Britain.[62] One of the few senior French-Canadian commanders was Georges Vanier, who had lost a leg in the First World War and whose career included both military and diplomatic postings. Later on, of course, he was a Governor General of Canada.

Advancement was difficult for French Canadians in the navy and air force too. One study shows that between 1920 and 1934 an average of 35 Anglophones took courses in Britain for every two Francophones. All courses were in English.[63] Among the few francophones was Vanier, who attended the British Army Staff College, while by contrast most French-speaking soldiers were relegated to small arms and physical training courses. There were no candidates at the Imperial Defence College, which meant that through the six years of the Second World War access to high command was choked off.[64] It was not until the very end of the war that Allard emerged as a brigadier and an officer who was headed for even higher command.*

Some said that the air force was the most difficult service for French Canadians.[65] The first RCAF recruiting centre in Quebec was not opened until the summer of 1941. In the early years of the war all training was in English and some bases even forbade speaking French on the station. It was 1942 before a mainly French-speaking squadron was formed, No. 425 (Alouette) Squadron.

As for the navy, a study during the war showed that while only 8 percent of the male population of Canada was born in the United Kingdom, 28 percent of RCN officers were British-born while in the Royal Canadian Naval Reserve it was 58 percent.[66] Even francophones who joined the RCNVR had to learn English and adapt. It was 1943 before there was an order that the RCN should provide facilities for teaching English to French-speaking recruits.[67] The most striking success story in the navy was Victor Brodeur who, as we saw earlier, took command of HMCS *Fraser* in 1937. By that time he was a veteran destroyer captain. He became the first French Canadian

---

* J.P.E. Bernatchez, a brigade commander as of 1944, was also on the very small list of French-speakers who went on to more senior postings just after the war.

to command a warship, taking charge of *Champlain* in 1930 and later commanding *Skeena*. His father had been the minister of marine and fisheries and one of the founders of the RCN. Like all francophones in the forces, Brodeur adapted by learning English and fitting in.[68] Perhaps a bit too much, since his nickname was "Scotty." Brodeur was later a rear admiral.

There were about 3 million French Canadians in 1939, roughly 29 percent of the Canadian population. The empire held no appeal for them. Every French Canadian remembered the conscription crisis of 1917–18, which was viewed as a symbol of English Canadian tyranny. Many francophones held a completely different perspective on the situation in Europe than did English Canadians.[69] Mussolini was respected because of the 1929 Lateran Treaty, which established the Vatican as a separate state, while Antonio Salazar of Portugal had returned the Catholic Church to prominence in Portugal. In the Spanish Civil War French Canadians had no interest in saving the Spanish Republic and its communist supporters, instead their sympathies were with Franco. The Roman Catholic Church in Quebec repeated relentlessly that communists were a much greater danger than fascists.[70] As Richard Jones notes, "throughout the critical years between the wars, a certain sympathy [arose] for the right-wing dictators who had seized power in several lands under the pretext of containing the communist threat."[71] Hitler was not revered, but at least he was anti-communist.

Meanwhile, there were many Nazi imitators, including Quebec's own Adrien Arcand, a Montreal journalist, federalist, anti-Semite, self-proclaimed Canadian fuhrer, and fanatical anti-communist.[72] Some prominent figures also expressed admiration for the strong leader. Lionel Groulx was one churchman who longed for a "chef," a leader to arouse enthusiasm and impose the policies which French Canada had always needed. "Happy are the people who have found their dictator," he said.[73]

Among the most prominent Quebec anti-communists was the popular tyrant Premier Maurice Duplessis who helped shape the province for two decades. After he won the 1936 election he launched an anti-communist and anti-socialist campaign. In 1937 his government passed the notorious Padlock Law which gave police wide powers to close down any establishment that promoted communism, and since communism was deliberately left undefined, any number of trade unions, journalists, Jehovah's Witnesses, and others were subject to attack.[74] The *Free Press* in Winnipeg called it "one of the most savage assaults upon freedom which Canada has ever seen."[75] King refused to have it either disallowed or referred to the courts, arguing that either move would play into Duplessis's hands.

Young Quebeckers generally held the view that the province was a kind of redoubt of the Catholic Church, but saying that did not exclude fascist or nationalist views. In 1936 one seventeen-year-old student at the prestigious Jean-de-Brebeuf Catholic school wrote an essay that portrayed himself as leading an army to create an independent and Catholic Quebec.[76] The same student was an admirer of Alexis Carrel, whose book *L'homme, cet inconnu* was a sensation in 1935. Carrel thought society was falling into ruin, women were ignoring children to pursue careers, and whites were genetically superior to blacks, but above all the principle of democracy was not only unfounded, but harmful. After the fall of France in 1940, he became a celebrated member of the Vichy regime.

Of course, the student referred to as admiring Carrel and wanting to lead the charge toward a Catholic and independent Quebec was Joseph Philippe Pierre Yves Elliott Trudeau. Later on Trudeau and many others changed their views but this was the state of debate in Quebec before the war. For Trudeau and his contemporaries the coming of the Second World War was of little interest. "The war was an undeniably important reality, but a very distant one. Moreover, it was part of current events, and ... they did not interest me very much ... we tended to think of this war as a settling of scores among the superpowers." Trudeau, as a wartime university student, was required to be a member of the Canadian Officer Training Corps and he took part in some military activities at that time, but without enthusiasm.

No one in Canada better understood the searing scars left by the 1917–18 conscription crisis than William Lyon Mackenzie King. He was among those Liberals who did not join Borden's coalition government in 1917.[77] King's own government relied heavily on support from the fifty-nine Quebec Liberal MPs. In spite of a whiff of support for dictators, when it came to French Canadians voting, there was strong support for King and the Liberal Party.

Actually, the vote was not so much for King as it was for Ernest Lapointe, the greatest Quebec political figure of his time and a man of enormous influence.[78]

Lapointe gave crucial backing to King in the 1919 Liberal leadership race, which King only won on the third ballot. Lapointe had a long history in cabinet, starting as minister of marine and fisheries in 1921 and later as minister of justice (1924–26, 1926–30, 1935–41). His influence was matched by his physical stature, standing six feet tall with massive shoulders, towering above his colleagues. He was a great speaker, but put so much effort into some addresses that by the end he was drenched in perspiration. His career was hampered by chronic health problems, with Lapointe saying even in July 1935 that he would not run again. Lapointe supported some rearmament, but he was dead against sending the army abroad. Most of all, there could be no conscription at any time for any reason. Lapointe's resignation was always a possibility, and if it happened it would most likely be fatal to King.

Munich had left a scar on many memories, but if another reminder of what was happening in Germany was needed, it came on November 9, 1938. The Kristallnacht rampage that night was triggered by the assassination of a German diplomat by a German-born Polish Jew. The Nazi response was a coordinated attack which left ninety-one Jews dead and put as many as 30,000 others in concentration camps. More than 200 synagogues were destroyed and thousands of homes and businesses were ransacked. The Canadian Jewish Congress organized a rally to express solidarity with German Jews, with the result that Maple Leaf Gardens was jammed while overflow meetings were held at other locations. The attacks forced many Christian churches in Canada and elsewhere to re-examine their commitment to pacifism.

CHAPTER TEN

WHO CAN HOPE TO APPEASE A BOA CONSTRICTOR?

Prime Minister William Lyon Mackenzie King spent New Year's Day 1939 worrying. The situation in Europe was getting more alarming by the week. "The dispatches I read this afternoon speak of Germany likely to force war.... It is all part of the madness of the dictatorships."[1] Two weeks later, King spoke to Parliament, delivering comments that shocked many, including MPs from Quebec.[2] He quoted Sir Wilfrid Laurier's famous dictum, "If England is at war, we are at war and liable to attack," but he said it would still be up to Parliament to decide the extent of participation. It was more evidence that King was growing to accept the likelihood of war, leaving isolationists, including his advisor O.D. Skelton, out of big decisions.[3]

On January 26, King received a cable from London marked "Most Secret." It was the latest summary of British intelligence about Hitler's intentions, saying that Britain now considered Hitler capable of almost anything and that war was possible even within weeks.[4] Canadians had already been through the wringer once during the Munich crisis and now here was a second outbreak of war fever. The summary said there was no definite evidence of what Hitler planned, but one possibility was a bolt-from-the-blue air attack on London, shades of *Things to Come*. The air attack, the paper went on, might be followed up by land and sea operations against Western powers. A highly placed German informant said those plans were being drawn up, but didn't know whether or not they would ever be implemented.[5] War scares started arriving with increasing frequency, and by April there had been twenty of them.[6] The increasing tensions prompted Britain to ditch its long-standing policy of not sending troops to France and instead began plans to put ground forces alongside the French army. One powerful cabinet member, Lord Halifax, admitted that while he had believed in keeping clear of a continental land war, now Britain must prepare an expeditionary force.[7]

At a cabinet meeting in Ottawa on January 27, the latest intelligence summaries and King's ringing speech earlier left queasy feelings around the table. Ernest Lapointe argued that cabinet should stick to its policy of no commitments. He agreed that if Britain were attacked Canada would be at war, but he started dropping heavy hints of resignation. It might be necessary, he said, for some French Canadian ministers to consider whether they could do a better job of steadying people outside the cabinet, rather than in.[8] This was sobering stuff. King replied that the greatest service anyone in the room could render in a crisis would be to keep the cabinet together. He said a break in the cabinet solidarity would bring demands for a national unity government and that "might lead to anything, conscription and all the rest." The "Boy Millionaire" George McCullagh, publisher of the *Globe and Mail* (the *Globe* merged with the *Mail and Empire* in 1931) was one of the men promoting a unity government, saying it was time for Liberals and Conservatives to bury their differences. Indeed, only a few weeks later Conservative Leader Robert Manion said he opposed any conscription if it involved sending young Canadians overseas. Manion said Canada could play its part in any upcoming struggle by recruiting volunteers. Since the Conservative leader had supported conscription during the First World War, this was a significant change.[9]

King wrote in his diary that his comments at cabinet "seemed to make an impression." He concluded, "I confess I felt proud of the Cabinet.... There was not an acrimonious word in the discussion but a keen sense of profound responsibility. As the members left, [Finance Minister Charlie] Dunning turned to me, and said I had done a great day's work."[10]

With the prospect of war looming, King summoned the chiefs of staff to the defence committee of cabinet on January 30, 1939. While the defence budget in November had increased spending from $35 million to $64 million, the chiefs argued that it would leave them far short of achieving even minimum goals.[11] When all three services added up what was needed, the total was a staggering $175 million beyond what had been in the 1939–40 estimates. Armed forces never get everything on their wish list, and certainly any hope of getting $175 million was sheer fantasy. Nevertheless, the requests simply represented a marker of how much catching up the armed forces had to do. It was one measure of the price to be paid for nearly two decades of neglect.

The navy was the most ambitious, looking for $68 million over several years. Admiral Nelles admitted that while the RCN had thought about acquiring new cruisers, it wasn't practical — the RCN was too small. He strongly urged the government to buy new Tribal destroyers as an alternative and beef up the fleet to nine destroyers on each coast. In addition there would be eight anti-submarine vessels, sixteen minesweepers, and two supply and repair vessels, as well as smaller craft.[12] In light of events only a few months later, when the navy suddenly realized the urgent need for small escort ships, the emphasis on destroyers in this plan is telling. The RCN was still thinking of big fleet actions and surface raiders. For its anti-submarine ships, the navy picked out British Halcyon-class minesweepers, but they were almost as complicated and expensive to build as a destroyer.

Buying enough planes for a twenty-three squadron air force would require $27 million more in spending. Thanks to the Americans, the planes that had been selected by the team that went to Washington earlier were still available. For the army, many re-equipment items such as tanks had been placed down in the priority list, but fully funding its coast defence, anti-aircraft, and mobile forces would cost $79 million.

So here was one of the important moments in the immediate pre-war period. In the time since Munich there was every indication that the European crisis could explode into war. The regular armed forces were still tiny, and while new money was beginning to make a difference, there were long lists of desperate shortages. Surely with all the evidence at hand, even if it had made only limited commitments before, this was the time for the King government to act decisively. If it could not address everything, perhaps, at least some of the most urgent needs could be dealt with.

The cabinet turned it all down — cold. As far as Prime Minister King was concerned the public simply wouldn't buy it. "Had we gone further," he said, "we would not have received the necessary support to get through our appropriations. We were conscious of the growing threat of war, and basing our policies upon it."[13] It was a stark message that the prime minister's commitment to rearmament was not open ended and, indeed, was limited.

Especially in the case of the air force, the decision was mainly party politics because at that point it looked like an election might be called.[14] Even though King himself had raised the prospect of buying U.S. aircraft, he argued that it would be unwise to spend money south of the border when the government was saying increased military spending would help Canadian industry.

I took the view which I think Council [cabinet] generally supported, that ... if orders were given in the States and no war came, we would be confronted through a[n election] campaign with having given order of millions to American factories instead of our own. It was better, therefore, to give orders in Canada though they would be about a year later in being delivered.[15]

King offered one consolation prize. Normally new budget money would not be available until it received parliamentary approval several months later. This time King got the Leader of the Opposition, Robert Manion, to allow the armed services to have early access to the money.

On March 14 and 15 Hitler sent troops into Prague and extinguished the remainder of the Czech state. No justification was offered. With this action the German dictator tore up the Munich agreement, repudiated earlier commitments to having no further territorial demands, and made a fool of Neville Chamberlain. The word "appeasement" had already been tarnished, but now it was utterly transformed. According to James Eayrs, "Munich ... entered the vocabulary of politics as a synonym for a spineless and shameless surrender of the rights of small nations in the unenlightened self-interest of larger nations unwilling and unready to make the necessary sacrifices themselves."[16]

In Calgary, Jeffery Williams, the young Highlanders officer, was standing in the radio department at Eaton's, the store where he worked, when he heard Hitler deliver a speech about the latest attack.[17] Williams thought the near hysteria of Hitler's voice and the roaring acclaim of the crowd seemed to come from "beyond the boundaries of reason."

The attack on Czechoslovakia outraged the British. The *London Daily Telegraph* asked, "who can hope to appease a boa-constrictor?" In a widely syndicated newspaper article, Winston Churchill wrote, "A veritable revolution in feeling and opinion has occurred in Britain, and reverberates through all the self-governing Dominions.... All are united in a resolve to meet the awful danger which threatens the civilization of the world."[18] Suddenly people were "up for war."

Within days Neville Chamberlain delivered a speech in Birmingham that marked one of the most dramatic foreign policy reversals in modern British history. He tried to justify his actions at Munich, but went on to say "any attempt to dominate the world by force was one that the democracies must resist." The British adopted a new policy of containment to support possible future victims — Poland, Romania, Greece, and Turkey. Limited compulsory military service was introduced in Britain but the sudden call up of men to create thirty-two divisions left the army in profound disarray.

King heard Chamberlain's speech on the radio. In the Commons on March 20, King delivered the strongest statement yet in support of Britain. "If there were a prospect of an aggressor launching an attack on Britain, with bombers raining death on London," he said, "I have no doubt what the decision of the Canadian people and parliament would be. We would regard it as an act of aggression, menacing freedom in all parts of the British Commonwealth." King said he was willing to sacrifice nearly everything for peace, but not liberty.[19] His speech did not go far enough for the *Globe and Mail*, but for *Le Devoir* his remarks represented cozying up to Britain.[20] King had not been informed ahead of time by the British about their plan to support Poland and the other countries. The Prime Minister was not pleased at the European commitments but in King-esque logic, it was better not to know, even though the result was that Canada was threatened with war and had nothing to say about it.[21]

In April the British High Commissioner called on King to say the Germans thought that the British would not fight and, even if they did, the dominions wouldn't support them. Would King make a statement in the House of Commons the next day saying Canada would stand by Britain in whatever course it took? King was indignant, writing in his diary, "were I to make such a statement, I would ... play right into the hands of the enemy. I told him how Lapointe and I had worked together to keep the Party united in Parliament and in the country by building a bridge that would unite the different parts; that this would be undoing all the good work we had done." Meanwhile, one of the most crucial decisions of all was what to do about conscription. It had been one of Lapointe's greatest worries. King confirmed in the Commons in March there would be no conscription.[22]

In the midst of all this, fishermen in Nova Scotia reported numerous U-boat sightings. The reports caused a brief sensation as one senator demanded the Halifax garrison be mobilized.[23] But they turned out to be false. King said the incidents justified warnings to Quebec that Canada could not stand aloof from a major war. "It is exactly what I would expect if war to be declared. The St. Lawrence would be closed almost immediately."[24]

Public opinion in English Canada was crystallizing in favour of war, especially in Ontario, in light of the German take-over of Prague.[25] The German invasion prompted the *Globe and Mail* to write "Czech Coup Opens Nazi Expansion Drive," although the paper did not abandon its support for appeasement until after Chamberlain's Birmingham speech.[26] On March 14, the Brantford *Expositor* asked, "Is Anything More Needed to Reveal the True Character of Hitler?"[27] The Calgary *Herald* headlined "German Troops Seize Czech Capital," while a later editorial said the time had come to oppose "Hitler's hordes."[28]

After the occupation of Prague a national vote by Canadian university students revealed that 54 percent of McMaster students in Hamilton favoured military action to stop the expansion of Germany, while 64 percent would go to war if Britain became involved. The University of Western Ontario in London recorded a 70 percent pro-intervention majority.[29] Students like Hammy Gray in British Columbia may have endorsed pacifism earlier, but their minds were undergoing a rapid change. It wasn't so much King who was galvanizing public opinion on or off university campuses in English Canada, but after hearing the news from Europe, Canadians were largely convincing themselves.

In May, after months of work, the army completed its provisional "War Book" detailing the immediate action the government and the army would take in an emergency.[30] At the same time senior officers abandoned any pretext that any mobilized divisions would be used for home defence. One assessment said flatly that there was simply no risk of a serious armed invasion of Canada. "There is, therefore, no military need to mobilize this force for the defence of Canada."[31]

Unusually, the military's plans became part of Ian Mackenzie's speech when he introduced the estimates in Parliament in April.[32] Mackenzie listed the tasks the army would have to perform in the event of war. While the first five dealt with home defence, two others said that the army should have "a reserve force available to meet the unexpected" and "should the eventualities of intensive conflict necessitate it … a substantial force [should] be ready for active service within six months after mobilization." The speech was also startling because it included numbers that showed how far the government's program fell short on rearmament. Historian Roger Sarty says:

> It was a striking performance. The government had laid bare the service chiefs' criticisms of the rearmament program and their dire warnings about the future. Here was stark notice that, should a major war break out, Canada could not escape a daunting, open-ended commitment. Here too was strong evidence that the general staff's campaign to bring the government to face the possibility that an expeditionary force might have to be dispatched was having effect.[33]

In the budget debate, leading Conservatives, including Tommy Church and Howard Green, denounced the government for its failure to do more to help Britain. The CCF's Grant MacNeil once again attacked the rearmament program as a step toward repeating the horrors of 1914–18.

In May came an event that, for a brief few days, transformed the country from the increasingly grim and depressing news. It was a royal visit, the first ever by reigning monarchs to Canada. It is difficult today, in a world jaded by jet travel and regular episodes of royal ribbon snipping, to re-capture the magic of it. It was a sensation. It would have an effect in rallying Canadians to stand with Britain at a crucial moment. Even decades later, Canadians who witnessed the tour could recall almost every detail of where they were and what they saw. Russell Bannock, who within months would join the RCAF as a pilot and become a Canadian war ace, remembered seeing the couple at the Alberta legislature on Friday, June 2. "I was fascinated to see royalty with all that publicity. I remember having a box camera and taking their picture."[34]

While Prime Minister King had originally proposed the idea as a some-thing to help bind the nation together, it is unlikely he imagined it would come at such a crucial time. King was at his meddling, micromanaging, paranoiac worst when it came to arrangements. The British Tories and the back room at the Palace were hiding behind every palm tree to make sure he got as little notice as possible. King wrote, "The Tory Court do not wish any liberal Administration to figure prominently with the King and Queen.

Lascelles [a Royal Secretary] has been loaded up against me."[35] Initial plans had the Governor General welcoming the royal couple as they first put foot on Canadian soil, but King elbowed him aside, the prime minister wheedling his way into every photo op.

For King George the very idea of the trip must have been terrifying. He had never expected to be king and in his many public speeches he had to overcome a persistent stammer, a subject notably explored in the movie *The King's Speech*. His wife, Queen Elizabeth, on the other hand, relished every moment. While she felt the people of the empire were doubtful about their new king, she said the tour "made us." At the last second it looked like the trip might have to be cancelled because the battle cruiser *Repulse*, which had been scheduled to bring the couple to Canada, could not be spared at such a sensitive moment. The Canadian Pacific liner *Empress of Australia* was substituted.

Requests from dozens of regiments, air squadrons and naval divisions to provide escort or to be reviewed rained down on Ottawa. For the Pacific coast portion of the trip, the B.C. minister, Ian Mackenzie was bombarded with entreaties, pleas, and demands. Retired colonels were either indignant or thrilled at each change of plan. Elderly generals were shocked or delighted that the king would or would not wear a particular uniform. The disputation reached such a fever that the king himself had to make some decisions about what uniforms he would wear. Most days, there would be several.

On May 17 the royal couple landed at Quebec City greeted by King and Ernest Lapointe. Three hundred members of the international press watched the crowd go wild. An estimated 1 million people lined a twenty-three mile parade route when the couple reached Montreal. On May 19, in Ottawa, the king personally signed a number of bills into law and received the credentials of the new American Minister. As many as 100,000 people witnessed one of the most solemn moments of the trip, the official unveiling of the national cenotaph in Ottawa. The seventy-foot high memorial featured twenty-three bronze figures representing people who had fought in the First World War, while overhead were winged figures symbolizing peace and liberty.

The couple travelled west with the *Free Press* headlining their arrival, "Winnipeg Roars Welcome to Happy King and Queen."[36] There was an unusual scene when the king and queen, along with Prime Minister King, were greeted by the Winnipeg mayor and his wife, who, in the circumstances, had the unlikely names Mr. and Mrs. John Queen. It has been reported that there was live radio coverage of the event, with the announcer having an increasingly difficult time coping with all the names. The complexity of the king meeting Mr. Queen, Mrs. Queen going inside with the queen, and Mr. King meeting Mr. Queen, eventually left the announcer referring to "Mr. Keen and the Quing." The broadcast ends, the story goes, with the commentator blurting out, "Oh, s---." No recording has ever surfaced.[37]

In Alberta, Second Lieutenant Jeffery Williams was on duty outside the banquet hall where the royal couple was being entertained. Williams and other army reservists had linked arms and leaned back against a surging crowd to keep the way clear for the guests of honour to leave. With his arms holding fast, a teenage girl behind him started to undo the buttons on his jacket. As the royal couple swept by the young girl planted a kiss on Williams's cheek but moments later, with the crowd melting away, the girl vanished.[38]

On June 7, the couple went to the United States, seeing Washington, D.C., and the New York World's Fair. The visit had its surprises. King George privately allowed at one point that he did not wish to appoint Winston Churchill to any office, "unless it is absolutely necessary in time of war."[39] King's paranoia about British conniving reached near new heights at a dinner for the president and Mrs. Roosevelt at the British embassy. King found himself seated well below the salt and left talking to "chauffeurs and others." He said it was deliberate.

The spectacular royal visit of 1939 included a stop at the University of Toronto. The tour was wildly successful, more so than King ever imagined.

The couple then returned to Canada on June 12, and sailed from Halifax three days later, their liner accompanied by Royal Canadian Navy destroyers, RCAF patrol planes, and every fishing boat within fifty miles. The tour had left Canadians bedazzled; its message of family ties with Britain had exceeded the prime minister's wildest dreams.

With the glamour of the royal tour over, the news turned again to the stark reality at hand. A frenzied German propaganda campaign against Poland began. Poland and Germany had long-standing disputes including the fact that Germany was split into two pieces, the western bulk of it separated from East Prussia. In between the two pieces was the Polish Corridor, an area jutting north from the central part of Poland which gave it access to the sea. Germany wanted a rail and highway link between the two parts, but Poland saw the plan as a thinly disguised attempt to undermine Polish independence.

Adding to the bonfire was the future of Danzig (now Gdansk) on the edge of East Prussia. The city and its surrounding areas had been a cut and paste creation of the Versailles Peace Conference to give Poland access to the sea, but also to recognize that East Prussia was mainly German-speaking. Its status was bizarre; it was not an independent state, not part of Germany, and not a part of Poland. It was a semi-autonomous "free city" under League of Nations protection, which, when push came to shove, meant absolutely nothing. In 1933 the Danzig government had been taken over by the local Nazi Party.

In July, the German-speaking citizens in Danzig began the classic Nazi pattern of a noisy campaign, demanding a return to the Reich. Border incidents increased. The Polish government was deaf to all pleas to work out a deal with Hitler but the Polish choices were grim. The Poles had seen what had happened to both Austria and Czechoslovakia. Meanwhile, the Russians offered to send troops to help, but the Polish knew what that meant.

In May, the Pact of Steel, a friendship and cooperation treaty between Italy and Germany, was signed. With that, Britain and France began focusing all their attention on Russia. It held the key to peace or war because if there were an alliance with Britain and France, it would present Germany with a two-front war. If the Russians stayed neutral or sided with the Germans, Hitler would have a one-front war.

Prime Minister Chamberlain was reluctant to seek a military alliance with the Soviet Union because he, along with most British people, was anti-communist and thought Stalin was a thug. The Russian leader's massive purges killed thousands of people, including virtually the entire top echelon of the military. However, much of Chamberlain's cabinet favoured an alliance out of necessity. The British and French sent a delegation to forge an agreement with Moscow, but instead of flying in and getting down to business, it took a slow liner to Russia.*

Then, on August 23, came the thunderbolt, the signing of the Molotov-Ribbentrop Non-Aggression Pact. After the treaty was announced, Prime Minister Chamberlain sent a letter to Hitler telling him that Britain was fully prepared to live up to its obligations to Poland. Hitler instructed his generals to prepare to invade Poland adding, "Our enemies are small worms. I saw them at Munich."

Unquestionably, two of the great problems facing the Canadian army in 1939 were armament and equipment.[40] Some new gear had begun to arrive, but for the most part it was still a threadbare existence. There were enormous shortages of vehicles, especially since a new British reorganization of its divisions (which Canada tried to follow) called for many more vehicles than the army had on hand. There were 122 trucks and transport vehicles of different types arriving, including one new tractor for hauling heavy artillery.[41] There were the fourteen new tanks, although they were only light Mark VI's, at least good for training. Five new mortars had been delivered and 130 more were on order.[42] The army had been able to buy some ammunition and equipment, still the deficiency of high explosive shells was about 95 percent.[43] The new ammunition cost $487,000 but as far back as 1935 the army had said it would actually cost more than $5.8 million to fully replenish stocks.[44]

Among the equipment most eagerly awaited were high-angle mountings for heavy coast guns and a number of medium guns and their mountings also for coast defence. Fire-control and searchlight equipment, all essential for their use, had still not arrived when war broke out. Some of the equipment that did arrive was in such small quantities as to be nearly useless. There were ten Bren guns,

---

* The head of the delegation was Admiral Drax, who in 1933 had arrived in Ottawa to reassure the government of the importance of the navy after McNaughton's attempt to wipe it out.

but none from the Inglis production line, which would not be producing finished guns for months. In the meantime, there were no significant changes in the strength of the Permanent Force which, as of March 31, remained at 446 officers, with 4,169 other ranks.[45]

There was at least a glimmer of new life in some new Canadian industry. That summer the British government contracted to have field guns manufactured in Canada, while just a couple of months earlier the Montreal Construction, Supply and Equipment Company was beginning to produce eighteen-pounder and 4.5 inch howitzer shells.[46]

The summer of 1939 provided the last chance for Canada's reserve forces to train for war. More than 40,000 members of the Non-Permanent Active Militia trained at camp even if only for a few days and without modern equipment.[47] The 15th Field Battery of Toronto still wore pith helmets and First World War uniforms, but Major Bruce Matthews said the 1938 and 1939 camps were different from earlier ones. Training was both realistic and effective and there was more ammunition to fire.[48] In Vernon, British Columbia, although some members of the British Columbia Dragoons brought their own cars for training, there were still far more horses. The drill, the route marches, the field tactics, and even the lectures on map reading had not changed very much in twenty years. Still, there were a few innovations — lectures on chemical warfare and on constructing anti-tank obstacles. At Camp Borden, Canada's first and only anti-tank gun, or at least a gun simulator, was a length of sewer pipe mounted on a Model T Ford. It was loaded with bags of powder and when fired belched clouds of black smoke. The firing was done electrically so that the gunner could stand well back out of harm's way. However, in one firing the sewer pipe tore loose and hurled past the ear of Lieutenant Colonel Worthington making for a narrow escape.[49]

At Camp Sarcee, just outside Calgary, summer training was enlivened by the RCAF No. 1 Fighter Squadron with its brand new eye-popping Hurricanes. The squadron was now commanded by Ernie McNab, the Rosthern, Saskatchewan native who had been a member of the Siskin aerobatic team years before. Joining McNab and his Hurricanes was No. 3 Bomber Squadron, with its less than impressive Westland Wapitis, operating from an airfield at nearby Currie Barracks.[50] One army drill involved responding to an air attack. The Calgary Highlanders' Jeffery Williams said when the instructor shouted "Aircraft Left!" a Hurricane flashed by before anyone had barely lifted his rifle. "It was the first demonstration of modern armament I had seen," said Williams.

All four battalions at Sarcee took part in the wind-up exercise. Near the end, a squadron of regulars from the Strathconas, all on horseback, moved into position to attack the infantry. They were followed by the horse-drawn guns of the artillery, both formations making a brave sight as they crossed a ford of the Elbow River at the trot. Then the Strathconas — in line and on command — charged across the field at a thunderous gallop. Even as late as 1939, the climax of the summer exercise was the big cavalry charge. Williams watched the gallant panorama. "I was standing beside Ed Langston, who commanded the Highlanders Vickers machine guns. He turned to me shaking his head. 'Unbelievable, isn't it.'"[51]

In an interview many years later, then Lieutenant Colonel George Pearkes was asked whether Canadian officers had learned new lessons from Ethiopia or from the Spanish Civil War to apply to summer training that year. Pearkes, who was at Sarcee in 1939, said, "I don't think we learnt anything." He added, "I think that our training was based a good deal on the 1918 methods … with a little more open warfare training."[52] All in all, the army was not the slightest bit ready for any kind of war against a first-class enemy. The sad picture resulted, said Reg Roy, from "Neglect, apathy, financial restrictions [and], isolationism." All those and more had contributed to the army's unpreparedness.[53]

MILESTONES

FEBRUARY 3, 1939 — The first contingent of Canadian veterans returns home from the Spanish Civil War.

MARCH 1939 — Britain provides first information to Canada of previously secret policies of aircraft detection, the first Canadian officials knew of progress in developing an effective radar system.

APRIL 29, 1939 — Adolf Hitler's fiftieth birthday.

AUGUST 1939 — U.S. President Roosevelt took a cruise along the Labrador coast, ostensibly on a holiday, but actually to spy out the land. None of the U.S. Navy officers, said the president, knew much about the area where submarines could hide and he wanted them to see the region.

In the weeks before the war the RCAF was still nowhere near being able to operate the number of squadrons it had planned, but at least the main RCAF organization was in place. The chief training base at Trenton was nearly complete, while Camp Borden was a secondary training base. Rockcliffe, near Ottawa, was greatly expanded and was getting $300,000 worth of improvements. The latest spending plans also included nearly a million dollars for hangars and runways at the land and seaplane base at Dartmouth, Nova Scotia.[54] The chain of civilian landing fields across the country and numerous emergency fields built as a relief measure were ready for use.

However, there were still chronic problems. The arrival of the Hurricane had been a big boost but most new aircraft in the planned twenty-three squadrons were not yet in service.[55] With the Hurricane, Ernie McNab and his pilots were at last able to start realistic training. Otherwise the RCAF was still basically flying the winged version of the halt and the lame. Ten Stranraers had been delivered by the fall of 1939, but, astoundingly, an entire year would pass before the eleventh one came off the production line. There was great finger pointing about that, the air force saying it was incompetence, the manufacturer blaming the British for delaying key parts. However, the plane had glaring limitations anyway. The cockpit was enclosed, but all three gunner's positions were open, making it near useless in winter. The Stranraer's bomb racks were so near the water they were prone to freezing. The plane did poorly in headwinds. For the longer term, the RCAF awaited the arrival of the first delivery of the Bolingbroke patrol bomber, which, as a further testament to the agony of the Canadian aircraft industry, was running months behind schedule.[56]

The air force also added ten Fairey Battle light bombers, but even as they arrived they were near obsolete. In France in 1940 RAF Battle aircraft were obliterated by the Luftwaffe. The RCAF was forced to keep its Wapitis and Shark torpedo bombers in service. The obsolete Grumman Goblin fighter, part of a cancelled foreign order, was taken on as an emergency measure after the war began.

After years of stalling and delay, the government finally agreed to the prototype air training plan the British had been clamouring for. The operation was started thanks to the $6 million the government had diverted from the RCAF budget. It was done on a small scale and was aimed at training 126 pilots — fifty for the RAF and the remainder for RCAF. Along with it came the introduction in Canada of the short service commission, which would have been extremely valuable if introduced years earlier. Young pilots would be regular air force members for four years, after which they would leave but remain in the air force reserve.[57] Still many Canadians were continuing to join the RAF because it was bigger and had more modern aircraft. David Albert Romans of Glace Bay, Nova Scotia, was accepted for pilot training in Britain and left Halifax on April 17, 1939. The shortage of pilots in the RCAF was glaring — still only 235 of them on the roster. For the RCAF, the government's rearmament program was simply running out of time.[58]

In July 1939, the four destroyers on the west coast held their final exercises before the outbreak of war. One of them simulated a destroyer attack on a cruiser, and following that there were other variations including several destroyers attacking a cruiser.[59] However, antisubmarine warfare received little attention. Meanwhile, the two east coast destroyers visited New York the same summer, causing the *Times* newspaper to run a cheeky article saying "about one-third of the Canadian Navy" was in town.[60] If the navy hoped for more destroyers, it was hard to imagine where they might come from. British shipyards were choked with Royal Navy orders. If there had been any thought of buying American ships, it was sobering to note that an American destroyer would cost in the order of $6 million, a sum not far below the entire RCN budget in 1939.

Admiral Nelles hoped to build destroyers in Canada, but at the outbreak of hostilities only one vessel of any size, an icebreaker, was under construction.[61] There were severe shortages of skilled technicians, draughtsmen, and labourers, along with general inexperience.[62] A royal commission report in 1940 said that Canada was "one of the least self-sufficient countries in the world" in ship building.[63]

However, even if the ships had magically appeared, there were no crews trained for them. The RCN was far too small to have crewed twelve new destroyers. In January the government had lifted the ceiling on the strength of the Royal Canadian Naval Reserve to 170 officers and 500 ratings.[64] However, while these men proved invaluable in the Battle of the Atlantic, many of them were not trained for combat, but only as civilian seamen. It would be months before reservists like Skinny Hayes (still in the Royal Naval Reserve at this point) could be trained to fight a ship. As the war broke out he was still aboard *Silverfir*, racing to its next port of call at a top speed of eight knots. [65]

In summarizing the strength of the RCN on the eve of war, historian Marc Milner said what Canada had was "a scrappy little fleet."[66] The Royal Canadian

Navy had its six good destroyers with well trained officers and crews, plus the four minesweepers.[67] However, in the years before the war, C.P. Stacey, for one, felt the navy had suffered the most. He said the RCN was unquestionably more effective than it had been, but "this is not saying a great deal."[68]

Events moved quickly after the middle of August. As early as August 19, Hitler ordered the German navy to begin moving to wartime stations, including pre-selected positions for the invasion of Poland. The pocket battleships *Admiral Graf Spee* and *Deutschland*, as well as numerous U-boats, cast off to take up positions at sea. On the 23rd came the Molotov-Ribbentrop Pact. On August 24, Neville Chamberlain recalled the British Parliament from its summer recess to approve a War Powers Act while the government put the Royal Navy on a war footing. Naval and coast defence reserves were called up including radar and anti-aircraft units. British and French private citizens in Germany were ordered home.

On August 25, in a move that was only realized years later, Hitler post-poned the invasion of Poland for five days because of worries expressed by Mussolini and because of surprise that the Chamberlain government had not already collapsed. In Canada on August 26, soldiers appeared outside the Burrard Street Armoury in Vancouver, while thousands of other reservists took up positions outside power stations, key office buildings, and armouries across the country. The Regina Rifles stood guard at the city's airport while other reg-iments did the same at similar airports.

On the 26th, the RCAF Wapiti bombers headed out from Calgary on their hapless journey to the east coast. On August 30, Poland began mobilizing its armed forces. On August 31, two Royal Canadian Navy destroyers on the west coast began their high-speed run to Halifax. On September 1, around dawn, the German battleship *Schleswig-Holstein* quietly slipped its moorings, drifted into the harbour, and began firing at a Polish army installation in Danzig. That same evening, at the start of the long Labour Day weekend, the 48th Highlanders had soldiers on duty at their armoury in Toronto. The phone rang and the orderly officer, Captain Eddie Ganong, Jr., reached for the receiver. He heard the order: "MOBILIZE!"

CHAPTER ELEVEN

FIXING TO CHAW THE GODDAM NAZIS TO DEATH

The Royal Canadian Navy began the first anti-submarine patrols even before the war was officially declared. By the time the Second World War was declared, patrols were operating on a wartime basis. Less than a week after that the first convoy — designated HX 1 — set out from Halifax for Britain. HMCS *St. Laurent*, freshly arrived from Vancouver, along with HMCS *Saguenay* and the British cruisers *Berwick* and *York*, provided escort for the eighteen merchant ships. The eight-inch gun cruisers were operating as a pair because of the threat from German surface ships and, in fact, the pocket battleship *Deutschland* did make a foray into the northwest Atlantic a few weeks later, getting as far as Greenland.

HX 1 (Homeward from Halifax-1) left with daylight air cover provided by Stranraers from No. 5 Bomber Reconnaissance Squadron working one or two at a time in relays. The patrol planes could at least provide warning of an attack. Many squadrons were operating with mostly inexperienced officers, but No. 5 Squadron was commanded by veteran officer Arthur Dwight Ross, a Winnipeg native who had graduated from RMC in 1928.*

In a few weeks, with the arrival of colder weather, the shortcomings of the Stranraer, including its balky bombs, would become even more obvious. In the meantime, the RCAF was not alone in having problems with weapons on its maritime patrol planes. Off the British coast, on September 5, a twin-engine Avro Anson spotted a submarine and dropped special anti-submarine bombs, but they bounced off the water, exploded in mid-air, and brought down the

---

* Ross was to play a heroic role in England in 1944. A bomber crashed onto the runway while trying to land and then plowed into a second aircraft, which touched off a series of fires and explosions from both fuel and bombs. Ross rushed to pull crew members from the wreckage, losing his right hand when one bomb went off. For his heroism he was awarded the George Cross.

attacking aircraft. If that were not disaster enough, it turned out the undamaged submarine belonged to the Royal Navy anyway.[1] On September 14 the same thing happened, with two Blackburn Skua dive-bombers from the aircraft carrier *Ark Royal*.

While the protection of convoy HX 1 was impressive, when it set out from Halifax, two days and about 400 miles out, the four escorting warships turned about and headed back to Halifax. A cruiser or battleship was supposed to stay with the merchant vessels all the way but such was the shortage of big ships that early HX convoys lost their escorts at mid-passage. Warships from the U.K. later picked up the convoy off the Irish coast.[2]

Even though the first convoy arrived safely in Britain, what about the next convoy and the one after that and the hundreds after them? Convoys would have to leave Halifax every six days heading for Britain and the Royal Canadian Navy's four Atlantic destroyers couldn't hope to accompany all them even for a couple of days at a time.[3] Through October and November only *St. Laurent* and *Fraser* were available for operations and they were at sea almost constantly. *Skeena* was in dry dock for refit and installation of asdic while *Saguenay*, at the

Library and Archives Canada

Convoys began in the first week of the war, although, as shown here, they became much larger as the war continued. The ships gathered in Bedford Basin, Halifax, before setting out for Britain.

request of the Royal Navy (which was providing the two cruisers in Halifax), was sent to the Caribbean to protect tankers there. The diminutive minesweepers *Fundy* and *Gaspe* provided the only Atlantic coast protection when the destroyers were on convoy duty. One officer, O.S. Robertson, says aboard *Fundy* even the most basic equipment was in short supply. There were only three duffel coats on the whole ship. No oilskins. No socks supplied. One pair of binoculars.

The Royal Canadian Navy, as one naval history has pointed out, while destined for a bitter war against German U-boats in the North Atlantic, was "singularly unprepared" for anti-submarine warfare.[4] That is despite the fact that the Royal Navy had indicated before the war it would be dependent on Canada for anti-submarine vessels in the western Atlantic.[5] Even a message from Admiral Nelles in September flatly stated, "four destroyers cannot defend our East Coast and focal areas."[6]

It is hard to understate the absolute necessity of keeping the convoy conveyor belt operating between Canada and Britain. Great Britain rivaled the United States as Canada's major trading partner in 1939.[7] Sixty-three percent of Canada's exports and 39 percent of imports moved by sea.[8] Britain relied heavily on such Canadian products as oil, food, bauxite, and nickel. Timber supplies were needed urgently because timber from other European countries had been cut off. For Britain, open sea lanes were life or death or, as British Admiral Dudley Pound put it later, if you lose the battle against the U-boats, you lose the war.[9] Even in the first months the shortage of shipping and Britain's inability to get resources from parts of continental Europe led to Britain's first food crisis. By mid-November 1939 some flour mills actually stopped work for lack of grain.

The Royal Navy's planning for putting merchant ships into convoys had been started as far back as 1937. The RN began to organize taking control of private shipping companies, setting up convoy collection ports, ocean routing, and allocating cargo. The merchant ships would also need fuel, repairs, and supplies. After the Munich crisis the Royal Canadian Navy had quietly reactivated retired Lieutenant Commander Richard Oland, an exceptionally capable officer, to develop secret convoy plans.[10] The enormous undertaking was complete, staff briefed and organization in place when war broke out.[11] The code word "FUNNEL" was the trigger for it all to begin and that had been sent out on August 31.

Meanwhile, on the same shores of the Atlantic, the U-boat attack on the liner *Athenia* on September 3 riveted the minds of the Royal Canadian Navy. Undersea killers were on the loose, as many as many as eighteen of them, somewhere in the Atlantic. The Royal Navy estimated that for the time being the threat to the Canadian coast was limited because of the relatively short range of many German boats. That was fortunate for Canadian coastal defences, but still it did not lessen the danger for transatlantic shipping.[12] Like *Athenia*, the juiciest U-boat targets were ships sailing independently, and the U-boats began picking them off at a rate of four a day.[13] Compounding all that on October 14 came the *Royal Oak* disaster. The British battleship was sunk in a U-boat attack in a supposedly protected refuge, and 830 British sailors were lost.

Given the small number of Royal Canadian Navy ships, everything for convoy protection and protection against surface raiders depended on the Royal Navy. Canada's maritime defence strategy was utterly dependent on the principle that the Royal Navy still ruled the waves, but very soon the RN would be stretched to the utmost. RN cruisers were supposed to provide convoy protection, but their shortage was clearly apparent in the very first convoy out of Halifax. In their absence, and for anti-submarine operations, the navy relied on the versatile destroyer, but destroyers, too, were in short supply. As Churchill found to his horror on becoming first lord of the Admiralty in 1939, the budget for the previous year had not included provision for building any destroyers, and only thirty-two were under construction.[14] The wastage from heavy operational use became obvious when Britain had to sign the "Destroyers for Bases" deal with the United States in 1940. Such was the state of the emergency with North Atlantic escorts that in November seven large French and British submarines arrived in Halifax to act as convoy escorts. They would remain on the surface and their deck guns would provide protection. The idea had to be scrapped after howling winter storms took such a toll on the boats that they were re-assigned to other duties.[15]

The shortage of escort vessels and the total reliance on the Royal Navy were by no means the only crippling problems. The low priority of anti-submarine training, mentioned earlier, now began to tell. Lieutenant Commander A.R.

Pressey was one of only two trained anti-submarine officers in the Royal Canadian Navy. His specialty was so obscure that at one point he had been seconded to help with the landing of an airship from Europe because someone had been under the impression that a note in his file, "A/S," meant he had been trained on airships rather than rather than in anti-submarine warfare.[16] Pressey had originally qualified in the 1920s, and when war broke out he was attending a refresher course in England. He returned to Halifax to take charge of both keeping anti-submarine equipment afloat and fixing harbour defences. It might be expected that his top priority would be training new asdic operators, but the most urgent need, he decided, was setting up a maintenance organization for the few asdics the RCN had. The RCN desperately needed to make good damage done by heavy seas and what he called the "the ravages of the enthusiastic amateur."[17] As for trained submarine detection ratings, there were eight in the RCN. In November a new group of twenty of them headed to England for asdic training.

While the port defences in Halifax had been mostly neglected to allow build up on the west coast, other east coast ports were, if possible, worse off. The navy's team in Sydney, Nova Scotia, the second principal start point for transatlantic convoys, was responsible for defending both the port and surrounding areas. The submarine threat was a sobering prospect. The Sydney defences consisted of one 4.7-inch gun on shore, five RCAF seaplanes, but no bombs for them, and two light RCMP patrol boats. When a U-boat sighting was reported, depth charges were improvised using ten-gallon milk drums filled with explosives, rigged to be pushed off the patrol boats. The sighting turned out to be false.

Once war began, the RCN's expansion plans included taking up both government and privately owned ships and converting them to auxiliary minesweepers or coastal patrol vessels. Of the forty vessels taken up on the Atlantic coast, only five turned out to be useful for minesweeping or anti-submarine work. They included the hydrographic survey ships *Acadia* and *Cartier*, both dating back to the First World War. Another ship in the ugly duckling fleet was the *Bras d'Or*.[18] It was a trawler built at Sorel, Quebec, in 1919 and the plan was to convert it to an auxiliary minesweeper. George Borgal, a reservist who had volunteered for full-time duty, concluded it was simply unseaworthy. "At the beginning of the war, anything that floated was bought for the navy.... The captain had no faith in it whatsoever; none of us did."[19] The RCN had to give up plans to commission four armed merchant cruisers on the east coast because it did not have enough crews. Instead the ships were handed over to the RN. A more successful part of the plan was to convert some west coast passenger liners into fighting ships. The *Prince Robert, Prince Henry,* and *Prince David* — each about 6,000 tons —later provided useful service, but their conversion took most of a year.[20]

It turned out that many of the Royal Canadian Navy Reserve and Royal Canadian Navy Volunteer Reserve officers did provide a treasure trove of experience and ability. Some members of the two organizations had taken early retirement from the regular British or Canadian navies and many were still relatively young. While a large number of these officers were assigned jobs ashore, others were headed for sea postings. One of them was Edgar Skinner who took command of the auxiliary minesweeper *Rayon d'Or.* Skinner had joined the naval reserve in 1929 but his career had also included time as a Newfoundland rum runner.[21] Later Skinner would work with Willard Bonner, a veteran of the RCMP marine division, who had often pursued Skinner.[22] In time 90 percent of the corvette captains were RCNR officers, including Skinner.

The most celebrated member of the "hidden reserve" was Chummy Prentice. James Douglas Prentice, whose appearance was accented by a monocle in his right eye, was one of the most colourful and outstanding captains of the war and, at the same time, a notorious slave driver. Dennis Timbrell, later an admiral, said Prentice was never without his monocle. "I've had to enter his cabin when he was asleep and there it was, in his eye. I'd say it was there when he was born. But I never saw him in his bathtub."[23]

Prentice was born in Victoria and as a youngster expressed an interest in a naval career. He was told it was better to join the Royal Navy rather than the RCN because "if he wished to join the navy he should join a real one."[24] Prentice had served in the RN for a number of years, attended the RN staff college and retired as a commander in 1934 for an unlikely alternative — farming in British Columbia.

Once war was declared there were frantic efforts to find room for any new recruits because existing shore bases were full. After riding east on an old colonist rail car with gas lamps, W.J. Roberts of Thunder Bay, Ontario, recalled sleeping on the floor his first night in Halifax.[25] Often finding equipment and supplies called for unusual methods. At the naval reserve division in Toronto a former Eaton's employee appealed to John David Eaton himself for help with bunk beds and cooking supplies for reservists who were volunteering for the regular navy. Eaton offered to pay for material supplied from his store, saying, "if anybody gives you any trouble, just refer it to me."[26] Eaton's was a part of the war effort in other ways. Herbie Little joined the RCNVR in Toronto in 1939 as an intelligence specialist. He had no uniform and worked in civilian clothing until December when his uniforms arrived from the Eaton's mail-order catalogue.[27]

Fewer than 200 RCNR ratings were ordered to either Halifax or Esquimalt. About 400 RCNVR ratings were called up but as it happened many of them were still undergoing summer training so they simply signed up for full-time service.[28]

In November a seventh destroyer arrived, HMCS *Assiniboine*. It was also an ex-RN ship that would have been most welcome, except that it had no steam heating system for the crew, a necessity for the North Atlantic winter. It was sent to the Caribbean to replace *Saguenay*, which then returned to Halifax.

J.D. "Chummy" Prentice, one of the most compelling personalities and outstanding leaders of the RCN in the Second World War. As a child he was told if he wanted to join the navy he should join the "real one," the Royal Navy.

One of the serious problems that became apparent in the first months of the war was that the air force and the navy were unable to knit together operationally, a symptom of a wider problem of the armed forces. One of the roadblocks in the anti-submarine campaign was the delay in getting navy and air force operations rooms physically next to each other in Halifax. In August, the boss of the RCAF's Eastern Air Command, Group Captain Norman Anderson, wanted to move his operations room next to the navy's ops room, but he couldn't find any available space. The nearest he could come was a building two miles away. The stalemate over which of the two services would move to close the gap continued for over three years.[29]

Throughout the fall and into the winter the RCN and RCAF coastal forces continued patrolling. One patrol on September 14 and 15 paid off when Stranraer flying boats shadowed the German merchant ship *Franz Klazen* until it was intercepted by RCN warships.[30] Much farther south, on October 23, the German-flagged tanker *Emmy Friederich* scuttled itself on encountering HMCS *Saguenay* and thus became the destroyer's first war conquest.

For those in khaki in September 1939 the challenge was to build an army that could fight and win on the battlefields of Europe. It was a colossal job. There was little knowledge of modern war, no organization that had ever worked together in the field, and no fighting doctrine. All arms co-operation was unknown. With the exception of F.F. Worthington, almost no one had any idea about tanks. Those and a thousand pieces of the puzzle had to be fitted together. Considering that the army had been starved for money and support for twenty years, none of this should have been a surprise. One recruit in the tank-less Ontario Regiment summed up the situation, saying that while his regiment had no armoured vehicles at least he and other soldiers had been able to go to an army dentist. "They're fixing us up so we can chaw the goddam Nazis to death," he said.[31]

Within forty-eight hours of receiving their mobilization phone calls, dozens of units in the army joined in a nationwide crash recruiting program. On the outbreak of war the Calgary Highlanders were the strongest reserve unit in Alberta even though it had only 200 men, not all of them physically fit. That changed very quickly. The regiment had so many would-be recruits that within two weeks the enlistment process completely bogged down.

Next day, the techniques of the horse sale came to personnel selection. At the northern end of the Armoury floor, some twenty prospective volunteers walked in a circle. In the centre, like a ringmaster, stood the erect figure of little Sgt.-Major Harvey of the Depot.... Outside the ring, the Colonel stood with the adjutant, eyeing the volunteers.... It did not take long. Out went the uncoordinated, the lame and the overweight, with a suggestion that they might try the artillery.[32]

That last was an unwarranted dig, and besides, the fifty-six artillery units called up were as jammed as the infantry. The 2nd Battery in Ottawa quickly became choosy, saying "only skilled truck-drivers of excellent physique, not under five feet ten inches, will be considered."[33] Among those lining up in Ottawa was Lloyd Lavigne of Cornwall, Ontario, who imagined he would get a uniform and a rifle immediately on enlistment and become a "real hero" in the eyes of his family. Instead, after signing up he was taken to the Central Canada Exhibition buildings where his first job was sweeping up the mess the horses and cows left behind when the fair closed. The barns were needed for barracks.[34]

By the end of September, the CASF numbered 61,500 men. At that point a slowdown was ordered for lack of equipment and because the government put the brakes on spending.[35]

It is frequently commented that many volunteers were unemployed men just looking for a job since the pay of $1.20 a day was nothing to sneer at.[36] However, records show that as many as 75 percent of recruits had quit a job to volunteer and almost half had been in either the Permanent Force or the reserve.[37] The 9th Field Ambulance, Royal Canadian Army Medical Corps in Montreal volunteered en masse with 89 percent of its personnel enlisting.

There were some unlikely volunteers and unusual reasons for joining up. Malcolm MacCrimmon, a farm boy from near Fort Saskatchewan, went all the way to Calgary to enlist because he was determined to play in the Calgary Highlanders' pipe band.[38] The mayor of Windsor, Ontario, David Croll, joined the Essex Scottish as a private. Croll was a lawyer and had been the first Jewish cabinet minister in the Ontario government.[39] Walter Dent had been with the International Brigades in Spain. "They taught me to knock off Fascists at one thousand yards," he boasted, "and when we go overseas I'm going to start doing it again."[40] Some Americans were told that without British citizenship they were not eligible while Polish immigrants were often rejected.[41]

Some regiments struggled to get enough recruits, including the regular PPCLI, which was 200 men under establishment at the end of September. It was same with the Royal 22e Regiment and Three Rivers Regiment.[42] In the end the TRR had to accept English-speaking volunteers and gradually became a mainly Anglophone regiment. On the other hand more than 2,000 men wanted to join the Maisonneuves while les Fusiliers Mont-Royal had 900 applications.[43] Some recruits had to be persistent. Jacques Dextraze had been working for Dominion Rubber Company as a salesman. He tried to enlist but was not accepted because he had flat feet. On a second try he was accepted as a private in the Fusiliers Mont-Royal. After the war Dextraze became a general and chief of the defence staff.[44]

According to Sidney Radley-Walters (in Normandy one of the great tank commanders of the army) the most unusual regiment was the Sherbrooke Fusiliers, which, later in the war, had two companies of French-speaking Catholics and two companies of English-speaking Protestants. The CO could not speak French, while another senior officer could not speak English. The adjutant was Jewish.[45]

The armed forces still limited the role of women only to nursing. So Margaret A. Briggs, originally from York Mills, New Brunswick, was one of only a few women volunteers accepted. She later served for three years overseas in hospitals in England and Italy.[46]

Most volunteers' shift from civilian life to the military was little noticed. However, one radio station announcer in Kirkland Lake, Ontario, made a spectacular exit from civilian life. He was on-air one night reading a commercial for Seymour's Men's Wear whose ads always ended "If Seymour's clothes don't fit, Seymour won't let you wear them." "Well, one night this chap had had it up to here with the station and with Seymour and he said, 'Remember, if Seymour's clothes don't fit, Seymour doesn't give a shit.' 'And,' he continued, 'neither do I.' With that he walked out of the station, [and] went to Toronto with the Queen's Own Rifles ..."[47]

One of the hallmarks of the period was sad, even painful — saying goodbye to the old guard. "The Non-Permanent Active Militia had its old war horses ... the colonels and brigadier generals of the last war who, sniffing gunpowder, gamely and gallantly wanted the opportunity to serve once more," noted Jack Granatstein.[48] But most were just too old and so out went many stalwarts of yesteryear. Numerous mobilized units had to find new commanding officers immediately. Lieutenant Colonel H.H. Riley may have won the Military Medal at Passchendaele in 1917, but he was overage and, within days of the outbreak of war, he was gone as commander of the Calgary Highlanders. Lieutenant Colonel Chipman, commanding officer of the 48th Highlanders, had started as a twelve-year-old bugle boy in a battalion commanded by his father. He was replaced.[49] Montreal's Black Watch diary recorded, "Many of the Regiment's originals unfortunately failed to pass the medical examinations.... These men, mainly veterans of the Great War 1914–1918, will be sadly missed."[50] Some Permanent Force officers were in the same fix. The commander of the new First Canadian Infantry Division artillery was supposed to be Colonel C.V. Stockwell, formerly commander of the artillery school in Kingston, but doctors pronounced him unfit for overseas service.[51] However, there is a paradox here. While dozens of First World War veterans were unfit for the CASF, some others, especially among the top ranks, were kept on of necessity. There were dozens of senior jobs that had to be filled, even if only third-rate or marginal commanders were available. Major General McNaughton referred to them as a "cover crop." The situation caused serious leadership problems early in the war.

The upside was that many officers, long stuck in the same rank, were soon promoted. In the Permanent Force, Guy Simonds, E.L.M. Burns, and Harry Crerar all went on to higher rank within months. Still, in 1939 the army could not hope to fill the hundreds of positions that were being created by the expansion. So, many third-rate or marginal commanders remained in their posts for months, sometimes years.

NCOs were forced to teach about weapons they had never actually seen, relying instead on what they had read in pamphlets.[52] Denis Whitaker, an RMC graduate and member of the Royal Hamilton Light Infantry, had only a diagram of a Bren gun to work with.[53] When a single Bren gun arrived in mid-October in Calgary, thirty Highlanders were given a chance to fire it before it was shipped on to Vancouver.[54] They also suffered from a shortage of helmets, trucks, small vehicles, medical supplies, and even field kitchens. Practically no mortars of any kind were available. There was little radio equipment. Al Stapleton from St. Mary's, in southwestern Ontario, joined up as soon as the war began. He was sent on signals training, but on semaphore flags, the same kind as used by boy scouts.[55]

When winter cold arrived, Signal Corps linemen had no gloves issued nor heavy wool coats.

Many regiments were short of rifles. The Edmonton Regiment received 500 new Lee-Enfields only on October 23.[56] There was a quantity of the dreaded Ross rifles and, as an emergency backup, 20,000 M1917 rifles were obtained from the U.S. These had limited use because of their non-standard .30-06 calibre and were relegated to local defence, reserves, and training. It was not until June 1940 that work began at Long Branch, now part of Greater Toronto, on a plant to produce 1,000 rifles a week.

In December, members of the 48th Highlanders saw a static display that included two borrowed tanks and five trucks. That was almost the only evidence of advances in weapons and equipment seen by the regiment since 1918.[57] Among the fifty-six artillery batteries called up most could only muster one or more old eighteen-pounders or 4.5 inch howitzers from the last war, which were outranged by new German guns.[58] Reg Roy, later a noted historian, was at this time a young officer in the Cape Breton Highlanders. He saw that one of the coast artillery guns at Victoria Park in Sydney bore the date 1895 on the breech block.[59] Artillery units had to rely on privately owned cars and hired commercial trucks to move their guns. Space on the parade square was often at a premium. At one location in Montreal, as many as six senior NCOs from several units could be seen, and heard, shouting simultaneously.

There was no commitment from the top brass to have any operational tank regiments at all or even to keep the armoured school at Borden.[60] Because of the uncertainty, no troops had been sent to the Armoured Fighting Vehicles School at Camp Borden for training. Finally, six weeks after the mobilization, that began to change as a handful of newly commissioned officers, including Ned Amy, finally arrived from the Royal Military College. Even though he had no idea about tanks, soon he and the others would be instructors. Amy said, "None of us had a clue about a car engine. The corporal instructor had an engine on the floor, and said to us 'There are the tools; take it apart.' When we had it in pieces, he told us to put it together again, and as we did he explained what the different parts were for. In no time at all we learned a hell of a lot about an engine."[61]

The civilian automobile industry pitched in to help. General Motors, Chrysler, and Ford sent cut down engines and spare parts to Camp Borden, while army instructors went to the auto plants for specialized courses. All stocks of First World War uniforms were quickly exhausted. None of the new battle dress had arrived, so soldiers on parade looked like they had just come back from a church rummage sale. Clothing companies including Tip Top Tailors in Toronto were working to deliver the new uniforms, but it would take weeks before even the first batch of them was ready. Some units didn't get battle dress uniforms until February 1940.

In Toronto many members of the Royal Regiment of Canada had only armbands to add to their civilian dress.[62] In the West Nova Scotia Regiment in Bridgewater burly lumberjack recruits might wear a First World War military hat but with a mackinaw shirt, a khaki web belt, and the usual woodsman's clothing — a pair of trousers cut off at the calf and long socks.[63]

Headgear at the Highlanders in Calgary ranged from straw hats to Stetsons. Cold weather arriving in the fall of 1939 meant "a nightmare spent in search of hats, boots, mittens and coats."[64] The regiment had to spend $270 of its own money to buy khaki glengarries and $235 for woolen mittens. Calgary ladies knit gloves and sweaters.[65]

It might have been expected that even if the army could do nothing else, at least it should be able to shoot and march. Most men had a rifle of some sort, but many in the army had no boots, so soldiers in most regiments had to wear civilian footwear. There were widespread reports of soldiers being unable to take part in field training or being excused from duty and there were numerous reports of medical problems with feet. The Royal Regiment of Canada, already confined to wearing armbands in place of uniforms, was further hampered by a shortage of boots. Only a gift of thirty pairs of boots and socks from the public-spirited Mrs. F. H. Phippin allowed it to march out of barracks.[66]

The title of the 1934 Cole Porter hit song "Anything Goes" aptly described the situation with barracks. The 2nd and 51st Field Artillery moved into Lansdowne Park in Ottawa. Soldiers like Lloyd Lavigne, who had to clean up after the horses, were sent to the Coliseum, while officers got the Horticultural Building.[67] Colin "Hefty" Ross, a stalwart of the Ottawa Roughriders football team, found the Lansdowne Park setting familiar. He donned the uniform of the Cameron Highlanders, while only a few days earlier he had been training for the football season at Lansdowne.[68] In Toronto, men in the 53rd Field Battery bedded down in the women's building of the Canadian National Exhibition grounds, while the officers set up their mess in the ladies washroom.[69] In Alberta, the 77th Field Battery used Moose Jaw College; in St. Catharines, the 10th Battery used a vacated macaroni factory.

Concentrating regular force units was not always a happy experience. All through the interwar years the PPCLI had been split between Work Point Barracks near Victoria and Fort Osborne Barracks in Winnipeg. On November 15, the two west coast companies moved to Winnipeg so the regiment could train together. PPCLI member George Grant remembered: "Was that ever a fight that night! They were rolling beer barrels all over the place…. It was a son-of-a-bitch of a battle … an awful bloody mess."[70]

The Fort Osborne Barracks were not suitable for field work, so PPCLI soldiers "learned nothing of small-unit tactics such as how to advance to contact with the enemy, use terrain to advantage, follow a barrage, or move into battle with tanks."[71] The Calgary Highlanders stuck to physical conditioning, drill, military law, map reading, and simple tactics, but there were no large-scale training schemes, little all arms co-operation work, and, apart from the odd dropped roll of toilet paper, little practice with air units.[72] For all regiments, it was a case of starting at the very beginning, which sometimes included things that were not in the training syllabus. Reg Roy said a recruit "learned never to refer to his rifle as a gun, and to be wary if someone asked him to go to the quartermaster stores for a repeating bayonet. If there was to be a short-arm inspection he soon realized that neither a revolver nor service knife was involved."[73]

At the start of the war the Royal Air Force had more Canadians among its flying crews than the entire number of officers in the RCAF, so it is not surprising that some of the first Canadians to see action in the war were in the RAF. On September 4, Roger Henderson, a Blenheim navigator, became the first Canadian to take part in an air sortie in the Second World War. A native of Winnipeg, Henderson was awarded a Distinguished Flying Cross for his actions in bombing German ships at Wilhelmshaven.[74] Another Canadian RAF member, Sergeant Albert S. Prince, a twenty-seven-year-old native of Vancouver, was killed only days later. His Blenheim failed to return from a shipping raid.[75]

The Royal Canadian Air Force itself suffered its first casualties on September 14, when a Delta aircraft piloted by James Edgerton Doan, aged thirty-four, of River Beach, Nova Scotia, and mechanic David E. Rennie crashed off the east coast. The plane, which had been on patrol, simply disappeared and the wreckage was not found until July 1958. It was discovered in thick bush, sixty kilometers north of Fredericton, but there was no trace of the crew.[76]

The program to rebuild and re-equip the RCAF had been the government's top defence priority for five years, but one history termed the results on the outbreak of war "pathetic."[77] The air force had 275 aircraft of twenty-three different types. The planned twenty-three squadrons had to cut back to fifteen, and the remainder were folded into other units.[78] Even among the squadrons that were left, some struggled to get operations going. The very first flight of No. 118 Squadron on November 11 had to be aborted after an Atlas aircraft had mechanical difficulties and encountered severe weather. It was forced to return to Saint John after only fifteen minutes in the air.[79] As September continued, Air Vice-Marshal Croil was still trying to scoop up whatever aircraft he could lay his hands on.

There was a political uproar when the prime minister found out the RCAF could not send any complete squadrons overseas immediately.[80] William Lyon Mackenzie King was "incensed" at the news because he wanted to preempt requests for large army formations. However, Air Vice-Marshal Croil said on September 15 that all qualified personnel were urgently needed as trainers.[81] Russell Bannock — the youth who photographed the king and queen in Edmonton — was a licensed commercial pilot when he enlisted in 1939. However, it was 1944 before he could plead and cajole his way into an overseas posting.[82]

Some reserve squadrons showed clearly how far the air force was from being equipped or combat ready. No. 119 Squadron in Hamilton was supposed

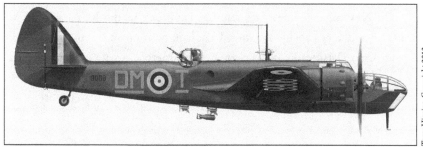

Terry Higgins, Copyright 2013

The Bolingbroke, built by Fairchild Aircraft in Longueuil, Quebec, was a testament to the RCAF's trials in rebuilding. The aircraft suffered long delays in delivery, and by the summer of 1940 its British equivalent, the Blenheim, was obsolete as a frontline aircraft.

to be a bomber squadron although few of its members had ever seen a bomber. In September the squadron was ordered to Vancouver for further training and nearly all of its light trainers were turned over to other squadrons. The one remaining aircraft was taking part in an army co-operation exercise dropping practice bombs when a wing touched the ground and the aircraft crashed. The squadron was left for weeks with no planes at all to train on while its transfer to Vancouver was inexplicably delayed.[83]

On September 14, in Longueuil, Quebec, a brand new twin-engine aircraft revved up for its maiden flight. At the controls was J. H. "Red" Lymburner, a former Canadian Airways pilot in northern Canada and a veteran of several daring Antarctic flights. Lymburner went through the check list then taxied the plane onto the runway and, shortly, shifted the Bristol Mercury VIII radial engines to full power. The Bolingbroke maritime patrol bomber lifted into the sky. The plane, the Canadian version of the Bristol Blenheim then in RAF service, was the first aircraft of its type built at Fairchild Aircraft. The maiden flight was a victory for the Bolingbroke and for Canada's tiny aviation industry, at least a victory of sorts. The maiden flight was supposed to have happened long before and the plane was meant to enter service in July 1939, but there had been a tangle of delays. The Bolingbroke had originally been ordered in November 1937.

While aircraft orders in Canada had totaled only 282 in 1938, as the war broke out the industry was beginning a turn around.[84] Contracts to build the Bolingbroke, the Hampden bomber (Canadian Associated Aircraft), and the Tiger Moth (de Havilland) would soon make an enormous difference. In northern Ontario, Canadian Car and Foundry had begun production work on forty Hawker Hurricanes.

On November 3 there was another landmark in the RCAF's build up. Ten new and very capable Lockheed Hudson patrol planes arrived at No. 11 Squadron in Dartmouth, Nova Scotia. The American-made Hudson was the first modern maritime patrol aircraft to go into service on the east coast. It had an effective range of 350 miles and a top speed 100 knots faster than the Stranraer.

Only days after war was declared, Prime Minister King got a clean bill of health from his personal physician. King would have to be at his best as he faced the monumental pressures of a wartime leader. Dr. George McCarthy called at Laurier House, finding the prime minister's blood pressure was 123/90 and King's circulation and colour were both good and his prostate normal. However, weighing in at 178 pounds, it was time for a little exercise.[85]

The first of those pressures confronted the government within days of the war declaration. As soon as hostilities began, the Royal Navy's top commander in the western Atlantic moved to take operational control of RCN warships. He wanted two RCN destroyers to join his squadron based in Jamaica. The RCN commander, Rear Admiral Nelles, was all in favour.[86] Nelles had pointed out earlier that Canada's destroyers were incapable of protecting the entire East Coast and the RN had helpfully sent two cruisers to Halifax. Nelles argued that to turn the British admiral down would mean that the RCN would gain its two destroyers but lose the two eight-inch RN cruisers.[87] Within days of the start of the war Canada had been given a sharp lesson in the price of dependence.

King bristled at the idea of complete British control. He and the cabinet were determined to avoid any appearance of committing Canadian ships to distant action, while King also believed that Canada had never given the Admiralty blanket authority over the Canadian fleet. However, in the end King found a way to give the RN most of what it wanted, but keep a fig leaf for appearances. On September 14 the cabinet passed an order-in-council directing RCN destroyers to "co-operate to the fullest extent" with Royal Naval forces, although they would not be under direct RN control.[88]

At the same time, King's government and the navy faced a crucial decision on long-term plans for the fleet. What kind of navy did Canada need to protect Atlantic convoys and the Canadian coast? For years the RCN had wanted only destroyers. Conveniently, while the navy felt that destroyers were the answer for both convoys and coastal protection, the unstated agenda was to have a fully manned professional fleet that would secure the service's future after the war.[89] However, a nasty reality upset this dream world. British shipyards were fully booked with Royal Navy orders while Canadian yards couldn't build big destroyers.

The decision on what ships to buy or build effectively determined the future of the RCN for the rest of the war. The navy was split into two. The more glamorous of the two would be the professional full-time navy with its spit and polish and destroyers cracking along at thirty knots. Most of the pre-war regular navy ended up in it. The second half would be the "Wavy Navy," so-called because most officers were reservists who wore "wavy" rings on their sleeves. Some also called it the "sheep dog" navy. They were a completely different breed. They were volunteers right off the street, teenagers who had never been to sea, former merchant seamen, and retired RN officers brought back for service. They wore anything that came to hand, a grab bag that might include a Maple Leafs hockey sweater, Grand Banks hip waders, or a baseball cap. They manned dinky ships that could do sixteen knots only if the wind was right and were stuck with the eternally boring work of coastal patrol.

Leonard Murray, later an admiral but in 1939 at naval headquarters in Ottawa, said in an interview in 1970 that the crucial event in the decision to build a small-ship anti-submarine navy was the sinking of the *Athenia*. He said he and other officers were able to convince Prime Minister King that an anti-submarine war was the one that the small Canadian navy could handle.[90] The navy nabobs, holding their collective noses, then looked around for a simple, cheap, and easy-to-build coastal patrol vessel. Earlier in 1939 the British had settled on a version of a ship called the *Southern Pride*, originally designed in 1895 and built for hunting whales. The RN had placed an order for one ship on July 25, 1939.

The whale catcher had several important plusses, including the same basic features as the Halcyon class. It was about 245 feet in length, 850 tons, and had steam-reciprocating engines that were an ancient but still serviceable design. Its worst feature was that it rolled and bucked and pitched at the merest hint of rough seas. The new ship only had one engine, one propeller, and one four-inch gun. That weapon had no sighting equipment of any note, resulting in the comment that since the gun really couldn't hit anything the main method of attack would be to ram an enemy submarine. In time, depth charges would make a difference. While the ship was slow, it could turn on a dime, tighter than any submarine. But most of all, the whale catcher could be built by the majority of small Canadian shipyards quickly and in large numbers.[91] The new ship would go on to naval immortality — the corvette. Louis Audette, who commanded several ships in the North Atlantic and Mediterranean, said, "For sheer worthiness, few ships have ever been better designed.... they were barely adequate in speed, their surface armament just met the needs of the moment, their anti-submarine asdic equipment was barely adequate and their living conditions made heroes of men destined to quite other roles in life."[92]

On September 18, only days after Canada got hold of the plans for the ship, a naval construction program was proposed to the federal cabinet. The next day the cabinet gave approval in principle to build both the corvette and another barebones design, the Bangor class minesweeper.[93] Between September 1939 and late 1940 more than 100 ships were ordered, seventy of them corvettes. Building the ships was a significant step forward, but it was not at all the complete solution to the U-boat threat. The navy needed to double its manpower, adding more than 7,000 officers and ratings. As late as November 1940 none of them had even been enlisted, the schools and depots required to train them had not yet been built, and in most cases the necessary land had not even been acquired.[94]

There was also another navy that was about to make its own heroic contribution to the war. Its members have been called the "forgotten veterans of the unknown navy." They were the sailors of the Canadian Merchant Marine and it has to be remembered that, after all, the merchant ships and their crews were the real targets of the U-boats.[95] In 1939 Canada had thirty-seven ocean-going merchant ships manned by 1,450 seamen. The merchant service greatly expanded as the war continued, most notably with the Park ships, the Canadian equivalent of the American Liberty ships. The merchant navy included tankers, troopships, and freighters, the last loaded with every imaginable product, including ammunition, guns, tanks, airplanes, and food.

Nearly fifty Canadian-registered merchant ships were lost to enemy action, and 1,146 Canadian merchant sailors perished at sea or in prison camps during the war.[96] In addition, six Canadian government-owned but British-registered merchant ships and eight Newfoundland-registered merchant ships were lost. Many others foundered or sank due to marine causes or accident. Members of the Merchant Navy have often said that the casualty rate for its members was higher than any branch of the Canadian armed forces during the Second World War. Later some cargo ships were armed with an obsolete gun or two — the DEMS, or defensively equipped merchant ships — but most were defenceless.

Experienced Royal Canadian Navy crews held the merchant sailors of many nations in high regard. James Lamb, a corvette veteran, said:

> You had hardly noticed them in Halifax in their shabby
> shoreside clothes, quiet men, generally, in their cloth caps
> and worn raincoats. At their Merchant Seamen's Club in

downtown Halifax they played pool, read magazines, wrote
letters home to families in Liverpool or London, Piraeus or
Bombay. In a city crowded with uniforms, loud with the bois-
terous tumult of brash young men, they passed unnoticed....
They wore no uniforms, but for all that they were the real
warriors of the Battle of the Atlantic... More than the fighter
pilots, the commandos, or the dashing torpedo-boat types
of our own service, these men truly deserve to be called the
Bravest of the Brave.[97]

Many of the merchant sailors, including Earle Wagner of Halifax, were
very young. Wagner tried to join the RCN but he was underage, so he left his
mother a note on the kitchen table and went off to sea.[98] His most harrowing
memory was off the U.S. coast in 1942, plowing through what amounted to a
shipping graveyard that had been left after U-boat attacks. As his vessel moved
along shallow waters, he could see the wreckage of ships strewn about, a mast
here, a funnel or part of a superstructure there. In one small area he counted
fourteen hulks, and those were just the ones with bits of wreckage still above
water level.[99] Wagner said, "but anyway, we were fearless at 18 years old."[100]

It is a dodgy business to say how many of the merchant ships from all
nations were lost in the vast Atlantic battleground due to the inadequacies
of the naval escort until later in the war. Robert Welland at least tried. "If we
had been decently prepared we probably would have lost only half the ships
in the Atlantic," he said.[101]

Among the less plausible ideas floated as the war began was that of a "limited liability" war. Canada would supply arms and support to Britain and perhaps even
airmen and aircraft or navy ships, but Canada would not go so far as to send
an expeditionary army to Europe or take an active part in any fighting on land.
Oscar Skelton argued, "If any military action is to be taken overseas, it should,
in the first instance, be in the air service rather than by military contingents....
A Canadian air force operating in France, would be effective from the stand-
points of both military value and of consolidation of public opinion."[102]

The idea had support in Quebec, but, most importantly, King supported
it. When the war began King had cabled Neville Chamberlain to ask what

Britain wanted from Canada. Initially, the British asked for a small Canadian army unit and technical troops. That pleased King, who wrote in his diary on September 6 that it would avert "the necessity of our thinking of an expeditionary force." King may not have had a plan of his own about what he wanted, but he knew what he didn't want. He didn't want an army expeditionary force.

Despite King's hopes, the military chiefs proposed sending ground troops. King saw it as a conspiracy. To his dismay the chief of the general staff, T.V. Anderson, wanted to send at least one division to Europe, while long-term army plans called for two divisions. However, by the time the cabinet met, King was surprised to find that some of his ministers were showing more support for the idea than he expected.[103] Before long even more support came when Britain urged that a strong ground force be sent. While King was ordinarily an astute reader of public opinion, one of the great misjudgments of his career may have been underestimating the strength of feeling about an expeditionary force. The public, most especially in Ontario, remembered the monumental contribution of the Canadian Corps in the First World War, demanded that ground troops be dispatched. On September 19 the government announced that one army division of about 18,000 men — to be called the First Canadian Infantry Division — would be sent to Europe.[104] Andy McNaughton would command it.

However, another part of the limited liability war policy survived for much longer. The government had to contend with a messy crash at the intersection of money and military build up. At a cabinet meeting on September 17, the military proposed spending $500 million in the first year of the war to build up equipment and manpower. The horrified finance minister, J.L. Ralston, pointed out that was nearly one-third of the total income of all levels of government, even with big tax increases. It could bankrupt the country. Ralston appealed to the Defence Department that "every effort should be made to spend less."[105] The government lowered the spending to $300 million, with the army receiving the brunt of the chopping. That was why the government suspended recruiting for a second division and cancelled plans for raising a third division altogether. Strangely enough, some of the army spending was held back in case of emergencies, as if the declaration of war was not emergency enough.

Of the $300 million, the RCAF's budget was pared to $77 million, meaning it could only buy a third of the 574 planes it wanted.[106] It would only be with the invasion of France in 1940 that the country turned from limited liability to an all-out war footing.

There was one other change that was overshadowed by other news headlines. King decided the time had come to strengthen the leadership in cabinet. Ian Mackenzie, who had blotted his copy book during the Bren Gun Scandal, was shuffled to a minor post. He was replaced by Norman Rogers, a lawyer and the MP for Kingston. Rogers was a Rhodes Scholar who had served in the army during the First World War and had been a private secretary to King in the 1920s. King had many quirks and failures, but he was ruthless in getting rid of cabinet liabilities — in his own good time. This was the moment for a heavy hitter in defence, and Mackenzie was out. In another change, the high-powered James Ralston became finance minister.

One of the most dramatic developments in the early months of the war was Britain's proposal for a sweeping air training plan in Canada. The Brits had had no luck with earlier plans. King was irked by the timing. If it had come a week or two before it could have been the centerpiece of Canada's war effort and he would have avoided having to send an army division. On September 28, King agreed to the plan in principle, a plan that ultimately became the renowned British Commonwealth Air Training Plan (BCATP), which proved to be one of the defining achievements in Canadian military history.[107] It would eventually train about 45 percent of all Commonwealth air crew in the war. In size it was near impossible to comprehend. It would require as many as 4,000 aircraft, at its peak graduating 3,000 air crewmembers per month from 107 training schools. About 131,000 men became pilots, navigators, air gunners, wireless operators, observers, air bombers, and flight engineers. By one estimate, enough concrete would be poured into new BCATP runways to build a two-lane highway from Ottawa to Vancouver. The plan would train flyers for Britain, Canada, Australia, and New Zealand, but also others from the United States, Belgium, France, Czechoslovakia, and Poland.

Getting a final agreement signed was an agony of competing agendas and worries about who would get stuck with the bill. The British hoped that Canada would supply most of the resources but that the Royal Air Force would run the show. King nixed that, saying it was "amazing how these people have come out from the Old Country and seem to think that all they have to do is to tell us what is to be done."[108] Finally, the deal was signed on December 17, 1939, King's sixty-fifth birthday. Canada would have a dominant role in running the plan but King and his colleagues had to accept the fact that many Canadian graduates would ultimately be absorbed into the RAF.

As if the war demands were not enough, William Lyon Mackenzie King faced two political crises, one in the fall of 1939 and another in 1940. Either of them could have ended his career. Immediately after the outbreak of the war, the Duplessis government in Quebec attacked King, saying the government's war measures infringed on provincial rights. Duplessis called a provincial election. If he was re-elected it could be fatal for the war effort. Led by Lapointe and Chubby Power, federal ministers threw themselves into the battle with decisive effect. Duplessis was defeated.[109] With that barely over, King was menaced by the supposedly Liberal government of Ontario led by Mitchell Hepburn. On January 18, 1940, Hepburn passed a resolution in the legislature condemning Ottawa for not prosecuting the war ardently enough. King trumped that attack, calling a snap federal election for March 26. That resulted in King winning the largest majority ever to that time. The three elections together confirmed that King's "moderate" war program was acceptable to the majority of Canadians.[110]

There was a lesser — and entirely bizarre — moment in Canada in the fall of 1939. In a Toronto newspaper on November 2, among the ads for bacon at twenty-seven cents a pound and men's suits for twenty-five dollars, was a notice advertising a speech at Massey Hall.[111] The address was entitled "What the German People are Thinking," and the speaker was William Patrick Hitler. It turned out that he was the nephew of the German Fuhrer. Willy Hitler was born in 1911, the son of the German leader's half brother Alois and his Irish wife. The other Hitlers had lived both in Ireland and Britain, and William Patrick was born in Liverpool. He lived in Germany for a time, but after an unsuccessful appeal to his uncle for a high-ranking job, he left Germany to live in Britain. In 1939 he was on a lecture tour.

Willy Hitler's comments to the Toronto audience and to news reporters were both wild and wildly inaccurate. A tip off might have been an earlier magazine article titled, "Why I Hate My Uncle." In his Toronto speech he said Adolf Hitler was mentally deranged, or, as he put it, "crackers." Willy predicted that Hitlerism would be stamped out in Germany in six to nine months, possibly by a coup. Willy Hitler later joined the U.S. Navy, and after the war changed his family name to Stuart-Houston.[112]

The Royal Canadian Air Force had an enormous new role in the British Commonwealth Air Training plan, but it soon became clear that the Canadian public demanded that air force planes and crews be sent to Europe. In October, Defence Minister Rogers complained to Air Vice-Marshal Croil that not sending squadrons would not "satisfy public sentiment."[113] The air force had proposals in hand but now the air force chief put together a new plan to deploy as many as twelve squadrons. The first unit sent would be No.110 (Army Cooperation) Squadron, to work with the First Canadian Infantry Division. However, even with the minister's prodding it was unable to leave until February 1940. The first fighter formation — No. 1 Squadron — didn't arrive in Britain until May 28, 1940, and then only after it had absorbed No. 115 Squadron from Montreal. The Battle of Britain awaited.

CHAPTER TWELVE

Ugly Surprises, Awful Miscalculations

No nation was prepared for war in Europe in 1939 — not Britain, not France, not Canada, and, in some respects, not even Germany. In contrast to the situation in 1914 no one wanted a European war. Top military and naval leaders in virtually all European capitals, including Berlin, were horrified at the prospect. The single exception was Adolf Hitler.

The British army had focused on Imperial defence and had lost leadership in armoured warfare. Its early operations in Norway, France and later North Africa showed it did not have a combat doctrine that could win battles.[1] Britain had begun large-scale rearmament two years before Canada, a program that had produced the Spitfire and Hurricane fighters, along with radar, but the Gloster Gauntlet, last of the RAF's open-cockpit fighter biplanes, did not go out of service until 1939.*

The Royal Navy, still the best in the world, boasted seven aircraft carriers at the start of the war, but gunnery officers held a death grip on the navy's leadership. Pre-war exercises were all meant to end with a climactic gun duel between two battle fleets.

France had gone through nineteen different governments between 1932 and the outbreak of war. The French Char B-1 tank was capable, but there were seventeen different engines developed for it, none in mass production.[2] In May 1940 many new fighters were left sitting on the runways awaiting engines that were being built by seventy small companies.[3] In 1939 the French Army was large, with about 900,000 regular soldiers and 5 million reservists, but many top generals were fixated on the protection provided by the Maginot Line.

---

* The Gloster Gladiator biplane fighter was still used in Malta in 1940, but it had an enclosed cockpit.

In Italy, King Victor Emmanuel told the foreign minister on August 24 that "we are absolutely in no condition to wage war" and that the army was in a "pitiful" state.[4] In 1938 Russia's Red Army had 1.6 million men under arms, but the Great Terror had purged three of five marshals and thirteen of fifteen army commanders. While not directly involved in the European war in 1939, Japan was bogged down in a costly war in China, and the United States had begun an oil embargo.

The United States itself was still gripped by isolationism. A poll in 1939 found that 67 percent of Americans wanted the country to remain neutral in a European war, while 12 percent wanted aid sent to the Allies. The figure for those who thought Americans should join the battle against the dictators was 2 percent. When Ernest King (later a five star admiral) became captain of the battleship USS *Texas* in 1940, he opened the safe aboard ship to see what war plans might be in it, but the only documents covered a possible war against Mexico.[5] Even in the summer of 1941, President Roosevelt was advised that the U.S. Navy was still not ready to take on Japan in the Pacific.[6]

In some crucial ways Germany was not prepared. While the German army had absorbed, as no other nation had, the importance of blitzkrieg warfare and inter-arms cooperation, in 1940 there were still serious equipment shortages. When the army rolled through the French area where the British Expeditionary Force had been, soldiers were astounded by the huge quantities of motor vehicles, guns, and armoured vehicles. One soldier wrote, "There lies the materiel of an army whose completeness of equipment we poor wretches can only gaze at with envy."[7] Fuel was scarce because Germany itself produced almost no oil. Mechanization was limited. Among many fatal German weaknesses, Hitler and other top leaders were completely focused on a short war, were unable to come up with a workable high command structure and were unable to manage the German economy without copious injections of foreign loot.[8]

The German navy did not expect to be ready for war until 1944. In a remarkable note on September 3, 1939, Grand Admiral Erich Raeder came close to criticizing Hitler for taking Germany into war prematurely, admitting that his force was nowhere near sufficiently armed.[9] It was only in January 1939 that Hitler had ordered Plan Z, the enormous naval re-equipment program that included building ten battleships, four aircraft carriers, and dozens of other surface ships along with 249 U-boats.

The Luftwaffe had made great progress since Hitler officially created it on February 26, 1935, incorporating about 20,000 officers and men and nearly 1,900 aircraft into the new service.[10] Still, questions remained about what aircraft were going to be needed, while under Hermann Goering the Luftwaffe was crippled by a lack of strategic vision. Some said the air force had a case of "Stuka Madness" — obsessed by tactical air power.[11] Meanwhile, a symbol of the disarray was the colossal German Air Ministry building in Berlin, the notorious home of back stabbing, turf wars, jealousies, endless paperwork, competing plans, obstruction, and acrimony.[12]

Nevertheless, Germany had a two-year head start on Britain or France in rearming, and, with enormous heaps of money, Germany was much better prepared for war in 1939 than any other European country. Even though his country was not fully ready, that did not deter Hitler from declaring war. He was convinced that the time to attack was not when Germany was ready, but rather when it had the maximum advantage over its adversaries.

It is difficult to compare Canada's rearmament situation with that of European countries because of wide differences in population, economy, political history, and colonial responsibilities. Canada's economy in 1939 was tiny and the Depression had knocked the stuffing out of government revenues and economic activity.[13] In military terms, Canada and Australia were comparable in some respects, including the fact that when the war began both were in the midst of a nationwide controversy about conscription. But there were big differences too. Australia had a bigger navy — six cruisers with about 10,000 officers and men in the regular, reserve, and merchant navies. It faced a different strategic threat than Canada did — the prospect of a possible Japanese naval attack on its homeland.[14] There were about 70,000 men in the Aussie army reserve. Australia was spending more on rearmament, but there was not enough time for it to make a big difference. In an assessment of the Australian situation in 1939, a newspaper article said, "no nation slept more foolishly, and more dangerously, than Australia."[15] The table below shows that, at the very least, Canada's defence spending was low among nations included. The newspaper that made that comment might wish to note the lower Canadian defence spending.

EXPENDITURE ON NATIONAL DEFENCE — VARIOUS COUNTRIES[16]

Country	Per capita 1937–38	Percent of budget 1937–38	Per capita 1938–39	Percent of budget 1938–39
Great Britain	$35.39	35.89%	$44.05	41.66%
Japan	$15.66	66.03%	$34.47	78.99%
France	$20.59	44.83%	$22.23	54.16%
Sweden	$7.52	14.23%	$11.44	23.34%
United States	$7.75	13.25%	$10.67	14.48%
Australia	$6.51	13.01%	$8.73	16.09%
Belgium	$6.48	11.81%	$7.56	16.36%
Italy	$7.24	25.04%	$7.37	23.98%
New Zealand	$4.04	4.67%	$5.33	5.85%
Norway	$4.45	10.32%	$4.49	9.88%
Denmark	$2.60	9.59%	$3.59	12.86%
Canada	$2.81	7.40%	$3.34	8.17%

Note: No figures for Germany were released after 1935.

Quite obviously, low defence spending was a principal reason why Canada's army, navy, and air force were unprepared for war in 1939.[17] Neither did the armed forces have the manpower, equipment, training, or leadership to face a first-rate power like Germany. The Canadian forces might have been able to make a contribution to an empire-wide challenge, but it would be a small and ineffective contribution and it would be many months before it would be more effective. The absolute best that might be said is that the three armed forces were in a better state than they had been three years earlier.

As for the army, Reg Roy, a historian with first-hand combat experience, described it in 1939 as being in a "shocking state of unpreparedness."[18] It had achieved important milestones with its 1936 reorganization and mobilization plan, but the failures were much greater. The army had been the government's third priority for rearmament, so the result was entirely predictable. At a time when a new war would be the most highly mechanized in history, the equipment situation was disastrous.[19] At least there might have been enough for one brigade — a unit highly trained and commanded by handpicked leaders. After three months the First Canadian Infantry Division was dispatched to

Europe armed with little more than personal rifles and small arms. The list of shortages seems endless: boots, anti-tank weapons, tanks, vehicles. The Division had only just been outfitted in the new battle dress.[20] On the west coast, but only on the west coast, the artillery was comparatively well off.

Lack of equipment, however, was only one measure of the army's weakness. In the regular army in the interwar years, the pay, conditions of service, and training were pathetic and the enlistment numbers were capped.[21] So the regular army of 1939 — 466 officers and 4,000 men — was simply too small to train itself for war or properly train the army reserve.[22] Anyway, as noted earlier, many of the officers were too old, too ill, or too inefficient for war service.[23] Chris Vokes said that in the interwar years, "Provided an officer, no matter how lazy or incompetent, could avoid sudden death or grave misbehavior, he could look forward to a ripe old age in the service."[24] In 1939 there were eighty-one officers in the rank of lieutenant colonel or above who were fifty years of age or older. By 1944 some major generals were as young as thirty-two.[25] Although he was a major in 1939, Bert Hoffmeister of the Seaforths had no idea of how to lead his men in battle and no clue about something as simple as writing an operations order.[26]

In a scathing critique of Canadian army leadership, historian John A. English says many Canadian senior officers were so out of touch with the latest developments in land warfare that once the Canadian army arrived in Britain, battle schools taught a near replication of the drills of 1917. On the same day, units of the First Canadian Infantry Brigade Group were patrolling and practicing dawn trench attacks, German panzers burst through the French front at Sedan and set out on their drive to the English Channel.[27]

While the failures in equipment were the result of government policy, poor training was result of both government penury and army leadership. As English said, if the will had been present much more could have been done in war games, tactical exercises without troops, and skeleton exercises. He singles out McNaughton himself as the worst (but by no means the only) offender. English argues that in the interwar years, "Keeping alive the art of warfighting especially against a first-rate enemy, was not accorded a high priority."[28] Instead,

> the Canadian regular force under McNaughton catered to politicians who, as blind as their electorates, could not envision another conflict. In actively seeking and assuming

politically attractive non-military roles ostensibly to ensure the survival of the militia as a fighting force, McNaughton virtually guaranteed the opposite: the continued erosion of whatever operational capability remained.... Least pardonable was McNaughton's assumption that military knowledge was mainly a matter of technical efficiency that any scientifically educated person could master probably better than a regular officer.[29]

The true weakness of the army leadership was exposed when General Bernard Montgomery, "the great house cleaner," examined the First Division in detail in 1942. Montgomery, while not much loved by his peers and often referred to in the British army as a "nasty little shit," was an excellent trainer. He combed through the senior leaders of the Canadian division and one after another were sent packing. Even though a hero of the First World War and a Victoria Cross winner, Major General George Pearkes was "unable to appreciate the essentials of a military problem ... a gallant soldier without ... brains."[30] He, in Monty's cruel words, "would fight his Division bravely till the last man was killed and ... the last man would be killed all too soon."

Except for the summers of 1938 and 1939, there was limited training because of the government's lamentable spending levels. Some years there was no ammunition for the artillery to fire. The First Canadian Division left Canada largely untrained, but even when individual training had been completed it would be impossible to throw 800 men together in a battalion and expect them to work together. The Calgary Highlanders' regimental history notes:

A well-drilled group of men, smart in their uniforms, who carry themselves with military bearing, are still not a fighting battalion. To become that they need to be taught how to work together on the battlefield.... In this stage of training, officers and NCOs are taught how to organize and lead men in battle; men are taught how to fight together in sections, platoons, companies, battalions. When a battalion has been trained well enough to function as a battalion, it must be trained with other battalions to fight as a brigade. Brigades are then trained to fight in divisions, divisions in corps, and corps in armies. As this type of training progresses, infantry learn how to fight with their supporting arms —mortars and heavy machine guns, artillery, engineers, and signals. They learn to fight alongside armour and how to best use tactical air power. They learn the incredibly complicated business of fighting and winning a modern war. In the late summer of 1939 the Calgary Highlanders embarked on this long process of learning the craft of war. They would be pre-occupied with it for almost five more years.[31]

Sometimes training had to start with the most mundane things. Today it is different, but for many soldiers in 1939 learning to drive and maintain a vehicle was a new experience. Jimmy Edwards, the young man with the phenomenal eyesight, wanted to be a fighter pilot. By 1939 he had still not flown a plane, but he had barely ever driven a car or truck either.[32] When Rifleman Alfred Babin arrived in Hong Kong, he was made an ambulance driver despite the fact that he had only driven a vehicle once before.

For the most part, the boring though essential infrastructure of the army was almost completely absent. In a division, 18,000 men had to be fed, have medical services, and their weapons and field radios repaired when they broke.[33] But those are just a few examples. Soldiers on the front lines required a multitude of specialists to keep them fighting, few of which existed in the army of 1939. Some men would have been trained for these jobs in civilian life, but many had to be trained by the army. A list of trades on the establishment in 1941 included: Armament artificer fitters, armament artificer wireless, RCA artificers, boilermakers, carpenters, clerks, coach trimmers, cooks, dispatch riders, draughtsmen, driver mechanics, electricians, engine artifacers, fitters, instrument mechanics, keyboard operators, machinists, mill construction crew, millwrights, motor assemblers, nursing orderlies, operations room assistants, photographers, precision grinders, sawfilers, shoemakers, signals linemen, signals operators, storemen, surveyors, tailors, toolmakers, vulcanizers, and welders.[34] Meanwhile, the Royal Canadian Electrical and Mechanical Engineers had not even been formed.

There was a glaring shortage of trained staff officers. Their role is to convert the ideas of the commander into orders and to work out how the orders will be executed. What formations will be assigned what jobs, when, and where? It has been said that a good staff officer can sometimes save even the most incompetent commander. At the outbreak of the war only forty-five regular staff officers had passed through British-run staff training programs at Quetta and Camberley.[35] There had been militia staff courses for reservists, and Howard Graham of the Hasty Pees and Jean Victor Allard had been among those who attended. By 1939, more than 400 officers had completed the course, with another twenty-nine taking an advanced certificate. However, most graduates had never had a chance to practice what they had learned, and they most emphatically could not organize or control a major combat operation.[36]

Apart from training there were other serious deficiencies. Neither the army nor the government had done much to encourage French Canadian soldiers to join up.[37] Not doing more to welcome French Canadians reinforced the perception that a European war was one fought by English Canadians for England's benefit. Jean Victor Allard said, "Shortly after a recruiting office opened in Shawinigan, a priest openly denounced the first volunteer from the pulpit as a traitor."[38]

In the face of these enormous problems, how did the army begin to rebuild and transform itself into the war-winning army of 1943–45? The Canadian army was a clone of the British army. This had some disastrous consequences as we will see shortly; however, it also was important because it meant Canadians did not have to undertake the much bigger task of putting together a completely independent army. It could count on British training, organization, and experience. One of the great strengths of the Canadian army was that it could also count on the courage, ability, and resourcefulness of the superb Canadian soldier who turned out to be masterful on the battlefield. There were many other factors, but among them were these three: first, the much sneered at part-time reservist; second, a steely core of regular officers; and third, blind luck.

While it is true that the reservists were only partly trained (to be generous about it), the reserve army in all those years of neglect and adversity made one priceless contribution to the wartime army. It kept the military spirit alive.[39] The reservists used their training and dedication to lift the rest, the thousands and thousands of totally green recruits. The soldiers who were new in 1939 and those who came on later in the war should collectively tip their tin hats in salute to the interwar reservist. Kim Beatty, the regimental historian of the 48th Highlanders, notes:

> it was the belittled and often maligned Friday-night soldiers who alone could be mobilized, and organized to fight. It was the non-permanent [i.e. reserve] units which created the infantry and armoured divisions and the tank brigades of the First Canadian Army, and which ultimately fought Canada's war on land…. A great debt, which is already largely dismissed and forgotten, is indeed owing to Canada's hard-tried [reserve] … officers and men, who had been scorned and derided, and called war-mongers to their faces. With only their sense of personal responsibility to motivate them, they rose to the need in 1939 with unswerving loyalty and an abiding patriotism. The manner of their whole-hearted response was only equaled by their magnificent final achievement.[40]

Later tank legend Sidney Radley-Walters had started his military training before the war and Jean Victor Allard had been in the army reserve for six years. Fred Woodcock from Winona, Ontario, was one of many employees at E.D. Smith jams who were active reserve members. From the part-time ranks sprang future battalion, brigade commanders, and generals of 1944 and 1945. They included, among many others, an outstanding artillery commander, Stanley Todd, and one of the most successful Canadian commanders of the war, Bert Hoffmeister. As has been pointed out, from 1939 the army reserve produced from within its ranks three of the five division commanders in the field in May 1945, three-quarters of all brigade commanders and nine in ten of the regimental and unit commanding officers. Over almost six years of war the one-night-a-week soldiers became the officers who led Canada's armies to victory.[41]

As for the regular army, it is true that there was plenty of dead-wood and there were notable failures in the early war years, but it was not *all* dead-wood.[42] So the army was saved, secondly, by those regular officers who had studied the military profession and prepared themselves for the future. This new group was mostly two decades younger than the leaders of 1939. While there were many reserve officers among the top ranks of the army in the later years of the war, there was also a crucial core of professionals who had used the years to great advantage. They might have been as few as 100 in number. Granatstein acknowledges that given the small number, it was a miracle of Biblical proportions that the army turned out to have as many competent generals as it did, let alone one or two who were brilliant.[43]

The poster boy of this group is Guy Simonds, who is almost universally praised as a superb, if supremely aloof, commander. Chris Vokes said Simonds was "the finest Canadian general we ever had," although as a leader of men he "wasn't worth a pinch of coonshit."[44] Simonds had developed reasonably comprehensive tactical theories before the war. Students at RMC in early1939, where he was an instructor, were struck by his powerful personality and obvious ability. Those students included Ned Amy, who called Simonds "very brilliant."[45] There were some other outstanding figures, including Harry Crerar, E.L.M. Burns, and Harry Foster (the Strathcona who had noted how much Calgarians reviled cavalrymen). In the meantime, Kenneth Stuart and Maurice Pope filled top administrative positions, acting as a bridge between the military and political worlds.

There is general agreement among commentators about at least one collective failure. Most conspicuously missing among the top army brass was any hint of charisma. While Worthington and Hoffmeister were dynamic personalities, they were the exceptions. For the most part, Canadian Second World War generals were, as Stacey said, "as grimly cold as codfish on a slab."[46]

So while the part-time reservists and a microscopic cadre of professional soldiers had made their contribution to the army in overcoming the failures of 1939, there was one other crucial factor — blind luck. Essentially, what Canada said to the Germans in 1939 was: "we're not ready yet, but you just wait three years and we will be." Canada said to the British: "we're not ready yet, and you and the French will have to hold the fort until we are." Meanwhile, the Canadian army, in the safety of Britain, had three years in which to train, be equipped, and find new leadership. It is extraordinary to have a national defence policy that relies on having three years from the outbreak of war to get ready for battle. However, as unsettling as this scenario might be, the strange reality is, it was not unknown. It also applied to Canada in 1914 and to the United States in 1939. The U.S. had from 1939 to near the end of 1941 to fire up its colossal industrial and military potential. Still, it is extraordinarily risky for the existence of any nation.

However, after noting the failures of equipment, the lack of training, and the multitude of leadership problems the army suffered, one other point should be stressed. Even after the war began, rearmament was put in jeopardy by the limits of military defence industry. There were some companies, such as Inglis (making Bren guns), National Steel Car Corporation (twenty-five-pounder guns and 3.7 inch shells), and Canadian Industries Limited (TNT explosives) producing war equipment. When full-scale Canadian production finally got underway, it reached astonishing levels. However, the production of the military equipment that Canada needed so desperately could only be rapidly cranked up in wartime on the basis of facilities set up in peacetime.[47] Stacey has called the puny industrial output at the start of the war as "the most fundamental ... the most difficult and controversial problem" Canada faced on the outbreak of war.[48]

So what?

So what if Canada's army was unprepared? So what if William Lyon Mackenzie King's military program amounted to rearmament lite? Did it really matter that it was ill-trained, poorly led, and equipped in 1939? The answer is yes, it did matter. Granatstein has singled out two devastating consequences: "the defeats at Hong Kong and Dieppe were the price we paid for our unpreparedness."[49]

In the fall of 1941, 1,975 Canadians, including two nursing sisters, were sent to Hong Kong to reinforce British and Imperial troops. Two infantry battalions, the Royal Rifles of Canada from Quebec and the Winnipeg Grenadiers, along with support forces and a brigade headquarters, made up a fighting formation called C Force. One of those in the ranks — his head sticking out above the others on parade — was six foot four inch George MacDonell, the Listowel, Ontario, soldier who had to lie about his age to enlist in the CASF in 1939. MacDonell was by this time nineteen, rock-solid, and a sergeant in the Royal Rifles.

By the fall of 1941 the Crown Colony was effectively surrounded by the Japanese army while the Americans had begun their potentially crippling oil embargo on Japan. If the Japanese chose to attack Hong Kong, it was apparent that the Crown Colony was indefensible. MacDonell called it "an isolated, unprepared military death trap."[50] The problem was that while Hong Kong was impossible to defend militarily, as a prestige possession, it was impossible to abandon politically.

For Canada, into what was a potentially explosive situation in the Far East in 1941, marched a human spark in the form of British Major General A.E. Grasett. He was Canadian-born but displayed some cartoonish British mannerisms, punctuating comments with the exclamation, "what, what." Grasett had been the Hong Kong garrison commander and while returning to Britain stopped in Ottawa for a chat with Major General Harry Crerar, by this time the chief of the general staff and the most important military advisor to the government. Both men were RMC old boys.

Grasett believed that the Japanese army could not fight effectively against white troops. It was a judgment typical of the times, so much so that author Brian Nolan calls it one of the "greatest propaganda deceits" of the Second World War. The propaganda depicted the Japanese soldier as "a bandy-legged, buck-toothed, myopic figure, who stared down the sights of his antiquated rifle through glasses as thick as the bottom of Coke bottles."[51] In any event, many British leaders did not think that an attack was likely, so one or two battalions of reinforcements would show the Japanese the colony would not be abandoned. For senior Canadian officers, the problem at Hong Kong was anything but new. As many as ten of them had attended British staff colleges before the war where possible attacks had been studied. Crerar had studied Hong Kong both at Camberley in 1922–24 and the Imperial Defence College in 1934.[52] In a series of war games at one of them, the conclusion was that if Hong Kong were attacked, any forces there would have no route of escape because the Royal Navy would be unable to mount any rescue force in time. George Pearkes said everyone at his course at the Imperial Defence College thought the same.[53] Author Carl Vincent in his searing book on Hong Kong called No Reason Why argues that in the history of the Second World War, the C Force members were the only Canadian soldiers and possibly the only Commonwealth soldiers ever sent into a position where there was absolutely no hope of victory, evacuation, or relief if fighting broke out.[54]

A short while after Grasett's visit, a British request to send one or two battalions to Hong Kong arrived in Ottawa. Prime Minister King and Defence Minister Ralston, after various discussions, eventually agreed to send troops. While Harry Crerar discussed the operation with generals Pope and Stuart, unquestionably Crerar as the chief of the general staff was the key figure in the approval. He told Ralston that "the Canadian Army should take this on."[55]

C Force arrived in Hong Kong on November 16, but because of a bureaucratic blunder its 212 vehicles and other equipment never arrived. That led Carl Vincent in *No Reason Why* to title one chapter "They've Dispatched J.K. Lawson [the commander] Without Even a Wheelbarrow."[56] The troops had barely settled in when the Japanese attacked on December 8 (local time), just hours after Pearl Harbor. The defending forces were gradually pushed back to parts of Victoria Island. However, even late in the battle George MacDonell felt "though bottled up on Stanley Peninsula in a hopeless position and running out of ammunition, food, and water, until the garrison surrendered we remained defiant."[57] Despite that, the Japanese advance continued and the government surrendered on December 25.

George MacDonell, Royal Rifles. MacDonell is pictured on his nineteenth birthday, August 5, 1941, only months before he was sent to Hong Kong. After the war he delivered a scathing assessment of government and military decision making in sending Canadian troops.

As a result, 290 Canadians were killed in combat, including some who were executed after being taken prisoner. The surviving Canadians, including MacDonell, endured three and a half years of torture, starvation, beatings, and disease in prisoner of war camps. In all, 550 members lost their lives in the fighting and the camps.

The disaster touched off a public outcry in Canada that resulted in the chief justice, Sir Lyman Duff, being appointed to head up a judicial inquiry. In the end Duff decided that, apart from the fiasco over trucks and equipment and the lack of training for 120 of the soldiers, there was no evidence anyone was to blame.[58] While some have judged that Duff's findings were the only ones possible in the circumstances, Vincent has expressed contempt for the entire Duff inquiry, while much later MacDonell condemned Duff's conclusion as a whitewash.[59]

As for other views about Hong Kong, British writer Basil Liddell Hart said that strategy and common sense had been vainly sacrificed in the name of prestige while historian George Stanley argued that Canadian and British officials displayed political naïveté if they thought that two additional battalions would deter Japan.[60] The most troubling question is why the force was sent at all. Indeed, Vincent's book is titled *No Reason Why* because he concluded there was no reason why the Canadians should have been sent. George MacDonell's view is that the government

> showed no concern for the actual military situation in the Far East and Hong Kong until the entire Canadian force had disappeared in the flaming wreckage of the defeated colony. General Harry Crerar, Canada's senior military officer and a man who spent his life as a professional soldier, should have advised against such utter folly. Why he did not is still unexplained.[61]

A central factor in the decision was that while the war had been going on for two years, and while the navy and air force had been fighting the Germans, the Canadian army had not fired a shot in anger. There was mounting political pressure on the government to "do something" and in the end the decision was essentially not military.[62] The pressure on the government started over its initial policy of limited liability war. The Conservative opposition and others including the Canadian Legion demanded "total war." There was a blizzard of pro-conscription editorials and service club resolutions in English-speaking Canada.[63]

It is hard to avoid the conclusion that General Crerar failed in his capacity as King's chief military advisor because he did not fully explain to the government the possible consequences of sending troops. Still, the final call was King's, and the prime minister must shoulder the blame for approving the expedition in the hope of deflecting political criticism.[64]

Since the Hong Kong attack did not occur until December 1941, one might ask what this has to do with the army being unprepared in 1939? To begin with, the top brass never did request either a military appreciation of Hong Kong's defences or the operation's viability, and neither was an appreciation prepared by the director of military operations and intelligence. The directorate was incapable of doing it.[65] The number of officers handling intelligence in the directorate of military operations and intelligence (which, incidentally, Crerar had headed before the war), had increased from one in 1940 to seven in 1941, but only one of these handled "foreign" intelligence.[66]

The Canadian army was essentially without the capacity to weigh, examine, probe, or analyze on its own. All assessments came from the British — a special monthly secret intelligence summary, a monthly confidential intelligence summary, and periodic secret summaries from Hong Kong, Singapore, and the Air Ministry. Those assessments discounted the probability of an attack almost to the end of November. The Hong Kong fiasco, therefore, brought into the harsh light the price to be paid for Canada being a branch plant operation.

As for the troops, a history of Canadian military intelligence concludes, "Ottawa could not and did not provide adequate information to the men it sent there to fight, and that, in itself is a condemnation of our lack of preparedness during peacetime."[67] This was compounded once C Force arrived in Hong Kong. A British assessment of the enemy was wildly off the mark.[68] The British estimated that there were only 5,000 enemy troops opposite the colony. In contrast, the Australians, before sending troops to Malaya, had issued a pamphlet warning that the Japanese were ruthless and had both good armament and technical training.[69] Even more than all the foregoing, the lack of independent risk assessment had, in fact, been discussed much earlier in Ottawa. Long before the war, King's advisor J.W. Pickersgill argued "that the

The Royal Rifles of Canada regiment was reconstituted in January 1942. After that time it served as a home defence regiment on the west coast.

principle of imperial uniformity meant that there was no critical analysis of defence issues in Canada and no independent thought about what was best" for the Canadian army.[70]

There is one further point. It has been said that having a separate Canadian intelligence assessment would have made no difference. Crerar biographer Paul Dickson argues that the general's "assessment of Japanese intentions was no worse, and no better, than that of the British or Americans."[71] It may be that the outcome would not have been any different, but Professor G.R. Perras says, for one thing, more still needs to be known about Crerar's actions.[72] As far as Crerar doing no worse than the British, he relied on British assessments and British information. He had worked with and been trained by the British army and he shared much of its world outlook, traditions, and values. The uniform he wore was indistinguishable from the British uniform. So it is hardly a surprise that he did no better or no worse than the British. No one questions his loyalty to Canada, but in many ways his viewpoint was a mirror image of the British viewpoint.

Only months after Hong Kong, Canadian troops were hurled into another inferno — Dieppe, the worst disaster in Canadian military history. More Canadians were killed there on August 19, 1942, than on any other single day of the war. At Dieppe a mainly Canadian force of about 6,100 troops supported by nearly 4,000 men at sea and in the air conducted a frontal assault on the heavily fortified port that was shaped like a Roman amphitheatre.

On the day of the battle pretty much everything went wrong.[73] Surprise was lost. When tanks arrived they had to contend with a shingle beach and couldn't get traction. Almost every radio taken ashore was blown up or failed to work. Later, the commander, Major General Roberts, acting on inaccurate information, committed his floating reserve to the battle, sending the Fusiliers Mont-Royal into the midst of a bloodbath.

By mid-morning it was obvious that the operation had failed. Courage the Canadians had shown in plenty, but it would be hopeless to remain any longer in Dieppe. In the end, almost 60 percent of the Canadians were killed, wounded, or captured. The Royal Regiment of Canada suffered 524 casualties, while only sixty-five members managed to get back to England. In the Royal Hamilton Light Infantry — the Rileys — Lieutenant Clement

Dick was wounded three times and was one of only three officers to return.[74] Before the war a company of the Rileys had come mostly from Winona, Ontario, site of the E.D. Smith plant. At Dieppe that company lost every man of fighting age.[75] Among them was thirty-seven-year-old Fred Woodcock, who was blinded and taken prisoner. Woodcock was repatriated and returned to Canada in 1944.[76]

Historian John Keegan said Dieppe "in retrospect, looks so recklessly hare-brained an enterprise that it is difficult to reconstruct the official state of mind which gave it birth and drove it forward."[77] The commando leader, Lord Lovat, whose force conducted the only successful part of the operation (attacking heavy gun emplacements), said the entire operation "was a bad plan and had no chance of success."[78]

Most commando operations were small but the idea of a "super raid" had been around for some time. "Like the flotsam and jetsam of so many other half-baked ideas, the super-raiding policy lay bobbing on the backwaters of the bay of doubtful options," said historian Brian Loring Villa.[79] The attack was planned by Combined Operations, whose commander, Vice-Admiral Lord Louis Mountbatten, had little experience in amphibious warfare. Support by bombers and big ships, originally key parts of the plan, were dropped because of RAF and RN opposition.

As with Hong Kong, politics was heavily involved. Winston Churchill wanted action everywhere and at all times. He picked Mountbatten to head Combined Operations (promoted from commodore to vice admiral in one jump) and undoubtedly expected fast results. Despite outrage by Stalin, Churchill was unable to deliver a second front in 1942 and considered big raids to be a substitute. However, several earlier attacks had been cancelled. Then, in July there was the disaster of the Russia-bound convoy PQ 17 that had been scattered, turning it into the worst convoy calamity of the war. Subsequent convoys to Russia were suspended.

As with Hong Kong, the British government needed "something," and so did the Canadian government. Ottawa was under tremendous pressure and it is clear that King's political requirements were in line with those of the chiefs of staff.[80] William Anderson, an artilleryman and later lieutenant general said, "You have to put yourself back in the context of 1942. The British were fighting all over the world. The Canadian army had done bugger-all. We were still just training and training. The pressure was on that we had to get into action!...

In that context it would have been unthinkable for any Canadian to say, 'We won't do it,' or 'We shouldn't try this.'"[81]

By this time the peripatetic General Crerar was commander of First Canadian Corps. Having delivered political advice in the Hong Kong fiasco, he lobbied furiously to have Canadians involved at Dieppe. While Canadians were eager participants, Operation Rutter/Jubilee was really run by the British, who did not relish senior Canadian officers trying to horn in on decision making. McNaughton made a number of attempts to have a direct liaison with General Paget's Home Forces headquarters, but was rebuffed.

The Second Canadian Division commander, Major General Roberts, the eventual scapegoat, knew that this was his first opportunity to prove himself and that another might not be coming for a long time. McNaughton at one point asked Crerar to review the entire plan because of questions raised. In a comment eerily similar to his advice on Hong Kong, Crerar said "I should have no hesitation in tackling it, if I were in Roberts' place."[82]

One of the enduring myths of Dieppe — certainly one promoted by both Mountbatten and Crerar — was that the operation at least taught lessons that were invaluable in the D-Day invasion of 1944. In retirement after the war Crerar talked publicly about many military issues, but only five times about Dieppe.[83] Those rare statements included his view that Dieppe was "probably the most valuable contribution of the war to the final, and decisive, Allied victory." In contrast, Generals Pearkes and Burns, for example, agreed that little was learned.[84] If there were lessons learned, said Jack Granatstein, they "would have been obvious to a second lieutenant fresh out of officer cadet classes."[85] Above all Dieppe showed that after three years of war the British and Canadian commanders still could not put together an operation that would succeed. Dieppe was simply more than the Canadian army could handle.

Winston Churchill once said about war,

> Never, never, never believe any war will be smooth and easy, or that anyone who embarks on the strange voyage can measure the tides and hurricanes he will encounter. The Statesman who yields to war fever must realize that once the signal is given, he is no longer the master of policy but the slave of unforeseeable and uncontrollable events. Antiquated War Offices, weak, incompetent or arrogant

Commanders, untrustworthy allies, hostile neutrals, malig-
nant Fortune, ugly surprises, awful miscalculations — all
take their seat at the Council Board on the morrow of the
declaration of war.[86]

The most unlikely escapee in the Dieppe disaster was Admiral Mountbatten, who went on to become the last Viceroy of India and an icon in
Britain. In the twelve hours of autobiographical film Mountbatten made for
the BBC in the 1960s, the Dieppe raid and its ugly surprises and awful miscalculations was allotted a total of three-and-a-half minutes.[87]

One of the greatest consequences of Canada being unprepared for war was
that the Royal Canadian Navy remained essentially a training navy until 1943.
Or at least most of it did. As noted earlier, the navy really split into two not
long after the war began: the "straight stripe" navy of regulars and the "wavy
navy" of reservists. While it started the war with its six destroyers and four
coastal minesweepers, by the conflict's end the navy grew to 775 ships and
92,000 men and women.[88] No navy in the world could have expanded fifty
times its size in six years and not suffered crippling growing pains.

There have been sharp differences characterizing the RCN of 1939, Marc
Milner arguing that the navy was much better off than most critics indicate and
that the "Canadian coast was not undefended in 1939."[89] In contrast, Joseph
Schull's assessment is that "of all Canadian fighting services in the Second
World War, the Royal Canadian Navy was in over its head from the first shot."[90]

Of course there would have been severe stresses and disasters in the
Royal Canadian Navy even if it had been bigger before the Second World
War. Still, the exceptionally small size of the pre-war navy and the pre-war
decision to not have smaller coastal patrol ships left the navy unable to make
even faint gestures toward expansion when it was needed. It was when the
corvettes began to arrive and totally green crews were thrown aboard and
pushed out to sea that convoy veteran James Lamb commented, "our object
was mere survival, pure and simple."[91] Keeping the ship afloat, not hunting
submarines, was the aim. As one new corvette captain wrote, "with more than
three-quarters of the complement as fresh to the sea as the ship herself, it was
hard to perform our simple task; hard to keep steam up, avoid the shoals or

even steer a straight course. Had anything warlike occurred there would have been a shambles."[92]

There were bound to be failures in leadership anyway, but the extraordinary speed and size of the RCN's expansion made the situation incomparably worse. Lieutenant H.D. Campsie left HMCS *Trillium* in late 1941, and those cleaning out his cabin found thirty-one empty liquor bottles, even though Campsie had been captain for only twenty-four days.[93] The captains who did manage to cope were often sent off to work with other ships they had never seen before and whose commanders they had never met.[94] Perhaps it was inevitable but many ratings were slotted into work they had not been trained for. In 1941 Harry Rhoades, a cook on HMCS *Trillium*, was also assigned duties as a sick berth attendant on the strength of his first aid course taken at Ogilvy's Department Store in Montreal before the war.[95] At the same time, some corvettes built in Canada for the Royal Navy made their way across the Atlantic with dummy wooden deck guns because no real guns were available, prompting crew member Ernie Adams of Dartmouth to comment that the dummy guns might "hopefully frighten the enemy to death."[96]

One of the consequences of the pre-war navy's size and manpower was not what happened after the war began, but what failed to happen. In the early days, U-boats were not being sunk in the numbers that would make a difference. Robert Welland pointed out, "the crews weren't properly trained. There was no time to train them. They were shoveled out — which was better than not putting them there at all."[97] One of the frequently cited evidence of the strain on the navy was convoy SC-7 (Slow Convoy Seven) of October 1940, which was attacked by sixteen U-boats. Fifteen of the forty-two merchant ships went to the bottom.

While there were no U-boats off Canada's Atlantic coast in the first months of the war, one naval history notes, "It was [still] over two years before the RCN recorded its first wartime-acknowledged U-boat kill. This was due to pre-war lack of preparedness and hands-on training against submarines, and a scarcity of even modestly suitable A/S [anti-submarine] vessels and asdic equipment."[98] The first kill known at the time was on SC-42 of September 1941. The convoy was escorted by HMCS *Skeena, Alberni, Kenogami*, and *Orillia*. Later *Chambly* and *Moose Jaw* caught up with the main force. Eleven U-boats attacked, sinking sixteen merchant ships. The Canadian victory was in sinking U-501. Despite that one successful attack, "the escort was too small, too dispersed, too badly equipped, too poorly trained and coordinated to effect any proper defence."[99] *Skeena* had no radar or high-frequency direction-finding equipment, *Kenogami* was manned by a green crew with a skipper on his first war patrol, and *Moose Jaw* had gone to sea without full provisions while most of the crew was incapacitated by sea sickness.[100]

As 1942 came to a close, allied shipping losses to U-boat attacks amounted to a staggering 7.8 million tons representing 1,664 ships. Eighty percent of ships torpedoed in the Atlantic in November and December of 1942 were hit while being escorted by Canadian groups. The famous British operational scientist P.M.S. Blackett produced several reports in early 1943, one of which argued that nearly a quarter of the merchant ship losses could have been saved by simply increasing the size of escort groups from six to nine ships.[101] Some early convoys had only a single escort vessel to protect them in the mid-Atlantic.

The Royal Navy was extremely critical of its Canadian juniors, and a portion of that criticism may have been deserved, but some comments were deeply resented. Among the most notorious allegations were those made by British anti-submarine commander Captain Donald Macintyre. He wrote, "Small warships ... are of little value without the trained and disciplined men to sail them. The experience of the Canadian navy in the war ... makes this abundantly clear."[102] What might Macintyre have expected given the size and training of the force in 1939? Beyond that, what Macintyre did *not* say was the Royal Navy stuck the RCN with much of the hard slogging in the slow convoys, which, by their very nature, were at greater risk than fast convoys. The British angled to have RN commanders and not RCN officers named as senior officer on many escort runs.[103] The Admiralty in London, using Ultra intelligence, sometimes pushed the RCN out of prospective U-boat areas of the eastern Atlantic, so lowering the opportunities for the RCN to sink more U-boats.

What about RCN losses? Could the loss of HMCS *Fraser* in a collision in 1940 be due to pre-war unpreparedness? No. It is difficult to say that unpreparedness was the direct cause that or other losses. However, it seems self evident that the total may well have been much lower with a bigger pool of pre-war officers, with more ships early on and with more shore support facilities. Would the toll of U-boats sunk by the RCN may have been higher and more merchant ships saved with better ships, and more of them and sooner? The answer to that one is, yes.

While the cause of individual losses may be difficult to pinpoint, in 1945 there was one, admittedly controversial, exception. Convoy veteran Lieutenant Commander Debbie Piers led an inquiry into the loss of the Bangor minesweeper HMCS *Esquimalt*.[104] The sinking was especially tragic because the ship went down in sight of the coast with heavy loss of life only two weeks before the end of the war. It appears the ship did not take some precautions to protect itself, but among the findings, the inquiry concluded that even at this time *Esquimalt* was equipped with a grab bag of anti-submarine and other gear that was long out of date. Piers and the inquiry board said the sinking also derived from pre-war policies of national unpreparedness, including inadequate equipment, tactics, training, and command and control.[105]

Then, once any ship had been in service and taken a beating in the North Atlantic, repairing it was near-impossible because there were so few repair facilities. Many ships required upgrading, but there were few yards able to do the work and a large number of Canadian ships became stuck with more and more obsolescent gear. Fortunately, after December 1941, a lot of repair work for both the Royal Navy and the Royal Canadian Navy was done in the United States. One thing that saved the navy was the unexpected success of the corvette. It turned out to be an ocean-going submarine beater.

A further consequence of unpreparedness was that the Royal Canadian Navy was long smothered in its efforts to become an independent navy. Fortunately, it was gradually able to build up the strength and experience — relying much less on the Royal Navy — but it took time. A great moment for the RCN came in 1943 when Rear Admiral Leonard Murray was appointed commander-in-chief, Canadian Northwest Atlantic. He was the only Canadian to command an Allied theatre of operations in the Second World War. Murray had joined the navy at the age of fourteen in the first intake of twenty-one recruits at the Royal Naval College of Canada in Halifax. His appointment in 1943 marked one of the greatest achievements of the Royal Canadian Navy during the entire war.

The hope of William Lyon Mackenzie King and others that civilians and civilian planes could put on war paint one day and be ready for battle the next was completely unrealistic. It takes years to build up a credible air force. It was a struggle for the Royal Canadian Air Force to make up for the Big

Cut and the lost years. The air force simply ran out of time in its rebuilding program so that in September 1939 it could only muster fifteen of its planned twenty-three squadrons.

It is striking that the RCAF was unable to send a single squadron to Britain on the outbreak of war. Apart from anything else, that inability meant the pilots missed months of operational training that might have been a priceless asset in the Battle of Britain. One of the principal arguments about making the air force the top rearmament priority was that it would be mobile, being able to move quickly to where it was needed. That had proved to be a lost hope in the Munich crisis, and the situation was only marginally better in 1939.

Even some of the new planes it received — the Fairey Battle being a vivid example — were good only for training.[106] The U.S. was beginning to have some very good aircraft, and while the neutrality laws were overcome by towing aircraft across the border, that still left the problem that U.S. equipment required a complete retooling of gear the RCAF had, and most weapons converted to American standards.

The most important operational role at the start of the war was coastal patrol on the Atlantic, but the RCAF was only capable of covering the approaches to Halifax and Sydney.[107] The Hudson and later the Bolingbroke both helped but RCAF anti-submarine aircraft were not effective in the mid-Atlantic until the latter part of 1943.[108] Both the navy and the air force were fortunate, indeed, that the U-boats did not start their attacks in the western Atlantic until 1940.

With the Canadian-made Bolingbroke finally having its first flight in the fall of 1939, the RCAF was closer to having a viable coastal patrol aircraft, but it would be months before the first Bolingbroke squadron would be ready for operations. One of the biggest handicaps was the failure to build aircraft engines in Canada, which left the RCAF only able to plead for the aircraft engines it needed in Britain and the U.S.

Very telling of the mindset of Britain in the opening days of the war was its request for reinforcements from the RCAF. The British did not want complete RCAF squadrons as a first priority; rather they wanted RCAF members as reinforcements for RAF squadrons.[109] Of course, soon the British said they would welcome individual squadrons but under more senior RAF control.

* * *

Perhaps the single greatest surprise for the RCAF and for Canada in the early months of the war was the British Commonwealth Air Training Plan. It is hard to imagine how the RCAF managed to cope with such a stupendous undertaking, far too large for Canada to handle. The BCATP fundamentally changed the direction of the air force. As many as 132,000 air crewmen were trained during the war, about 55 percent of them Canadians. One of King's significant contributions was his determination to shape the BCATP to promote Canadian identity. While it is true that many graduates ended up serving in the RAF or in RAF squadrons, King was determined that it would have a Canadian face.[110] So fierce was his opposition to British negotiators dictating the terms of the plan that the British High Commissioner in Ottawa, Sir Gerald Campbell, was moved to call him "the narrowest of the narrow Canadian nationalists."[111]

The massive commitment to the BCATP began, but both the government and the public demanded the air force have a part in the air battles of Europe. However, less than a year after the war began there was one demonstration of the dire effects of pre-war RCAF failures — the Battle of Britain. A shortage of pilots, more than a shortage of aircraft, turned out to be a decisive factor in the Battle of Britain. With the fall of France, Britain had been aware of the looming aircrew shortage and combed through the air and naval staffs to search for more trained pilots. In June, seventy-five semi-trained Royal Navy pilots were transferred to the RAF. Operational training was cut from six weeks to three, resulting in pilots saying the first time they fired their guns was at the enemy. The situation reached a crisis between August 24 and September 6, when the RAF was losing 120 pilots per week, killed or wounded, out of a fighting strength of just less than 1,000. By one description, "Experienced pilots were like gold-dust, and each one lost had to be replaced by an untried man."[112]

Pilots from several nations took part in the battle, including 140 from Poland and 129 from New Zealand.[113] About 100 Canadian pilots participated, many of them either enlisted in the RAF or RCAF members assigned to RAF squadrons. A dozen Canadian pilots served in the RAF's No. 242 Squadron, including Squadron Leader Fowler Gobeil, who in 1927 had been so impressed by the dashing pilot instructor uniforms at Camp Borden. Gobeil was credited with the first aerial victory by a member of the RCAF, a Messerschmitt 110 shot down on May 25, 1940.[114] The squadron gained fame when led by Douglas Bader and members included Stan Turner, who had joined the RAF in 1938. Johnny Kent, originally from Winnipeg and a legend in the RAF, fought in No. 303 Squadron.

The RCAF's principal contribution to the battle was No. 1 Squadron, which was sent to Britain soon after Dunkirk, but before it left Canada even that single squadron had to be brought up to strength by absorbing No. 115 Fighter Squadron. This was all the RCAF had. No. 1 Squadron — later re-numbered 401 — was made up of twenty-seven officers, 314 ground crewmembers, and pretty much Canada's entire fleet of Hurricanes. That left the Canadian homeland without any fighter force except the obsolete Goblin biplane for a year and a half.[115] No. 1 Squadron, led by the formidable Ernie McNab, was the RCAF's first unit to take part in combat during the war. It joined the battle on August 26. Even then, McNab said his pilots went into the fight with only twenty hours on their planes, and most had fired their guns only once at a moving target. By mid-October the squadron had accounted for thirty-one enemy aircraft shot down for the loss of sixteen aircraft and three pilots killed.

The casualties sustained by No. 1 Squadron, although not large, created a difficult problem. With no operational training units in Canada and the flow of Canadian trainees barely underway, there were no fighter pilots to replace the dead or wounded.[116] Pilots from Nos. 110 and 112 Squadrons volunteered to make up for the shortages. Still, No. 112 Squadron had only arrived in June and it was flying Lysander army cooperation aircraft, so crews had to be retrained and re-equipped. The RCAF recognized the depth of the crisis and rushed over many of the thirty-nine pilots who were among the first graduates from the British Commonwealth Air Training Plan. They were dispatched the moment they received their wings, even though they had been expected to be BCATP instructors. They arrived too late to take a decisive role in the battle.[117]

It is hard to argue that more Canadians would have turned the Battle of Britain in late August from a crisis to a certain victory. However, a larger number of Canadian fully trained pilots, aircrews, and planes would have contributed to the margin of victory, and air crew would have gained valuable combat experience. Two flying veterans have commented on the pilot shortage. Former Spitfire pilot and icon of the RCAF, Lieutenant General William Carr was a BCATP graduate and had his wings pinned on by Air

Vice-Marshal Billy Bishop.[118] The Ottawa native flew 143 reconnaissance missions over Malta, Italy, and other battlefields during the war and afterward became the first commander of Canadian Forces Air Command in 1975. Carr says that Canada should have been able to do more. Those comments are supported by Russ Bannock, who had witnessed the royal visit in Edmonton in 1938, and who later went on to become a Mosquito pilot. Bannock says Canada could have been rearmed sooner. He said, "we were quite slow and late in doing that."[119] The glittering legend that was the Battle of Britain demonstrated the less glittering reality that the RCAF was able to contribute only a limited number of pilots, crews, and aircraft at one of the turning points of the war.

Of Canada's three armed services, the RCAF had the hardest time in taking control of its own destiny, remaining intertwined with the RAF through most of the war. Establishing a Canadian identity — Canadianization — became an issue as the war continued. It became a priority of the government and of King especially. However, the greatest difficulty was that the Air Training Plan diverted so many resources that it took a long time to build up to a size in Europe that merited independent command. So the BCATP virtually guaranteed that Canadianization would be extremely difficult.

The army had fared better. The decision to send Canadians to Sicily in 1943 meant the Canadian army would be split so valuable combat experience was gained, but having the entire overseas army fighting together was delayed.[120] However, it finally did happen as the First Canadian Army continued its attacks into Germany late in the war. Meanwhile, the navy gained a good deal of independence, with the appointment of Rear Admiral Murray as a theatre commander, marking one important milestone. Canadians were fighting in Canadian ships and many times under Canadian command.

However, in the RCAF, Canadianization was not completed by the end of the war. So many Canadians were scattered throughout the RAF in the early war years that transferring them into RCAF formations proved to be an intractable problem. Some Canadians had worked together with pilots and ground crew from both Britain and other Commonwealth countries, and once they had bonded as a team they were reluctant to leave. Lieutenant General Carr said he was "as proud to serve in an RAF squadron as I was in an RCAF squadron." One barrier was that it was harder to appoint Canadians to senior air positions until RCAF squadrons were formed into wings and groups.* By the middle of the war approximately 60 percent of all RCAF personnel overseas spent some or all of their careers scattered among 700 different British formations, becoming known in the process as the "Lost Legion."

Apart from the prime minister, others who promoted Canadianization in the RCAF included Chubby Power, the boozing but still formidable minister of national defence for air.[121] At one point Power, in no uncertain terms, ordered commanders to "put the RCAF on the map." Another advocate was Air Marshal Gus Edwards, the air officer commander-in-chief, RCAF overseas in Britain, whose forceful personality took on inertia and opposition.[122] The RCAF had to overcome outraged hostility from some top British commanders, including Air Marshal "Bomber" Harris. He was alarmed at the prospect of a separate Canadian Bomber Group and at the same time denigrated Canadian commander Air-Vice Marshal G. E. Brookes as "Babbling Brookes."[123] An important date was October 25, 1942, when eleven bomber squadrons were brought together to form No. 6 Bomber Group, the first all Canadian formation of that size in the RCAF. The Group at its peak included fourteen squadrons. Sadly, today its grim casualty rates are sometimes forgotten by Canadians, but it made a vital contribution to the bombing campaign against Germany. By D-Day 1944, there were three RCAF Spitfire wings, wing-flying dive-bombing Typhoons, and a reconnaissance wing of Spitfires and Mustangs. Eventually, forty-seven RCAF squadrons were sent overseas.

---

* One important move toward "Canadianization" came on April 1, 1943, when Canada began to assume the entire cost of the RCAF overseas. In 1943–44 that amounted to $383.9 million.

CHAPTER THIRTEEN

PULL DOWN THE BLINDS AND HIDE UNDER THE BED

Canada was unprepared for the Second World War because of a web of failures and circumstances. In addition to the failures of William Lyon Mackenzie King and the inadequate training and leadership on the part of the military, there were jagged divisions between French and English Canada, the Depression, the searing memories of the last war, and the country's long-standing aversion to the military (except in the actual moment of crisis). Each of these failures and circumstances warrants a closer examination, beginning with the role of King himself, along with his government.

As far back as 1921 and again between 1926 and 1930, the conjuror from the Canadian Berlin led governments that emphatically opposed anything but the barest military spending. The funding base in the 1920s that was so low it became impossible to properly arm and equip the armed forces afterward. The army of the 1920s lived on its shining reputation and the equipment hauled back from Europe, while the air force scraped along as a mostly civilian outfit, and the navy similarly lived on the brink of extinction.

The 1935 election gave the Liberals a strong mandate but as King took office the League of Nations was looking more and more like a house of cards, Germany was rearming, and there was a growing sense of crisis. With all that King began still only a tepid rearmament program. Presenting rearmament to the public as home defence was a crablike response to isolationist opinion in Quebec and elsewhere, but it was a politically shrewd decision. Making the RCAF the government's top priority is not surprising given the theories of the time, but, above all, it suited King's political agenda. Still, it is a telling measure of the limited scope of rearmament that the RCAF's rebuilding program was still incomplete in September 1939.

Prime Minister King's personal leadership was a crucial reason for Canada's slow march toward rearmament. By one description an enduring strategy that later Canadian prime ministers inherited from him was "to ignore a crisis as long as possible (or even longer) in the hope that some day it will just go away."[1] Bruce Hutchison in his King biography said that "the first and gravest failure of his life was his misunderstanding of the world's drift to war and anarchy, his refusal to admit Canada's inevitable place in this process or to prepare his people for it."[2] King championed appeasement to the extent that one biographer called him "the ultimate appeaser,"[3] while George MacDonell, who spent gruelling years as a Japanese prisoner of war, referred to King in more recent times as "the world's greatest fence-sitter."[4] MacDonell said King "was paralyzed with the belief that Britain would talk its way out of the coming confrontation with Germany."

King supported appeasement for several reasons, but among them was his view that if Hitler could be bought off there would be no war and therefore no problem. Many Canadians and many Britons thought the same, including Neville Chamberlain (actually, a more likely holder of the title "the ultimate appeaser"), but King did so long after it was obvious that war was probable. There was a lack of urgency throughout the period because, in his heart of hearts, King did not believe it would actually, finally, definitely, positively come to a fight. His 1937 statement that "I think it is extremely doubtful if any of the British Dominions will ever send another expeditionary force to Europe" was the height of denial.[5]

King was far from alone in being hypnotized by Adolf Hitler (King Edward VIII comes to mind), but the prime minister's assessment of him had far-reaching consequences. The contrasting appreciation of Harry Crerar is stark. It is axiomatic that governments must plan on the capabilities of potential enemies rather than on their intentions. King bet on Hitler's intentions and lost. As late as August 22, 1939 — only days before the war broke out — King commented that if there was going to be an attack this was the moment but, as far as Hitler's dream of world domination was concerned, "I have never believed this was his aim."[6] Later that same day news of the Nazi-Soviet Non-Aggression Pact broke. Neither isolationism nor the Depression, nor the anti-conscription views of French Canada, could account for King's fundamental misreading of the danger.

King did recognize maritime defence as an essential pillar of Canadian nationhood. He also had a hard edged view of the danger that Americans posed in the event of a Japanese attack. A lot of money was poured into Pacific defence while at the same time it is not surprising that King dallied over construction of the Alaska Highway. (It was finally built in 1942.) King said in January 1939 that without strong protection from British naval forces on the east coast Canada would be part of the United States. While King understood the importance of coast defence, he failed to approve enough money for rearmament on both coasts. He was content to leave Atlantic defence to two destroyers, a few archaic aircraft and guns, but, most of all, to the Royal Navy. The government did not mind leaving Canada's Atlantic defence to the empire defence shield. King was forever railing about British interference and the colonialist attitudes in London, but when it suited him, the defence of the Atlantic coast could be handed over to British admirals and British fleets.

King's policy of "no commitments" virtually guaranteed that the Canadian military would not be ready when war came.[7] No commitments meant no joint equipment purchases with the British, but it was impossible to re-equip the Canadian forces and build an industrial foundation in Canada to supply arms and munitions without them. Canadian needs were small so it was uneconomic to supply them independently. Industrial co-production deals were badly needed, but were much delayed, in the case of the Bren gun for two years from 1936 to 1938. The Bren Gun Scandal was shattering. It is no wonder that Canada had such limited industrial capacity or so few shipbuilding or ship repair facilities in 1939.

It was particularly unfortunate that King never really understood the military. Charles Stacey once said King's interest in military matters was so limited that he "would have understood those Chinese intellectuals, who, we are told, regard soldiers as an inferior race of beings whose proceedings deserve only the contempt of civilized men."[8] Before the war King rarely visited military or naval bases. Going to Camp Borden in 1939, for instance, was conveniently on the way to a political event. He disliked reviewing troops and the fact that he was always late left fury in the ranks.[9] It was possibly King's lack of military awareness that resulted in Canada having no share, or virtually none, in the higher direction of the war later on. The Canadian government was sometimes not consulted even on special matters — Dieppe for one. To quote Lester B. Pearson, King normally "accepted the situation with a mild complaint or none at all."[10]

King failed to prepare the Canadian people for war. He did deliver a few important addresses to Parliament, particularly in early 1939, which sounded the alarm bell. In a speech in the Commons on January 16 he said, "If Britain is at war, we are at war and liable to attack." King was torn between the feeling that he must prepare Canadians for the worst and the contrary advice of the isolationists on his staff and his French Canadian colleagues.[11] After war broke out he reviewed his pre-war speeches and regretted that he had not gone further in "stating [the] possibility of war and of Canada's probable part in any conflict." He thought the best parts of his speeches were ones he included in the face of opposition.[12]

The role of a prime minister in an emergency is to reach out to Canadians and explain the depth of a crisis. He has a unique power to command national attention.[13] U.S. President Harry Truman once said "the principal power the President has is to … try to persuade people to do what they ought to do without persuasion."[14] In the immediate period before the war, there were no cross-country speaking rallies, no important appearances in major cities to achieve a greater national consensus in English Canada. Any such addresses would have to have been carefully crafted because of the political danger in Quebec, but King chose to wait for public opinion to change and then act. The distinguished academic R. MacGregor Dawson has commented, "King's leadership would have been improved had he been more venturesome and more willing to offer forthright guidance to the nation…. King was always reluctant to venture into the unknown. He avoided taking risks."[15]

One writer has described King's rearmament program in 1937 as "an act of political courage."[16] Defence spending was unpopular with most Canadians and was not popular with any finance minister either. The statement is likely accurate. King does deserve credit for facing down opposition and leading his government in advocating rearmament. However, saying his program was an act of political courage in 1937 is not saying that his rearmament failures by 1939 should be excused. The international situation became worse and worse, public opinion in English Canada began to crystallize and French Canada began to gravitate toward the view that participation in war might be acceptable as long as there was no conscription. King still dallied, still misjudged Hitler, and still failed to grip the gravity of the situation. The expansion of armed forces at the beginning of the war would have been impossible without the preparations made in 1937–39, but King failed to do what was required.

While it is true that King did more for Canadian security than any other peacetime ministry, the real test is to look at where rearmament ended up in 1939. Charles Stacey still said that defence spending before the war was "inadequate to the circumstances."[17] Even the increases for 1939–40 "were not so large as the desperate world situation of the day demanded." In the period between 1935 and the outbreak of war, defence spending tripled but that must be put into context: three times almost nothing is still almost nothing.[18] The rearmament campaign never approached the level that would allow for adequate training, re-equipment or manpower.

In September 1939 King was still hoping for a limited liability war. He envisioned sending supplies, air force members and planes and perhaps ships but not a large army force. Oscar Skelton was adamant that soldiers *not* be sent to Britain. Recruiting for the Second Division was put off for the astonishing reason that it was too expensive — a part of the limited liability policy. Canadian industry as a whole was drastically underutilized for the first eight months of the war. It was only with the collapse of France in May 1940 and with the Germans on the Atlantic looking westward, that everything changed.

It would be wrong to say that King made all the decisions on defence and wrong to give him blame — or in some cases, credit — for decisions on rearmament. Other players were part of the unfolding drama. Defence Minister Ian Mackenzie provided an able link between the military and government and later claimed, "I have done more in two years, than any minister will ever do in the Dominion of Canada."[19] However, with the exception of approving Defence Scheme No. 3 on his own account, Mackenzie never had free rein on defence policy and, besides, was seriously damaged by the Bren Gun Scandal.

Ernest Lapointe usually set the boundaries of what was acceptable to French Canada. Lapointe was King's closest political associate and the prime minister rarely made any important decision on defence or much else without consulting him.[20] Lapointe's power came from his enormous prestige in Quebec and the fear that if he ever resigned in anger, the King ministry might well collapse. Added to that was the fact that King knew little French, never much understood French Canada, and along with most English protestants was hostile to the Catholic church. There were other influential cabinet members. including Charlie Dunning, the finance minister, and James Ilsley, the Nova Scotia native and minister of national revenue. Ilsley was among those who favoured strong League of Nations action against Italy in 1936 and was a "hawk" during the Munich crisis.[21] Outside the cabinet Oscar Skelton, King's close advisor, played a central role in defence and foreign affairs. Skelton was suspicious of British imperialism and anything that smacked of sending an expeditionary force to Europe. As the war neared though, Skelton's voice was frequently ignored.

In Canada a number of people in government and a few outside it had influence but unfortunately there was no "Canadian Churchill." There was really no one to sound the alarm and galvanize public opinion. King's actions may have been constrained by having to keep his team together, but when it came right down to it, King was the driving force on defence and foreign affairs. He proposed and others disposed. He had the enormous clout of being the boss and he was a wily and experienced political operator. Most often King had the last word.[22]

In addition to the leadership weaknesses of King, the Depression, the small size of government, and the hideous memories of the First World War were critical factors in Canada's rearmament failures. In some ways the 1930s were the most disastrous decade of the century. At one point more than 1.5 million Canadians were on relief. In 1936 Alberta defaulted on provincial debts twice and Saskatchewan and Manitoba were effectively bankrupt.[23] Canada was small and weak economically, completely dependent on a short list of exports, chiefly newsprint for American newspapers and wheat.[24] The prairies especially relied on producing wheat but in 1930 world prices collapsed because of overproduction then drought wiped out crops for several years. Canada's Gross National Product fell from $4.7 billion in 1929 to $2.4 billion in 1932.[25]

In the depths of the Depression defence spending for all three service sank to $13 million. Prime Minister R.B. Bennett had been Honorary Colonel of the Calgary Highlanders since 1924, and while he may have wanted to do more for the military that was extremely difficult as the Depression deepened. Meanwhile, the relief camps were a fiasco, which helped make Bennett's government the most unpopular in Canadian history. In terms of recovery, it was only in 1939 that the prairies experienced a bumper wheat crop. By that time some of the worst of the U.S. protectionist laws had been curbed, but too late for thousands of prairie farmers who had gone bankrupt in the meantime. Just before the war the newsprint industry also made a modest recovery.[26]

Such was the wreckage of the Depression that only in 1939 did Canada's Gross National Product surpass its 1929 levels, reaching $5.6 billion.[27]

Federal government revenue just before the war amounted to only about $600 million. Federal income rested mainly on customs duties (23 percent), excise tax (15 percent), and sales taxes (27 percent). All of these depended to a degree on the consumption of goods that sharply declined in the Depression. Income tax made up only about 22 percent of federal revenue. The national government in the 1930s was tiny, the federal civil service having only 45,000 employees, of whom nearly 12,000 were delivering the mail.[28] The First World War aside, governments had neither the revenues nor the willingness to take on the management of the economy.[29]

If all that was not enough, the government was saddled with staggering debts. Canada had built far more railway lines than would ever be economic. Between 1930 and 1936 the federal government spent more money to service the debt of Canadian National Railway than it did on unemployment relief.[30] At the same time Prime Minister King was a fiscal conservative who desperately wanted balanced budgets and avoided Keynesian deficit spending policies.[31] He believed that economic recovery was chiefly in the hands of private enterprise.

The ghosts of the First World War hung over the interwar years. With vivid memories of the horrors of war there were demands for peace, almost at any price. Disarmament was the hope of many and rearmament, a dreaded prospect. Among many disarmament campaigns, between 1930 and 1932 half a million Canadians supported a petition organized by the Women's International League for Peace and Freedom. It said in part, "The nations have renounced war. Let us also renounce the instruments of war. The undersigned men and women ... STAND FOR WORLD DISARMAMENT."[32] It is not difficult to understand why appeasement was such a popular policy and why Neville Chamberlain was still an admired British leader in the first months of the war.

A greater factor in explaining the poor state of the Canadian forces in 1939 was, quite simply, that national unity trumped rearmament. Prime Minister King's rearmament plans were limited by what was acceptable to French Canada and by King's large and influential Quebec caucus in Parliament. It is easy to forget that in the conscription crisis of 1917 Canada had teetered on the brink of civil war. In the 1930s French Canada was anti-imperialist, anti-conscription, anti-communist, and pro-fascist while public debate in the province was largely driven by church opinion.[33] The anti-military views of the teenaged Pierre Trudeau were typical of those in Quebec. There was also the small but burgeoning fascist movement of Adrien Arcand and Premier Duplessis's infamous Padlock Laws.[34]

French-English divisions in the King government were also apparent from 1935 onward. In 1936 the cabinet debated what to do about the Italian invasion of Ethiopia. Ernest Lapointe threatened to resign at once if Canada supported a League of Nations military intervention. Fortunately, as it turned out, the issue did not come to that. Earlier, King had written in his diary that his first priority was "what will serve to keep Canada united."[35] He used almost the same words at the time of Munich. It will be recalled that Chubby Power, King's English Quebec lieutenant and a man whose eye was always on the next election, said the 1936 military spending increases would cost the Liberals the entire province of Quebec. Ian Mackenzie was in London in 1937 telling the British that Canada could not spend a cent more on national defence because if it did so, it risked a national implosion. Perhaps he was right. As late as February 1939 Lapointe was holding meetings to prevent King from breaking the "Parliament will decide" strictures.[36]

The outline of a modus vivendi gradually became clear. If Anglos wanted to get themselves killed in Europe, that was acceptable to French Candians, as long as they didn't have to do the same. In other words, war but no conscription. A cabinet meeting on January 27, 1939, turned out to be a watershed. Ernest Lapointe told the men around the table that a war declaration might mean the resignation of some Quebec cabinet members. King was decisive in response. "A break in the Cabinet," said King, "would mean an inevitable demand for National Government ... if they wished to avoid a situation of that kind, it would be for all of us to stay together."[37] "National Government" was a clear reference to the introduction of conscription in the First World War. Similarly on March 20, after the German occupation of the rest of Czechoslovakia, King told Parliament "if there were the prospect of an aggressor launching an attack on Britain, with bombers raining death on London, I have no doubt what the decision of the Canadian people and Parliament would be."

There were two other crucial dates in terms of resolving the conflicts between French and English Canada. On March 30 and 31 Lapointe and King delivered speeches to Parliament in which the two, in essence, traded promises.

King pledged "no conscription" and Lapointe pledged "no neutrality" in a war involving Britain.[38] As a result King felt he and Lapointe had built substantial support for Canadian unity. "Together, our speeches constituted a sort of trestle sustaining the structure which would serve to unite divergent parts of Canada, thereby making for a united country," said King.[39] Then when Hitler signed the Nazi-Soviet pact in August, 1939 the influential Cardinal Villeneuve, for one, began to support going to war against Germany.[40] As war approached the aim of the generals, admirals, and air marshals was to defeat Nazi Germany. The aim of King was to keep the country together.[41]

Why did Canada go to war in 1939, anyway? The Americans didn't. In some ways, the French Canadian point of view made perfect sense. Germany was not threatening to invade Canada. What Canadian national interests were threatened? Why was it that every twenty years Canadians had to be summoned to another bloodbath in Europe? Was there no end to the European squabbles? Was Canada located in Europe after all?

The short answer was that in 1939 Canada went to war because it was still a British colony. Not literally, but emotionally. Canada had begun to shape its own destiny on the battlefields of the First World War while at the same time the Statute of Westminster moved Canada a long way toward being an independent nation. So in some respects Canada was an independent nation. But the reality was that economic, imperial, historic, and family ties between Canada and Britain were overpowering for English-speaking Canadians.[42] Canada went to war "because Britain went to war. Not for democracy, not to stop Hitler, not to save Poland."[43] No politician dared suggest that Canada abandon the Union Jack. The prime minister knew that English-speaking Canadians controlled the country and they would never allow a Canadian government to stand idly by while Britain was attacked.[44] The conflict over rearmament came because the English Canadian mindset was completely at odds with the views of most French Canadians, not to mention many newer immigrants from Poland, Norway, Ukraine, or Germany.

Professor David Bercuson says historians are still struggling with the question of whether or not military readiness was more important to Canada in 1939 than national unity.[45] But there is plenty of evidence that King put rearmament second and national unity first. Let's recognize it for what it was:

an exercise in realpolitik. It was clear to him and many in Ottawa that another conscription crisis would tear the country apart. In that reality you do what you have to do. King's focus through the entire period was to limit rearmament principally because it was pure poison in French Canada. From 1936 on, each new defence spending proposal created smouldering opposition that threatened to break into a conflagration.

By the end of March 1939 both English and French Canadians had largely been reconciled to the possibility that Canada would participate in a war. In the next weeks the royal visit helped further galvanize support. On September 10, Canada declared war and there were no resignations in cabinet, no Liberal MPs defecting, no rioting in French Canada. King was able to get both a Canadian declaration of war *and* preserve unity.

One must stand back a bit to realize that that was a monumental achievement. Mainly as a result of King's finesse, the crisis that could have split the country in two passed with muted opposition. According to Hutchison, "his greatest work, by his own estimate, [was that] he found the old racial gulf of Canada newly widened and he bridged it where even Laurier had failed."[46] King brought the country into the conflict "with a quietude and peace almost comparable to that of a vessel sailing over a smooth and sunlit lake ... we had kept down all passion and faction, and now were united country."[47] In the end it is hard to leave King as only a hiss-able villain on rearmament. The reality is more complicated.

Desmond Morton is among historians who trumpet what King did, commenting, "In all of King's long political career, perhaps no achievement was as remarkable or as improbable as bringing Canada united into the Second World War."[48] In one survey of twenty-five leading Canadian historians, fourteen of them put King as first or tied for first among Canada's greatest prime ministers while another puts him third. Of course his later achievements in introducing a sweeping program of social programs were still ahead and they were monumental in themselves but whether he was first or third, he was certainly among Canada's greatest prime ministers.[49]

Also in the long term King was successful in delaying a national division on conscription. There was a conscription crisis in 1942, it did divide the government, and there had to be a plebiscite to release the government from earlier promises. But by that time French Canada had collectively realized the government had tried extraordinary measures to avoid conscription and it went ahead in 1944. There was still outrage, but it did not cause the collapse of the government or divide Canada irrevocably.[50]

A footnote of sorts is a reminder that while King's achievement was monumental, it was not entirely altruistic. His decision making was also about raw political power — winning it and keeping it. King was, after all, a ruthless, cold-blooded politician. He understood that leadership meant retaining power almost at any price. King's promotion of the British Commonwealth Air Training Plan was meant to be a contribution to winning the war, but as the air force history notes, it came with "clear political advantages" that King would certainly have seen.[51] On September 28, 1939, he came close to confessing that his decision to trim British proposals for air co-operation in 1938 was, first of all, about politics. The opposition Conservatives could not be seen pushing him too close to the "Imperialist" camp.[52] King had an enormous capacity for self justification and re-shaping events in his mind but, interestingly, on this matter he expresses "regret" in his diary. He also admits trying to avoid undue expenditure and criticism by Parliament in twice stopping the purchase of American aircraft."[53] He did not want to have to defend American purchases in any election campaign leaving the Royal Canadian Air Force left to buy cheap leftovers from the Royal Air Force and, as one officer said, "the British built some bad airplanes."[54]

One of the odd things about King (and there were many) was that if historians count him among the greats, he never looked or sounded the part. He seems not larger than life but smaller, not a heroic figure like Churchill, nor a leader who could radiate warmth. Canadians might have wished for a man of destiny, a figure of greatness; alas, King is the anti-charisma candidate. Bruce Hutchison said that once the war began, despite any hopes for more, Canadians had to be satisfied with a "steady candle flame of competence."[55]

But there is more to it. The personality of King, the Depression, the legacy of the First World War, and the French-English divide still do not entirely explain the failures of the 1930s. There is more to be seen in the soul of the nation itself. Few in any part of the country were clamouring for rearmament. Most Canadians knew little and cared less about the armed forces. As David Bercuson has said, if we want to find a villain, Canadians should look in the mirror.[56] However, the issue is even broader than that. In a kind of "a plague on all their houses" comment, Bercuson says the "guilty" men at Dieppe and

Hong Kong were Canadians and their government who starved their military forces for years on end and then one day sent them off against well-equipped enemies, in pursuit not of national interests as defined by Canadian politicians but of international interests defined by external authorities. Hong Kong was not the first example of this happening, nor was Dieppe the last. It is, he says, "the Canadian way of war."

Jimmy "Stocky" Edwards. In 1939 he barely knew how to drive a car, but by 1942 he had become Canada's highest-scoring ace in the Middle East.

Department of National Defence

Canada has never been a military-minded country. It has a superb record in war but that is not the same thing. In the twentieth century Canada was more or less locked in a cycle: ignore the military, build up frantically when war breaks out, dismantle quickly when the war ends, and ignore again.[57] Canada has never learned to maintain institutional knowledge or military readiness, making it abundantly clear that Canada does not value its armed forces in peacetime. Harry Crerar believed one of the goals of the military in the Second World War was that "the country needed a greater appreciation of the costs of sovereignty."[58] As Bruce Hutchison said, "As a result of … foolish economies, Canada entered the war virtually defenceless, not only by King's leadership, or lack of it, but by general consent of Parliament and people. All this was an ostrich policy, or no policy at all…. Canada pulled down the blinds and hid under the bed."[59]

After a few years Jimmy Edwards, the Battleford, Saskatchewan, teenager turned into Wing Commander "Stocky" Edwards, an RCAF fighter pilot in North Africa and one of the deadliest aces of the air force. The airmen who were joining up by the thousands included Russ Bannock from Edmonton, who had watched the king and queen from the steps of the Alberta Legislature. Later in the war he had the hair-raising job of chasing V-1 rockets and shooting them down. Very successfully, too. Ned Amy never grew much taller but still became a battle-savvy tank officer in Normandy, and after the war a brigadier general. After winning a Distinguished Service Cross at Dunkirk, Skinny Hayes went on to service in the Royal Canadian Navy in the Battle of the Atlantic. Later in the war he was commander of the corvette HMCS *Guelph*. Robert Welland went from being a junior officer on HMS *Fame* to being the youngest commander of an RCN destroyer at age twenty-five. On being told of the appointment, his mother, reflecting the worries of mothers everywhere, wrote "Bobby, aren't you a bit young to be a destroyer captain?"[60] By the end of the war Welland would declare that he was the best-looking lieutenant commander from Oxbow, Saskatchewan, and before he was finished in the navy he would declare that he was the best-looking admiral from Oxbow, Saskatchewan.

Despite the woeful limits of the rearmament program — and Canadians hiding under the bed — the battles in the early going of the Second World War would rely heavily on those who had made their commitments to the army, navy, and air force in the interwar years or in the immediate months after war was declared. Call them The Originals, if you will. They're the ones we've been talking about. The men who put on uniforms (if they could find them) in the pre-war years came from Truro, Nova Scotia, and Rossland, British Columbia, and towns and cities strung in a thin line across Canada from east to west. Those who enlisted in the Canadian Active Service Force in 1939 included every type imaginable. They were the underaged, the immigrants from Eastern Europe and ex-Brits, men in business suits and old guys from the last war just itching to get in. They were divided about evenly in coming from farms, small towns, big towns, and cities.[61] Many had quit their jobs but some had been scrounging for a living, unemployed for months — men called the "breadliners."[62] The first thing when the breadliners signed up was to get rid of the lice. On the fortieth anniversary of the landing on the moon, Walt Cumming, one of the Apollo astronauts remarked, "there are things worth risking your life for."[63] The Originals would have agreed.

Many who joined up in 1939 were just kids who looked like they should be in school. They were jumping to the Dorsey Brothers or Glenn Miller or maybe Glen Gray's Casa Loma Orchestra — the last name perhaps coming from a Toronto night club that never opened. In his book, On The Triangle Run, James Lamb has a wonderful description of some of them enjoying their music, even though living in the shadow of war. "Couples would dance so closely that you couldn't tell where he ended and she began. Life was unbearably sweet and you simply perceived it would not always be thus."[64]

The Originals faced a thousand different turns ahead: good fortune, bad, promotion, illness, separation from loved ones, fear, injury. Worse. In the North Atlantic corvettes spent day after day heaving and sloshing their way to Derry and back. Boredom was as much the enemy as the submarine. One of the most famous messages of the war was sent from HMCS Coaticook to HMCS Levis during just such a time. It simply said "12 HEBREWS 8," which on checking the Bible read, "Jesus Christ, the same yesterday and today, and forever."

General McNaughton was dumped as commander of the First Canadian Army. McNaughton proclaimed the day of the scientific soldier but in the end he flamed out. He had helped to revolutionize artillery warfare in the First World War and was without doubt the most compelling military personality of the 1930s. Despite those achievements one examination of his leadership in the early years of the Second World War was titled "A Study in Failure."[65]

He had not acknowledged that his first responsibility was to prepare himself to lead troops into battle. Another assessment said "time demonstrated irrefutably that McNaughton's flaws as a commander, trainer, and national commander were serious indeed."[66] When it came to his obsession with equipment, some junior officers said he was forever having "attacks of the gadgets."[67] His genius lay elsewhere.

While some generals may have had their careers wrecked by being part of either the Hong Kong or Dieppe debacles, Harry Crerar, uniquely, survived both. Crerar being allowed to testify in writing at the Hong Kong inquiry rather than in person was a measure that there was still a war going on. But by1945 the two defeats seem to have been repressed in the collective memory while Crerar established himself as an army commander. One officer reflected the common thought in the army that Crerar, while not the best captain of the battlefield, still "spoke for Canada very effectively."[68] He was no Patton, but was still, as Granatstein said, a "competent soldier in a good, middle-ground Canadian way."[69]

Despite the horrors of Hong Kong, George MacDonell successfully rebuilt his life afterward. The children of Brian Carr-Harris, the pilot of the daring rescue in the high Arctic in the 1920s, would only have childhood memories of him. He died in an air crash in Quebec in 1942. Fred Woodcock, blinded at Dieppe, had to somehow rebuild his life. While Rear Admiral Murray became the only Canadian to command a theatre of operations during the war, his career was smashed by the ugly Halifax riots on VE Day. Hammy Gray put aside his university studies and his pacifist views to become Lieutenant Hampton Gray, an RCNVR pilot flying Corsair fighters in the Pacific. He was among the posthumous winners of the Victoria Cross.[70]

Even as soldiers, sailors, and airmen mobilized for war, Canada was still suffering painful reminders of the earlier war. On October 11, 1939, at Winnipeg's Victoria Hospital, Charlotte Wood died at seventy-eight. The mother who lost five sons. The Winnipeg *Free Press* wrote, "honoured by King and Country, Mrs. Charlotte S. Wood, Winnipeg's War Mother, was paid silent tribute as the body was lowered to its last resting place at Brookeside Cemetery." She had sent eleven sons to serve in the Great War and was Canada's first Silver Cross Mother.[71]

Skip ahead a few years when weaknesses in equipment, training, and leadership had been ruthlessly exposed and the penalties for those weaknesses paid — think Dieppe or Hong Kong for a start. The Originals and

Library and Archives Canada

Hampton Gray, VC. From pacifist student to Pacific war pilot. Like many young people of the time, Hampton Gray's attitudes toward war changed dramatically within a few years.

those who came later set about learning how to win a war. By the time the war ended Canada could boast the fourth largest air force in the world. Canadians paid a fearful price in the wartime air battles. Of the 249,662 Canadians who served in the air force's war, 17,101 died. In air raids over Germany alone, it is sometimes forgotten that almost 10,000 Canadians were killed. One of many ironies of the times was that King supported air force rearmament because he thought there would be fewer casualties than in a ground war, but the casualties among air crews were far higher than he or most experts expected.

The RCN lost thirty-three ships and close to 2,000 officers and men. Canadian sailors fought the Battle of the Atlantic for 2,055 days, learning how to run a warship but also learning about the navy's pride, traditions, and its mystique. By 1944 it had faster frigates and improved corvettes, better radar, asdic, and weapons with the result that by the end of the war the RCN had acquitted itself with distinction. It sank or captured forty-six of the 632 German U-boats lost at sea. The Royal Canadian Navy and Canada had every reason to be proud of what it achieved, especially in light of the stupendous obstacles it overcame in the early years. By the way, one of the most dreadful statistics of the time shows the effectiveness of the allied navies by 1945. By one reckoning three out of every four U-boat sailors did not survive the war.

Women had to wait a long time to contribute their full share in the armed forces. It was only in 1942 that the Women's Royal Canadian Naval Service was formed. Finally all three services had women's divisions. That, of course, says nothing of the role women played on the home front.

As for the army, by the end of 1943 it had more than a quarter of a million men and women in it. Victories in many places including Normandy, Holland, and the Hitler and Gothic Lines in Italy were a demonstration that Canadians had no peers in action. In Normandy Sidney Radley-Walters thought Canadians had risen above the calamity of unpreparedness to become the best soldiers on any battlefield in the Second World War.[72] Rad's comments (he was Major Rad, then Lieutenant Colonel Rad, and eventually all the way up to Brigadier General Rad after the war) may be unsurprising. What else would a Canadian soldier say? But his opinion comes with some clout: he had seven tanks shot out from under him and survived. He became the best known Canadian tank commander and one of the most honoured men of the war. Not to be taken lightly. Meantime, Ned Amy summarized his feelings about the army on the outbreak of war, saying "I think that we did what we could with what we had."[73] That so many young volunteers turned out to be sterling soldiers, quick to learn, grousing a lot certainly, not a few of them with some time in the pokey for misbehaving, but nevertheless, smart and with a spirit of dedication, is miraculous. John A. English summed them up — and it would be just as true of the navy and the air force — by saying, "Canada possibly never deserved such an army, the likes of which it will probably never see again.[74]

In an address in honour of Remembrance Day, Jack Granatstein said:

> Canadians faced and defeated the best army in the world and that says much. The same must be said of the aircrew who delivered wholly justifiable retribution on the Reich and the sailors who learned on the job and swept the North Atlantic clean of U-boats. The record in [both] World War One and World War Two was stellar, astonishing for a small country mainly fighting for others' national interests — but in defence of our values.[75]

In the same speech he also included comments that applied to the First World War and conflicts after 1945, including the most recent in Afghanistan. "We live in relative peace, in freedom, in prosperity because Canadians have been willing to fight and die to keep this country secure. This matters every day. We must never forget this."

One by one the units of the First Canadian Infantry Division made final preparations to go overseas. On November 1, 1939, the 48th Highlanders of Canada, Canadian Active Service Force, were inspected by Major General McNaughton at the University Avenue Armoury in Toronto. Only a month later, its new commanding officer, Lieutenant Colonel Eric Haldenby, along with the battalion's Headquarters Company and D Company boarded trains for Halifax. A second train with senior battalion officers and A, B, and C companies aboard pulled out of the Toronto station an hour later. The regiment's advance party, which included the newly married Trum Warren, the officer who had been headed for a stag party the night the regiment was mobilized, was already in England. His wedding to Mary Wigle of Hamilton went ahead on September 9 just as planned.[76] Trum Warren was in Europe as his father, Captain Trumbell Warren, had been before him. Captain Warren had been killed in France on April 20, 1915, only a few weeks before his son was born back in Canada. So in 1939 another generation was returning to the battlefields of Europe. The younger Trum Warren became an intelligence specialist and a most unusual job awaited him later in the war. He became an aide-de-camp to General Bernard Montgomery who revered Warren almost as his own son.

Any close observer watching the troops in the 48th Highlanders and other regiments leaving for Britain would have found the scene revealing. There were signs of how much still had to be done. A civilian raincoat here and a civilian suitcase there. Many men were still wearing First World War webbing and one man wore a First World War hat. There were still no tanks in the division. Some artillerymen hoped to have the new twenty-five-pounder gun/howitzer with them but there were none in Canada and no factories tooled up to produce them. Britain held the patents and restricted the manufacturing of the twenty-five-pounder so it was only after horrendous losses of May 1940, that the patents were released. As for the training of the troops before they left, Felix Carriere of the PPCLI would later recall how much he had not encountered and how little he had. "The only training I did encounter was firing a .303 rifle at the ranges to see if we could hold a rifle."[77]

The 48th Highlanders was not the first battalion to leave but among the first. Earlier almost 7,500 soldiers had left on December 10, while the last members of the division did not arrive in Britain until February 1940. The Calgary Highlanders were disappointed because they were not in the First Division but that wasn't all. Most of the regiment's web equipment and rifles had to be handed over to the Edmonton Regiment which was in the First Division. Worse, the Calgarys had to send a large draft of men to the Edmontons to bring them up to strength.[78]

Once the 48th Highlanders arrived in Halifax the battalion became part of convoy TC-2 with seven troop ships in all. Those arriving would have been reassured to see their escorts including the battleship HMS *Revenge* (with Vice-Admiral Holland aboard), two big French ships, the *Dunkerque* and *Gloire*, along with the Canadian destroyers *Ottawa*, *Fraser*, *Restigouche*, and *St. Laurent*. *St. Laurent*, by the way, had a new captain on the bridge, Lieutenant Commander Harry DeWolf, later famous as captain of HMCS *Haida*. Somewhere in among the khaki crowd was Eddy Ganong, who had earlier answered the phone to hear the historic order, "Mobilize." That seemed like a long time ago. Ganong was now Major Ganong and in 1942 he would command the regiment.[79] Ganong and the other Highlanders boarded His Majesty's Transport *Reina del Pacifico*, a former Pacific Steam Navigation liner.

The convoy set sail on December 22. For air cover, the Lockheed Hudsons of the RCAF were at the ready. The twin stacks of *Reina del Pacifico* blackened with smoke and, with troops all along the rail, the liner slowly gained way. As the land off Halifax stepped into the sea, on the upper deck of *Reina*, the 48th Highlanders' pipe band played and played until the ship was reduced to a smudge in the distance.

Some of the men did not return for six years. Others never did.

APPENDIX

MILITARY ENLISTMENTS BY PROVINCE

Province	Male Population (18–45)	RCN	Army	RCAF	Total	% Male Population (18–45)
Prince Edward Island	19,000	1,448	6,333	1,528	9,309	48.18%
Nova Scotia	123,000	6,837	45,020	7,498	59,355	48.31%
New Brunswick	94,000	2,737	35,947	6,453	45,137	48.17%
Quebec	699,000	12,404	138,269	24,768	175,441	25.69%
Ontario	830,000	40,353	266,937	90,518	397,808	47.77%
Manitoba	159,000	7,782	48,542	20,120	76,444	48.12%
Saskatchewan	191,000	6,472	52,306	21,827	80,605	42.38%
Alberta	178,000	7,360	50,844	19,499	77,703	43.11%
British Columbia	181,000	11,925	58,246	20,805	90,976	50.47%
Outside Canada	-	893	5,892	5,900	16,278	-
Not Stated	-	263	191	-	454	-
TOTAL	**2,474,000**	**98,474**	**708,535**	**222,501**	**1,029,510**	**41.15%**

Source: C.P. Stacey. *Arms, Men and Governments: The War Policies of Canada 1939–1945*. Ottawa: The Queen's Printer for Canada, 1970, 590. Note that the Quebec figures included many English speaking Quebeckers but there is no breakdown between English and French Quebeckers included.

NOTES

CHAPTER ONE

1. Kim Beattie, *Dileas: History of the 48th Highlanders of Canada, 1929–1956* (Toronto: 48th Highlanders of Canada, 1957), 37ff.

2. Jack Batten, *The Spirit of the Regiment: An Account of the 48th Highlanders from 1956 to 1991* (Toronto: 48th Highlanders of Canada, 1991), 30.

3. Bruce Hutchison, *The Incredible Canadian* (Toronto: Longmans Canada, 1953), 249.

4. *Canada Gazette*, vol. LXXXIII, no. 11, 728.

5. W.A.B. Douglas, Roger Sarty, et al., *No Higher Purpose: The Official Operational History of the Royal Canadian Navy in the Second World War, 1939-1943*, vol. 2, part 1 (St. Catharines, Ontario: Vanwell Publishing Ltd., 2004), 52.

6. Major E. G. Weeks's diary in J.L. Granatstein and Norman Hillmer, *Battle Lines: Eyewitness Accounts from Canada's Military History* (Toronto: Thomas Allen Publishers, 2004), 240.

7. Howard Graham, *Citizen and Soldier: The Memoirs of Lieutenant-General Howard Graham* (Toronto: McClelland & Stewart, 1987), 99.

8. Farley Mowat, *The Regiment* (St. Catharines, Ontario: Vanwell Publishing Ltd., 2007), 4.

9. George S. MacDonell, *One Soldier's Story: 1939–1945: From the Fall of Hong Kong to the Defeat of Japan* (Toronto: Dundurn, 2002), 21.

10. David J. Bercuson, *The Patricias: The Proud History of a Fighting Regiment* (Toronto: Stoddart Publishing, 2001), 149.

11. E.A.C. Amy, interview by Larry D. Rose, April 8, 2008.

12. Reginald H. Roy, *The Seaforth Highlanders of Canada, 1919–1965* (Vancouver: Seaforth Highlanders of Canada, 1969), 51.

13. John Marteinson and Michael R. McNorgan, *The Royal Canadian Armoured Corps: An Illustrated History* (Toronto: Royal Canadian Armoured Corps Association, 2000), 76ff; Roger V. Lucy, *Early Armour In Canadian Service* (Ottawa: Service Publications, 2009), 18.

14. Roger Sarty, *The Maritime Defence of Canada* (Toronto: Canadian Institute of Strategic Studies, 1997), 232ff.

15. Stewart A. Mein, *Up the Johns!: The Story of the Royal Regina Rifles* (Regina: Senate of the Royal Regina Rifles, 1992), 91.

16. "The Week We Went to War," *Toronto Star*, August 30, 2009, anniversary article. Horst Wessel, an SA officer in Berlin, was an unlikely Nazi martyr. He was beaten up and killed by communist thugs. They had been called in because of a dispute Wessel and his prostitute girl friend had over unpaid rent. David Clay Large, *Berlin* (London: Basic Books, 2001), 237.

17. *Globe and Mail*, September 2, 1939.

18. Brian Nolan, *King's War: Mackenzie King and the Politics of War, 1939–1945* (Toronto: Random House of Canada, Ltd., 1990), 46ff.

19. N. Robertson Papers, "Statistics on Internment," January 3, 1941, in J.L. Granatstein, *A Man of Influence: Norman A. Robertson and Canadian Statecraft* (Toronto: Deneau Publishers, 1981), 90. According to Statistics Canada there were about 474,000 ethnic Germans in Canada, 98,000 Italians, 146,000 Polish, and 225,000 Ukrainians. See J.H. Thompson, *Ethnic Minorities During Two World Wars* (Ottawa: Canadian Historical Association, 1991), 14. As many as 35,000 Ukrainians later served in the armed forces at an enlistment rate that matched Canada as a whole.

20. Nolan, *King's War*, 48. Houde was an outspoken opponent of conscription and registering with the government for possible conscription.

21. Much later, after the Japanese attack on Pearl Harbor and Hong Kong, thousands of Japanese Canadians on the west coast were rounded up and spent the remainder of the war in camps and abandoned mining communities in the British Columbia interior and Alberta.

22. C.P. Stacey, *Six Years of War: The Army in Canada, Britain and the Pacific*, vol.1 (Ottawa: Department of National Defence, 1955), 40–42; Douglas et al., *No Higher Purpose*, 49–50.

23. W.A.B. Douglas, *The Official History of Royal Canadian Air Force*, vol. 2, *The Creation of a National Air Force* (Toronto: University of Toronto Press, 1986), 151.

24. D.J. Goodspeed, ed., *The Armed Forces of Canada 1867–1967: A Century of Achievement* (Ottawa: Canadian Forces Headquarters, Directorate of History, Queen's Printer, 1967), 96; Also Sarty, *The Maritime Defence of Canada*, 233.

25. John Gordon Quigley, *A Century of Rifles, 1860–1960: The Halifax Rifles* (Halifax: William McNab and Son, 1960), 111ff.

26. After the Second World War, the New Brunswick Rangers reorganized as part of the Royal New Brunswick Regiment.

27. Jeffrey A. Keshen, *Saints, Sinners, and Soldiers: Canada's Second World War* (Vancouver: UBC Press, 2004), 35.

28. James A. Boutilier, ed., *The RCN in Retrospect, 1910–1968* (Vancouver: UBC Press, 1982), 71.

29. Marc Milner, *Canada's Navy: The First Century* (Toronto: University of Toronto Press, 1999), 81. Milner says the boilers of both ships collapsed once they reached Halifax.

30. Douglas et al., *No Higher Purpose*, 53.

31. Headlines from the *Ottawa Journal* and the *Ottawa Citizen*, September 2, 1939.

32. *Toronto Telegram*, September 4, 1939.

33. Barbara Hehner, *The Desert Hawk: The True Story of Stocky Edwards, World War II Flying Ace* (Toronto: Harper Trophy Canada, 2005), 7–11.

34. J.L. Granatstein and Desmond Morton, *A Nation Forged in Fire: Canadians and the Second World War, 1939–1945* (Toronto: Lester and Orpen Dennys, 1989), 2; Stacey, *Six Years of War*, 46.

35. Lemp was killed in U-110 on May 9, 1941.

36. Robert Welland, interviews by Larry D. Rose, January 11, 2008, and May 17, 2008. Robert Welland, *This Will Have to Do*, unpublished memoir.

37. Account of *Athenia* sinking from I. Miller, "Toronto's Response to the Outbreak of War — 1939," *Canadian Military History*, Winter 2002, 8; Nathan Miller, *War At Sea: A Naval History of World War II* (Oxford: Oxford University Press, 1995) 17–20.

38. Bill McNeil and Morris Wolfe, *Signing On: The Birth of Radio in Canada* (Toronto: Doubleday, 1982), 72.

39. Michael L. Hadley, *U-Boats Against Canada: German Submarines in Canadian Waters* (Montreal: McGill-Queens University Press, 1985), 13.

40. Granatstein and Morton, *A Nation Forged in Fire*, 173.

41. Stacey, *Six Years of War*, 35.

42. J.L. Granatstein, *The Generals* (Toronto: Stoddart Publishing, 1993), 9.

43. Chris Vokes with John P. Maclean, *Vokes: My Story* (Ottawa: Gallery Books, 1985), 63.

44. Amy, interview.

45. Stacey, *Six Years of War*, 34.

46. *Ibid.*, 57.

47. G. Drew, "Canada's Defence Farce," *Financial Post*, March 26, 1938.

48. Granatstein and Morton, *A Nation Forged In Fire*, 13.

49. Stacey, *Six Years of War*, 57.

50. G. Nicholson, *The Gunners of Canada*, vol. 2 (Toronto: McClelland & Stewart, 1972), 37–38.

51. Stacey, *Six Years of War*, 36.

52. *Ibid.*, 41.

53. G. Nicholson, *The Gunners of Canada*, vol. 2 (Toronto: McClelland & Stewart, 1967), 37-38.

54. As dreadful as the army's situation was, one view is that it was worse in the navy. C.P. Stacey, *The Military Problems of Canada: A Survey of Defence Policies and Strategic Conditions Past and Present* (Toronto: Ryerson Press, 1940), 116. Also see Footnote 52. Marc Milner, however, says the navy was better prepared than some believe. See Marc Milner "On a War Footing: Navy," *Legion Magazine*. January 1, 2007.

55. Tony German, *The Sea Is at Our Gates: A History of the Canadian Navy* (Toronto: McClelland & Stewart, 1990), 71; Douglas et al., *No Higher Purpose*, 32.

56. M. Lynch, *Salty Dips*, vol. 1 (Ottawa: Naval Officers' Association of Canada, Ottawa Branch, 1985), 112; Also, Douglas et al., *No Higher Purpose*, 32–33.

57. Joseph Schull, *The Far Distant Ships: An Official Account of Canadian Naval Operations in the Second World War* (Toronto: Stoddart Publishing, 1987), 34.

58. One example with comic overtones came in 1943. The RCN promoted HMCS *Haida*'s Harry DeWolf from commander to captain. The British then had to promote the "senior officer" of the flotilla DeWolf was working with so the RN officer would not be outranked. The RN officer was delighted. Fraser McKee and Robert Darlington, *The Canadian Naval Chronicle, 1939-1945* (St. Catharines, Ontario: Vanwell Publishing Ltd., 1996), 143.

59. National Defence Headquarters, Bulletins on the Development of the RCAF, August 25–December 31, 1939, Directorate of History and Heritage, 181.003 (D3868), as quoted in Douglas, *The Official History of Royal Canadian Air Force*, 343.

60. Douglas, *The Official History of Royal Canadian Air Force*, 150.

61. Brereton Greenhous et al., *The Crucible of War 1939-1945*, vol. 3 (Toronto: University of Toronto Press, 1994), 16.

62. S. Kostenuk and J. Griffin, *RCAF Squadrons Histories and Aircraft: 1924-1968* (Toronto: Samuel Stevens Hakkert, 1977), 24.

63. W.A.B. Douglas and Brereton Greenhous, *Out of the Shadows: Canada in the Second World War*, revised edition (Toronto: Dundurn, 1996), 34.

64. *Ibid.*

65. Nora Bottomley, *424 Squadron History: A Detailed Pictoral History of 424 Squadron (RCAF) From Its Origins in 1935 to Modern Times* (Belleville, Ontario: Hangar Bookshelf, 1985), 17.

66. Douglas, *The Official History of Royal Canadian Air Force*, 346; C.L. Annis interview, 1977, C.L. Annis biographical file, Department of History and Heritage.

67. Stacey, *Canada and the Age of Conflict*, 254.

68. William Lyon Mackenzie King, "Diaries of Prime Minister William Lyon Mackenzie King," Library and Archives Canada, www.collectionscanada.gc.ca/databases/king/index-e.html, August 24, 1939.

69. King sometimes called Roosevelt "Franklin," but more often "Mr. President." Churchill copied Roosevelt in addressing King as "Mackenzie." H. Reginald Hardy, *Mackenzie King of Canada*, 2nd edition (Westport, Connecticut: Greenwood Press, 1970), 176.

70. Nolan, *King's War*, 53.

71. Stacey, *Canada and the Age of Conflict*, 307.

72. Tweedsmuir was more famous as John Buchan, author of the thriller *The Thirty-Nine Steps*. He had earlier been a colonial administrator and an MP in Britain.

73. Naval Service Headquarters to COAC, COPC, *Fraser, St Laurent*, etc., memo, Dist, NHS1650 (Operations General) pt 2.

CHAPTER TWO

1. Hugh A. Halliday, "The Imperial Gift," *Legion Magazine*, September 1, 2004.

2. The Avro 504K used a Clerget engine that had one unpleasant characteristic — its lubricant leaked through the cylinders and valves and covered the aircraft. The lubricant was castor oil, notorious for its unpleasant dead fish odour. Everything reeked of castor oil, and since it splashed all over the pilot too, no flyer was in danger of suffering from constipation. N. Marion ed., *Camp Borden: Birthplace of the RCAF, 1917–1999* (Borden, Ontario: 16 Wing, 2004), 57.

3. W.A.B. Douglas, *The Official History of Royal Canadian Air Force*, vol. 2, *The Creation of a National Air Force* (Toronto: University of Toronto Press, 1986), 47–64.

4. Tim Cook, *Shock Troops: Canadians Fighting the Great War 1917–1918* (Toronto: Penguin Books Canada, 2008), 54.

5. Cook, *Shock Troops*, 611.

6. Serge Bernier, *The Royal 22e Regiment, 1914–1999* (Montreal: Art Global, 1999), 77ff; Also J.L. Granatstein, *The Generals* (Toronto: Stoddart Publishing, 1993), 14.

7. John Swettenham, *McNaughton*, vol. 1, *1887–1939* (Toronto: Ryerson Press, 1968), 189; George F.G. Stanley, *Canada's Soldiers, 1604–1954: The Military History of an Unmilitary People* (Toronto: Macmillan, 1960), 339, 345.

8. Stewart A. Mein, *Up the Johns!: The Story of the Royal Regina Rifles* (Regina: Senate of the Royal Regina Rifles, 1992), 78.

9. Bradley T. Shoebottom, "The Disposal of Canadian Equipment After World War One," *The Royal Military College*, 1993, 1–12.

10. The early history from Marc Milner, *Canada's Navy: The First Century* (Toronto: University of Toronto Press, 1999), 72.

11. James A. Boutilier, ed., *The RCN in Retrospect, 1910–1968* (Vancouver: UBC Press, 1982), 64.

12. C. Lancaster, "The Little Known Navy," *Starshell*, No. 57, Winter 2011/12, 22.

13. Mac Johnston, *Corvettes Canada: Convoy Veterans of WWII Tell Their True Stories* (Toronto: John Wiley & Sons, 2008), 15.

14. Donald E. Graves, *In Peril on the Sea: The Royal Canadian Navy and the Battle of the Atlantic* (Toronto: Robin Brass Studio Inc., 2003), 44.

15. House of Commons Debates, June 16, 1920, 3646. Other material in this section from Desmond Morton, *Canada and War: A Military and Political History* (Toronto: Butterworths, 1981), 92.

16. Morton, *Canada and War*, 92–93.

17. House of Commons Debates, 1927, 2203.

18. Harry Foster was later a major general and divisional commander. Tony Foster, *Meeting of Generals* (Toronto: Methuen, 1986), 62; J.L. Granatstein, *Canada's Army: Waging War and Keeping the Peace* (Toronto: University of Toronto Press, 2002), 147.

19. John Page, interview, February 11, 1992. Toronto Scottish Regiment Archives.

20. Granatstein, *The Generals*, 280.

21. Mein, *Up the Johns*, 78ff.

22. Kim Beattie, *Dileas: History of the 48th Highlanders of Canada, 1929–1956* (Toronto: 48th Highlanders of Canada, 1957) 34.

23. Marion, *Camp Borden*, 46.

24. C.R. Slemon, interview, October 20, 1978, Slemon File, Department of History and Heritage.

25. Marion, *Camp Borden*, 57.

26. Douglas, *The Official History of Royal Canadian Air Force*, 109.

27. Robert Carr-Harris's children and nephews include Captain F.F. Carr-Harris, DSO, MC, a medical missionary in China, and a doctor in the First World War; Major G.M.M. Carr-Harris, who served in both the First and Second World War; Lieutenant Colonel L.H. Carr-Harris, OBE, of the Royal Artillery; and Brian, an RMC graduate in 1924. Information from: R. McKenzie, RMC Museum, e-mail messages to author, February 2010; M.P. Carr-Harris (son of Brian Carr-Harris), interview by Larry D. Rose, May 30, 2010. B. Carr-Harris Service Record, DND. There is still a Carr-Harris hockey game played between RMC and Queen's every year.

28. C.P. Stacey, *Canada and the Age of Conflict*, vol. 2, *1921–1948, The Mackenzie King Era* (Toronto: University of Toronto Press, 1981), 61.

29. James Eayrs, *In Defence of Canada*, vol. 1, *From the Great War to the Great Depression* (Toronto: University of Toronto Press, 1965), 173–84; C.P. Stacey, "From Meighen to King: The Reversal of Canadian External Policies, 1921–1923" *Transactions of the Royal Society of Canada*, series IV, 7 (Ottawa: Royal Society of Canada, 1969), 233–46.

30. Graves, *In Peril On The Sea*, 35. Eayrs, *In Defence of Canada*, vol. 1, 271, gives credit to "the energetic" James Ralston.

31. Larry Milberry, *Canada's Air Force at War and Peace*, vol. 1 (Toronto: CANAV Books, 2000), 50 and 98ff.

32. F. Gobeil, "Siskin Pilot," in Marion, *Camp Borden*, 58.

33. Douglas, *The Official History of Royal Canadian Air Force*, 122.

34. J.S. Brown service record, Department of National Defence.

35. Stacey, *Canada and the Age of Conflict*, 155ff; Eayrs, *In Defence of Canada*, vol. 1, 70ff.

36. While Admiral Ernest J. King was rabidly against British imperialism, he was not alone in examining the British threat. Thomas B. Buell, *Master of Sea Power: A Biography of Fleet Admiral Ernest J. King* (Annapolis, Maryland: Naval Institute Press, 1995), 145.

37. Stacey, *Canada and the Age of Conflict*, 156–57.

38. Stephen John Harris, *Canadian Brass: The Making of a Professional Army, 1890–1939* (Toronto: University of Toronto Press, 1988), 205.

39. *New York Times*, April 16, 1995. Brown's conduct has been much criticized, but Granatstein says that while Brown was very anti-American he was far from "barking mad." Granatstein, *Canada's Army*, 169. John A. English says Brown's portrayal as "a bigoted blockhead" is almost certainly unfair. John A. English, *The Canadian Army and the Normandy Campaign: A Study of Failure in High Command* (Westport, Connecticut: Praeger, 1991), 271, Footnote 36.

40. W.W. Goforth, a young militia lieutenant from Montreal, won the *Canadian Defence Quarterly* essay prize in 1932 by arguing that preparing only for another European war would be "narrow-sighted." Should home defence become necessary, he argued, the "close" conditions of Europe were no guide to the defence of Canada's wide open spaces. Harris, *Canadian Brass*, 205.

41. Eayrs, *In Defence of Canada*, vol. 1, 258.

42. John Nelson Rickard, *The Politics of Command: Lieutenant-General A.G.L. McNaughton and the Canadian Army, 1939–1943* (Toronto: University of Toronto Press, 2010), 4.

43. Swettenham, *McNaughton*, 106–07; G. Nicholson, *The Gunners of Canada*, vol. 1 (Toronto: McClelland & Stewart, 1967), 314–15.

44. Swettenham, *McNaughton*, 107. McNaughton's account gives the range of the railway gun as 68,000 yards.

45. Nicholson, *The Gunners of Canada*, vol. 1, 282.

46. Rickard, *The Politics of Command*, quoting Bill Rawlings "Surviving Trench Warfare," 111–12.

47. Such British generals as Bernard Montgomery did have brigade and command experience. Also see Rickard, *Politics of Command*, 23–24.

48. W.A.B. Douglas and Brereton Greenhous, *Out of the Shadows: Canada in the Second World War*, revised edition (Toronto: Dundurn, 1996), 27.

Chapter Three

1. Pierre Berton, *The Great Depression: 1929–1939* (Toronto: McClelland & Stewart, 1990), 24.

2. Dr. Irving Fisher, quoted in the *Globe and Mail*, November 17, 2010. It's the fourth on the list of "Worst Predictions of all Time," http://shareranks.com/499,The-Worst-Predictions-Ever#b.

3. John Marteinson and Michael R. McNorgan, *The Royal Canadian Armoured Corps: An Illustrated History* (Toronto: Royal Canadian Armoured Corps Association, 2000), 66.

4. Berton, *The Great Depression*, 23. Berton says the police violently broke up many of the events, despite the fact that most were completely peaceful.

5. Bruce Hutchison, *The Incredible Canadian* (Toronto: Longmans Canada, 1953), 156–57.

6. C.P. Stacey, *Canada and the Age of Conflict*, vol. 2, *1921–1948, The Mackenzie King Era* (Toronto: University of Toronto Press, 1981), 122; Berton, *The Great Depression*, 71.

7. Stacey, *Canada and the Age of Conflict*, 103. Woodsworth was at this time a member of the Independent Labour Party but became leader of the CCF after its formation in 1932. Macphail, the first woman Member of Parliament in Canada, was a member of the Progressive Party but later also joined the CCF.

8. Memo, March 23, 1931, in James Eayrs, *In Defence of Canada*, vol. 1, *From the Great War to the Great Depression* (Toronto: University of Toronto Press, 1965), 288.

9. Another union strike was at Sydney Mines, Nova Scotia in 1925. Among the army troops was Guy Simonds, a later lieutenant general, but at this time a young artillery officer. J.L. Granatstein, *The Generals* (Toronto: Stoddart Publishing, 1993), 149.

10. Morton, *Canada and War*, 97; Eayrs, *In Defence of Canada*, vol. 1, 288.

11. Ray Stouffer, "Air Chief Marshal Frank Miller — A Civilian and Military Leader," *Canadian Forces Journal*, vol. 10, no. 2. www.journal.forces.gc.ca/vol10/no2/08.

12. Miller was able to re-join the air force in 1933. He became an air chief marshal after the war, and later chairman of the chiefs of staff committee.

13. M. Carr-Harris, interview by Larry D. Rose, May 30, 2010.

14. Memorandum for Chief of Defence Staff by the Deputy Minister, Department of National Defence, December 19, 1932.

15. Eayrs, *In Defence of Canada*, vol. 1, 298.

16. Max Braithwaite, *The Hungry Thirties, 1930–1940* (Toronto: Natural Science of Canada, Ltd., 1977), 59.

17. W.A.B. Douglas, *The Official History of Royal Canadian Air Force*, vol. 2, *The Creation of a National Air Force* (Toronto: University of Toronto Press, 1986), 124–25.

18. Larry Milberry, *Sixty Years: The RCAF And CF Command, 1924–1984* (Toronto: CANAV Books, 1984), 47.

19. S. Kostenuk and J. Griffin, *RCAF Squadrons Histories and Aircraft: 1924–1968* (Toronto: Samuel Stevens Hakkert, 1977), 18.

20. Jeff Noakes, "Air Marshal Wilfred Curtis," in Bernd Horn and Stephen Harris, eds., *Warrior Chiefs: Perspectives on Senior Canadian Military Chiefs* (Toronto: Dundurn, 2000), 237ff.

21. George Randolph Pearkes, interviews by Reginald Roy, 1966. University of Victoria Archives.

22. Report of the Chief of the General Staff on the Imperial Conference, 1930, McNaughton Papers, in John Swettenham, *McNaughton*, vol. 1, *1887–1939* (Toronto: Ryerson Press, 1968), 226.

23. Desmond Morton, *Canada and War: A Military and Political History* (Toronto: Butterworths, 1981), 96; Marteinson and McNorgan, *The Royal Canadian Armoured Corps*, 68.

24. Roger V. Lucy, *Early Armour in Canadian Service* (Ottawa: Service Publications, 2009), 10.

25. *Ibid.*, 11.

26. Morton, *Canada and War*, 96.

27. Swettenham, *McNaughton*, 229.

28. Address to the United Services Institute, Montreal, December 10, 1921, in Swettenham, *McNaughton*, 229; John A. English, *The Canadian Army and the Normandy Campaign: A Study of Failure in High Command* (Westport, Connecticut: Praeger, 1991), 45–46.

29. John A. English, *Lament for an Army: The Decline of Canadian Military Professionalism* (Toronto: Irwin, 1998), 21; English, *The Canadian Army and the Normandy Campaign*, 240.

30. See, for instance, the role of Guderian in Ronald E. Powaski, *Lightning War: Blitzkreig in the West, 1940* (Toronto: John Wiley and Sons, 2002), 45ff.

31. Both Guy Simonds and E.L.M. Burns, among others, commented in *Canadian Defence Quarterly*; Also see, for example, Lieutenant Colonel H.F. Letson, "The Influence of Mechanization and Motorization Application on the Organization and Tactics of the Non-Permanent Active Militia," *Canadian Defence Quarterly*, 1933.

32. Granatstein, *The Generals*, 19.

33. Lieutenant Colonel N.O. Carr, CAA Annual Report, 1932, in G. Nicholson, *The Gunners of Canada*, vol. 2 (Toronto: McClelland & Stewart, 1972), 38.

34. Eayrs, *In Defence of Canada*, vol. 1, 311.

35. A.A.G. Smith letter in J.L. Granatstein, *Canada's Army: Waging War and Keeping the Peace* (Toronto: University of Toronto Press, 2002), 161.

36. Fred Woodcock, referred to in *Toronto Star*, August 31, 1989.

37. Douglas E. Harker, *The Dukes* (Vancouver: The British Columbia Regiment, 1974), 169.

38. George F.G. Stanley, *Canada's Soldiers, 1604–1954: The Military History of an Unmilitary People* (Toronto: Macmillan, 1960), 399.

39. Eayrs, *In Defence of Canada*, vol. 1, 311–12.

40. Stephen John Harris, *Canadian Brass: The Making of a Professional Army, 1890–1939* (Toronto: University of Toronto Press, 1988), 152ff.

41. Swettenham, *McNaughton*, 205.

42. Roger Sarty, *The Maritime Defence of Canada* (Toronto: Canadian Institute of Strategic Studies, 1997), 91.

43. English, *The Canadian Army and the Normandy Campaign*, 43. English describes McNaughton as a close personal friend of Bennett.

44. Eayrs, *In Defence of Canada*, vol. 1, 261.

45. Swettenham, *McNaughton*, 227.

46. Eayrs, *In Defence of Canada*, vol. 1, 274; Harris, *Canadian Brass*, 156.

47. Swettenham, *McNaughton*, 316.

48. The description of Hose from Eayrs, who interviewed him. Eayrs, *In Defence of Canada*, vol. 1, 238. This section also based on William Glover, "Commodore Walter Hose: Ordinary Officer Extraordinary Endeavour," in Michael Whitby et al., *The Admirals: Canada's Senior Naval Leadership in the Twentieth Century* (Toronto: Dundurn, 2006), 55ff.

49. Eayrs, *In Defence of Canada*, vol. 1, 266–67.

50. *Ibid.*, 272–83.

51. Marc Milner, *Canada's Navy: The First Century* (Toronto: University of Toronto Press, 1999), 69.

52. Swettenham, *McNaughton*, 26.

53. Admiral Sir Ernle Chatfield, August 1936, in Lawrence R. Pratt, *East of Malta, West of Suez: Britain's Mediterranean Crisis, 1936–1939* (Cambridge, U.K.: Cambridge University Press, 1975), 3.

54. Richard J. Gwyn, *John A: The Man Who Made Us, The Life and Times of John A, Macdonald* (Toronto: Random House, 2007), 264.

55. M. Pope, *Soldiers and Politicians* (Toronto: University of Toronto Press, 1962), 99.

56. Norman Hillmer, "Defence and Ideology: The Anglo-Canadian Military 'Alliance' in the 1930s," *International Journal*, vol. XXXIII, Summer, 1978, 588, 591–92.

57. This section based on Whitley et al., *The Admirals*, 69ff; Milner, *Canada's Navy*, 70ff.

58. Kenneth Hansen, "The Destroyer Myth," *Canadian Naval Review*, vol. 3, no. 3, 2006, 6.

59. *Ibid.*

60. *Ibid.*, 5. The recommendation of Admiral Sir Ernle Chatfied made to the Canadian government in 1939. Hansen suggests the 900-ton Grimsby class escorts could have been purchased for one-third the cost of a Tribal destroyer.

61. Milner, *Canada's Navy*, 74.

62. See for example English, *The Canadian Army and the Normandy Campaign*.

63. Roman Jarymowycz, *Tank Tactics: From Normandy to Lorraine* (Mechanicsburg, Pennsylvania: Stackpole Books, 2009), 34.

64. McNaughton to Ralston, November 25, 1927, in Swettenam, *McNaughton*, 241.

65. C.P. Stacey, *Six Years of War: The Army in Canada, Britain and the Pacific*, vol.1 (Ottawa: Department of National Defence, 1955), 2, 21–22.

66. Morton, *Canada and War*, 96.

67. Stacey, *Six Years of War*, 22.

68. *Ibid.*

69. Harris, *Canadian Brass*, 167, 178.

70. Major General A.G.L. McNaughton, "The Defence of Canada," Memorandum, May 28, 1935, copy in Ian Mackenzie Papers, Library and Archives Canada, vol. 29, file x-4.

CHAPTER FOUR

1. William Lyon Mackenzie King, "Diaries of Prime Minister William Lyon Mackenzie King," Library and Archives Canada, www.collectionscanada.gc.ca/databases/king/index-e.html, October 13, 1935.

2. Sir John A. Macdonald had been the first prime minister to return to office back in 1878, while Pierre Trudeau became the third leader to do so in 1980.

3. Charles Ritchie, *The Siren Years: A Canadian Diplomat Abroad, 1937–1945* (Toronto: Macmillan, 1974), 187.

4. C.P. Stacey, *Mackenzie King and the Atlantic Triangle* (Toronto: Macmillan of Canada, 1976), xiii.

5. Desmond Morton, "Self Centeredness," *International History Review*, XVIII, February 1996, 207.

6. F.R. Scott, *The Eye of the Needle: Satire, Sorties, Sundries* (Montreal: Contact Press, 1957).

7. King's Diary, July 27, 1927.

8. C.P. Stacey, *Canada and the Age of Conflict*, vol. 2, *1921–1948, The Mackenzie King Era* (Toronto: University of Toronto Press, 1981), 17, 49.

9. C.P. Stacey, *A Very Double Life: The Private World of Mackenzie King* (Toronto: Macmillan of Canada, 1976), frontispiece.

10. J.L. Granatstein, CPAC Television interview, "William Lyon Mackenzie King."

11. Regrettably, today the room where the table sat holds the air conditioning equipment.

12. Stacey, *A Very Double Life*, 198. Stacey says, "Did he conduct the affairs of Canada in accordance with what he believed to be advice from the Beyond…. the answer is quite clearly No."

13. Granatstein, CPAC-TV interview.

14. Bruce Hutchison, *The Incredible Canadian* (Toronto: Longmans Canada, 1953), 155.

15. *Ibid.*, 5.

16. Stacey, *Mackenzie King and the Atlantic Triangle*, xv. Stacey says King was politically shrewd and had a retentive memory, but was not a first-rate intellect.

17. Ferns quoted in Allan Levine, *King: William Lyon Mackenzie King: A Life Guided by the Hand of Destiny* (Vancouver: Douglas & McIntyre, 2012), 270.

18. Hutchison, *The Incredible Canadian*, 3ff.

19. The stone bust of Kaiser Wilhelm mysteriously disappeared during the anti-German fever of the First World War and was never seen again. The plinth remains.

20. Ulrich Frisse, "The Missing Link: Mackenzie King and Canada's 'German Capital,'" in John English et al., eds. *Mackenzie King: Citizenship and Community* (Toronto: Robin Brass Studio, 2002), 18–34.

21. There has been criticism that King avoided First World War service. However, he was forty in 1914 and engaged in work that aided the war effort.

22. John Porter, *The Vertical Mosaic: An Analysis of Social Class and Power in Canada* (Toronto: University of Toronto Press, 1965), 135.

23. C.P. Stacey, *Arms, Men and Governments: The War Policies of Canada, 1939–1945* (Ottawa: The Queen's Printer, 1970), 70–71; George Randolph Pearkes, interviews by Reginald Roy, 1966, University of Victoria Archives; Stacey, *Canada and the Age of Conflict*, 100.

24. Ashton to Mackenzie, April 22, 1936, Ian Mackenzie Papers, Library and Archives Canada, vol. 29, file x-4; vol. 30, x-11.

25. C.P. Stacey, *Six Years of War: The Army in Canada, Britain and the Pacific*, vol.1 (Ottawa: Department of National Defence, 1955), 8.

26. This summary from C.P. Stacey, *The Military Problems of Canada: A Survey of Defence Policies and Strategic Conditions Past and Present* (Toronto: Ryerson Press, 1940), 96ff.

27. Department of National Defence figures. Stacey, *The Military Problems of Canada*, 173.

28. Stacey, *Six Years of War*, 8.

29. King's Diary, October 29, 1935.

30. H. Blair Neatby, *The Politics of Chaos: Canada in the Thirties* (Toronto: Macmillan of Canada, 1972), 170–71.

31. House of Commons Debates, 1937, 1142-3. The conclusion that the Ethiopian conflict was likely an excuse for King's inaction is in Stacey, *The Military Problems of Canada*, 98–99.

32. James Eayrs, *In Defence of Canada*, vol. 3, *Appeasement and Rearmament* (Toronto: University of Toronto Press, 1967), 135.

33. Larry Milberry, *Canada's Air Force at War and Peace*, vol. 1 (Toronto: CANAV Books, 2000), 98; Stacey, *The Military Problems of Canada*, 113.

34. W.A.B. Douglas, *The Official History of Royal Canadian Air Force*, vol. 2, *The Creation of a National Air Force* (Toronto: University of Toronto Press, 1986), 141.

35. Carl Vincent, *Canadian Aircraft of WWII* (Kitchener, Ontario: Aviaeology, 2009), 43–45.

36. Stacey, *The Military Problems of Canada*, 113.

37. Gerry Bell was later posted to No. 119 Squadron and after that, 424 Squadron. Nora Bottomley, *424 Squadron History: A Detailed Pictoral History of 424 Squadron (RCAF) From Its Origins in 1935 to Modern Times* (Belleville, Ontario: Hangar Bookshelf, 1985), 10.

38. Later Harry George DeWolf was the celebrated commander of the destroyer HMCS *Haida* and still later a vice-admiral.

39. Roger Sarty, "Rear-Admiral L.W. Murray and the battle of the Atlantic," in Bernd Horn and Stephen Harris, eds., *Warrior Chiefs: Perspectives on Senior Canadian Military Chiefs* (Toronto: Dundurn, 2000), 168.

40. *Maclean's*, July 1, 1935, 11. Keightley's type of business is not indicated.

41. Eayrs, *In Defence of Canada*, vol. 3, 177; Stacey, *Canada and the Age of Conflict*, 226.

42. Norman Hillmer, et al., *A Country of Limitations: Canada and the World in 1939* (Ottawa: Canadian Committee for the History of the Second World War, 1996), 220; King's Diary, July 31, 1936; Also see House of Commons Debates, November 12, 1940, 55–56.

43. "Hearings before the Committee on Military Affairs," Directorate of History and Heritage 74/256, vol. 2, 72, in Douglas, *The Official History of Royal Canadian Air Force*, 128.

44. "Appreciation of Canada's Obligations with Respect to the Maintenance of Neutrality in Event of War between the United States of America and Japan," October 14, 1936, Directorate of History and Heritage, 74/256, 211–19.

45. R.M. Lower, "The Defence of the West Coast," *Canadian Defence Quarterly*, vol. 16, October 1938, 32–35; and Defence Scheme No 2, April 11, 1938, Directorate of History and Heritage, 322.016 (D 12).

46. Douglas *The Official History of Royal Canadian Air Force*, 129–30; *Ottawa Citizen*, April 1935.

47. Eayrs, *In Defence of Canada*, vol. 3, 49.

48. M. Pope, *Soldiers and Politicians* (Toronto: University of Toronto Press, 1962), 91.

CHAPTER FIVE

1. W.A.B. Douglas, *The Official History of Royal Canadian Air Force*, vol. 2, *The Creation of a National Air Force* (Toronto: University of Toronto Press, 1986), 131; Blair Neatby, *William Lyon Mackenzie King: The Prism of Unity*, vol. 3, *1933–1939* (Toronto: University of Toronto Press, 1975), 182.

2. William Lyon Mackenzie King, "Diaries of Prime Minister William Lyon Mackenzie King," Library and Archives Canada, www.collectionscanada.gc.ca/databases/king/index-e.html, August 25, 1936.

3. *Ibid.*, August 26, 1936.

4. *Ibid.*; Neatby, *William Lyon Mackenzie King*, 182.

5. James Eayrs, *In Defence of Canada*, vol. 3, *Appeasement and Rearmament* (Toronto: University of Toronto Press, 1967), 138.

6. "An Appreciation of the Defence Problems Confronting Canada With Recommendations for the Development of the Armed Forces," Joint Staff Committee, Department of National Defence, September 5, 1936.

7. J.L. Granatstein, *The Generals* (Toronto: Stoddart Publishing, 1993), 83ff. Granatstein's chapter on Crerar is titled "Ambition Realized."

8. "An Appreciation of the Defence Problems," Joint Staff Committee.

9. Canadian Liaison Letter No. 4, Major General A.G.L McNaughton to Field Marshal Sir George Milne, December 3, 1932, Ian Mackenzie Papers, Library and Archives Canada, vol. 30; Quoted in M.A. Hooker, "Serving Two Masters: Ian Mackenzie and Civil-Military Relations in Canada, 1935–1939," *Journal of Canadian Studies*, vol. 21, no. 1, 39.

10. A crippling limitation was that total government revenues were small. Even in 1939 they were only $600 million. Further discussion in chapter thirteen.

11. The previous budget minus the amount spent on unemployment relief was about $23 million. C.P. Stacey, *Canada and the Age of Conflict*, vol. 2, *1921–1948, The Mackenzie King Era* (Toronto: University of Toronto Press, 1981), 201.

12. Stacey, *Canada and the Age of Conflict*, 201.

13. King's Diary, September 10, 1936.

14. Robert A. MacKay and E.B. Rogers, *Canada Looks Abroad* (London: Oxford University Press, 1938), 363–69.

15. House of Commons Debates, 1937, 893–98.

16. *Ibid.*, 907.

17. Eayrs, *In Defence of Canada*, vol. 3, 56.

18. King to Massey, March 17, 1937, King Papers, Library and Archives Canada.

19. There may have been disappointment in the military about spending, but Colonel Maurice Pope at least thought it was the first positive statement on defence policy from a government leader since Confederation. M. Pope, *Soldiers and Politicians* (Toronto: University of Toronto Press, 1962), 124.

20. George Drew to R. K. Finlayson, January 4, 1937, in Eayrs, *In Defence of Canada*, vol. 3, 142.

21. House of Commons Debates, 1937, 954-65.

22. Norman Hillmer, "Defence and Ideology: The Anglo-Canadian Military 'Alliance' in the 1930s," *International Journal*, vol. XXXIII, Summer, 1978, 599.

23. "Folly of Canadian Rearmament," *Canadian Forum*, vol. XVI, no. 193, 1937, 6–7.

24. C.P. Stacey, *The Military Problems of Canada: A Survey of Defence Policies and Strategic Conditions Past and Present* (Toronto: Ryerson Press, 1940), Appendix C, quoting "Canada: Estimates for the Fiscal Year ending March 31, 1937, 26."

25. King's Diary, October 23, 1936.

26. Stacey, *Canada and the Age of Conflict*, 200.

27. See for instance Reginald H. Roy, *The Seaforth Highlanders of Canada, 1919–1965* (Vancouver: Seaforth Highlanders of Canada, 1969), 45.

28. C.P. Stacey, *Six Years of War: The Army in Canada, Britain and the Pacific*, vol.1 (Ottawa: Department of National Defence, 1955), 13; C.P. Stacey, *Arms, Men and Governments: The War Policies of Canada, 1939–1945* (Ottawa: The Queen's Printer, 1970), 3.

29. House of Commons *Debates*, 1939, 3253ff.

30. Marc Milner, *Canada's Navy: The First Century* (Toronto: University of Toronto Press, 1999), 70–71.

31. Farley Mowat, *The Regiment* (St. Catharines, Ontario: Vanwell Publishing Ltd., 2007), xi.

32. M. Lynch, *Salty Dips*, vol. 1 (Ottawa: Naval Officers' Association of Canada, Ottawa Branch, 1985), 1.

33. Donald E. Graves, *In Peril on the Sea: The Royal Canadian Navy and the Battle of the Atlantic* (Toronto: Robin Brass Studio Inc., 2003), 45; F. Sherwood quoted in, Lynch, *Salty Dips*, 11–12.

34. George F.G. Stanley, *Canada's Soldiers, 1604–1954: The Military History of an Unmilitary People* (Toronto: Macmillan, 1960), 346; Granatstein, *The Generals*, 26.

35. Stephen John Harris, *Canadian Brass: The Making of a Professional Army, 1890–1939* (Toronto: University of Toronto Press, 1988), 181ff.

36. G. Nicholson, *The Gunners of Canada*, vol. 2 (Toronto: McClelland & Stewart, 1972), 36.

37. The 24th Field Brigade was one of the units moved to Calgary on mobilization in 1939. Today it is the 44th Field Engineer Squadron.

38. John Marteinson and Michael R. McNorgan, *The Royal Canadian Armoured Corps: An Illustrated History* (Toronto: Royal Canadian Armoured Corps Association, 2000), 72.

39. *Ibid.*, 71.

40. *Ibid.*

41. *Ibid.*, 69.

42. Brereton Greenhous, *Dragoon: The Centennial History of the Royal Canadian Dragoons, 1883–1983* (Belleville, Ontario: Guild of the Royal Canadian Dragoons, 1983), 287.

43. *Ibid.*, 286; Marteinson and McNorgan, *The Royal Canadian Armoured Corps*, 70–71.

44. Greenhous, *Dragoon*, 287.

45. Howard Graham, *Citizen and Soldier: The Memoirs of Lieutenant-General Howard Graham* (Toronto: McClelland & Stewart, 1987), 101. The examiner was Churchill Mann, later a major general.

46. Brigadier General R.T. Bennett, Granatstein Interviews, May 22, 1991.

47. Nicholson, *The Gunners of Canada*, vol. 2, 37–38.

48. *Ibid.*, 38.

49. Chris Vokes with John P. Maclean, *Vokes: My Story* (Ottawa: Gallery Books, 1985), 57.

50. Lieutenant General Howard Graham in Reginald H. Roy, *For Most Conspicuous Bravery: A Biography of Major-General George R. Pearkes, V.C., Through Two World Wars* (Vancouver: UBC Press, 1977), 124.

51. David Bercuson, *Battalion of Heroes: The Calgary Highlanders in World War II* (Calgary: Calgary Highlanders Regimental Funds Foundation, 1994), 8ff.

52. This section, including the summary of Welland's tour of the Middle and Far East, from an obituary, "Rear-Admiral Bob Welland," in the *London Telegraph*, August 10, 2010; Robert Welland, interview by Larry D. Rose; Robert Welland, *This Will Have to Do*, unpublished memoir.

53. Welland, interview. Welland died on May 28, 2010.

54. Ralph Hennessy, interview by Larry D. Rose, May 7, 2008.

55. Another 1936 cadet was Tom Pullen, who became an RCN captain and later a noted authority on the Arctic.

56. Account from *Daily Telegraph*, September 27, 2011.

57. Welland, interview.

58. G. "Skinny" Hayes, "Days of Endeavour," *Starshell*, vol.VII, Winter 2007–Spring 2008, 19.

59. "The Elibank Incident," August 19, 1936, King Papers, in Hooker, "Serving Two Masters," 38–56.

60. A lengthy account in Douglas, *The Official History of Royal Canadian Air Force*, 193–204. Also see Hillmer, "Defence and Ideology," 605. Eayrs, *In Defence of Canada*, vol. 3, 91ff.

61. Len Deighton, *Fighter: The True Story of the Battle of Britain* (London: Triad/Panther, 1979), 56.

62. This section from Hillmer, "Defence and Ideology," 596–612.

63. *Ibid.,* 600

64. See Hellfire Corner, www.fylde.demon.co.uk/welcome.htm. Also Suzanne Evans, *Mothers of Heroes, Mothers of Martyrs: World War I and the Politics of Grief* (Kingston: McGill-Queens University Press, 2007), 163.

CHAPTER SIX

1. See, for instance, B. Holman, "The Air Panic of 1935: British Press Opinion Between Disarmament and Rearmament," *Journal of Contemporary History*, April 2011, vol. 46, no. 2, 288–307.

2. Donald Cameron Watt, *How War Came* (New York: Pantheon Books, 1989), 592.

3. House of Commons Debates, November 10, 1932, col. 632.

4. Sir Frederick Hugh Sykes, *Aviation in Peace and War* (London: E. Arnold, 1922), 100–03.

5. Giulio Douhet, *Command of the Air*, translation (New York: Arno Press, 1972).

6. *Ibid.,* 7. In another work, Douhet describes a fictional war between France and Belgium on one side and Germany on the other. Germany gains air superiority and wins the war in a few days.

7. W.A.B. Douglas, *The Official History of Royal Canadian Air Force*, vol. 2, *The Creation of a National Air Force* (Toronto: University of Toronto Press, 1986), 120, describes Trenchard as adopting a "modified version of Sykes' theories."

8. John Terraine quoted in Ross Wayne Mahoney, "The RAF, Combined Operations Doctrine and the Raid on Dieppe" (master's thesis, University of Birmingham, August 19, 1942), 117.

9. Douglas, *The Official History of Royal Canadian Air Force*, 63, 120–21.

10. G. Howsam, *Canadian Defence Quarterly*, vol. III, April 1931, 356–60, in Douglas, *The Official History of Royal Canadian Air Force*, 121. Howsam was later an air vice-marshal.

11. Jeffrey A. Keshen, *Saints, Sinners, and Soldiers: Canada's Second World War* (Vancouver: UBC Press, 2004), 35.

12. "Canada's Present Defence Policy," July 1938, Directorate of History and Heritage, 181.02 (D107) in Douglas, *The Official History of Royal Canadian Air Force*, 131.

13. A discussion of military developments of the period in Donald Cameron Watt, *Too Serious a Business: European Armed Forces and the Approach to the Second World War* (Berkeley, California: University of California Press, 1975), 60.

14. B.H. Liddell Hart, *Strategy: The Indirect Approach* (London: Faber & Faber, 1967), 267.

15. Major General D.C. Spry, June 15, 1967. Reginald H. Roy, *For Most Conspicuous Bravery: A Biography of Major-General George R. Pearkes, V.C., Through Two World Wars* (Vancouver: UBC Press, 1977), 124.

16. Stephen John Harris, *Canadian Brass: The Making of a Professional Army, 1890–1939* (Toronto: University of Toronto Press, 1988), 203; E.L.M. Burns, "A Division that Can Attack," *Canadian Defence Quarterly*, vol. XV, April 1938, 282–98; G.G. Simonds, "An Army that Can Attack — A Division that Can Defend," *Canadian Defence Quarterly*, vol. XV, no. 4, July 1938, 413ff.

17. J.L. Granatstein, *The Generals* (Toronto: Stoddart Publishing, 1993), 151.

18. J.L. Granatstein, *Canada's Army: Waging War and Keeping the Peace* (Toronto: University of Toronto Press, 2002), 166–67.

19. Victor Wheeler, "The 50th Battalion in No Man's Land" (pamphlet, Alberta Historical Resources Foundation, 2000), 201.

20. John S. Moir ed., *History of the Royal Canadian Corps of Signals 1903–1961* (Ottawa: Corps Committee, Royal Canadian Corps of Signals, 1962), 45ff.

21. Terry Copp, *The Brigade: The Fifth Canadian Infantry Brigade in WWII* (Mechanicsburg, Pennsylvania: Stackpole Books, 1992), 37. Megill was a brigade commander during the Second World War.

22. Moir, *History of the Royal Canadian Corps of Signals*, 62.

23. Donald E. Graves, *In Peril on the Sea: The Royal Canadian Navy and the Battle of the Atlantic* (Toronto: Robin Brass Studio Inc., 2003), 36.

24. Percy Nelles, "Defence of Trade," memorandum, February 12, 1937, Library and Archives Canada, III, B5, vol. 37, file D-26, in Marc Milner, *The North Atlantic Run: The Royal Canadian Navy and the Battle for the Convoys* (Toronto: University of Toronto Press, 1985), 9.

25. This section based on Graves, *In Peril on the Sea*, 112–13.

26. John Keegan, *The Price of Admiralty: The Evolution of Naval Warfare from Trafalgar to Midway* (New York: Penguin Books, 1990), 267. French and Polish scientists worked on the same ideas, says Keegan.

27. Graves, *In Peril on the Sea*, 37.

28. M. Lynch, ed., *Salty Dips*, vol. 6 (Ottawa: Naval Officers' Association, Ottawa Branch, 1999), 153.

29. Marc Milner, *Canada's Navy: The First Century* (Toronto: University of Toronto Press, 1999), 82.

30. Colonel William Murray quoted in Harold A. Skaarup, *Out of Darkness — Light: A History of Canadian Military Intelligence*, vol. 1 (New York: iUniverse, 2005), 99.

31. S.R. Elliot, *Scarlet to Green: A History of Intelligence in the Canadian Army, 1903–1963* (Toronto: Canadian Intelligence and Security Association, 1981), 81.

32. Skaarup, *Out of Darkness — Light*, 98. Also C. Allen, "A Minute Bletchley Park: Building a Canadian Naval Operational Intelligence Centre," in Michael Hadley et al., eds., *A Nation's Navy: In Quest of a Canadian Naval Identity* (Montreal: McGill-Queen's University Press, 1996), 158.

33. F.W. Winterbotham, *The Ultra Secret* (New York: Dell, 1974).

34. Marc Milner, *Battle of the Atlantic* (St. Catharines, Ontario: Vanwell Publishing Ltd., 2011), 79.

35. John Marteinson and Michael R. McNorgan, *The Royal Canadian Armoured Corps: An Illustrated History* (Toronto: Royal Canadian Armoured Corps Association, 2000), 71.

CHAPTER SEVEN

1. Prime Minister King can be seen briefly in a Pathe film of the coronation. The film was a first.

2. The number in Allan Levine, *King: William Lyon Mackenzie King: A Life Guided by the Hand of Destiny* (Vancouver: Douglas & McIntyre, 2012), 263.

3. *Ibid.*

4. Kim Beattie, *Dileas: History of the 48th Highlanders of Canada, 1929–1956* (Toronto: 48th Highlanders of Canada, 1957), 23.

5. James Eayrs, *In Defence of Canada*, vol. 3, *Appeasement and Rearmament* (Toronto: University of Toronto Press, 1967), 55.

6. Eayrs, *In Defence of Canada*, vol. 3, 84–90.

7. Notes in King Papers, in Eayrs, *In Defence of Canada*, vol. 3, 86.

8. Eayrs, *In Defence of Canada*, vol. 3, 87.

9. K. Martin, "Is the British Empire in Retreat?" *Yale Quarterly*, Autumn, 1937; Blair Neatby, *William Lyon Mackenzie King: The Prism of Unity*, vol. 3, *1933–1939* (Toronto: University of Toronto Press, 1975), 219.

10. C.P. Stacey, *Canada and the Age of Conflict*, vol. 2, *1921–1948, The Mackenzie King Era* (Toronto: University of Toronto Press, 1981), 209.

11. Stacey, *Canada and the Age of Conflict*, 207–08.

12. Keith Feiling, *The Life of Neville Chamberlain* (Toronto: Macmillan, 1946), 303.

13. King to Tweedsmuir, July 10, 1937, King Papers, Library and Archives Canada.
14. Letter to Viscount Greenwood in Eayrs, *In Defence of Canada*, vol. 3, 60.
15. Stacey, *Canada and the Age of Conflict*, 209ff.
16. *Ibid.*
17. Eayrs, *In Defence of Canada*, vol. 3, 42.
18. Toronto *Globe*, September 9, 2006. William Shirer said Ribbentrop was possibly the stupidest of the leading Nazis. William L. Shirer, *The Nightmare Years 1930–1940* (New York: Little Brown & Co., 1984), 157. Ribbentrop was executed as a war criminal on October 16, 1946.
19. William Lyon Mackenzie King, "Diaries of Prime Minister William Lyon Mackenzie King," Library and Archives Canada, www.collectionscanada.gc.ca/databases/king/index-e.html, June 29, 1937.
20. *Ibid.*
21. *Ibid.*
22. Stacey, *Canada and the Age of Conflict*, 211. King had had the same reaction following his 1928 visit with Italian fascist dictator Benito Mussolini. King was "filled with admiration" that Mussolini had dealt with the communists and cleaned the streets of beggars and prostitutes. Levine, *King*, 180–81.
23. Eayrs, *In Defence of Canada*, vol. 3, 45.
24. "Minute of July 25, 1937," quoted in Stacey, *Canada and the Age of Conflict*, 21.
25. King to Tweedsmuir, July 10, 1937, King Papers, in Eayrs, *In Defence of Canada*, vol. 3, 46.
26. Bruce Hutchison, *The Incredible Canadian* (Toronto: Longmans Canada, 1953), 225.
27. H.D.G. Crerar, "Visit to Germany June 16–21, 1937," Crerar Papers, in Paul Douglas Dickson, *A Thoroughly Canadian General: A Biography of General H.D.G. Crerar* (Toronto: University of Toronto Press, 2007), 110.
28. W.A.B. Douglas, *The Official History of Royal Canadian Air Force*, vol. 2, *The Creation of a National Air Force* (Toronto: University of Toronto Press, 1986), 139.
29. "The Direct Defence of Canada Considered from an Air Force Aspect," Directorate of History and Heritage, vol. I, 74.256, in Douglas, *The Official History of Royal Canadian Air Force*, 139.
30. On the outbreak of the Second World War, Birchall flew coastal patrols off the east coast with No.5 Squadron. On April 4, 1942, then Squadron Leader Birchall was flying a PBY Catalina patrolling off Ceylon's southern coast when the crew spotted a large Japanese fleet, including five aircraft carriers, heading for Ceylon. The crew managed to send out a radio warning before being shot down. Three crewmen were killed and the others, including Birchall, became prisoners of war. Birchall repeatedly risked his life to stand up to the Japanese to demand better treatment for prisoners. After the war he became an air commodore.
31. George Brown and Michael Lavigne, *Canadian Wing Commanders* (Langley, British Columbia: Battleline Books, 1984), 2ff.
32. While the casualty rate among the early pilots was very high, Arthur survived the war.
33. Douglas, *The Official History of Royal Canadian Air Force*, 141.
34. Larry Milberry, *Canada's Air Force at War and Peace*, vol. 1 (Toronto: CANAV Books, 2000), 103.
35. Douglas, *The Official History of Royal Canadian Air Force*, 1339.
36. Milberry, *Canada's Air Force*, 103–04.
37. S. Kostenuk and J. Griffin, *RCAF Squadrons Histories and Aircraft: 1924–1968* (Toronto: Samuel Stevens Hakkert, 1977), 18.
38. Nora Bottomley, *424 Squadron History: A Detailed Pictoral History of 424 Squadron (RCAF) From Its Origins in 1935 to Modern Times* (Belleville, Ontario: Hangar Bookshelf, 1985), 12.
39. John P.D. Dunbabin, "British Rearmament in the 1930s: A Chronology and Review," *Historical Journal*, vol. XVII, no. 3, 1975, 587–609.
40. Galen Perras, "'Future Plays Will Depend on How the Next One Works': Franklin Roosevelt and the Canadian Legation Discussions of January 1938," *Journal of Military and Strategic Studies*, Summer 2006, vol. 8, issue 4, 13.

41. *Ibid.*, 15.

42. *Ibid.*

43. "Canadian Defence Weakness 'Menace' to U.S. Security," *Ottawa Citizen*, January 6, 1938.

44. King's Diary, October 29, 1936, and July 31, 1936. Douglas, *The Official History of Royal Canadian Air Force*, 130.

45. Perras, "Future Plays," 3.

46. C.P. Stacey, *The Military Problems of Canada: A Survey of Defence Policies and Strategic Conditions Past and Present* (Toronto: Ryerson Press, 1940), 105.

47. C.P. Stacey, *Six Years of War: The Army in Canada, Britain and the Pacific*, vol.1 (Ottawa: Department of National Defence, 1955), 28.

48. Harris, *Canadian Brass*, 182ff.

49. M.A. Hooker, "Serving Two Masters: Ian Mackenzie and Civil-Military Relations in Canada, 1935–1939," *Journal of Canadian Studies*, vol. 21, no. 1, 41.

50. Harris, *Canadian Brass*, 179.

51. Stacey, *Six Years of War*, 32–33.

52. *Ibid.*, 30; Harris, *Canadian Brass*, 183.

53. Harris, *Canadian Brass*, 183. While Ian Mackenzie signed off on this, it is likely Mackenzie King did not know.

54. Pope to Duguid, November 3, 1943, in Harris, *Canadian Brass*, 183.

55. Hooker, "Serving Two Masters," 44.

56. Jeffery Williams, *Far From Home: A Memoir of a 20th Century Soldier* (Calgary: University of Calgary Press, 2003), 91–92.

57. *Ibid.*, 88.

58. *Ibid.*

59. *Vancouver Sun*, September 3, 1937.

60. Brereton Greenhous, *Dragoon: The Centennial History of the Royal Canadian Dragoons, 1883–1983* (Belleville, Ontario: Guild of the Royal Canadian Dragoons, 1983), 289.

61. David J. Bercuson, *The Patricias: The Proud History of a Fighting Regiment* (Toronto: Stoddart Publishing, 2001), 136.

CHAPTER EIGHT

1. Williamson Murray, *The Change in the European Balance of Power, 1938–1939: The Path to Ruin* (Princeton, NJ; Princeton University Press, 1984), 32ff.

2. B.H. Liddell Hart, *The Other Side of the Hill* (London: Pan Books, 1999), 77.

3. William Lyon Mackenzie King, "Diaries of Prime Minister William Lyon Mackenzie King," Library and Archives Canada, www.collectionscanada.gc.ca/databases/king/index-e.html, March 12, 1938.

4. Paul Douglas Dickson, *A Thoroughly Canadian General: A Biography of General H.D.G. Crerar* (Toronto: University of Toronto Press, 2007), 110.

5. *Ibid.*, 112.

6. Robert Welland, *This Will Have to Do*, unpublished memoir, 31.

7. G. "Skinny" Hayes, "Days of Endeavour," *Starshell*, serialized, 2007–2008 Issues.

8. A summary in David Mackenzie, "The Bren Gun Scandal and the Maclean Publishing Company's Investigation of Canadian Defence Contracts, 1938–1940," *Journal of Canadian Studies*, vol. 26, no. 3, 1991, 140–62; Also C.P. Stacey, *The Military Problems of Canada: A Survey of Defence Policies and Strategic Conditions Past and Present* (Toronto: Ryerson Press, 1940), 130–31.

9. C.P. Stacey, *Six Years of War: The Army in Canada, Britain and the Pacific*, vol.1 (Ottawa: Department of National Defence, 1955), 11–12.

10. Mackenzie, "The Bren Gun Scandal," 141.

11. *Ibid.*, Skelton to LaFleche April 23, 1937, 142.

12. *Ibid.*, 141.

13. James Eayrs, *In Defence of Canada*, vol. 3, *Appeasement and Rearmament* (Toronto: University of Toronto Press, 1967), 117.

14. *Ibid.*

15. *Milwaukee Journal*, February 12, 1939.

16. *Ottawa Citizen*, September 27, 1929.

17. J.L. Granatstein, *The Generals* (Toronto: Stoddart Publishing, 1993), 244. After various posts, LaFleche entered the King cabinet as minister of national war services in 1942.

18. Stacey, *Six Years of War*, 37. The person is not identified in the records.

19. Blair Neatby, *William Lyon Mackenzie King: The Prism of Unity*, vol. 3, *1933–1939* (Toronto: University of Toronto Press, 1975), 279ff; Stacey, *Six Years of War*, 25–26.

20. Mackenzie, "The Bren Gun Scandal," 144–45.

21. *Ibid.*, 144.

22. George A. Drew, "Canada's Armament Mystery," *Maclean's*, September 1, 1938, 8ff.

23. *Ibid.*

24. *Milwaukee Journal*, February 12, 1939.

25. Mackenzie, "The Bren Gun Scandal," 146–47.

26. *Report of the Royal Commission on the Bren Machine Gun Contract, 1939*, Library and Archives Canada, 45–46.

27. King's Diary, February 9, 1939.

28. *Milwaukee Journal*, February 12, 1939.

29. Stacey, *Six Years of War*, 26.

30. *Ibid.*, 25.

31. Eayrs, *In Defence of Canada*, vol. 3, 122.

32. Stacey, *Six Years of War*, 26; Doug Knight ed., *Tools of the Trade: Equipping the Canadian Army* (Ottawa: Service Publications, 2005), 15.

33. W.A.B. Douglas, *The Official History of Royal Canadian Air Force*, vol. 2, *The Creation of a National Air Force* (Toronto: University of Toronto Press, 1986), 147.

34. John P.D. Dunbabin, "British Rearmament in the 1930s: A Chronology and Review," *Historical Journal*, vol. XVII, no. 3, 1975, 587–609.

35. Douglas, *The Official History of Royal Canadian Air Force*, 147.

36. C.R. Slemon, interview, September 6, 1976, C.R. Slemon Biographical file, Directorate of History and Heritage.

37. Department of National Defence Report, Directorate of History and Heritage181.003 (D3868).

38. Douglas, *The Official History of Royal Canadian Air Force*, 147.

39. *Ibid.*, 149.

40. Terry Strocel, *440 Squadron History* (Stittsville, Ontario: Canada's Wings, 1983), 8.

41. Larry Worthington, *Worthy* (Toronto: Macmillan, 1961), 147; Marteinson and McNorgan, *The Royal Canadian Armoured Corps*, 71.

42. Worthington, *Worthy*, 150.

43. *Ibid.*, 149; John Marteinson and Michael R. McNorgan, *The Royal Canadian Armoured Corps: An Illustrated History* (Toronto: Royal Canadian Armoured Corps Association, 2000), 74.

44. The terminology of Field Marshal Claude Auchinleck, in J. Connell, *Auchinleck: A Critical Biography: A Biography of Field-Marshal Sir Claude Auchinleck* (London: Cassell, 1959), 81.

45. "Canadian Defence Requirements, 1935–38," Ian Mackenzie Papers, Library and Archives Canada, vol. 29.

46. E.A.C. Amy, interview by Larry D. Rose, April 8, 2008.

47. King's Diary, August 19, 1938.

Notes

48. P. Worthington, note to the author, April 10, 2010.

49. Worthington, *Worthy.*

50. Roman Jarymowycs, "General Guy Simonds: The Commander as Tragic Hero," in Bernd Horn and Stephen Harris, eds., *Warrior Chiefs: Perspectives on Senior Canadian Military Chiefs* (Toronto: Dundurn, 2000), says Worthington was a graduate of the University of California. Peter Worthington called the claim "nonsense." Peter Worthington, message to Larry D. Rose, May 4, 2012.

51. Worthington, *Worthy,* 147. Early in the war Worthington commanded a division in Britain, but when the time came for combat he was fifty-six and considered too old.

52. Amy, interview.

53. Major General D.C. Spry, Roy Interview, June 15, 1967, 5, University of Victoria Collection.

54. D.B. Smith, interview by J. Granatstein, September 14, 1991.

55. Reginald H. Roy, *For Most Conspicuous Bravery: A Biography of Major-General George R. Pearkes, V.C., Through Two World Wars* (Vancouver: UBC Press, 1977), 124–25.

56. Brereton Greenhous, *Dragoon: The Centennial History of the Royal Canadian Dragoons, 1883–1983* (Belleville, Ontario: Guild of the Royal Canadian Dragoons, 1983), 290; J.L. Granatstein, *Canada's Army: Waging War and Keeping the Peace* (Toronto: University of Toronto Press, 2002), 168.

57. Permanent Force Collective Training. Directorate of History and Heritage 324.009 (D449).

58. Stephen John Harris, *Canadian Brass: The Making of a Professional Army, 1890–1939* (Toronto: University of Toronto Press, 1988), 198; Abridged Report on Permanent Force Collective Training, Camp Borden, 1938, Department of National Defence, 1939, Directorate of History and Heritage 324.00 (D449); Greenhous, *Dragoon,* 291.

59. Greenhous, *Dragoon,* 293.

60. Granatstein, *Canada's Army,* 168.

61. Carolyn Gossage, *Greatcoats and Glamour Boots: Canadian Women at War, 1939–1945* (Toronto: Dundurn, 2001), 30–31.

62. During the Second World War almost 50,000 Canadian women volunteered for military service. Close to 22,000 of them enlisted in the CWAC (Canadian Women's Army Corps), 17,000 in the RCAF (Royal Canadian Air Force Women's Division), and 6,781 in the Wrens (Women's Royal Canadian Naval Service). An additional 4,518 served in the medical corps. Gossage, *Greatcoats and Glamour Boots,* 24.

Chapter Nine

1. King to Tweedsmuir, King Papers, Library and Archives Canada, September 6, 1938.

2. William Lyon Mackenzie King, "Diaries of Prime Minister William Lyon Mackenzie King," Library and Archives Canada, www.collectionscanada.gc.ca/databases/king/index-e.html, August 31, 1938.

3. *Ibid.*

4. *Ibid.,* September 12, 1938.

5. Derek Wood and Derek Dempster, *The Narrow Margin: The Battle of Britain and the Rise of Air Power, 1939–40* (London: Hutchinson, 1961), 91.

6. John MacFarlane, *Ernest Lapointe and Quebec's Influence on Canadian Foreign Policy* (Toronto: University of Toronto Press, 1999), 11.

7. W.A.B. Douglas, *The Official History of Royal Canadian Air Force,* vol. 2, *The Creation of a National Air Force* (Toronto: University of Toronto Press, 1986), 143.

8. Senior Air Officer to Western Air Command, memo, January 12, 1939, Directorate of History and Heritage, 181.003 (D3868); National Defence Headquarters, *Bulletins on the Development of the RCAF.*

9. King's Diary, January 11, 1938.

10. Roger Sarty, *The Maritime Defence of Canada* (Toronto: Canadian Institute of Strategic Studies, 1997), 221ff.

11. Sarty, *The Maritime Defence of Canada*, 221.

12. King's Diary, September 27, 1938.

13. David Faber, *Munich: The 1938 Appeasement Crisis* (New York: Simon & Shuster, 2008), 2–5.

14. Harold Nicholson quoted in W.K. Wark, "Diplomatic Revolution in the West," in Norman Hillmer, et al., *A Country of Limitations: Canada and the World in 1939* (Ottawa: Canadian Committee for the History of the Second World War, 1996), 35ff.

15. The building where the leaders met still exists and is now a music school.

16. Faber, *Munich*, 2–5.

17. Chamberlain's appearing on the balcony was much criticized later because it showed the king apparently endorsing appeasement.

18. C.P. Stacey, *Canada and the Age of Conflict*, vol. 2, *1921–1948, The Mackenzie King Era* (Toronto: University of Toronto Press, 1981), 215.

19. Bruce Hutchison, *The Incredible Canadian* (Toronto: Longmans Canada, 1953), 239.

20. James Eayrs, *In Defence of Canada*, vol. 3, *Appeasement and Rearmament* (Toronto: University of Toronto Press, 1967), 70.

21. A.J.P. Taylor, *The Origins of the Second World War* (New York: Simon & Shuster, 1996), 187ff.

22. Quoted in W.K. Wark, "Diplomatic Revolution," in Hillmer et al., *A Country of Limitations*, 41.

23. As late as 1939 Mackenzie King used the phrase to describe Churchill. Stacey, *Canada and the Age of Conflict*, 298. Later, of course, King changed his mind.

24. Hutchison, *The Incredible Canadian*, 239.

25. L. Worthington, *Worthy* (Toronto: Macmillan, 1961), 151.

26. John Dafoe, "What's the Cheering For?" Winnipeg *Free Press*, October 3, 1938.

27. H. Blair Neatby, *The Politics of Chaos: Canada in the Thirties* (Toronto: Macmillan of Canada, 1972), 175. Blair Neatby, *William Lyon Mackenzie King: The Prism of Unity*, vol. 3, *1933–1939* (Toronto: University of Toronto Press, 1975), 274.

28. G. Case, "The Lessons of Munich: Mackenzie King's Campaign to Prepare Canada for War," *Canadian Military Journal*, vol. 3, no. 4, 1; King's Diary, October 29, 1935.

29. Stacey, *Canada and the Age of Conflict*, 231–36. Case, "The Lessons of Munich," 1.

30. In T. Copp, "Ontario 1939: The Decision for War," in Hillmer et al., *A Country of Limitations*, 109.

31. E. Soward, *A Formidable Hero* (Toronto: CANAV Books, 1984), 14.

32. Quoted in Richard Jones "Politics and Culture: The French Canadian and the Second World War," in Sidney Aster ed., *The Second World War as a National Experience* (Ottawa: The Canadian Committee for the History of the Second World War, 1981), 5.

33. Stacey, *Canada and the Age of Conflict*, 235. Also King's Diary, September 12, 1938.

34. "Back Stage in Ottawa," *Maclean's*, November 1, 1938, in Eayrs, *In Defence of Canada*, vol. 3, 71.

35. King's Diary, October 24, 1938.

36. Stacey, *Canada and the Age of Conflict*, 233.

37. King's Diary, December 16, 1938.

38. Stacey, *Canada and the Age of Conflict*, 219–20; C.P. Stacey, *The Military Problems of Canada: A Survey of Defence Policies and Strategic Conditions Past and Present* (Toronto: Ryerson Press, 1940), 103; C.P. Stacey, *Six Years of War: The Army in Canada, Britain and the Pacific*, vol.1 (Ottawa: Department of National Defence, 1955), 13; Also see House of Commons Debates, March 24, 1938. Figures used are quoted in Sarty, *The Maritime Defence of Canada*, 225.

39. It had actually been ordered in 1936 but seven more were ordered in 1937. Douglas, *The Official History of Royal Canadian Air Force*, 144.

40. *Ibid.*

41. *Time* Magazine, December 4, 1939.

42. Sarty, *The Maritime Defence of Canada*, 220–21.

43. Douglas, *The Official History of Royal Canadian Air Force*, 135.

44. *Ibid.*, 137. Western Air Command became operational on April 15, 1938.

45. S. Kostenuk and J. Griffin, *RCAF Squadrons Histories and Aircraft: 1924–1968* (Toronto: Samuel Stevens Hakkert, 1977), 18.

46. Sarty, *The Maritime Defence of Canada*, 226.

47. Eayrs, *In Defence of Canada*, vol. 3, 153.

48. Anderson to Minister, December 19, 1938, file D-2000, Queens University Archive, C.G. Powers Papers, vol. 67, in Sarty, *The Maritime Defence of Canada*, 226.

49. Eayrs, *In Defence of Canada*, vol. 3, 152.

50. J.L. Granatstein, *Canada's Army: Waging War and Keeping the Peace* (Toronto: University of Toronto Press, 2002), 161.

51. George S. MacDonell, *One Soldier's Story: 1939–1945: From the Fall of Hong Kong to the Defeat of Japan* (Toronto: Dundurn, 2002), 20ff.

52. David Bercuson, *Battalion of Heroes: The Calgary Highlanders in World War II* (Calgary: Calgary Highlanders Regimental Funds Foundation, 1994), 40.

53. J.L. Granatstein, *The Generals* (Toronto: Stoddart Publishing, 1993), 25–26.

54. Jean V. Allard, *The Memoirs of General Jean V. Allard* (Vancouver: UBC Press, 1988). Allard was the first French Canadian to become chief of the defence staff and hold the accompanying rank of general.

55. *Globe and Mail*, January 7, 2001. Gilles Turcot was later a major general.

56. As a captain Paul Triquet was awarded the Victoria Cross in 1943 in Italy, the first Canadian V.C. winner of the Second World War.

57. At Dieppe 584 men of the Fusiliers Mont-Royal were commanded by Lieutenant Colonel Dollard Menard, who was wounded five times.

58. J. Gouin ed., *Bon coeur et bon bras*, quoted in Terry Copp, *The Brigade: The Fifth Canadian Infantry Brigade in WWII* (Mechanicsburg, Pennsylvania: Stackpole Books, 1992), 16.

59. Allard, *Memoirs*, 20.

60. "Armed Forces Historical Study," in J.L. Granatstein and J.M. Hitsman, *Broken Promises: A History of Conscription in Canada* (Toronto: Oxford University Press, 1977), 112.

61. Jean Pariseau and Serge Bernier, *Les Canadiens français et le bilinguisme dans les Forces armée canadiennes* (Ottawa: Department of National Defence, 1987), 95ff.

62. Granatstein, *The Generals*, 250.

63. Pariseau and Bernier, *Les Canadiens français*, 98–99, 106.

64. Granatstein, *The Generals*, 242.

65. Floyd Williston, *Through Footless Halls of Air: The Stories of a Few of the Many Who Failed to Return* (Renfrew, Ontario: General Store Publishing, 1999), 40; Pariseau and Bernier, *Les Canadiens français*, 102.

66. Study by David Zimmerman in Marc Milner, *Canada's Navy: The First Century* (Toronto: University of Toronto Press, 1999), 72–73.

67. "Manpower problems of the Royal Canadian Navy during the Second World War," Report No. 71, Historical Section (GS), July 20, 1954, 10; Pariseau and Bernier, *Les Canadiens français*, 131, quotes a J.M. Hitsman study for the Directorate of History and Heritage.

68. Tony German, *The Sea Is at Our Gates: A History of the Canadian Navy* (Toronto: McClelland & Stewart, 1990), 143; Milner, *Canada's Navy*, 73.

69. Desmond Morton, *A Military History of Canada* (Toronto: McClelland & Stewart, 2007), 178.

70. Jones, "Politics and Culture."

71. *Ibid.*, 10.

72. Pierre Berton, *The Great Depression: 1929–1939* (Toronto: McClelland & Stewart, 1990), 461. Arcand also had his supporters in English-speaking Canada holding rallies in Toronto and other cities.

73. L. Groulx (under the pseudonym of J. Brassier), "Pour qu'on vivre," *L'Action nationale*, January 1934 (Trans.), in Neatby, *The Politics of Chaos*, 183.

74. MacFarlane, *Ernest Lapointe*, 82–89.

75. Allan Levine, *King: William Lyon Mackenzie King: A Life Guided by the Hand of Destiny* (Vancouver: Douglas & McIntyre, 2012), 276.

76. This section based on Nemni, Max and Monique, *Young Trudeau: 1919–1944: Son of Quebec, Father of Canada*, translated by William Johnson (Toronto: McClelland & Stewart, 2006), 58–76.

77. J.W. Pickersgill, *The Mackenzie King Record*, vol. 1, *1939–44* (Toronto: University of Toronto Press, 1960), 22–23.

78. This section based on Macfarlane, *Ernest Lapointe*, 11ff.

CHAPTER TEN

1. William Lyon Mackenzie King, "Diaries of Prime Minister William Lyon Mackenzie King," Library and Archives Canada, www.collectionscanada.gc.ca/databases/king/index-e.html, December 31, 1938.

2. House of Commons Debates, January 1939; C.P. Stacey, *Canada and the Age of Conflict*, vol. 2, *1921– 1948, The Mackenzie King Era* (Toronto: University of Toronto Press, 1981), 237.

3. John MacFarlane, *Ernest Lapointe and Quebec's Influence on Canadian Foreign Policy* (Toronto: University of Toronto Press, 1999), 123.

4. Stacey, *Canada and the Age of Conflict*, 238.

5. *Ibid.*

6. W.K. Wark, "Diplomatic Revolution in the West," in Norman Hillmer, et al., *A Country of Limitations: Canada and the World in 1939* (Ottawa: Canadian Committee for the History of the Second World War, 1996),

7. Williamson Murray, *The Change in the European Balance of Power, 1938–1939: The Path to Ruin* (Princeton, NJ; Princeton University Press, 1984), 278.

8. Stacey, *Canada and the Age of Conflict*, 238.

9. R. Plamondon, Manion Obituary, *National Post*, April 8, 2009.

10. King's Diary, January 27, 1939.

11. Roger Sarty, *The Maritime Defence of Canada* (Toronto: Canadian Institute of Strategic Studies, 1997), 226.

12. Marc Milner, *Canada's Navy: The First Century* (Toronto: University of Toronto Press, 1999), 80.

13. J.W. Pickersgill, *The Mackenzie King Record*, vol. 1, *1939–44* (Toronto: University of Toronto Press, 1960), 15–20.

14. Sarty, *The Maritime Defence of Canada*, 228.

15. *Ibid.*

16. James Eayrs, *In Defence of Canada*, vol. 3, *Appeasement and Rearmament* (Toronto: University of Toronto Press, 1967), 70.

17. Jeffery Williams, *Far From Home: A Memoir of a 20th Century Soldier* (Calgary: University of Calgary Press, 2003), 117.

18. Quoted in W. Wark, "Diplomatic Revolution in the West," 48.

19. King's Diary, March 20, 1939.

20. *Globe and Mail*, March 21, 1939; *Le Devoir*, March 21, 1939.

21. O.D. Skelton, "Memorandum for the Prime Minister," August 25, 1939, Memorandum, April 12, 1939, in Stacey, *Canada and the Age of Conflict*, 240.

22. *Toronto Telegram*, March 27, 1939.

23. Sarty, *The Maritime Defence of Canada*, 232.

24. King's Diary, April 14, 1939.

25. This section based on T. Copp, "Ontario 1939: The Decision for War," in Hillmer et al., *A Country of Limitations*, 113.

26. *Globe and Mail*, March 16, 1939.

27. *Brantford Expositor*, March 16, 1939, in Copp, "Ontario 1939," 113.

28. *Calgary Herald*, March 15–24, 1939.

29. Copp, "Ontario 1939," 116; G. Case, "The Lessons of Munich," *Canadian Military Journal*, vol. 3, no. 4, 14.

30. C.P. Stacey, *Six Years of War: The Army in Canada, Britain and the Pacific*, vol.1 (Ottawa: Department of National Defence, 1955), 33.

31. Sarty, *The Maritime Defence of Canada*, 229.

32. *Ibid.*, 230.

33. *Ibid.*, 231.

34. R. Bannock, interview by Larry D. Rose, March 29, 2010.

35. King's Diary, February 28, 1939.

36. Winnipeg *Free Press*, May 24, 1939.

37. The story, true or not, has been retold in L. Perreaux, *National Post*, October 9, 2002.

38. Williams, *Far From Home*, 119.

39. Stacey, *Canada and the Age of Conflict*, 246.

40. C.P. Stacey, *The Military Problems of Canada: A Survey of Defence Policies and Strategic Conditions Past and Present* (Toronto: Ryerson Press, 1940), 125.

41. Stacey, *Six Years of War*, 20; George Randolph Pearkes, interviews by Reginald Roy, 1966, University of Victoria Archives.

42. D.J. Goodspeed, ed., *The Armed Forces of Canada 1867–1967: A Century of Achievement* (Ottawa: Canadian Forces Headquarters, Directorate of History, Queen's Printer, 1967), 95.

43. Captain G.P. Morrison to chief of the general staff, memorandum, November 8, 1935, in G. Nicholson, *The Gunners of Canada*, vol. 2 (Toronto: McClelland & Stewart, 1972), 42.

44. House of Commons Debates, 1939, 3243-4; Stacey, *Six Years of War*, 29.

45. "Report of the Department of National Defence … 1939," in Stacey, *The Military Problems of Canada*, 122.

46. Stacey, *The Military Problems of Canada*, 138.

47. J.L. Granatstein, *The Generals* (Toronto: Stoddart Publishing, 1993), 26.

48. *Ibid.*, 182. Matthews was later a major general.

49. Larry Worthington, *Worthy* (Toronto: Macmillan, 1961), 153–54.

50. Williams, *Far from Home*, 119.

51. *Ibid.*, 112–13.

52. Pearkes, quoted in Reginald H. Roy, *For Most Conspicuous Bravery: A Biography of Major-General George R. Pearkes, V.C., Through Two World Wars* (Vancouver: UBC Press, 1977), 113.

53. *Ibid.*, 134.

54. Stacey, *The Military Problems of Canada*, 109.

55. *Ibid.*, 112.

56. *Ibid.*, 115.

57. *Ibid.*, 114.

58. *Ibid.*, 115; W.A.B. Douglas and Brereton Greenhous, *Out of the Shadows: Canada in the Second World War*, revised edition (Toronto: Dundurn, 1996), 32. The results were described as "pathetic."

59. Joseph Schull, *The Far Distant Ships: An Official Account of Canadian Naval Operations in the Second World War* (Toronto: Stoddart Publishing, 1987), 35–38.

60. *New York Times*, June 29, 1939.

61. Dean Chappelle, "Building a Bigger Stick: The Construction of Tribal Class Destroyers in Canada, 1940–1948," *The Northern Mariner*, January 1995, 1–17.

62. Stacey, *Six Years of War*, 36.

63. *Report of the Royal Commission on Dominion-Provincial Relations, Book One: Canada 1867–1939* (Ottawa: Government of Canada, 1940), 179.

64. Milner, *Canada's Navy*, 46. Apart from their small size, the minesweepers were coal-fired, leaving stokers on board to shovel what they called "Sydney Shit," the low-grade Cape Breton coal, to power the vessels.

65. G. "Skinny" Hayes, "Days of Endeavour," *Starshell*, 2008–10. Hayes transferred to the RCNR. He then transferred again to the Royal Canadian Navy after the war continuing his service. He retired as a captain.

66. Milner, *Canada's Navy*, 75.

67. James B. Lamb, *On The Triangle Run: The Fighting Spirit of Canada's Navy* (Toronto: HarperCollins, 1987), 53.

68. Stacey, *The Military Problems of Canada*, 116.

Chapter Eleven

1. Len Deighton, *Blood, Tears and Folly: In the Darkest Hour of the Second World War* (London: Jonathan Cape, 1993), 67.

2. This section based on W.A.B. Douglas, Roger Sarty, et al., *No Higher Purpose: The Official Operational History of the Royal Canadian Navy in the Second World War, 1939–1943*, vol. 2, part 1 (St. Catharines, Ontario: Vanwell Publishing Ltd., 2004), 38ff.

3. By the end of 1939, 527 vessels had crossed the Atlantic in twenty-five HX convoys, for the loss of only four ships: two to mines, one to a U-boat, and one to collision. The real test in the Battle of the Atlantic was to come after the fall of France in May 1940.

4. Douglas et al., *No Higher Purpose*, 38.

5. Roger Sarty, *The Maritime Defence of Canada* (Toronto: Canadian Institute of Strategic Studies, 1997), 237.

6. Nelles to Minister, September 12, 1939, Library and Archives Canada, RG 24, 3842, NSS 1017 10–23, part 1.

7. In the 1920s the United States had overtaken Britain as the number one importer of Canadian goods. However, with the depression and high tariffs in the U.S. and with Empire Preference, imports of Canadian goods by Britain had increased relative to the U.S. A.E. Safarian, *The Canadian Economy in the Great Depression* (Toronto: McClelland & Stewart, 1970), 153.

8. Joseph Schull, *The Far Distant Ships: An Official Account of Canadian Naval Operations in the Second World War* (Toronto: Stoddart Publishing, 1987), 10.

9. W.A.B. Douglas and Brereton Greenhous, *Out of the Shadows: Canada in the Second World War*, revised edition (Toronto: Dundurn, 1996), 42.

10. Stephen Kimber, *Sailors, Slackers and Blind Pigs: Halifax at War* (Toronto: Doubleday Canada, 2002), 15–16.

11. James B. Lamb, *On The Triangle Run: The Fighting Spirit of Canada's Navy* (Toronto: HarperCollins, 1987), 38.

12. As late as February 1940, Hitler categorically refused permission for submarines to patrol waters off the coast near Halifax because of the psychological effect that any ship sinking might have on the United States. Ian Kershaw, *Fateful Choices: Ten Decisions that Changed the World* (New York: Penguin Group, 2007), 395.

13. Douglas et al., *No Higher Purpose*, 62.

14. Martin Gilbert, *Winston S. Churchill: Finest Hour, 1939–1941* (London: Heinemann, 1983), 18.

15. Douglas et al., *No Higher Purpose*, 64.

16. Robert Welland, interviews by Larry D. Rose, January 11, 2008, and May 17, 2008.

17. Pressey in Douglas et al., *No Higher Purpose*, 69–70.

18. Ken Macpherson and John Burgess, *The Ships of Canada's Naval Forces, 1910–1981* (Toronto: Collins, 1981), 144.

NOTES

19. G. Borgal, in Blake Heathcote, *Testaments of Honour: Personal Histories from Canada's War Veterans* (Toronto: Doubleday Canada, 2002), 49. *Bras D'Or* sank in a storm in the Gulf of St. Lawrence on October 19, 1940, with all hands lost. Details of the ship's service and sinking in Fraser McKee and Robert Darlington, *The Canadian Naval Chronicle, 1939–1945* (St. Catharines, Ontario: Vanwell Publishing Ltd., 1996), 21–22.

20. Milner, *Canada's Navy*, 26.

21. Edgar Skinner was later commander of HMCS *Arrowhead* and an outstanding corvette captain.

22. Lamb, *On The Triangle Run*, 115

23. M. Lynch, ed., *Salty Dips*, vol. 2 (Ottawa: Naval Officers' Association of Canada, Ottawa Branch), 32.

24. Milner, *Canada's Navy*, 29.

25. Roberts's later service included time on the corvette *Oakville*. M Mac Johnston, *Corvettes Canada: Convoy Veterans of WWII Tell Their True Stories* (Toronto: John Wiley & Sons, 2008), 5.

26. M. Lynch, *Salty Dips*, vol. 1 (Ottawa: Naval Officers' Association of Canada, Ottawa Branch, 1985), 8.

27. M. Lynch, ed., *Salty Dips*, vol. 2, 11–13.

28. Douglas et al., *No Higher Purpose*, 53.

29. *Ibid.*, 378

30. Hugh A. Halliday, *Legion Magazine*, January–February 2006.

31. The soldier is not named. Lex Schragg, *History of The Ontario Regiment, 1866–1951* (Oshawa, Ontario: The Ontario Regiment), 49.

32. Jeffery Williams, *Far From Home: A Memoir of a 20th Century Soldier* (Calgary: University of Calgary Press, 2003), 127.

33. George Blackburn, *Where The Hell Are the Guns?: A Soldier's View of the Anxious Years, 1939–44* (Toronto: McClelland & Stewart, 1999), 31.

34. *Ibid.*, 39–41. Lavigne became mayor of Cornwall in post-war years.

35. C.P. Stacey, *Six Years of War: The Army in Canada, Britain and the Pacific*, vol.1 (Ottawa: Department of National Defence, 1955), 53.

36. Desmond Morton, *Canada and War: A Military and Political History* (Toronto: Butterworths, 1981), 105.

37. *Toronto Star*, September 14, 1939.

38. David Bercuson, *Battalion of Heroes: The Calgary Highlanders in World War II* (Calgary: Calgary Highlanders Regimental Funds Foundation, 1994), 16.

39. S. Anthal and K. Hackleton, *Duty Nobly Done* (Walkerville, Ontario: Walkerville Publishing, 2006), 354. David Croll finished the war as a lieutenant colonel, later becoming an MP, and after that Canada's first Jewish senator.

40. Bercuson, *Battalion of Heroes*, 16.

41. *Toronto Star*, September 13, 1939.

42. Stacey, *Six Years of War*, 54; Jean V. Allard, *The Memoirs of General Jean V. Allard* (Vancouver: UBC Press, 1988), 19.

43. Terry Copp, *The Brigade: The Fifth Canadian Infantry Brigade in WWII* (Mechanicsburg, Pennsylvania: Stackpole Books, 1992), 16; Jeffrey A. Keshen, *Saints, Sinners, and Soldiers: Canada's Second World War* (Vancouver: UBC Press, 2004), 13.

44. Bernd Horn and Stephen Harris, eds., *Warrior Chiefs: Perspectives on Senior Canadian Military Chiefs* (Toronto: Dundurn, 2000), 303.

45. S. Radley-Walters, interviews by Larry D. Rose, January 31, and February 5, 2008.

46. After an illness, Briggs died on February 22, 1945. Sixty years after her death her name was added to the cenotaph at Harvey Station, New Brunswick.

47. C. Strange in Bill McNeil and Morris Wolfe, *Signing On: The Birth of Radio in Canada* (Toronto: Doubleday, 1982), 94.

48. J.L. Granatstein, *The Generals* (Toronto: Stoddart Publishing, 1993), 29.

49. Miller quotes *Toronto Star*, October 31, 1939; Also see B. Greene, *Who's Who in Canada, 1940–41* (Toronto: International Press, 1941), 448.

50. 1st Battalion, Black Watch of Canada, *War Diary*, September 21, 1939.

51. G. Nicholson, *The Gunners of Canada*, vol. 2 (Toronto: McClelland & Stewart, 1972), 53.

52. See for example Reginald H. Roy, *The Seaforth Highlanders of Canada, 1919–1965* (Vancouver: Seaforth Highlanders of Canada, 1969), 54.

53. Denis Whitaker and Shelagh Whitaker, *Dieppe: Tragedy to Triumph* (Toronto: McGraw-Hill Ryerson, 1992), 63. General Denis Whitaker participated in the Dieppe operation.

54. Copp, *The Brigade*, 6.

55. Al Stapleton, interview by Larry D. Rose, March 12, 2008.

56. Douglas and Greenhous, *Out of the Shadows*, 26.

57. Kim Beattie, *Dileas: History of the 48th Highlanders of Canada, 1929–1956* (Toronto: 48th Highlanders of Canada, 1957), 63.

58. Blackburn, *Where the Hell Are The Guns?*, 30–31.

59. R. Roy in Terry Copp, *No Price Too High: Canadians and the Second World War* (Toronto: McGraw-Hill Ryerson, 1996), 34.

60. John Marteinson and Michael R. McNorgan, *The Royal Canadian Armoured Corps: An Illustrated History* (Toronto: Royal Canadian Armoured Corps Association, 2000), 80.

61. *Ibid.*, 81. Also E.A.C. Amy, interview by Larry D. Rose, April 8, 2008.

62. D.J. Goodspeed, *Battle Royal: A History of the Royal Regiment of Canada 1862–1962* (Toronto: Royal Regiment of Canada Association, 1962), 356.

63. Robert Thexton, *Times To Remember: Some Recollections of Four and a Half Years Service with the West Nova Scotia Regiment During 1940–1944* (self-published, 2008), 26, footnote 7.

64. Bercuson, *Battalion of Heroes*, 18.

65. Copp, *The Brigade*, 6.

66. Goodspeed, *Battle Royal*, 356.

67. H.M. Jackson, *The Royal Regiment of Artillery, Ottawa, 1855–1952* (self-published, 1952), 166.

68. Blackburn, *Where the Hell are the Guns*, 24.

69. Lieut. R.J. Peterson in *ibid.*, 47.

70. David J. Bercuson, *The Patricias: The Proud History of a Fighting Regiment* (Toronto: Stoddart Publishing, 2001), 153.

71. *Ibid.*, 154–55.

72. Williams, *Far From Home*, 129.

73. Roy, *The Seaforth Highlanders of Canada, 1919–1965*, 56.

74. Arthur Bishop, *Courage in the Air: Canada's Military Heritage*, vol. 1 (Toronto: McGraw-Hill Ryerson, 1992), 174. Henderson was killed in action in July 1940.

75. Floyd Williston, *Through Footless Halls of Air: The Stories of a Few of the Many Who Failed to Return* (Renfrew, Ontario: General Store Publishing, 1999), 10.

76. *Ibid.*

77. Douglas and Greenhous, *Out of the Shadows*, 32.

78. W.A.B. Douglas, *The Official History of Royal Canadian Air Force*, vol. 2, *The Creation of a National Air Force* (Toronto: University of Toronto Press, 1986), 344.

79. S. Kostenuk and J. Griffin, *RCAF Squadrons Histories and Aircraft: 1924–1968* (Toronto: Samuel Stevens Hakkert, 1977), 51.

80. Sarty, *The Maritime Defence of Canada*, 235.

81. *Ibid.*

82. Russell Bannock, interview by Larry D. Rose, March 29, 2010; L. Gray, *Canada's World War II Aces: Heroic Pilots & Gunners of the Wartime Skies* (49th Shelf Publishing, 2006), 24ff. Russell Bannock

became one of the outstanding Mosquito pilots of the war, taking on the dangerous occupation of shooting down V-1 rockets.

83. Nora Bottomley, *424 Squadron History: A Detailed Pictoral History of 424 Squadron (RCAF) From Its Origins in 1935 to Modern Times* (Belleville, Ontario: Hangar Bookshelf, 1985), 17–19.

84. *Time* Magazine, December 4, 1939.

85. William Lyon Mackenzie King, "Diaries of Prime Minister William Lyon Mackenzie King," Library and Archives Canada, www.collectionscanada.gc.ca/databases/king/index-e.html, September 15, 1939.

86. Tony German, *The Sea Is at Our Gates: A History of the Canadian Navy* (Toronto: McClelland & Stewart, 1990), 73.

87. Nelles to Minister, September 12, 1939, NAC RG 24, 3842, NSS 1017-10-23, part 1, in Douglas et al., *No Higher Purpose*, 57.

88. Douglas et al., *No Higher Purpose*, 55, 56.

89. Sarty, *The Maritime Defence of Canada*, 119; also Milner, *Canada's Navy*, 80.

90. Marc Milner, "Rear Admiral Leonard Murray," in Michael Whitby et al., *The Admirals: Canada's Senior Naval Leadership in the Twentieth Century* (Toronto: Dundurn, 2006), 102–03.

91. K. Macpherson and M. Milner, *Corvettes of the Royal Canadian Navy, 1939–1945* (St. Catharines, Ontario: Vanwell Publishing Ltd., 2002), 6.

92. *Ibid.*

93. Johnston, *Corvettes Canada*, 3.

94. Marc Milner, *Battle of the Atlantic* (St. Catharines, Ontario: Vanwell Publishing Ltd., 2011), 41.

95. Hansard, Committee on Veterans Affairs, Nova Scotia House of Assembly, November 9, 2006.

96. Robert G. Halford, *The Unknown Navy: Canada's World War II Merchant Navy* (St. Catharines, Ontario, Vanwell Publshing Ltd., 1995), 26. The book contains a list of ship losses in Appendix 3.

97. Lamb, *On The Triangle Run*, 41–44.

98. Earle Wagner, The Memory Project, Digital Archive, Dominion Institute.

99. J. MacInnis, CTV report, Halifax, September 23, 2008.

100. Wagner, The Memory Project; Hansard, Nova Scotia House of Assembly, November 9, 2006.

101. Welland, interview.

102. Skelton, "Canadian War Policy," August 24, 1939, Library and Archives Canada, file 388, part 2, NA, RG 25 D-1, vol. 780. Also King's Diary, August 25, 1939.

103. Sarty, *The Maritime Defence of Canada*, 235.

104. *Ibid.*, 236.

105. Douglas et al., *No Higher Purpose*, 74; Memo from Ralston to Rogers, September 21, 1939, Directorate of History and Heritage NHs 8200 (1939–45), pt 3; C.P. Stacey, *Arms, Men and Governments: The War Policies of Canada, 1939–1945* (Ottawa: The Queen's Printer, 1970), 11.

106. Stacey, *Arms, Men and Governments*, 11–12; Also Department of National Defence Estimates, 1939–40, Directorate of History and Heritage 181.009 (D3658).

107. A full account of the British Commonwealth Air Training Plan in Douglas, *The Official History of Royal Canadian Air Force*, 191ff.

108. King's Diary, October 17, 1939.

109. Stacey, *Arms, Men and Government*, 10–11.

110. *Ibid.*, 11.

111. *Toronto Star*, November 2–3, 1939; *Globe and Mail*, November 3, 1939.

112. David Gardner, CNN interview, February 6, 2002.

113. Douglas, *The Official History of Royal Canadian Air Force*, 344.

CHAPTER TWELVE

1. M. Postan et al., *History of the Second World War: Design and Development of Weapons: Studies on Government and Industrial Organization* (London: H.M. Stationery Office, 1964), 308–10; Donald Cameron Watt, *Too Serious a Business: European Armed Forces and the Approach to the Second World War* (Berkeley, California: University of California Press, 1975), 81.

2. Jean-Marie d'Hoop, *La politique française du rearmament (1933–1939)*, quoted in Watt, *Too Serious a Business*, 37.

3. Lieutenant Colonel F. R. Kirkland, "The French Air Force in 1940," *Air University Review*, U.S. Department of the Air Force, September–October 1985.

4. Ian Kershaw, *Fateful Choices: Ten Decisions that Changed the World* (New York: Penguin Group, 2007), 141.

5. Thomas B. Buell, *Master of Sea Power: A Biography of Fleet Admiral Ernest J. King* (Annapolis, Maryland: Naval Institute Press, 1995), 129. Admiral King's rabidly anti-British views were noted in chapter two of this book.

6. William L. Langer and S. Everett Gleason, *The Undeclared War, 1940–1941* (New York: Harper & Brothers Ltd., 1953), 845–46.

7. David Edgerton, *Britain's War Machine: Weapons, Resources, and Experts in the Second World War* (London: Oxford University Press, 2011), 61–62, quoting General Fedor von Bock. Montgomery held the exact opposite view, "weapons and equipment ... were quite inadequate." Bernard Law Montgomery, *The Memoirs of Field-Marshal Montgomery* (London: World Publishing, 1958), 47.

8. Watt, *Too Serious a Business*, 81; Williamson Murray, *The Change in the European Balance of Power, 1938–1939: The Path to Ruin* (Princeton, NJ; Princeton University Press, 1984), 49.

9. Charles S. Thomas, *The German Navy in the Nazi Era* (Annapolis, Michigan: Naval Institute Press, 1990), 187.

10. Len Deighton, *Blood, Tears and Folly: In the Darkest Hour of the Second World War* (London: Jonathan Cape, 1993), 350.

11. Derek Wood and Derek Dempster, *The Narrow Margin: The Battle of Britain and the Rise of Air Power, 1939–40* (London: Hutchinson, 1961), 7.

12. The building is still in use by the German government.

13. M. Urquhart and K. Buckley, *Historical Statistics of Canada* (Toronto: Macmillan, 1965).

14. G.H. Gill, *Royal Australian Navy, 1939–1945* (Canberra: Australian War Memorial, 1957), 47ff.

15. G. Sheridan, *The Australian*, May 12, 2012.

16. House of Commons Debates, April 26, 1939, 3253.

17. A discussion of the definition of "military readiness" and the meaning of the term in M. R. Voith, "Military Readiness," *Army Doctrine and Training Bulletin*, Department of National Defence, vol. 4, no 2., Summer 2001, 4–48.

18. Roy joined the pre-war reserves and then served in Europe with the Canadian Scottish Regiment. Reginald Roy, *Sinews of Steel* (Kelowna, British Columbia: Whizzbang Association, 1965), 102.

19. C.P. Stacey, *The Canadian Army, 1939–1945: An Official Historical Summary* (Ottawa: King's Printer, 1948), 2.

20. House of Commons Debates, April 26, 1939, 3255.

21. J.L. Granatstein, *The Generals* (Toronto: Stoddart Publishing, 1993), 8.

22. John A. English, *The Canadian Army and the Normandy Campaign: A Study of Failure in High Command* (Westport, Connecticut: Praeger, 1991), 242. In the course of the war the regular army had to expand to fifty times its original size (fifteen-fold for the British).

23. Granatstein, *The Generals*, 259.

24. *Ibid.*, 21.

25. *Ibid.*, 20–21.

26. B. Hoffmeister, Granatstein interview, March 2, 1992.

27. John A. English, *Lament for an Army: The Decline of Canadian Military Professionalism* (Toronto: Irwin, 1998), 31.

28. English, *The Canadian Army and The Normandy Campaign*, 240.

29. *Ibid.* McNaughton biographer John Rickard also says "McNaughton remained CGS for seven years.... In that time he failed to prepare the army for modern war." John Nelson Rickard, *The Politics of Command: Lieutenant-General A.G.L. McNaughton and the Canadian Army, 1939–1943* (Toronto: University of Toronto Press, 2010), 28.

30. English, *The Canadian Army and the Normandy Campaign*, 135.

31. David Bercuson, *Battalion of Heroes: The Calgary Highlanders in World War II* (Calgary: Calgary Highlanders Regimental Funds Foundation, 1994), 18–19.

32. J. Edwards, interview by Larry D. Rose, June 25, 2008.

33. The number of soldiers in a Canadian infantry division increased as the war continued, up to about 18,000 members. Some allied divisions, reinforced for D-Day, numbered up to 30,000.

34. A partial list from "The Gentlemen in Battledress," an address by Lieutenant Colonel James Mess, November 28, 1941, Department of National Defence. A copy is in the Royal Regiment of Canada Museum, Toronto.

35. English, *The Canadian Army and the Normandy Campaign*, 57ff.

36. *Ibid.*, 66.

37. Jean V. Allard, *The Memoirs of General Jean V. Allard* (Vancouver: UBC Press, 1988), 25.

38. *Ibid.*, 24–25.

39. D.J. Goodspeed, ed., *The Armed Forces of Canada 1867–1967: A Century of Achievement* (Ottawa: Canadian Forces Headquarters, Directorate of History, Queen's Printer, 1967), 96.

40. Kim Beattie, *Dileas: History of the 48th Highlanders of Canada, 1929–1956 (Toronto: 48th Highlanders of Canada, 1957)*, 35.

41. Granatstein, *The Generals*, 180.

42. Granatstein lists Victor Odlum and Basil Price as among the early failures.

43. Granatstein, *The Generals*, 259.

44. Interview with Major General Vokes, in Granatstein, *The Generals*, 159.

45. E.A.C. Amy, interview by Larry D. Rose, April 8, 2008.

46. C.P. Stacey, *The Military Problems of Canada: A Survey of Defence Policies and Strategic Conditions Past and Present* (Toronto: Ryerson Press, 1940), 143.

47. Doug Knight ed., *Tools of the Trade: Equipping the Canadian Army* (Ottawa: Service Publications, 2005), 16.

48. Stacey, *The Military Problems of Canada*, 125.

49. J.L. Granatstein, *Notes for Address to the Royal Canadian Military Institute, October 28, 2011*. For an excellent summary and critique of the Hong Kong disaster see Galen Perras, "Defeat Still Cries Aloud For Explanation: Explaining C Force's Dispatch to Hong Kong," *Canadian Military Journal*, Autumn 2011, 37–47.

50. George S. MacDonell, *One Soldier's Story: 1939–1945: From the Fall of Hong Kong to the Defeat of Japan* (Toronto: Dundurn, 2002), 68.

51. Brian Nolan, *King's War: Mackenzie King and the Politics of War, 1939–1945* (Toronto: Random House of Canada, Ltd., 1990), 56.

52. Paul Dickson, "Crerar and the Decision to Garrison Hong Kong," *Canadian Military History*, vol. 3, 1994, 97–110.

53. George Randolph Pearkes, interviews by Reginald Roy, 1966. University of Victoria Archives.

54. Carl Vincent, *No Reason Why: The Canadian Hong Kong Tragedy* (Stittsville, Ontario: Canada's Wings, 1981).

55. *Ibid.*, 33. Vincent calls Crerar's action a "virtual rubber stamp approval," 25.

56. *Ibid.*, 79ff.

57. MacDonell, *One Soldier's Story*, 159.

58. L. Duff, *The Report on the Canadian Expeditionary Force to the Crown Colony of Hong Kong* (Ottawa: King's Printer, 1942).

59. MacDonell, *One Soldier's Story*, 159. Vincent, *No Reason Why*, 223. On the only possible verdict see Galen Perras, "Defeat Still Cries Aloud for Explanation."

60. B.H. Liddell Hart, *History of the Second World War* (London: Cassell, 1970), 219; George F.G. Stanley, *Canada's Soldiers, 1604–1954: The Military History of an Unmilitary People* (Toronto: Macmillan, 1960), 380–81.

61. MacDonell, *One Soldier's Story*, 90.

62. C.P. Stacey, *Arms, Men and Governments: The War Policies of Canada, 1939–1945* (Ottawa: The Queen's Printer, 1970), 41.

63. Morton, *Canada at War*, 117.

64. John English et al., eds. *Mackenzie King: Citizenship and Community* (Toronto: Robin Brass Studio, 2002), 148. Clearly, King was worried that sending a force might later be used as an argument for conscription. After the war King falsely claimed that he had "strenuously" opposed sending troops. William Lyon Mackenzie King, "Diaries of Prime Minister William Lyon Mackenzie King," Library and Archives Canada, www.collectionscanada.gc.ca/databases/king/index-e.html, February 25, 1948.

65. S.R. Elliot, *Scarlet to Green: A History of Intelligence in the Canadian Army, 1903–1963* (Toronto: Canadian Intelligence and Security Association, 1981), 374. Also James Eayrs, *In Defence of Canada*, vol. 1, *From the Great War to the Great Depression* (Toronto: University of Toronto Press, 1965), 77 and 91–93 says the department relied "too exclusively upon Imperial sources and too little upon its own." Dickson, "Crerar and the Decision to Garrison Hong Kong," 170.

66. Dickson, "Crerar and the Decision to Garrison Hong Kong," 105.

67. Elliot, *Scarlet to Green*, 377–78.

68. *Ibid.*, 375.

69. *Ibid.*, 375.

70. S. Harris, "The Canadian Way of War, 1919–1939," in Bernd Horn ed., *The Canadian Way of War: Serving the National Interest* (Toronto: Dundurn, 2006), 207.

71. Paul Douglas Dickson, *A Thoroughly Canadian General: A Biography of General H.D.G. Crerar* (Toronto: University of Toronto Press, 2007), 173.

72. Galen Perras, "Defeat Still Cries Aloud for Explanation," 37–47.

73. J.L. Granatstein, *Canada's Army: Waging War and Keeping the Peace* (Toronto: University of Toronto Press, 2002), 210.

74. Clement Dick interview, May 7, 1991, for Granatstein, *The Generals*.

75. Letter from A.A.G. Smith to Granatstein, January 4, 1994, in Granatstein, *Canada's Army*, 211.

76. *Toronto Star*, August 31, 1989.

77. John Keegan, *Six Armies in Normandy: From D-Day to the Liberation of Paris* (London: Jonathan Cape Ltd., 1982), 120–21.

78. Brian Loring Villa, *Unauthorized Action: Mountbatten and the Dieppe Raid* (Oxford: Oxford University Press, 1991), 3.

79. *Ibid.*, 232.

80. Professor Anthony Verrier in Denis Whitaker and Shelagh Whitaker, *Dieppe: Tragedy to Triumph* (Toronto: McGraw-Hill Ryerson, 1992), 59.

81. *Ibid.*, 97.

82. Villa, *Unauthorized Action*, 191.

83. Dickson, *A Thoroughly Canadian General*, 161.

84. Reginald H. Roy, *For Most Conspicuous Bravery: A Biography of Major-General George R. Pearkes, V.C., Through Two World Wars* (Vancouver: UBC Press, 1977), 172–73; E.L.M. Burns, *General Mud: Memoirs*

of Two World Wars (Toronto: Irwin Publishing, 1970), 115; C.P. Stacey, *Six Years of War: The Army in Canada, Britain and the Pacific*, vol.1 (Ottawa: Department of National Defence, 1955), 400–01, lists the "lessons learned" official and otherwise. Stacey says: "yet it had not been necessary to attack Dieppe in order to learn them."

85. The conclusion of Granatstein, "Dieppe 60 Years On," *National Post*, 2002.

86. Winston Churchill, *My Early Life: 1874–1904* (New York: Scribner, 1996), 232.

87. Anrew Roberts, *Eminent Churchillians* (London: Weidenfeld and Nicholson, 1994), 69.

88. Mac Johnston, *Corvettes Canada: Convoy Veterans of WWII Tell Their True Stories* (Toronto: John Wiley & Sons, 2008), 1

89. Marc Milner, "On A War Footing," *Legion Magazine*. January 1, 2007.

90. Joseph Schull, *The Far Distant Ships: An Official Account of Canadian Naval Operations in the Second World War* (Toronto: Stoddart Publishing, 1987), 10–11.

91. James B. Lamb, *The Corvette Navy: True Stories from Canada's Atlantic War* (Toronto: Macmillan, 1979), 58.

92. Watt, *Too Serious a Business*, 55.

93. Mac Johnston, *Corvettes Canada: Convoy Veterans of WWII Tell Their True Stories* (Toronto: John Wiley & Sons, 2008), 272.

94. *Ibid.*, 25.

95. *Ibid.*, 8–9.

96. *Ibid.*, 6.

97. Robert Welland, interviews by Larry D. Rose, January 11, 2008, and May 17, 2008.

98. Fraser McKee and Robert Darlington, *The Canadian Naval Chronicle, 1939–1945* (St. Catharines, Ontario: Vanwell Publishing Ltd., 1996), 33.

99. Marc Milner, *Canada's Navy: The First Century* (Toronto: University of Toronto Press, 1999), 95–96; McKee and Darlington, *The Canadian Naval Chronicle*, 33–36. As the authors point out, the phrase "wartime acknowledged sinking" refers to the fact that it was only long after the war that records showed HMCS *Ottawa* had very likely sunk an Italian submarine in November 1940.

100. Marc Milner, *Battle of the Atlantic* (St. Catharines, Ontario: Vanwell Publishing Ltd., 2011), 137. Many later convoys had additional escorts but a much larger contingent of merchant ships that did not appreciably increase the risk.

101. *Ibid.*

102. Donald Macintyre, *U-Boat Killer: Fighting the U-Boats in the Battle of the Atlantic* (London: Weidenfeld & Nicholson, 1956), 173.

103. J. Rohwer, review of "The U-Boat Hunters," *International Historical Review*, vol. XVIII, no. 1, February 1996, 209.

104. Piers was later a rear-admiral.

105. Michael L. Hadley, *U-Boats Against Canada: German Submarines in Canadian Waters* (Montreal: McGill-Queens University Press, 1985), 292.

106. On May 10, 1940, thirty-two Battles were sent against the Luftwaffe in France, of which thirteen were lost and all the rest damaged.

107. W.A.B. Douglas, *The Official History of Royal Canadian Air Force*, vol. 2, *The Creation of a National Air Force* (Toronto: University of Toronto Press, 1986), 466.

108. *Ibid.*

109. Brereton Greenhous et al., *The Crucible of War 1939–1945*, vol. 3 (Toronto: University of Toronto Press, 1994), 16ff.

110. B. Dalke, "Canada's Greatest Contribution — National Identity and the Role of Prime Minister W.L. Mackenzie King in Negotiating the BCATP Agreement," *Canadian Defence Journal*, vol. 9, no. 4.

111. J.L. Granatstein and Desmond Morton, *Canada and the Two World Wars* (Toronto: Key Porter, 2003), 231.

112. Wood and Dempster, *The Narrow Margin*, 212.

113. The exact numbers vary. These are cited by R. Hough and D. Richards, *The Battle of Britain* (London: Norton, 1990), 191.

114. W.A.B. Douglas and Brereton Greenhous, *Out of the Shadows: Canada in the Second World War*, revised edition (Toronto: Dundurn, 1996), 180. Gobeil was the first RCAF member to shoot down a German aircraft. Canadians in RAF service had previously done the same. In 1943 Gobeil was part of a trial to use towed gliders to carry cargo across the Atlantic. He flew a glider tethered to a DC-3. Robert Farquharson, *For Your Tomorrow: Canadians and the Burma Campaign, 1941–1945* (Toronto: Trafford Publishing, 2004), 143.

115. Carl Vincent, *Canadian Aircraft of WWII* (Kitchener, Ontario: Aviaeology, 2009), 18.

116. Hugh A. Halliday, "The Battle of Britain," Part 17, *Legion Magazine*, September 1, 2006.

117. N. Marion ed., *Camp Borden: Birthplace of the RCAF, 1917–1999* (Borden, Ontario: 16 Wing, 2004), 78.

118. William Carr, interview by Larry D. Rose, January 19, 2008.

119. R. Bannock, interview by Larry D. Rose, March 29, 2010.

120. R. Wakelam, "No Easy Thing — Senior Command in the Canadian Army, 1939–45," *Canadian Military History*, Winter 2011, 23.

121. While Mackenzie King's name was frequently reviled by armed forces members, Jim "Stocky" Edwards was outspoken in King's support on Canadianization. Edwards said King wanted all the squadrons to be Canadian, but it took a long time. Edwards, interview.

122. Suzanne K. Edwards, "The Leadership of Air Marshal Harold (Gus) Edwards," *Canadian Aerospace Power Studies*, vol. 1, March 2009, http://airforceapp.forces.gc.ca/CFAWC/eLibrary/pubs/SicIturAdAstra-Vol1_e.pdf.

123. S. Dunmore and W. Carter, *Reap The Whirlwind* (Toronto: McClelland & Stewart, 1991), 14.

CHAPTER THIRTEEN

1. Susan Kelman, *Globe and Mail*, November 12, 2010. On the other hand, Charles Vining wrote of King in 1934, "He has a tendency to procrastinate until a crisis is upon him and he then improvises under fire with a skill which sometimes has transported his follows from desperation to delight." C. Vining in John English et al., eds. *Mackenzie King: Citizenship and Community* (Toronto: Robin Brass Studio, 2002), xiii.

2. Bruce Hutchison, *The Incredible Canadian* (Toronto: Longmans Canada, 1953), 7.

3. Allan Levine, *King: William Lyon Mackenzie King: A Life Guided by the Hand of Destiny* (Vancouver: Douglas & McIntyre, 2012), 278.

4. MacDonell, interview by Larry D. Rose, July 20, 2008 and March 31, 2011.

5. House of Commons Debates, March 25, 1937.

6. William Lyon Mackenzie King, "Diaries of Prime Minister William Lyon Mackenzie King," Library and Archives Canada, www.collectionscanada.gc.ca/databases/king/index-e.html, August 22, 1939.

7. D. Bercuson, *Globe and Mail*, October 14, 2009.

8. C.P. Stacey, *Canada and the Age of Conflict*, vol. 2, *1921–1948, The Mackenzie King Era* (Toronto: University of Toronto Press, 1981), 275.

9. J. Pickersgill, Granatstein Interview.

10. C.P. Stacey, *Mackenzie King and the Atlantic Triangle* (Toronto: Macmillan of Canada, 1976); also M. Pope, *Soldiers and Politicians* (Toronto: University of Toronto Press, 1962), 175.

11. Stacey, *Canada and the Age of Conflict*, 237.

12. *Ibid.* Generally speaking, King was the first to blame others for any failure and the last to offer credit to anyone else for success.

13. T. Hockin, "The Prime Minister and Political Leadership: An Introduction to Some Restraints and Imperatives," in Thomas A. Hockin ed., *The Apex of Power: The Prime Minister and Political Leadership in Canada* (Scarborough, Ontario: Prentice-Hall of Canada, 1971), 18–21.

14. *Ibid.*, 20.

15. R. MacGregor Dawson in Hockin, *Apex of Power*, 94.

16. Roger Sarty, *The Maritime Defence of Canada* (Toronto: Canadian Institute of Strategic Studies, 1997), 17ff.

17. C.P. Stacey, *The Military Problems of Canada: A Survey of Defence Policies and Strategic Conditions Past and Present* (Toronto: Ryerson Press, 1940), 143.

18. This comparison was suggested by Stephen Harris in a message to the author, May 26, 2009.

19. James Eayrs, *Selected Papers from the Transactions of the Institute, 1937–38*, no. 33, Canadian Military Institute, 20.

20. Blair Neatby, *William Lyon Mackenzie King: The Prism of Unity*, vol. 3, *1933–1939* (Toronto: University of Toronto Press, 1975), 128.

21. Stacey, *Canada and the Age of Conflict*, 216.

22. King's power was by no means absolute, but he was the only figure who spoke for the entire country while his cabinet ministers tended to have regional power bases. King was not as powerful on all issues. He was sometimes anti-Semitic but felt some Jews fleeing Europe should be allowed into Canada. The cabinet, and in particular Lapointe, were adamantly opposed and King gave way. Levine, *King*, 15 and 286ff; Blair Neatby, *William Lyon Mackenzie King: The Prism of Unity*, vol. 3, *1933–1939* (Toronto: University of Toronto Press, 1975), 304.

23. Neatby, *William Lyon Mackenzie King*, 160.

24. K. Norrie et al., *A History of the Canadian Economy* (Toronto: Nelson College Indigenous, 2008), 296.

25. Unless otherwise noted, statistics in this section based on M. Urquhart and K. Buckley, *Historical Statistics of Canada* (Toronto: Macmillan, 1965), and M. Horn, "The Great Depression of the 1930s in Canada" (booklet, Canadian Historical Society, 1984).

26. Neatby, *William Lyon Mackenzie King*, 188.

27. Norrie, *A History of the Canadian Economy*, 317.

28. *Ibid.*, 344.

29. Bennett had moved toward a bigger role for Ottawa with the establishment of the Bank of Canada in 1934, along with the Canadian Broadcasting Corporation and Trans Canada Airlines.

30. Pierre Berton, *The Great Depression: 1929–1939* (Toronto: McClelland & Stewart, 1990), 10.

31. Horn, "The Great Depression of the 1930s in Canada." Norrie, *A History of the Canadian Economy*, 342. Neatby, *William Lyon Mackenzie King*, 153.

32. Quoted in J.L. Granatstein and J.M. Hitsman, *Broken Promises: A History of Conscription in Canada* (Toronto: Oxford University Press, 1977), 123.

33. John MacFarlane, *Ernest Lapointe and Quebec's Influence on Canadian Foreign Policy* (Toronto: University of Toronto Press, 1999), 14, challenges this view saying French Canadian opinion was much more complex and varied.

34. Berton, *The Great Depression*, 364.

35. King's Diary, October 29, 1935.

36. Lapointe was most notably meeting with O.D. Skelton. MacFarlane, *Ernest Lapointe*, 144.

37. King's Diary, March 31, 1939.

38. MacFarlane, *Ernest Lapointe*, 140–41.

39. King's Diary, March 31, 1939.

40. MacFarlane, *Ernest Lapointe*, 150. Even though most of the Catholic clergy remained adamantly against the war, Villeneuve later held huge masses in support of the army and encouraged the faithful to buy Victory bonds. However, in 1937 Villeneuve had said, "Dictatorship is far better than revolution." in Richard Jones, "Politics and Culture: The French Canadians and the Second World War," in Sidney Aster ed., *The Second World War as a National Experience* (Ottawa: The Canadian Committee for the History of the Second World War, 1981).

41. Neatby, *William Lyon Mackenzie King*, 175; Also Dickson said "Mackenzie King ... believed his goal was to bring Canada though the war intact" in "Harry Crerar and an Army for Strategic Effect," *Canadian Military History*, Winter 2008, vol. 17, no.1, 37.

42. J.L. Granatstein, *Canada's War: The Politics of the Mackenzie King Government, 1939–1945* (Toronto: University of Toronto Press, 1975), 19. Copp has challenged the view, at least in the case of Ontario. "The people of Ontario supported a declaration of war out of their informed convictions that fundamental issues were at stake." T. Copp, "Ontario 1939: The Decision for War," in Norman Hillmer, et al., *A Country of Limitations: Canada and the World in 1939* (Ottawa: Canadian Committee for the History of the Second World War, 1996), 109ff.

43. Granatstein, *Canada's War*, 19.

44. G. Case, "The Lessons of Munich: Mackenzie King's Campaign to Prepare Canada for War," *Canadian Military Journal*, vol. 3, no. 4, 2.

45. D. Bercuson, *Globe and Mail*, October 14, 2009. Also see George F.G. Stanley, *Canada's Soldiers, 1604–1954: The Military History of an Unmilitary People* (Toronto: Macmillan, 1960), 353–54.

46. Hutchison, *The Incredible Canadian*, 7.

47. King's Diary, September 12, 1939.

48. Desmond Morton, *A Military History of Canada* (Toronto: McClelland & Stewart, 2007), 178.

49. J.L. Granatstein and Norman Hillmer, "Historians Rank the Best and Worst Canadian Prime Ministers," *Maclean's*, April 21, 1997; J.L. Granatstein and Norman Hillmer, *Prime Ministers: Ranking Canada's Leaders* (Toronto: HarperCollins Canada, 1999), 84ff ;and *Maclean's*, June 20, 2011. It is notable that one of Canada's greatest public servants, Norman Robertson, who worked closely with King for many years, was much less charitable. On the occasion of King's death Robertson remarked to a startled friend, "I never saw a touch of greatness in him." J.L. Granatstein, *A Man of Influence: Norman A. Robertson and Canadian Statecraft* (Toronto: Deneau Publishers, 1981), 202.

50. J.L. Granatstein and Desmond Morton, *Canada and the Two World Wars* (Toronto: Key Porter, 2003), 308–10.

51. W.A.B. Douglas, *The Official History of Royal Canadian Air Force*, vol. 2, *The Creation of a National Air Force* (Toronto: University of Toronto Press, 1986), 191.

52. King's Diary, September 28, 1939.

53. *Ibid.*

54. J. Edwards, interview by Larry D. Rose, June 25, 2008. Of course, there were some very good planes built too, including the Spitfire and Lancaster.

55. Hutchison, *The Incredible Canadian*, 7.

56. David J. Bercuson, "The Valour and the Horror: An Historical Analysis," in David J. Bercuson and S.F. Wise eds., *The Valour and the Horror Revisited* (Montreal: McGill-Queen's University Press, 1994), 122.

57. Mac Johnston, *Corvettes Canada: Convoy Veterans of WWII Tell Their True Stories* (Toronto: John Wiley & Sons, 2008), 296.

58. Paul Dickson, "Harry Crerar and an Army for Strategic Effect," *Canadian Military History*, vol. 17, issue 1, 37.

59. Hutchison, *The Incredible Canadian*, 228.

60. A. Lawlor, Welland Obituary, *Globe and Mail*, June 16, 2010.

61. Reginald Roy, "Morale in the Canadian Army in Canada during the Second World War," *Canadian Defence Quarterly*, Autumn, 1986.

62. W.A.B. Douglas and Brereton Greenhous, *Out of the Shadows: Canada in the Second World War*, revised edition (Toronto: Dundurn, 1996), 36.

63. W. Cumming in Tariq Malik, "Astronauts Mark Apollo 11 Anniversary," July 20, 2009, www.space.com/7022-astronauts-mark-apollo-11-anniversary-spacewalk.html.

64. James B. Lamb, *On The Triangle Run: The Fighting Spirit of Canada's Navy* (Toronto: HarperCollins, 1987), 1.

65. Bill Rawling, "The Generalship of Andrew McNaughton: A Study In Failure," in Bernd Horn and Stephen Harris, eds., *Warrior Chiefs: Perspectives on Senior Canadian Military Chiefs* (Toronto: Dundurn, 2000), 73–88.

66. J.L. Granatstein, *The Generals* (Toronto: Stoddart Publishing, 1993), 263.

67. Tony Foster, *Meeting of Generals* (Toronto: Methuen, 1986), 165.

68. W.A.B. Anderson, Granatstein Interviews, May 21, 1991.

69. Granatstein, *The Generals*, 263.

70. E. Soward, *A Formidable Hero* (Toronto: CANAV Books, 1984).

71. Ceris Schrader, "Lady Lost Five Sons," www.hellfire-corner.demon.co.uk/ceris.htm. It was not until June 2003 that the Department of Veterans Affairs saw fit to place a headstone marking her sacrifice.

72. S. Radley-Walters, interviews by Larry D. Rose, January 31, and February 5, 2008.

73. E.A.C. Amy, interview by Larry D. Rose, April 8, 2008.

74. John A. English, *The Canadian Army and the Normandy Campaign: A Study of Failure in High Command* (Westport, Connecticut: Praeger, 1991), 63.

75. Granatstein, *Address to the Royal Canadian Military Institute*, November 9, 2011.

76. *Hamilton Spectator*, October 3, 2001.

77. F. Carriere, Roy Interview.

78. Jeffery Williams, *Far From Home: A Memoir of a 20th Century Soldier* (Calgary: University of Calgary Press, 2003), 131.

79. Kim Beattie, *Dileas: History of the 48th Highlanders of Canada, 1929–1956* (Toronto: 48th Highlanders of Canada, 1957), 32.

SELECTED BIBLIOGRAPHY

ABBREVIATIONS

CDQ — *Canadian Defence Quarterly*
CMH — *Canadian Military History*
CMJ — *Canadian Military Journal*
DHH — Directorate of History and Heritage
LAC — Library and Archives Canada
Legion — *Legion Magazine*

INTERVIEWS

Brigadier General E.A.C. "Ned" Amy, March 3, and April 17, 2008.
Wing Commander Russell Bannock, March 29, 2010.
Alfred Babin, July 20, 2008.
Robert Billings, July 7, 2010.
Lieutenant General William Carr, January 19, 2008.
Michael Carr-Harris, May 29, 2010.
Lieutenant Colonel James "Stocky" Edwards, June 24, 2008.
Charley Fox, June 20, 2008.
Norman F. Green, June 8, 2008.
Wallace Harrington, July 15, 2008.
Vice Admiral R.L. Hennessy, May 7–8, 2008.
George MacDonell, July 20, 2008, and March 31, 2011.
Bruce O'Connor, May 21–22, 2008.
Frederick Price, Letters, May 28, 2008, and July 20, 2008. Interview, May 31, 2008.
William John Quinsey, June 15, 2008.

Grant Radley-Walters (son of Sydney Radley-Walters), July 10, 2010.

Brigadier General Sydney Radley-Walters, January 31, 2008, and February 5, 2008.

Al Stapleton, March 12, 2008.

Harry Watts, January 10, 2008.

Lieutenant Commander Eugene Weber, May 5, 2008.

Rear Admiral Robert Welland, January 11, 2008, and May 12, 2008.

Peter Worthington, Letter April 10, 2010. Interview April 23, 2008.

OTHER INTERVIEWS

J.L. Granatstein. Interviews for *The Generals*, DHH 00093 93/9.

George Randolph Pearkes. Interviews by Reginald Roy, 1966. University of Victoria Archives.

ARTICLES

Burns, E.L.M. "A Division That Can Attack." *CDQ* XV (April 1938).

Copp, Terry. "The Defence of Hong Kong December 1941." *CMH* 10, no. 4 (Autumn 2001).

Dafoe, John. "What's the Cheering For?" Winnipeg *Free Press* (October 3, 1938).

Delaney, D. "Looking Back on Canadian Generalship in the Second World War." *Canadian Army Journal* 7.1 (Spring 2004): 13–22.

Dickson, Paul Douglas. "Harry Crerar and an Army for Strategic Effect." *CMH* 17, no. 1 (Winter 2008): 37–48.

Dickson, Paul Douglas. "Crerar and the Decision to Garrison Hong Kong." *CMJ* 3 (1994).

Drew, George A. "Canada's Armament Mystery." *Maclean's* (September 1, 1938).

Drew, George A. "Canada's Defence Farce." *Financial Post* (March 26, 1938).

Granatstein, J.L. "Arming the Nation: Canada's Industrial War Effort 1939–1945." Canadian Council of Chief Executives (May 27, 2005).

Halliday, Hugh A. "The Imperial Gift." *Legion Magazine* (September 2004).

Hansen, Kenneth. "The Destroyer Myth." *Canadian Naval Review* 3, no. 3 (2006).

Hillmer, Norman. "Defence and Ideology: The Anglo-Canadian Military 'Alliance' in the 1930s." *International Journal* XXIII (Summer 1978): 588–12.

Hooker, M.A. "Serving Two Masters: Ian Mackenzie and Civil-Military Relations in Canada, 1935–1939." *Journal of Canadian Studies* 21, no. 1: 38–56.

Keightley, B.W. "The Germany I Saw." *Maclean's* (July 1, 1935).

McAndrew B. "Operational Art and the Northwest European Theatre of War, 1944." *CDQ* 21 (Winter 1991): 19–26.

Mackenzie, David. "The Bren Gun Scandal and the Maclean Publishing Company's Investigation of Canadian Defence Contracts, 1938–1940." *Journal of Canadian Studies* 26, no. 3 (1991).

Miller, I. "Toronto's Response to the Outbreak of War, 1939." *CMH* (Winter 2002).

Perras, Galen. "Defeat Still Cries Aloud for Explanation: Explaining C Force's dispatch to Hong Kong." *CMJ* (Autumn 2011).

Schrader, Ceris. "Lady Lost Five Sons." www.hellfire-corner.demon.co.uk/ceris.htm.

Simonds, Guy. "An Army that Can Attack — A Division that Can Defend," *CDQ* XV, no. 4 (July 1938): 413ff.

Wakelam, R. "No Easy Thing: Senior Command in the Canadian Army, 1939–45." *CMH* 20, no. 1 (Winter 2011): 21–30.

Wentzell, T. "Brigadier J.K. Lawson and Command of "C" Force at Hong Kong." *CMH* 20, no. 2 (Spring 2011): 15–26.

DIARY

William Lyon King. *Diaries of Prime Minister William Lyon Mackenzie King.* LAC, MG26J13.

BOOKS

Allard, Jean V. *The Memoirs of General Jean V. Allard.* Vancouver: UBC Press, 1988.

Aster, Sidney, ed. *The Second World War as a National Experience.* Ottawa: The Canadian Committee for the History of the Second World War, 1981.

Batten, Jack. *The Spirit of the Regiment: An Account of the 48th Highlanders from 1956 to 1991.* Toronto: 48th Highlanders of Canada, 1991.

Beattie, Kim. *Dileas: History of the 48th Highlanders of Canada, 1929–1956.* Toronto: 48th Highlanders of Canada, 1957.

Bercuson, David. *Battalion of Heroes: The Calgary Highlanders in World War II.* Calgary: Calgary Highlanders Regimental Funds Foundation, 1994.

Bercuson, David J. *The Patricias: The Proud History of a Fighting Regiment.* Toronto: Stoddart Publishing, 2001.

Berton, Pierre. *The Great Depression: 1929–1939.* Toronto: McClelland & Stewart, 1990.

Blackburn, George. *Where The Hell Are the Guns?: A Soldier's View of the Anxious Years, 1939–44.* Toronto: McClelland & Stewart, 1999.

Boutilier, James A., ed. *The RCN in Retrospect, 1910–1968.* Vancouver: UBC Press, 1982.

Brown, George and Michael Lavigne. *Canadian Wing Commanders.* Langley, British Columbia: Battleline Books, 1984.

Copp, Terry. *The Brigade: The Fifth Canadian Infantry Brigade in WWII.* Mechanicsburg, Pennsylvania: Stackpole Books, 1992.

Davis, Justice H. *Report of the Royal Commission on the Bren Machine Gun Contract, 1939.* King's Printer, 1939.

Dickson, Paul Douglas. *A Thoroughly Canadian General: A Biography of General H.D.G. Crerar.* Toronto: University of Toronto Press, 2007.

Douglas, W.A.B. *The Creation of a Natonal Air Force.* Vol. 2. Toronto: University of Toronto Press, 1986.

Douglas, W.A.B. and Brereton Greenhaus. *Out of the Shadows: Canada in the Second World War.* Revised edition. Toronto: Dundurn, 1996.

Douglas, W.A.B., Roger Sarty, et al. *No Higher Purpose: The Official Operational History of the Royal Canadian Navy in the Second World War, 1939–1943.* Vol. 2, Part 1. St. Catharines, Ontario: Vanwell Publishing Ltd., 2004.

Douhet, G. *Command of the Air.* New York: Arno Press, 1972 (trans.)

Duff, Justice L. *Report on the Canadian Expeditionary Force to the Crown Colony of Hong Kong.* Ottawa: King's Printer, 1942.

Dunmore, S. and Carter, W., *Reap The Whirlwind.* Toronto: McClelland & Stewart, 1991.

Eayrs, J. *In Defence of Canada: From the Great War to the Great Depression.* Vol. 1 and vol. 3. Toronto: University of Toronto Press, 1965.

Elliot, S.R. *Scarlet to Green: A History of Intelligence in the Canadian Army, 1903–1963.* Toronto: Canadian Intelligence and Security Association, 1981.

English, John A. *The Canadian Army and the Normandy Campaign: A Study of Failure in High Command.* Westport, Connecticut: Praeger, 1991.

English, John A. *Lament for an Army: the Decline of Canadian Military Professionalism.* Toronto: Irwin, 1998.

English, John A. et al. *Mackenzie King: Citizenship and Community.* Toronto: Robin Brass Studio, 2002.

German, Tony. *The Sea Is at Our Gates: A History of the Canadian Navy*. Toronto: McClelland & Stewart, 1990.

Goodspeed, D.J. *Battle Royal*. Toronto: Royal Regiment of Canada Association, 1962.

Gossage, Carolyn. *Greatcoats and Glamour Boots: Canadian Women at War, 1939–1945*. Toronto: Dundurn, 2001.

Graham, Howard. *Citizen and Soldier: The Memoirs of Lieutenant-General Howard Graham*. Toronto: McClelland & Stewart, 1987.

Granatstein, J.L. *A Man of Influence: Norman A. Robertson and Canadian Statecraft*. Toronto: Deneau Publishers, 1981.

Granatstein, J.L. *Canada's Army: Waging War and Keeping the Peace*. Toronto: University of Toronto Press, 2002.

Granatstein, J.L. *The Generals*. Toronto: Stoddart Publishing, 1993.

Granatstein, J.L. and Norman Hillmer. *Battle Lines: Eyewitness Accounts from Canada's Military History*. Toronto: Thomas Allen Publishers, 2004.

Granatstein, J.L. and Norman Hillmer. *Prime Ministers: Ranking Canada's Leaders*. Toronto: HarperCollins Canada, 1999.

Granatstein, J.L. and J.M. Hitsman. *Broken Promises: A History of Conscription in Canada*. Toronto: Oxford University Press, 1977.

Granatstein, J.L. and Desmond Morton. *A Nation Forged in Fire: Canadians and the Second World War, 1939–1945*. Toronto: Lester and Orpen Dennys, 1989.

Graves, Donald E. *In Peril on the Sea: The Royal Canadian Navy and the Battle of the Atlantic*. Toronto: Robin Brass Studio Inc., 2003.

Greenhous, Brereton. *Dragoon: The Centennial History of the Royal Canadian Dragoons, 1883–1983*. Belleville, Ontario: Royal Canadian Dragoons, 1984.

Greenhous, Brereton et al. *The Crucible of War 1939–1945*. Vol. 3. Toronto: University of Toronto Press, 1994.

Hadley, Michael L. *U-Boats Against Canada: German Submarines in Canadian Waters*. Montreal: McGill-Queens University Press, 1985.

Harker, Douglas E. *The Dukes*. Vancouver: The British Columbia Regiment, 1974.

Harris, Stephen John. *Canadian Brass: The Making of a Professional Army, 1890–1939*. Toronto: University of Toronto Press, 1988.

Hillmer, Norman, et al. *A Country of Limitations: Canada and the World in 1939*. Ottawa: Canadian Committee for the History of the Second World War, 1996.

Horn, Bernd and Stephen Harris, eds. *Warrior Chiefs: Perspectives on Senior Canadian Military Chiefs.* Toronto: Dundurn, 2000.

Hutchison, Bruce. *The Incredible Canadian.* Toronto: Longmans Canada, 1952.

Jarymowycz, Roman. *Tank Tactics: From Normandy to Lorraine.* Mechanicsburg, Pennsylvania: Stackpole Books, 2009.

Johnston, Mac. *Corvettes Canada: Convoy Veterans of WWII Tell Their True Stories.* Toronto: John Wiley & Sons, 2008.

Kostenuk, S. and J. Griffin. *RCAF Squadrons Histories and Aircraft: 1924–1968.* Toronto: Samuel Stevens Hakkert, 1977.

Lamb, James B. *The Corvette Navy: True Stories from Canada's Atlantic War.* Toronto: Macmillan, 1979.

Levine, Allan. *King: William Lyon Mackenzie King: A Life Guided by the Hand of Destiny.* Vancouver: Douglas & McIntyre, 2012.

Lynch, M. *Salty Dips.* Vols. 1–7. Ottawa: Naval Officers' Association, 1983–2000.

MacDonell, George S. *One Soldier's Story: 1939–1945: From the Fall of Hong Kong to the Defeat of Japan.* Toronto: Dundurn, 2002.

MacFarlane, John. *Ernest Lapointe and Quebec's Influence on Canadian Foreign Policy.* Toronto: University of Toronto Press, 1999.

McKee, F. and R. Darlington. *The Canadian Navy Chronicle.* St. Catharines, Ontario: Vanwell Publishing Ltd., 1996.

Marion, N., ed. *Camp Borden: Birthplace of the RCAF.* Borden, Ontario: 16 Wing, 2004.

Marteinson, John and Michael R. McNorgan. *The Royal Canadian Armoured Corps: An Illustrated History.* Toronto: Royal Canadian Armoured Corps Association, 2000.

Mein, Stewart A. *Up the Johns! The Story of the Royal Regina Rifles.* Regina: Senate of the Royal Regina Rifles, 1992.

Macpherson, Ken and John Burgess. *The Ships of Canada's Naval Forces, 1910–1981.* Toronto: Collins, 1981.

Milberry, Larry. *Sixty Years: The RCAF and CF Command, 1924–1984.* Toronto: CANAV Books, 1984.

Milberry, Larry. *Canada's Air Force at War and Peace.* Vol. 1. Toronto: CANAV Books, 2000.

Milner, Marc. *Battle of the Atlantic.* St. Catharines, Ontario: Vanwell Publishing Ltd., 2011.

Milner, Marc. *Canada's Navy: The First Century.* Toronto: University of Toronto Press, 1999.

Milner, M. and Vandervort, B. *The Maritime Defence of Canada.* Toronto: Canadian Institute of Strategic Studies, 1997.

Morton, Desmond. *Canada and War: A Military and Political History.* Toronto: Butterworths, 1981.

Mowat, Farley. *The Regiment.* St. Catharines, Ontario: Vanwell Publishing Ltd., 2007.

Neatby, Blair. *The Politics of Chaos: Canada in the Thirties.* Toronto: Macmillan of Canada, 1972.

Neatby, Blair. *William Lyon Mackenzie King: the Prism of Unity, 1933–1939.* Toronto: University of Toronto Press, 1975.

Nemni, Max and Monique. *Young Trudeau: 1919–1944: Son of Quebec, Father of Canada.* Translated by William Johnson. Toronto: McClelland & Stewart, 2006.

Nicholson, G. *The Gunners of Canada.* Vol. 1, vol. 2. Toronto: McClelland & Stewart, 1967, 1972.

Pariseau, Jean and Serge Bernier. *Les Canadiens français et le bilinguisme dans les Forces armée canadiennes.* Ottawa: Department of National Defence, 1987.

Pickersgill, J.W. *The Mackenzie King Record,* vol. 1, *1939–44.* Toronto: University of Toronto Press, 1960.

Pope, M. *Soldiers and Politicians.* Toronto: University of Toronto Press, 1962.

Quigley, John Gordon. *A Century of Rifles, 1860–1960: The Halifax Rifles.* Halifax: William McNab and Sons, 1960.

Rickard, John Nelson. *The Politics of Command: Lieutenant-General A.G.L. McNaughton and the Canadian Army, 1939–1943.* Toronto: University of Toronto Press, 2010.

Ritchie, Charles. *The Siren Years: A Canadian Diplomat Abroad, 1937–1945.* Toronto: Macmillan, 1974.

Roy, Reginald H. *For Most Conspicuous Bravery: A Biography of Major-General George R. Pearkes, V.C., Through Two World Wars.* Vancouver: UBC Press, 1977.

Roy, Reginald H. *The Seaforth Highlanders of Canada, 1919–1965.* Vancouver: Seaforth Highlanders of Canada, 1969.

Roy, Reginald. *Sinews of Steel.* Kelowna, British Columbia: Whizzbang Association, 1965.

Safarian, A.E. *The Canadian Economy in the Great Depression.* Toronto: McClelland & Stewart, 1970.

Sarty, Roger. *The Maritime Defence of Canada.* Toronto: Canadian Institute of Strategic Studies, 1996.

Schragg, Lex. *History of The Ontario Regiment, 1866–1951.* Oshawa, Ontario: The Ontario Regiment.

Schull, Joseph. *The Far Distant Ships: An Official Account of Canadian Naval Operations in the Second World War.* Toronto: Stoddart Publishing, 1987.

Skaarup, Harold A. *Out of Darkness — Light: A History of Canadian Military Intelligence.* Vol. 1. New York: iUniverse, 2005.

Soward, E. *A Formidable Hero.* Toronto: CANAV Books, 1984.

Stacey, C.P. *Canada and the Age of Conflict,* vol. 2, *1921–1948, The Mackenzie King Era.* Toronto: University of Toronto Press, 1981.

Stacey, C.P. *Mackenzie King and the Atlantic Triangle.* Toronto: Macmillan of Canada, 1976.

Stacey, C.P. *The Military Problems of Canada: A Survey of Defence Policies and Strategic Conditions Past and Present.* Toronto: Ryerson Press, 1940.

Stacey, C.P. *The Official History of the Canadian Army in the Second World War,* vol. 3, *The Victory Campaign.* Ottawa: Department of National Defence, 1960.

Stacey, C.P. *Six Years of War: The Army in Canada, Britain and the Pacific.* Vol. 1. Ottawa: Department of National Defence, 1955.

Stacey, C.P. *A Very Double Life: The Private World of Mackenzie King.* Toronto: Macmillan of Canada, 1976.

Stanley, George F.G. *Canada's Soldiers 1604–1954: The Military History of an Unmilitary People.* Toronto: Macmillan, 1960.

Sweetenham, J. *McNaughton,* Vol. 1. Toronto: Ryerson, 1968.

Urquhart, M. and K. Buckley. *Historical Statistics of Canada.* Toronto: Macmillan, 1965.

Vincent, Carl. *No Reason Why, The Canadian Hong Kong Tragedy.* Stittsville, Ontario: Canada's Wings, 1981.

Villa, Brian Lorring. *Unauthorized Action: Mountbatten and the Dieppe Raid.* Oxford: Oxford University Press, 1991.

Vokes, Chris, with John P. Maclean. *Vokes: My Story.* Ottawa: Gallery Books, 1985.

Whitaker, Denis and Shelagh Whitaker. *Dieppe: Tragedy to Triumph.* Toronto: McGraw-Hill Ryerson, 1992.

Whitby, Michael, et al. *The Admirals: Canada's Senior Naval Leadership in the Twentieth Century.* Toronto: Dundurn, 2006.

Williams, Jeffery. *Far From Home: A Memoir of a 20th Century Soldier.* Calgary: University of Calgary Press, 2003.

Worthington, L. *Worthy.* Toronto: Macmillan, 1961.

INDEX

Numbers in italics refer to images and their captions.